KNOWLTON NASH

Prime Time at Ten

Behind-the-Camera Battles of Canadian TV Journalism

M&S

McClelland and Stewart
The Canadian Publishers
481 University Avenue
Toronto, Ontario
M5G 2E9

Canadian Cataloguing in Publication Data

Nash, Knowlton.
  Prime time at ten

Includes index.
ISBN 0-7710-6703-8 (bound). ISBN 0-7710-6704-6 (pbk).

1. Nash, Knowlton. 2. Broadcasters – Canada –
Biography. 3. Television broadcasting of news –
Canada. 4. Canadian Broadcasting Corporation.
I. Title.

PN4913.N38A3 1987   070.1′9′0294   C87-094292-1

Printed and bound in Canada

Prime Time at Ten

CONTENTS

*To Jesse and Robert, who are teaching me
what life is really all about*

PREFACE

There is no doubt that journalism is hasty, incomplete, sometimes inaccurate, occasionally misleading, and frequently flawed. It's an imperfect necessity. I also believe that journalism is the hinge of democracy: it is the only way we're going to find out about the events and issues that dominate our lives. In this increasingly complex, confusing, and interrelated world, the public's growing dependence on the media imposes new demands on journalists. The challenge for those of us in the news business is to strive continually to come as close as we can to providing a true reflection of reality so people can understand and cope with that reality. Telling it "the way it is," as Walter Cronkite used to end his newscasts, has given contemporary journalism a power unknown before in history.

Years ago Walter Lippmann wrote of journalism, "The power to determine each day what shall be seen important and what shall be neglected is a power unlike any that has been exercised since the Pope lost his hold on the secular mind." Nowhere is that power exercised with more impact than on television, where most of us now get our news. TV has become the most potent instrument of journalism the world has ever known. But the bigger the platform, the bigger the responsibility. Thus, of all forms of journalism, TV news bears the greatest accountability to the public.

The battle for better television journalism has been my lodestar for more than three decades as a correspondent, executive, and anchor of *The National*. This book is about the behind-the-camera fights, successes, and failures that led to the on-camera revolution in the quest to improve television journalism, a revolution that is epitomized in *The National* at 10:00 and *The Journal*. It is, I think, a story that needs to be told so people can measure our original intentions against our accomplishments in the pursuit of a better-informed society. Along the way the reader can sit in on the boardroom battles, view the private wars, and share the off-camera secrets of the backstage power-pullers as well as the stars of television journalism. My sources have been the recollections of scores of participants and the thousands of old memos, letters, clippings, and tapes that are a result of my pack-rat habits. The people, events, and issues flowing through these pages are essentially as seen through my eyes and inevitably others will have different perspectives. They are, however, as I saw and heard and felt them.

I've enjoyed every facet of my more than four decades of journalism, from the time I sold newspapers on a Toronto streetcorner to my years as a foreign correspondent, boardroom combatant, and anchorman. I still retain a "Gee Whiz!" sense of wonder at having a box seat at the passing parade of history. Journalism is an odd business of watching other people do things. I came into it, perhaps, for the same reason people become cowboys: too lazy to work and too nervous to steal. At any rate, my professional passage has been enriched by shared experiences with many colleagues, friends, and even sometime adversaries. And the invigorating anticipatory joy in this business of news is that there are always new challenges.

As with my first book about life as a foreign correspondent, *History on the Run*, I am immeasurably indebted to my editor, Rick Archbold, for his patient insistence on structure and theme and for his continual demand for more validating facts and anecdotes. Neither book would have happened at all without Jack McClelland, whose enthusiastic urging kept me lashed to my word processor until the manuscript popped out. I also owe a great debt to the many colleagues who helped to call back yesterday in giving of their time and their memories. But I'm particularly indebted to CBC chief news editor John Owen and former CBC-TV managing director Norn Garriock, who read the early draft and provided so much valuable advice, along with other colleagues who read all or part of the manuscript. It would take almost as many pages as there are in the book itself to list those who have stimulated, challenged, and helped me through the years: Bill Hogg, who hired me in the first place for CBC News; Gene Hallman, who brought me into the executive suite; Trina McQueen, who took me out of it and into *The National*; executive colleagues like Peter Herrndorf, Denny Harvey, Jack Craine, Bill Morgan, Thom Benson, Don MacPherson, Don Ferguson, Don Macdonald, and program partners like David Nayman, Mark Bulgutch, David Bazay, Fred Parker, Tony Burman, Mark Starowicz, Barbara Frum, and so many others. To my wife Lorraine my debt is incalculable, for both her professional advice and personal succour in the couple of years of working on this book. Without her sensitive understanding neither the book nor anything else would be as fulfilling.

PROLOGUE

September 9, 1985

The National's newsroom seemed somehow subdued as I walked in. The jumble of desks was still piled high with newspapers and books, the floor still cluttered with paper, and the cables and wires still snaked across the thinning, flat, grey broadloom to the phones and TV cameras at the front end. The phones were still ringing, the teletypes buzzing, the computers clicking, the typewriters clacking. But the usual across-the-room shouts were missing; the smiling, joking camaraderie absent. Then I noticed a dozen of my jeans and sports shirt-clad colleagues clustered quietly around the assignment desk. As I got closer I could see their lips were tightened and their eyes focused on an NBC news feed coming in from New York on one of the bank of TV monitors high on the side wall.

"God, his camera was still running," grimaced Graham Ritchie, our tall, thin, balding senior producer. "Just like Neil."

I looked up and saw a picture of several men lying dead or wounded on a Bangkok street while another crawled away, dodging bullets fired by a couple of tanks seen in the background. It was the tail end of a failed coup by dissident soldiers in Thailand.

"Neil who?" I asked, sensing that I already knew the answer.

"Neil Davis," said Graham. "He's dead."

Neil Davis. If anyone was, he was the quintessential TV foreign correspondent. He had been in more wars, revolutions, and crises, had been wounded more times, had interviewed more presidents, prime ministers, generals, and dictators than anyone else I'd ever known in the news business. Most of his professional life had been spent in Asia, Africa, and the Middle East. And I'd first met him when I was a CBC foreign correspondent on assignment in Vietnam in late 1967, where he was a correspondent-cameraman for Visnews, the international TV news agency. He had been my cameraman. As I looked up at the TV pictures of Neil lying dead on a Bangkok street, my mind reeled back twenty years to when I'd climbed two dimly lit flights of stairs to a cramped, equipment-strewn office in a ramshackle building in downtown Saigon just after I had arrived in Vietnam. "Hi mate!" Neil cheerily smiled as I entered his lair. "Welcome to the Paris of the Orient. First thing you'll want is to change some money at my Indian friend's office down the hall. Hell of a lot better than the official exchange rate."

The man I met that day was a tall, thin, devilishly handsome, thirty-three-year-old lady killer of Tasmanian birth whose knack for getting things done was exceeded only by his reputation as a journalistic professional. I soon discovered he was one of the world's heaviest smokers of other people's Marlboro cigarettes. He always wanted to be where the action was, but in the field you felt safe with him because while he loved to gamble on cricket, tennis, and boxing, he rarely gambled in a fire fight, as Vietnam jungle skirmishes were called. He was careful, never a crazy "war lover" as some journalists were, and one of the first things he taught me was the life-saving difference between the sounds of outgoing and incoming fire.

But these thoughts of Vietnam were suddenly replaced by more immediate concerns. Assignment editor Bob Waller's loud shout of "Meeting! Meet! Meet! Meet!" echoed through the newsroom and my colleagues and I drifted away from the TV monitors, shuffling into a small boardroom just down the hall for our regular hour-long review of the day's news.

"Pretty dull day," I heard foreign assignment editor George Hoff say. "Reagan's brought in some minor sanctions against South Africa. Bishop Tutu says it's not enough. There's a car bombing in Madrid, and, of course, there's the revolution attempt in Thailand that failed."

Domestic assignment editors Bob Waller and Suzanne Howden droned on about Parliament reopening, a bank crisis in Canada, worries about Canadian sovereignty in the Arctic, and a trawler fire in St. John's. Usually I would be following every word in the discussion, already beginning to get a sense of the shape of *The National* for that night. But today my mind plunged back to Neil Davis and Vietnam.

I remembered the two of us tramping along a dusty road near Danang on a patrol with some "grunts," the U.S. Marines. We were on a "search and destroy" mission with the Marines but hadn't seen any action yet. "No, I don't want to go down that trail tomorrow morning," he said to me. "I just don't like the look of it." Instead we went back to Danang. Later, I learned that one member of the patrol had stepped on a land mine, badly wounding himself and three others.

Neil wasn't a crazy risk-taker, but he wanted to be on the leading edge of life. "I would always try to go to the extreme front line," he told me once. "You can't get the spontaneity of action if you're not there. . . . You don't see the faces, the expressions. You don't feel the compassion."

When the Communist forces finally triumphed in Vietnam, journal-

10

ists joined the helicopter evacuation from Saigon, but not Neil. He stayed behind to record the takeover, and it was he who took the famous shot of the first North Vietnamese tank crashing through the front gates of the presidential palace. He kept on filming as excited Viet Cong and North Vietnamese soldiers waving their guns ran up to him screaming in Vietnamese, "Stop! Stop! Stop!" Neil flashed a broad smile and spoke the Vietnamese words he'd been practising for days: "Welcome to Saigon, comrades. I've been waiting to film the liberation." The soldiers hesitated, and then ran past him into the presidential palace.

"Always keep your camera running, no matter what," he'd told me once when we were helicoptering over a Viet Cong base near Pleiku. "You never can tell what you'll get."

What he got on this September day in 1985 on a downtown Bangkok street was, in a horrible irony, his own death. He'd been focusing his lens on four rebel tanks firing their 76-mm cannons at a radio station behind him. Suddenly, two shells exploded against a nearby wall and shrapnel tore into his left side, killing him instantly. His camera fell from his hands still running, but now pointed toward him.

Neil had always been philosophical about mortality, and he'd told me often he would rather be killed than paralysed by a wound. "I was never afraid of being killed because that's that.... You're done," he had said. "I didn't want to be badly wounded." Several times I'd heard him quote a Buddhist saying, "Death is a lady who greets you softly."

In an apartment in Singapore, one of his many temporary homes in Southeast Asia, he had hung a plaque that seemed to sum up his own philosophy: "When you walk with me, do not walk behind me for I may not always lead. Do not walk in front of me for I may not always follow. Walk beside me and be my friend." It was a philosophy he acted out in his own remarkable life.

As I sat there in our CBC boardroom hearing only faint echoes of the discussion around me about the efforts of correspondent Joe Schlesinger in Washington to get a story on new economic sanctions President Reagan had just imposed on South Africa, and on Brian Stewart in Johannesburg trying to get reaction to the Reagan move, I slipped from thinking of Neil to thinking of myself and my own two decades as a foreign correspondent based in Washington. As anchorman of *The National*, I no longer did much journalistic barnstorming around the world, and, frankly, I didn't mind one bit. As exhilarating as it may be to be shot at and missed, I'd been shot at more than enough in Vietnam and elsewhere in covering crises from Santo Domingo to Paris to Colombia. In Vietnam and other Indochina fighting, more than eighty correspondents had been killed, and that sobering statistic diluted much of my yearning for the unique excitement that comes with living on the edge. Aside from the dangers, there also was the wrenching personal toll as family life took a back seat to the endless news assignments and constant travel.

Thinking of Neil Davis, I reflected on how much my life had changed in the two decades since I'd first met him in Saigon. A couple of years after dodging bullets in Vietnam, I'd left the peripatetic correspondent's life to join the behind-the-scenes battle to give Canadians more and better television journalism. Then, after nearly ten years of boardroom warfare, I'd switched hats again to step into the camera's unrelenting stare as anchor of *The National*. From my anchor chair, I found life was in its own way just as exciting as it had been when I roamed the world in search of a story.

My meditating mind snapped back to the present as the daily editorial meeting broke up. Graham Ritchie, who had worked with Neil when they were both at Visnews, came up to me and, with his English accent not hiding the emotion he felt, said, "I hope tonight you're not going to make Neil sound like one of those crazies . . . one of those war-loving characters."

"Don't worry, I know he wasn't," I responded and went off to my office to quietly write a closing to our report on the failed revolution and the death of fifty-one-year-old correspondent-cameraman Neil Davis. As I typed, I saw his impish smile, heard his twangy "Hi mate!," and remembered a courageous and gentle friend.

"He was a good professional," I said that night on *The National*, "and more important, he was a good man."

Then, pushed by the inexorable pressure of the nightly newscast, I went on to the next story, on the travels of Pope John Paul II. Whatever else happens, the news goes on.

1 *LEAVING MOTHER*

It's hard to know where to begin this story – 1966, when I first thought of quitting my job as Washington correspondent; 1969, when I did quit to enter the bureaucratic wars of the CBC; or 1974, when Pierre Berton's *The National Dream* finally hit the television screens of the nation. But as I reflect back, the right place seems to be the late spring of 1976 with a phone call about the Montreal Summer Olympics. By late May of that year the games loomed on the near horizon as the most spectacular Canadian event of the year.

On the phone was my boss, Denis Harvey, the CBC assistant general manager, whose twinkling eyes, thick blond hair, and chunky build concealed a rock-hard core. It seemed the Sports producers wanted Lloyd Robertson, anchorman of *The National*, to host the two and a half weeks of CBC Olympics coverage, and Harvey thought it was a good idea. I didn't.

"I don't like it," I responded. "With all the planning and rehearsals, plus nearly three weeks in Montreal, Lloyd would be off *The National* for too long. Besides, doing sports will dilute his identification with news, which we're trying to emphasize. He'll seem like a 'Jack of all trades.'"

As director of CBC-TV News and Current Affairs programming, I'd planned extensive news coverage of the Olympics to supplement the overall presentation of the event itself, which was being handled by the Sports area. Now, Sports wanted to cut into the effectiveness of our news coverage by taking Lloyd away for their programming.

"It's not just sports, you know," Harvey snapped. "It's a very big story, too, dammit!"

"Would Walter Cronkite host the Olympics if they were held in the States?" I shot back.

"Who cares?" Denny replied with characteristic briskness. "We're talking about Lloyd! Look, call me at the end of the day." This was typical of his aggressively enthusiastic style, coming on with all guns firing and wanting direct, simple "Yes" or "No" answers, impatient with nuanced subtleties. Denny had once been a very young sports editor at the *Hamilton Spectator* – the "toy department," he called it – and, following a spectacularly successful newspaper career, had been the best chief news editor CBC-TV ever had before moving into the management hierarchy. As I hung up the phone, I remembered a comment by columnist Charlie Lynch when Denny had first joined CBC three and a half years earlier. "When he spits, ball bearings come out," Charlie had said.

Today, Denny was relatively mild, but I got up from my desk, picked up a file full of problems about the 1976-77 program season that started in September, and stomped over to a couch at the other end of my office. God knows, I had enough headaches without this one: we were in the midst of a whole new approach to Current Affairs programming, including hard-hitting documentaries, *the fifth estate*, the controversial and successful *Marketplace* and *Ombudsman* programs, as well as an innovative late-night talk show that I felt would knock the socks off the viewing nation. Each of the literally dozens of other programs under my wing was fighting for budgets, talent, facilities, and scheduling. All that, plus the usual Byzantine bureaucratic infighting of the CBC, the regular parliamentary inquisitions, and the random other political pressures of the job.

"The CBC is probably the toughest corporation in the country to run," I was told years later by Sheelagh Whittaker, a new CBC vice-president who had just come in from the private sector where she'd been a business consultant. She was right. With its parliamentary mandate for public enlightenment as well as public amusement, while at the same time having to compete in a ferociously competitive broadcasting environment, not only was the CBC "probably the toughest corporation in the country to run" but also it likely was the toughest broadcasting organization in the world to manage. After leaving Washington in January, 1969, to take on my job as director of News and Current Affairs, I'd soon discovered just how complex and pressurized life was in the CBC. The Corporation spent half a billion dollars a year at the time, had more than 10,000 employees in radio and TV stations scattered across the country, and operated full French and English radio and TV services as well as the Northern Service and the International Service. On top of that, CBC was dependent for about a third of its audience on private commercial affiliates whose basic motivation was profit and who thus added to the philosophical dilemma of the CBC. It was always trying to be both a public broadcaster and a commercial revenue earner because, as well as government grants, the CBC needed this revenue to finance its programming. No other broadcasting organization around the globe had the same combination of political pressures, economic demands, cultural expectations, and regional obligations. It all resulted in a pressure-cooker bureaucracy and my part of this bubbling stew encompassed all the English-language TV journalistic programming, and that put me on the leading edge of controversy twenty-four hours a day. Lloyd Robertson was now one more problem to handle – a big one.

For me, *The National* was the single most important program the CBC aired and by far my most important responsibility. And the anchorman was critical. Audiences wanted the consistent presence of the same face, someone steady, friendly, and reliable, an "anchor" in a chaotic world. To lose Lloyd for the Olympics as well as for his normal summer holidays would, I felt, seriously damage that link with the audience. Our backup announcers did a fine job, but too much use of them seriously undermined the effectiveness of Lloyd's steady, reliable television presence.

Stretching out on my office couch, I mulled over the implications of Lloyd's hosting the Olympics. Then I got up, idly flipped through the news copy tapping out on the news agency teletypes along the side wall of the office, glanced over at the TV monitors to see *Take Thirty* begin its daily half hour of light information and interviews, and went back to my desk to phone my chief news editor, Mike Daigneault, to get his reaction. A tough, thin reed of a young man – he was in his early thirties – Daigneault covered his sensitivity about being so young and holding such a senior job with a sometimes combative assertiveness, but he had a quick-witted intelligence and managerial daring that I'd admired when I had named him to his position a couple of years earlier.

To my surprise, Mike wasn't as worried about Lloyd hosting the Olympics as I was. And I couldn't deny the games were going to be a very big story. Still, I was reluctant. I knew *The National* would suffer even if the CBC in general gained by having Lloyd host the Olympics. By the end of the day, with Mike not too concerned and Harvey insistent, I acquiesced. As it turned out, that was one of the biggest mistakes I made as a senior CBC executive.

Lloyd Robertson and I went back a long way together. Shortly after

I'd come up from Washington to take over CBC News and Current Affairs, I'd decided to make him the anchor of *The National*. Peter Trueman, now a Global anchorman but then my head of TV News, was uncomfortable with Lloyd as anchor. "Plastic and shallow," said Trueman. "He needs experience as an honest-to-God reporter." It was true that Lloyd had not come up through the journalistic ranks and had never had experience as a Parliament Hill reporter or a foreign correspondent. But through his years as an announcer he had anchored not only *The National* as a backup but also every possible kind of news special, election, political convention, space shot, and political crisis. And he had developed a deep personal interest in news. After such programs he would gossip over drinks in a bar across the street from the CBC with producers, reporters, and correspondents, talking about news stories and reportorial hijinks. So in spite of the thinness of his journalistic roots, I felt Lloyd could do the job better than anyone else in sight.

Before the final decision was made, Trueman and I argued heatedly over Lloyd, but since he offered no alternative, Peter reluctantly accepted my decision and Lloyd went into *The National*'s anchor chair, where he quickly became a major success. Audience ratings went up with his friendly, confident air. And his eagerness to please his colleagues contrasted sharply with the more contentious style of his immediate predecessors in the job.

LLOYD HAD BEGUN his broadcast career as a $50-a-week announcer with his hometown station in Stratford, Ont., and then a station in Guelph, Ont., before joining the CBC in 1954 when television in Canada was only two years old. But he quickly switched over to TV, working at CBC stations in Windsor, Winnipeg, and Ottawa before he arrived in Toronto in 1962. At the CBC he developed a love for news and, more than any other CBC announcer, he got involved with journalists and journalism. Many a time in the late 1960s I would come up from Washington to co-anchor news specials with Lloyd Robertson or do reports on news programs he was hosting. After the programs we'd often go out for a drink and I'd kid him about the conservative suits he favoured, trying to offset his youthful appearance.

On the night of the Olympics opening, July 17, 1976, Lloyd was to anchor *The National* out of Montreal, his last time before plunging all his efforts into hosting the Olympics. It turned out to be a bad omen for me.

That night we wanted to open *The National* with Lloyd standing on the roof of the CBC building against a panoramic view of Montreal. To

16

have a dramatic nighttime scene, the shot was to be taped shortly after sunset and just before the Atlantic edition of *The National* began. The timing would be tight, but we figured Lloyd would have more than enough time to go down the dozen or so floors to the studio to be there when the program began. So as dusk fell, Lloyd, attired in his pumpkin-coloured Olympic jacket, stood on the rooftop smiling into the camera as a brisk wind tousled his normally neat hair. But every time the taping began, he had to stop because the video signal, being sent from the rooftop camera to a mobile truck in the parking lot below and then to the control room in Toronto, was not getting through. As the clock ticked toward 10:00 p.m., the director became increasingly alarmed. Finally, he ordered Lloyd to get down to the studio fast and do his opening from there. Lloyd raced off the rooftop and down the first flight of stairs with his camera crew and floor director close behind. But when they tried to get out into the top floor hallway, they found the door locked.

As the usually imperturbable anchorman of *The National*, whom most Canadians looked on as the personification of calm, authoritative news, pounded on the door in rising panic and shouted for assistance, all hell was breaking loose in *The National* control room in Toronto. Three minutes to air and no Lloyd.

Meanwhile Lloyd and his colleagues raced back up to the roof to call the control room on their audio line to ask that someone be sent up to unlock the door.

Two minutes to go and still no Lloyd in the studio. But David Halton, who was then the CBC's Quebec correspondent, was doing a report for *The National* that night and suddenly he was hauled out of the newsroom and shoved into the anchor seat, the news script thrust into his hands just before the program went on the air.

Back at the locked door with the seconds ticking away, a janitor arrived to open it and Lloyd raced down to the studio, visualizing the empty anchor desk that would greet the viewers of Atlantic Canada.

"Good evening," said David Halton a little nervously as he introduced the first news report and viewers gave a start as this familiar face looked back at them in an unfamiliar role.

Three minutes after the program began, Lloyd burst into the studio and in a brief break while a report was running, David handed the anchoring duties over to a slightly breathless Robertson. Expecting a blast from the control room when the newscast was over, Lloyd was relieved when the only thing the producer in Toronto said was, "Did you have to wear that damn pumpkin jacket?"

Fortunately, there were no more problems of this ilk and in the ensuing days of the Olympics Lloyd did a superb job. In fact, from my point of view, he was simply too damned good.

Sitting at home in Toronto watching the CBC coverage, CTV news head Tom Gould saw Lloyd as "not just a pretty face" but as a smooth, knowledgeable anchor with a sharp ad-lib capability. Gould later said that the one thing he particularly liked was when Lloyd commented that a Canadian boxer didn't need more experience, but did need more manners in the ring. "We phoned Lloyd the next day," Gould said.

Ever since it had begun a decade and a half earlier, CTV had been trying to catch up to the CBC in its news programming. With the twelve-year anchoring veteran Harvey Kirck, they had come within range of *The National's* audience, but for the past few months CTV had been worried about falling ratings and felt it needed something to try to overtake CBC's *National*. Gould and his deputy, an old friend and former colleague of mine, Don Cameron, felt Robertson might be just the ticket. If they got him, it would be a double whammy; CTV would get a superb news anchor while CBC would suffer a heavy loss.

Both Gould and Cameron had quit the CBC for CTV feeling, among other things, that the Corporation was failing to give a high enough priority to its news programming. In fact, they were right at the time. For years before their departure we had been fighting side by side to change things. But Tom and Don had left in mid-battle nursing their own grievances about ill treatment. At the time Gould, a one-time Vancouver newspaperman, was *The National's* tough-talking Ottawa reporter, and Don had been executive producer of the CBC's *Newsmagazine* and later executive producer of local Toronto news programming. At the CBC Cameron was known as a sabre-toothed teddy bear because of his demanding professionalism but marshmallow soul. Now, Tom and Don saw revenge looming enticingly before them.

For Gould, this prospect was doubly attractive. Not only had he resigned in anger, charging CBC with journalistic misjudgement and mismanagement, but I also happened to be married to his ex-wife. Thus, his cup was running over and, for him, the phone call to Lloyd couldn't have come at a better time.

Aiding their cause was the fact that Lloyd was embittered about the union situation at the CBC, which prevented him from doing some reporting as well as anchoring. Announcers were in one union and journalists in another, and at that time the unions were adamant that you couldn't do both jobs. It was a ridiculous and unprofessional attitude but reflected a deep and grasping attachment to jurisdictional territory and a failure by me and my CBC management colleagues to work out a compromise acceptable to both unions. And it was only part of the long history of prickly labour-management relations at the CBC with its many different unions representing different groups such as technicians, announcers, news people, office staff, producers, and others, a situation resulting in inter-union rivalries as well as the occasional demonstration of solidarity.

Lloyd was never a forceful union man but went along with his union peers. He'd been especially upset during a strike in 1972 that saw several unions walking out in support of the contract demands of striking technicians. He'd gotten deeply involved, trying to be a middleman between the two sides, but without any success. During that bitter strike, as a management man, I'd sat in on *The National* as Lloyd's replacement. My car was damaged and a few eggs thrown at my front door at home. More of a nuisance, though, was a continuous flow of telephone calls at two, three, and four in the morning, which I determined came from the news union. The problem was solved, however, when I decided to activate the "call forwarding" system on my home telephone and all my early morning calls were forwarded to the home telephone of the president of the union. He later complained of management harassment.

Four years later Lloyd was in the middle of another union fight when the news union – the Canadian Wire Service Guild – objected vociferously to some reporting of a recent British election Lloyd had done, even though the union had no jurisdiction outside Canada. Lloyd also roused union ire when he sought to do some reporting at the Habitat Conference in Vancouver in the spring of 1976. The local CBC newsroom had walked out in protest. A grievance in that case was pending when Cameron phoned Lloyd to suggest lunch.

But Lloyd was busy and lunch kept getting put off. Finally, in late August, Cameron called again and suggested Gould would join them for lunch. "That's when I first realized CTV might want to talk business," Lloyd said later. "So I suggested we meet privately."

They met for lunch the day after Labour Day at Gould's home in downtown Toronto and in the genial atmosphere of old friends, as they were, Gould and Cameron gave Lloyd an offer they hoped he couldn't refuse. It was by far the most money ever offered a network news anchor in Canada, and much more than Lloyd was then making at the CBC. But even so, he hesitated. At forty-two, Lloyd had spent more than half his life with the CBC – twenty-two years – and his heart and soul were with "Mother Corp." even if he was angry at the union situation. He told Gould and Cameron he'd have to think about it.

They gave him a deadline of one week.

OBLIVIOUS TO THESE GOINGS-ON, I was wondering how we might mark the fortieth anniversary of CBC Radio going on the air. In reading through old memos, speeches, and statements, I had been struck with how much broadcast news had changed since the CBC was first heard on November 2, 1936. The leisurely, gentle, and often haphazard style of newscasts and their relative unimportance in the scheme of broadcasting in those days contrasted sharply with the intensely competitive, fast-paced, high profile of broadcast news in the fall of 1976.

The CBC didn't even have have a News Service in the first five years of its life. It simply had announcers read a newscast prepared by Canadian Press. "Here is the National News bulletin . . . a summary of the day's news," said the precise, rich-voiced announcer Charles Jennings, the father of Peter Jennings, now anchor of the ABC news in the U.S. Each weeknight in the late 1930s Jennings would riffle through the flimsy pages of a script written by Canadian Press and delivered to the CBC shortly before air time by a messenger on a bicycle or in a taxicab. It wasn't until New Year's Day, 1941, that the CBC News Service was born and produced the first newscast of its own. The BBC and American networks had been broadcasting their own newscasts for well over a decade.

Dan McArthur, the creative, driving, and sometimes eccentric first chief news editor for CBC, organized five newsrooms across the country in Halifax, Montreal, Toronto, Winnipeg, and Vancouver. McArthur, who was born in Brooklyn, spent his young childhood in England, and was educated in rural Ontario schools, battled for a dozen years on behalf of his editors against the bureaucracy he once called in a memorandum, "that fungus growth that now covers the whole CBC like a green mildew." He battled, too, against a government that sometimes wanted the CBC as its mouthpiece, and a senior management that was not imbued with an overabundance of sensitivity to the idea of journalistic independence in dealing with the authorities. In those early days, CBC's journalistic credibility rested almost exclusively on McArthur's shoulders. He was shrewd, stubborn, and irreverent, and he won more battles than he lost in his determination to build a CBC News Service of integrity, independence, and reliability.

When television came along in 1952, McArthur thought the new medium was frivolous, phoney, and couldn't be trusted with the news, and he handed over the News Service to Bill Hogg, his sensitive, conscientious associate. There could hardly have been a greater difference between the two: one a flamboyant confrontationalist always battling his bosses with an unmatched capacity for invective; the other a gentle soul who flinched at the word "darn." Unlike McArthur, Hogg also was exceptionally careful in spending money, his own or the Corporation's. He once invited a half dozen CBC foreign correspondents to his home for an evening of conviviality for which he had bought a twelve-pack of beer as the liquid refreshments. The beer lasted all of fifteen minutes and the party broke up unusually early. But both McArthur and Hogg shared one attribute – each had an acute capacity for spotting talent and determinedly went after what they wanted. What Hogg wanted was what the Americans and the British already had, a nightly TV newscast.

The BBC had been the first with television news, experimenting with it in the late 1930s. In the fall of 1937, the legendary American correspondent Edward R. Murrow sat at home in his London apartment and entertained a tall, heavy-shouldered young newspaperman named Eric Sevareid by watching a TV set the BBC had given him. "That's television," Murrow said. "That's the future, my friend." A year later, Neville Chamberlain's return from Munich was seen on television by Murrow and a few hundred Londoners who watched Chamberlain wave his piece of paper signed by Hitler and promise "Peace in our time."

The television future arrived slowly in Canada. The first CBC-TV news program went on the air at 7:30 p.m., September 8, 1952, under the banner of *Newsmagazine*, a program that would carry on for another three decades. The CBC Montreal station, which had opened two days before Toronto, did not carry *Newsmagazine* at first but instead aired at 8:00 p.m. twice a week a fifteen-minute "CBC Newsreel," one in English and one in French, reflecting the fact that there was only one station for both languages. The "Newsreel" was like an old-fashioned movie newsreel with talking dogs, fashion shows, funny monkeys, and a few fires. There were more serious news discussion programs about the United Nations and world affairs, but in the early years of Canadian television, news for the most part was an afterthought in what was essentially an entertainment medium. By today's standards, the news programs then were mostly ponderous productions with stilted commentators, awkward journalists, and not much film of news events. But there was hope that CBC would soon show what was happening in the country as well as just talking about it. "In time," the CBC announced in its annual report in that first television year, "we would like to see a daily news program with material flowing in from scores of news conscious film cameramen."

In March of 1953 the first CBC daily newscast began on television, inserted into a thirty-minute nightly program called *Tabloid* that presented "news, sports, weather in picture stories of wide appeal." The program was seen at first only in Toronto and three months later in Ottawa.

On Monday, January 25, 1954, TV news began a life of its own with a telecast to Toronto, Ottawa, and Montreal at 6:45 p.m. just before *Tabloid*. Larry Henderson was hired as the CBC's first regular news anchorman.

Four months later, Henderson was seen in a new 11:00 p.m. newscast in Toronto, Ottawa, and Montreal, becoming one of Canada's first television stars as each night viewers were welcomed to the "CBC Television News . . . *The National* Edition, with Larry Henderson." By the end of 1955, Henderson was seen on CBC stations in Toronto, Ottawa, Montreal, Halifax, and Winnipeg and on seventeen private affiliates. A year later, Vancouver was also on the air and the television news went from coast to coast. Since this was before CTV was born, Henderson was the only source of national television news for English Canadians from coast to coast.

But within a few years Henderson wanted to spend more time out in the field reporting, especially in the Middle East, and after failing to get a raise up to the princely sum of $25,000, he quit and was replaced by the Gibraltar-like, solid, stolid, unflappable Earl Cameron.

"As Canadian as wheat," one CBC executive had exclaimed at Cameron's selection. But Cameron couldn't have cared less about writing, reporting, or editing. One time in the early 1960s I ran into Earl in the CBC parking lot right after a newscast and asked him some detail about one of the stories. "I don't know," he smiled. "I just read the words." What did interest Earl was his professionalism as an announcer, his careful enunciation and calm demeanour providing the sound of authority. He became, for a time, the most trusted man in Canada. If Earl said it, the country believed it.

While Earl calmly read the news, big changes were brewing in Canadian broadcasting. With the birth of CTV in 1961, CBC television was no longer the only game in town. And CBC-TV news soon had some direct competition. *CTV News* began on September 24, 1962, from its Ottawa base at CJOH at 10:30 p.m. It borrowed the Huntley-Brinkley style of NBC – a fifteen-minute newscast co-anchored by a very young and journalistically tender Peter Jennings and an only slightly more experienced Baden Langton. Both eventually went to the American networks, Langton as an occasional anchor and reporter and Jennings as a visibly inexperienced twenty-six-year-old anchor of ABC news. Within a short time Peter quit in embarrassment to become an ABC reporter and, later, the network's chief European correspondent. Now, with maturity, sophistication, and experience under his belt, he once again has the job as the ABC news anchor, the best, to my mind, of all the American network anchors with his informal but polished delivery and his wide knowledge of international affairs.

The Canadian tradition of news anchors has, over the years, become less British and more American, which means increasingly we have journalists at the helm, not just news readers. Now even the staid old BBC has begun to follow the North American model. But back in the early sixties, *The National* was pretty staid, too, and with a brash new kid on the block in the form of *CTV News*, it was inevitable that something would change.

After seven years as anchor of *The National*, Earl was unceremoniously dumped from that job by executive producer Bill Cunningham, who wanted a journalist and not just a voice in the job. Cunningham offered the anchor seat to the handsome, crinkly-faced Paris correspondent, Stanley Burke, and Stan took it. Stan fitted the bill perfectly. As a CBC correspondent he had covered wars, revolutions, and political crises. He'd been the CBC's correspondent at the United Nations and London as well as Paris. He had credibility and he was a familiar news face. But even as a journalist, Stan faced the same union problems Lloyd Robertson would later encounter.

As a member of the announcer's union, Burke was not allowed to write or edit *The National*, which was the jurisdictional territory of the news union. That infuriated Stan, who always preferred to attack any problem in head-on confrontation. He might have achieved more by quiet persistence, but that wasn't his style. In the end, he was beaten down and grumpily acquiesced in his role largely as a reader of *The National* without much journalistic input. His untapped energy went elsewhere and in 1969, about seven months after I had taken on the job of director of News and Current Affairs, he became inflamed with a passionate public commitment to, among other things, the Biafrans in their rebellion against the government of Nigeria.

In so doing, Burke broke a fundamental journalistic rule. He was so committed to the Biafrans and so outraged at what he felt was a cowardly, do-nothing attitude by the Canadian government, that he began making public statements attacking Ottawa. By late summer I felt he had gone too far, especially with his plan to lead a delegation to Ottawa to protest government policy. In spite of his deep and honest outrage, Stan was destroying his impartiality as anchor of *The National* by taking such a public posture on a highly controversial issue. How could he be credible in presenting a report from Biafra when the audience knew he was actively promoting one side in the argument?

Late one afternoon in August, 1969, I called him over to my office and told him he had to make a choice: stop speaking out publicly for Biafra, or stop anchoring *The National*. Public and press interest was high in what was happening to Stan: in the middle of our conversation, I had a phone call from a reporter from *The Toronto Star* asking me what we were talking about. Apparently someone had seen him coming into my office and had called the reporter. I stalled, hung up, and continued my conversation. It went pleasantly enough for an hour, although initially Stan said he couldn't see any conflict of interest. In the end, he told me his conscience wouldn't let him stop speaking out about Biafra, and he'd have to leave the $30,000 anchor job. I tried to argue him out of it, but he insisted. I told him to think about it overnight. That evening Stan spoke to a conference of young people and announced to them that he was quitting *The National* because he wanted to spend full time fighting for Biafra. A Canadian Press reporter covering the meeting flashed the story to the newspapers and radio and TV stations. I wasn't distressed by this public resignation because I was used to Stan's often free and easy style. When I heard it, I simply asked our public relations people to put out a news release confirming the story and expressing my regrets at Stan's departure. Just after midnight that same night, he called me to say that he'd changed his mind and now wanted to stay. He hadn't known a reporter was covering his remarks. And he was dismayed that I'd issued a confirming press release.

"Oh," he said. "Well. Hmmm. Well. Well. Oh well." And off he went to champion the cause of the Biafrans in speeches, news conferences, and petitions. Stan was happy leading a cause and certainly his efforts on behalf of Biafra at least got the issue more public attention than it might have had. He didn't miss the spotlight of *The National*, and eventually he went on to publish weekly newspapers on the West Coast.

After considerable internal debate, we settled on Warren Davis as Stan's replacement. He was a staff announcer with strong broadcast journalism credentials. He had the talent, as did Burke, to do more than simply read the news well, for he had high skills in producing reports and a strong news sense, too. Those talents could be used, I thought, in strengthening *The National*, although they had to be used carefully, slowly, and subtly because of the union jurisdictional sensitivities. When I offered him the job Davis only somewhat reluctantly agreed. And as it turned out he was not entirely comfortable with a careful, slow approach in the touchy union jurisdiction area. As anchor of *The National*, he was clearly an unhappy man. As the weeks went by his frustration mounted, occasionally causing him to punch his fist through walls, throw furniture around, and scream mightily. After a few months he quit and so we launched yet another talent search. That was when we hired Lloyd Robertson.

SIX YEARS LATER at that lunch on Tuesday, September 7, 1976, Gould and Cameron dangled before Lloyd more money than he'd ever dreamed of, promised significant improvements at CTV News, and most important of all for Lloyd, said he could report as he wanted. There were no unions to worry about at CTV. Lloyd countered that he'd been told the CBC might be able to work out a deal with the unions to let him do reporting. "Hell," said Gould, "they'll never change that so you can report. Never!" Lloyd was receptive. As it happened his $50,000 CBC contract was up at the end of September, so for him the timing was perfect.

Their offer included a salary of $85,000 a year for five years and promises to extend the length of the news, possibly to thirty minutes; the hiring of more senior journalists; more resources and wider news coverage. Gould and Cameron weren't sure how Lloyd and Harvey Kirck would share the anchoring and one idea discussed was for them to split the week. But that was discarded in favour of a two-man anchor arrangement.

One thing Lloyd worried about was Harvey's reaction. "If Kirck doesn't agree, I don't want it," Lloyd told them. Wisely, he insisted as part of any deal that Harvey's salary be substantially raised. Lloyd knew the public relations bombshell that would explode in his face if Harvey quit or was fired, as some CTV people had been thinking. Lloyd knew, too, that he wanted to work with a happy, well-paid co-anchor, not one soured at Robertson's bigger paycheque. CTV agreed.

On the day after his lunch, Wednesday, with dollars and freedom dancing in his head, Lloyd met with his immediate boss, chief news editor Mike Daigneault, and then the two of them came along to my office in the late afternoon. Mike had called me earlier in the day to alert me to this new crisis and I hoped I could talk Lloyd out of quitting. I didn't want to lose him, so I gave it my best shot. We talked of his career hopes, his immediate desires, and generally about what CTV was offering.

"Sure, you'll get more money right now, Lloyd," I said. "But your long-term interests are here." I told him of the value of his CBC pension; the value of the strength of CBC News against "the nickel and dime" CTV news operation. "They're just not going to spend the money on gathering the news. . . . You'll be a puppet," I told him.

"No," he said. "They're planning some real changes." And most important of all to Lloyd, he said they would "give me freedom to report."

With a nervous laugh Lloyd then mentioned Barbara Walters, who had just gotten a well-publicized U.S. news anchor contract for $1 million a year, and he smiled. "So, we're 10 per cent of their population and 10 per cent of their money seems fair."

"Well, who knows," I smiled back noncommittally, and I privately reflected on a conversation I'd had a few days earlier with the head of news at the BBC, Andrew Todd. He'd told me that he had just finished tough negotiations with his news anchor at the time, Angela Rippon, who was holding out for more money. They finally agreed on a big raise, lifting her salary all the way up to $14,000 a year. (It's hard to believe these figures now. British anchor salaries have exploded into the $200,000-$300,000 range while the Americans are hitting $2 million. In Canada, we currently range from $100,000 to $200,000.)

I promised Lloyd I'd put together a deal that was better than CTV's, if not in money at least in benefits and opportunity for advancement. I was encouraged when Lloyd said, "Look, it's not so much the money anyway. I figure it's worth at least 20 per cent difference to work at the CBC."

Nine hours later, at 3:00 a.m. Thursday, I was in an Ottawa hotel room working on a counterproposal to Lloyd – an offer I'd still have to sell to my immediate bosses and to the executive vice-president, Pierre Desroches, and the president, Al Johnson. I was dog-tired from one of those endless days that had come to be almost a routine feature of my bureaucratic existence. The day had begun in Toronto at 8:15 a.m. with dictation, phone calls, preparation for a 10:30 meeting on the budget for News, followed by lunch with an Ottawa executive pro-ducer, a three-hour session with my network colleagues arguing over what programs would be in our 1977-78 schedule, and then the worri-some meeting with Lloyd. I'd rushed from that session to a suite in a nearby hotel for a VIP dinner with a couple dozen prominent Canadian businessmen and a screening of a drama-documentary we were previewing for them on the life and times of Lord Beaverbrook. Actor John Colicos portrayed Beaverbrook with marvellous dramatic flare and I was delighted at the burst of applause as the credits rolled and at the favourable comments I heard after the lights came on as our guests sipped their cognac and puffed their cigars. From there, I raced to the

Toronto airport to catch a midnight plane to Ottawa, and now I sat at my hotel room desk putting the finishing touches on the counter-proposal to Lloyd.

After our meeting, Lloyd had gone from my office to meet his lawyer and accountant to evaluate the CTV offer and work out some modifications. One change he wanted was a ten-year deal – a straight five years with his option to extend it by another five years. CTV had agreed and sweetened the money offer even more: $85,000 in the first year, rising by $5,000 a year to $100,000 in the fourth year. Meanwhile, Lloyd waited for CBC to respond.

A few hours before dawn on Thursday, I finally put away my pen and grabbed four hours' sleep before an eight o'clock breakfast meeting with an Ottawa producer. Then I grabbed a cab out to the CBC headquarters in the Ottawa suburbs for a day-long conference of English and French network executives and CBC head office vice-presidents on programming and policy issues facing the CBC. In the late afternoon, I took a taxi back into downtown Ottawa to meet Dick O'Hagan, Prime Minister Trudeau's communications adviser and an old friend, who had been the information minister at the Canadian embassy in Washington when I was posted there as a correspondent. I wanted to touch base with him since he was a source of information on what the government was up to.

Then it was out to the airport and back to Toronto to plunge into meetings planning our 1977-78 TV schedule and discussing immediate program problems with the upcoming 1976-77 schedule. We would be launching the new schedule at a big media event the next week. Such is the life of the CBC bureaucrat.

The next night, Friday, I met again with Lloyd, who was getting impatient with the delay in getting the CBC proposal. As we sat in a hotel bar across the street from the CBC, he said, "Well, when is it coming? When will there be something on paper?"

"Soon . . . soon," I said. "I'm working on it with Ottawa and it looks good."

Saturday I spent working on budgets and TV schedules for the next season and making phone calls to Ottawa seeking approval of my proposals for Lloyd. Meanwhile, Lloyd was stewing at home.

Sunday night, doubting my optimism, Lloyd met with his old friend, CBC vice-president Don MacPherson, at Don's suburban Toronto home. He told Lloyd, "Keep your shirt on."

Monday involved another plane trip to Ottawa for a screening and more meetings, more phone calls to Lloyd's friends asking them to tell

Lloyd not to jump to CTV, and more phone calls to my bosses about our counterproposals. Finally, late Monday I got approval for the offer to Lloyd and handed it to him.

Tuesday morning was a kaleidoscope of meetings for me: a staff crisis in News, a program problem in Agriculture and Resources, a budget panic in Current Affairs, and another review of our 1977-78 program schedule plans with my network associates. My regular noon editorial meeting (for some inexplicable reason called "the noon balloon") was followed by detailed discussion on new plans for several Current Affairs programs. Finally, at four o'clock, an apprehensively grinning Lloyd Robertson walked into my office along with, to my surprise, his grey-suited lawyer, an accountant, and a pension expert. Since we were old friends, I'd naively expected him to come alone. This seemed like overkill.

Lloyd plopped down on my couch, his lawyer and accountant on either side of him and the pension expert in a chair. We chatted awkwardly for a few minutes until Mike Daigneault arrived, increasingly worried about losing Lloyd. I sat behind my big mahogany desk, facing Lloyd and company. Mike sat quietly in a chair along the side wall. I toyed nervously with a wine glass filled with Diet Pepsi, my standard office libation, while Lloyd and his colleagues sipped from coffee mugs and Lloyd began to speak. He described a meeting at the back end of a downtown bar that he'd had a few hours earlier with a couple of key members of his union nemesis, the Canadian Wire Service Guild.

"You what?" I asked sharply, fearing the union would have tried to scare Lloyd away from the CBC because it didn't want him trying to do any reporting. With a sinking feeling I began to imagine facing all the TV critics the next day who would be here for the annual "launch" of the CBC television season, and somehow telling them that everything at Mother Corp. was rosy.

"Well, I wanted to know what would happen if the Guild lost its grievance against me for reporting in Vancouver," he explained.

"Yeah ... and they said?" I responded. But I already knew the answer.

"They said, 'It wouldn't matter a damn,' " he replied, shrugging his shoulders dejectedly. "They were adamant ... they told me they would fight against me doing any reporting and that the battle might become personal."

"Well, they'll probably lose the grievance, so it won't matter anyway," I replied grimly, but I knew now my cause was nearly lost. I was furious about the meeting because, of course, the Guild was trying to frighten Lloyd and they'd succeeded. (Ironically, the Guild gave up its grievance a couple of months later and the issue never again was a problem.) But it was still a problem for Lloyd, and as I looked at him sitting on my couch he clearly was a discouraged man. His advisers were fidgeting as we continued to talk while Mike sat listening quietly.

"Let's talk about our proposal, Lloyd," I said, mustering as much surface confidence as I could. "It's a good one, better than I'd really expected to get."

The proposed deal was $65,000 a year, rising to $85,000 after five years, a handsome benefits package of medical and hospital care, four weeks' vacation rising to five, and a pension of "at least $26,500" within ten years if he wanted to retire. I knew the money was not as good as that offered by CTV, but I felt we could offer much better long-term career potential for him, especially if Lloyd wanted to move into the management side of broadcasting, which he'd told me was one possibility for him down the road.

As I spoke, Lloyd's lawyer, accountant, and pension expert whispered into his ear, shook their heads, and nodded once or twice. At that moment I could have murdered them.

Mike Daigneault and I looked at each other, smiled tightly, and waited.

"Well, the money's not too bad," he said. "Not as good as CTV, but not too bad."

"Ahh," I muttered.

"But I'd like it to be ten years, not a five-year contract," he said.

"No," I said. "I can't do that, although that might very well happen in time."

"Don't you think I'll be good enough to last ten years?" he asked, his voice rising from petulance to angry shrillness for the first time in our negotiations. Normally Lloyd was a placid individual, and I'd seen him lose his temper only rarely, when he felt under intense pressure. Obviously he was being torn in two by the whole process.

"It's not that at all," I said. "Of course you are and will be, but I just don't feel it's right to make an absolute ten-year guaranteed commitment."

Then I offered to extend his five-year contract another five years, conditioned on both CBC and him agreeing to it.

His accountant smirked and said, "That's not good enough. Besides, we can get Lloyd much better tax advantages with the other offer." He explained that Lloyd could set up his own company and sell his services to CTV, thereby saving a lot of tax money.

"But look at the CBC pension plan and the health care plan," I countered with all the forcefulness I could muster. But I knew it wasn't much.

"Lloyd can do better than that on his own," the pension expert said.

If only I could have talked to Lloyd alone, I thought wishfully. Every time he said something hopeful about my offer, one of his advisers would leap in with a "But, the other deal is better because . . ." To me, they already seemed totally persuaded Lloyd should take the CTV offer, and I saw Lloyd's loyalties to the CBC dissolving before my eyes. As the meeting continued, Lloyd became increasingly impatient. "I knew it was pretty well over by then," he later told me. At the end of an hour or so of more inconclusive to-ing and fro-ing, we all got up, shook hands, smiled as best we could, and Lloyd said, "Well, I'll think about it and let you know."

But in my heart, I already knew. We were beaten by the union, by the accountant, lawyer, and pension expert (whose advice on tax advantages eventually turned out to be decidedly disadvantageous when the government cracked down on what it called a loophole), and, of course, by the CTV offer.

As Lloyd and his phalanx of associates trooped out of my office, I sank back in my chair, depressed and apprehensive. I ruminated on what I would say if we lost Lloyd when, the next morning at nine, I would walk into a room full of TV critics at the fall launch. But I couldn't muse to myself too long. In a boardroom down the hall some producers were waiting for me to discuss a new agricultural program idea. Then I had a six o'clock hand-holding session with an executive who wanted a pay raise and wasn't going to get it, and then later there was a party with Al Waxman on the *King of Kensington* set.

Meanwhile, Lloyd and his advisers went off to have dinner and discuss the two proposals. Lloyd was too keyed up to eat; he drank a glass of milk but pushed away his spiced beef sandwich. Then they drove down to the lawyer's office where he paced the floor while the accountant argued that he should take the CTV offer and the lawyer advised him to consider the CBC offer seriously. Although the money was less, the benefits package offset that, he felt. Finally the accountant won the day, although in the end Lloyd probably made his decision more on the basis of his freedom to report at CTV than on the bigger money. Lloyd swallowed hard and decided to jump. Then he called Mike Daigneault. It was just before 10:00 p.m.

"Mike, I'm sorry, but I'm going," he said.

Then the lawyer called Tom Gould and handed the phone to Lloyd, who said in an oddly detached fashion, "Lloyd Robertson has just agreed to co-anchor *CTV News* with Harvey Kirck." It was as if, even though he'd made up his mind, he was trying to distance himself from the decision.

"Lloyd," said Gould, "you'll never be sorry."

Robertson drove over to Gould's house where they drank champagne, and then, exhausted but super-hyper, he went home. He couldn't sleep and his wife Nancy woke up at 4:00 a.m. to hear him pacing the floor. "My God," he told her, "I've made the wrong decision." He told me later, "That night ... I felt as though I'd kicked my mother in the stomach." Nancy calmed him down, but he stayed awake, troubled and restless, till dawn.

So did I. Daigneault had called me at home about 10:00 p.m., minutes after he put down the phone from Lloyd, and I immediately began trying to figure out how to control the damage the next morning when I faced the TV critics with the fall lineup. They didn't know it yet, but one of the things we wouldn't be offering for the 1976-77 season was Lloyd Robertson. I knew his defection to CTV would become front-page news across the country and I tried to figure out my right move.

I decided the best defence was an offence. My plan was to make a pre-emptive strike by announcing Lloyd's defection before CTV did. That way, I'd take some steam out of their news conference announcement and be able to put my own "spin" on the story. After a late-night phone call to check the idea with Denny Harvey, who said, "Hell of a good idea! Do it!" I then fell exhausted into bed around 2:00 a.m.

Wednesday morning at eight I walked into Studio One in the CBC Jarvis Street complex in downtown Toronto where the launch was being held. It was here that CBC's first programs were produced when TV began in Canada, and it remains active to this day as the studio for *The Journal*. I picked up a phone and called Lloyd at home. "You're absolutely sure?" I asked. "Yes," he said wearily. Then I told him I was going to announce his departure at the launch in half an hour. "What? You are? Gee ..." and he trailed off.

The launch got under way with people arriving late, as usual, clutching styrofoam cups of coffee in one hand and note pads in another. The critics, CBC producers, executives, and public relations staff settled into their uncomfortable folding chairs on the studio floor and, as I had for half a dozen years at these press launches, I introduced a tape showing excerpts of the new season of information programming. But in a painful irony, this was one narrated by none other than Lloyd Robertson.

In my introductory comments I laid heavy emphasis on the importance of depth in CBC journalism, noting our news triumphs, the number and quality of our foreign correspondents, our resources, and our commitment to first-class journalism. I was trying to lay the groundwork for my announcement about Lloyd's departure by emphasizing the importance of "the news machine" and not just the anchor. I knew that Lloyd as anchor was the personification of the news and had, in a way, been "Mr. CBC" for years, that most viewers seemed to think he was responsible for everything. He wasn't, of course, but they thought so, and thus I was trying to dispel that notion in order to soften the coming blow and to demonstrate that CBC News would remain the strong news leader without him. As I talked on, I noticed some of the critics looking at me quizzically, wondering why I was going on at such length about "the news machine."

When the tape was over and the lights came on, I strode out to centre stage, looked out at the critics, and said, "The tape you just saw is now a collector's item. That was Lloyd Robertson's last appearance on CBC."

I could hear a mass intake of breath and the studio suddenly became silent because this was news not only to the critics and entertainment reporters, but to most of the CBC staff present as well. Everybody had their eyes glued on me. "Lloyd is leaving us for CTV," I said. "I'm sorry to lose him and we'll miss him. I wish him luck, but not too much."

About half of the thirty or so critics rushed to the phones and the others came rushing up to me yelling, "What do you mean? ... When? ... What happened."

"Well," I said, "maybe when the BBM audience report came out showing CBC had a 50 per cent lead over *CTV News*, they decided they better do something."

"Why did he go?" another reporter asked.

"For a million different reasons," I smiled as enigmatically as I could, thinking of ten years at about $100,000 a year. I said I didn't know exactly what the CTV offer was, but that it must have been high and irresistible, and I thought it was for ten years. But I added that CTV still did not have anything like the News Service resources the CBC had. In an aside to a colleague, I whispered, "Lloyd's now a million-dollar baby in a five-and-ten-cent store."

A sharp-eared critic with a fast pencil overheard the remark and, of course, it landed on the front pages, somewhat to my embarrassment and much to Lloyd's and CTV's distress. To be honest, I wasn't really upset about the money CTV was paying Lloyd since it simply recognized market realities. And it was paltry compared to American anchor pay. Besides, it gave me leverage in pushing for higher salaries for some of our own journalists. But we were playing hardball in a very competitive game and as a weapon in our competitive war, it was too good not to exploit.

CTV was stunned by my pre-emptive announcement of Lloyd's departure and scheduled a noon news conference to try to regain the offensive. Listening to reports of the event, I savoured its awkward inconclusiveness and low impact. It was a symphony in grey with Tom Gould standing there in his dull grey suit and the similarly clad co-anchors on either side. Harvey Kirck, a gruff but amiable bear of a man, looked bleary-eyed, having flown in overnight from Calgary where he'd been on a public relations tour, unaware of Lloyd's move until the last minute. He was not too thrilled at the prospect of sharing the anchor desk he'd manned alone for a dozen years.

The news conference was edgy and at times antagonistic as Gould and Lloyd vigorously denied reporters' accusations that big money was the reason for Lloyd's switch.

"It'll be the greatest powerhouse up front in any network in the world," Gould said defiantly.

"We're just going to be gangbusters together," said Kirck gamely. ". . . One of the basic factors behind this is that we've been working for years to break that bloody habit of people watching the CBC."

"It was not the money," said Lloyd defensively. "It was a wrenching blow." Describing himself as "a child of the CBC," Lloyd added, "I simply had no assurance [from CBC] that some long-standing [union] jurisdictional disputes could be resolved. . . . Now I'm going to be a practising newsman and broadcast journalist."

Then, trying to brighten the heavy atmosphere, Lloyd looked over at a dour Harvey and quipped, "We're going to call it the Happy and Grumpy Hour." A wan smile creased Harvey's glum face.

Money was clearly the focus of the news stories about Lloyd's move, a fact both CTV and Lloyd resented because it tarnished what they had hoped would be a public relations knockout success. The matter was raised in the House of Commons, where NDP leader Ed Broadbent called it "scandalous," urged special taxes on big salaries, and added, "He's making more than the Prime Minister of Canada. Would you say that his responsibility to this nation is as great as that of the Prime Minister?" The money issue was taken up in editorials and columns and got especially big play because the government had just launched a wage restraint program. Within CTV there was envious hostility among many of the journalists. Bruce Phillips, Ottawa bureau chief (who's now a key aide to Prime Minister Mulroney), was particularly loud and bitter in his criticism to colleagues and Press Club friends, and later he even made an embarrassingly scathing speech about it to a Parliamentary Press Gallery dinner. He was especially angry about Lloyd's lack of reportorial background.

While the headlines and emotions still were hot from Lloyd's announced move to CTV, he remained on the CBC payroll for another couple of weeks. He had, however, been off the air since the negotiations had begun, with back-up announcer George McLean filling in. I breathed a sigh of relief that even though we'd lost Lloyd, at least it was all over. Although it seemed much longer, the whole Lloyd Robertson drama had lasted exactly one week.

As part of CTV's open purse-string campaign to catch up with CBC News and the promises to Lloyd, Gould and Cameron immediately struck again. In a blow not as visible but equally damaging to CBC News, they wooed and won Tim Kotcheff, the executive producer of CBC news specials and the weekly *Newsmagazine*. Kotcheff, a dynamic, hard-working, baby-faced tough guy, had beaten the pants off CTV on every major event from space shots to elections. Losing him was like losing a right arm after the right leg had gone with Lloyd's departure. (Eleven years later he became vice-president of CTV News.)

A month later, on October 18, the Lloyd and Harvey show, the "Happy and Grumpy Hour," began on CTV. The two shared a big desk, Harvey in a blue suit looking stern and, I thought, uncomfortable, while Lloyd, in brown, was at his old smoothie best. Harvey squinted less at the Teleprompter since he had decided to give up his contact lenses and go back to his horn-rimmed glasses, but he refused to lower his chair so that he and the shorter Lloyd could appear at the same height.

As the weeks went by, Lloyd discovered he was missing "Mother Corp.," missing the editorial depth of the CBC news, and missing old friends.

In early December, the Canadian Wire Service Guild, knowing it would lose the case anyway, finally dropped its pending grievance against Lloyd for doing reporting at the Vancouver Habitat Conference the previous spring when he was with the CBC. With that, one of my colleagues called Lloyd and they started conversations about the possibility of him coming back to the CBC. At the time, Lloyd's wife Nancy told a reporter, "After twenty-two years, he still hasn't lost his love for the CBC."

But Lloyd's contract was iron-clad for five years and CTV wasn't going to let him out of it. Nonetheless, there were several informal conversations with CBC News executives - one too many, in fact. And someone – I've never known who – leaked the story to the Toronto *Globe and Mail*. It was a Friday and I'd been to a late-night retirement party for one of my colleagues. About 3:00 a.m. I was catapulted out of bed by an uncharacteristically apoplectic Lloyd Robertson, who was almost incoherent as he fulminated about the front-page banner *Globe and Mail* story detailing the possibility of his returning to CBC. He thought I'd leaked the story to force his hand. That was the last thing I would have done, knowing it would destroy any possibility of getting him back. Someone at CBC who didn't want him back may well have been the leaker.

But there was no use explaining all this to my outraged ex-anchorman. "You're trying to destroy me, for God's sake!" he shouted. "Destroy me!"

"For Heaven's sake, calm down, Lloyd," I said. "The last thing in the world I want to do is to destroy you. I want you to come back. I'm just as angry as you are about the story. Maybe the union did it to keep you away from the CBC. I'd be crazy as hell to tell anyone about the conversations."

Finally, after about fifteen minutes of this sort of thing, Lloyd calmed down, but he was not entirely reassured. Three hours later, the Saturday *Globe* thumped down outside my apartment door and the front-page headline blared out at me. In the story, Lloyd admitted there had been conversations with the CBC about returning, but he added, "I have no intention of returning to CBC." He had called the paper three times after he heard they were publishing the scoop to make sure they knew he wasn't quitting CTV.

I was never part of the conversations with Lloyd about coming back but I had been kept aware of them and advised that he was serious about coming home to "Mother" now that the union grievance was cleared. It would have been a tremendous coup for us, a monumental black eye for CTV, and it might have worked.

After this incident, Lloyd's umbilical cord to "Mother Corp." was finally cut, although he retained a continuing affection for CBC and kept contact with his friends, including me. A couple of years later, after CTV had delivered on only some of the promises made to him, Lloyd wrote me a note saying, "Departing my beloved CBC was the most traumatic event of my life. That is not an overstatement of my reaction." Little did we realize that a few years later Lloyd and I would be amiable on-camera adversaries as opposing anchors of *CTV News* and *The National*.

With the tempest abated, I reflected with some amazement on all the headlines and internal CBC upheaval that Lloyd's departure had caused. Larry Henderson's departure back in 1959 certainly hadn't created such a fuss, nor had Stanley Burke's ten years later, in spite of their high profile. While I could certainly live without such crises, I also realized the storm over Lloyd's leaving was in many ways a good sign. It demonstrated clearly that inside and outside the CBC people were placing a very high value on *The National*, and by extension on all CBC television journalism.

IT'S HARD TO BELIEVE NOW – from the vantage point of 1987 – the sad state TV journalism was in back in the winter of 1969 when I packed up my typewriter and trenchcoat to come home to Toronto to a CBC desk job. The Corporation was still reeling from the upheaval of the death nearly three years earlier of the extraordinarily popular and controversial *This Hour Has Seven Days*. With Patrick Watson, one of the best interviewers in the nation, and Laurier LaPierre, with his stormy emotional impact on the audience, the program was the most talked about, loved, and hated that's ever been aired in Canada. While it was only on the screens for a couple of years, it made a searing impression with its hot-seat interviews, crusading documentaries, and brash reporting, and it has affected all Canadian current affairs programming for the last two decades. (It affected U.S. programming, too, for after seeing *This Hour Has Seven Days*, CBS people developed their own version called *60 Minutes*."Riveting," said former CBS president Bill Leonard after he saw *Seven Days*, although he added, "The investigative journalism seemed to us questionable, to say the least." In his autobiography Leonard said CBS decided to copy *Seven Days*, but to do so "responsibly.") *Seven Days* also set afire the long-simmering rivalry between the News Service and the Current Affairs producers, a rivalry that began when CBC television was born. The first squabble arose around the end of 1953 when news producer Gunnar Rugheimer demanded an expansion of TV news to fifteen minutes within the dinner-hour program *Tabloid*. Ross McLean, executive producer of *Tabloid*, refused to give up the time and the newscast was withdrawn altogether from the show to begin a life of its own a few months later. That prickly News and Current Affairs relationship continued with varying intensity up to recent times.

To outsiders, disputes between the two kinds of information programming at the CBC may seem arcane at best. But to those of us who were there during this period, it seemed, at times, like a life-and-death struggle. In a way it was, because as long as we were fighting each other over the same resources, reporting the same stories, and criticizing each other's approach to those stories, we only added ammunition to those inside the CBC who wanted to reduce the Corporation's commitment to journalism. As it was, most of the CBC senior management regarded broadcast journalism as a necessary nuisance, something to be tolerated but not encouraged. In the mid-1960s as we struggled behind the scenes to give news more clout within the CBC, the public explosion over *This Hour Has Seven Days* broke out.

In a fit of pique and folly in the winter of 1966, CBC senior management had ordered Watson and LaPierre fired from their hosting jobs on *Seven Days* for getting the CBC into so much political and public controversy with the program. The program unit fought back with a public campaign to "save Watson and LaPierre" and "Save *Seven Days*." If the power-tripping *Seven Days* rebels were not seeking a coup d'état, they at least were seeking a coup d'Corp., facing, they claimed, a Corporation management mortally wounded by a fatal blend of ignorance and arrogance. Judy LaMarsh, the lovable and mercurial Secretary of State at the time, agreed with that assertion and publicly scolded and privately mutilated CBC president Alphonse Ouimet. With all the considerable passion she could muster, she lambasted Ouimet and his senior echelon for "rotten management," saying, "absolutely appalling things . . . have gone on in the Corporation." Her source for most of her charges was, of course, the *Seven Days* program unit. She flirted with the idea of the host of *Seven Days*, Patrick Watson, being named president of the CBC, a role in which Patrick could comfortably envisage himself and for which he lobbied personally among cabinet ministers.

From our vantage point in News, we felt *Seven Days* was at times too sensational, too confrontational, and too loose with the CBC's journalistic policies. It was always great theatre, but sometimes it became questionable journalism. On a more selfish and pragmatic basis, we were also frightened by the huge popularity of the program and feared it might expand and even take over many of the functions of the News Service.

There were sharp words and sometimes near fisticuffs between the two sides, with much private grumbling about "stodgy news" on *The National* and "yellow journalism" on *Seven Days*. News even barred *Seven Days* from access to its film library. Late one Saturday night a particularly enterprising *Seven Days* researcher actually broke into our library by climbing over the transom and making off with a piece of archival film. The news union immediately demanded "these pilferers of pictures and slap-happy exponents of the sly lie" be forbidden access to the News department.

But what we in the News Service worried most about was that *Seven*

Days was, in effect, becoming a second news service within the CBC, which meant duplication and wasted resources. Certainly the internal war between the two sides was wasteful, embarrassing, and stupid. We should be working together, not against each other, some of us argued, because only through a united effort could CBC journalism get the kind of priority from the Corporation's senior management that would bring us more resources and ultimately lead to a better TV journalistic service for Canadians.

At this point I got directly involved. From my Washington base as president of the CBC Correspondents Association, I had joined my colleagues in arguing for more clout for the News Service. Our efforts had been ineffective, and anyway, I was always travelling around the world chasing news stories. But one late winter night in 1966 arriving back at my Washington home after covering a Lyndon Johnson dinner speech, I picked up the ringing phone in my study.

"Look, we're getting screwed . . . things have just got to change," said the voice from Toronto.

"Yeah," said a second voice. "We need a revolution, for Chrissakes! Now!" On the phone were Don Cameron, then executive producer of *Newsmagazine* and later the architect of the Lloyd Robertson snatch by CTV, and Bill Cunningham, then executive producer of *The National*. They were agitators par excellence in the internal politics of CBC News as well as the best pair of producers in CBC journalism.

"We've got to change the place around, and we need a candidate, and we want you," said Cunningham.

"Hang on!" I shouted back. "What are you talking about and why me?"

For half an hour Cameron and Cunningham, who through their careers have done more than anyone I know to enhance Bell Telephone profits, and who were known as "The Gold Dust Twins" of CBC journalism for their high-flying personal and professional lifestyle, outlined their grievances and ideas: with the *Seven Days* crisis and our own News Service frustrations over inadequate resources, morale had been plummeting. In those grim days, the CBC *National* newsroom was rapidly becoming "a boneyard of broken dreams," to quote Senator Keith Davey in his 1969 Senate Report on the Mass Media.

It was an old story that I and my colleagues had echoed repeatedly in conversations, meetings, and petitions. Now, Cameron and Cunningham proposed something new: a continuing co-ordinated assault on senior CBC management to force a fundamental change in attitude by giving news the highest priority.

"There's got to be a vice-president of News, if we're to have any real power and make real changes," said Cunningham. "And we figure you for it."

But it wasn't realistic to talk about a vice-president for News at CBC at that time, especially since Bill knew little or nothing about the hierarchical structure of the CBC. What he wanted was for the News Service to make its decisions autonomously without constant reference "up the line." Besides, I felt what really mattered was not the title, but the power and influence on senior management. Also, on a personal basis, while wanting to see the changes Cunningham and Cameron talked about, the bureaucratic thickets of CBC management had never attracted me.

"No, look, talk about the need for clout, for power to change," I responded. "Let's concentrate on fighting for ways to get more internal respect for News and more money to cover stories."

We began to talk about tactics. I felt we had to involve not only key reporters, correspondents, and producers, but the French network, too, and CBC News management, which was as unhappy as we were at the lack of priority for news. They agreed and we started organizing.

Five months of endless hotel room meetings among a small key group of news people, incessant phone calls, and a lot of memos led us to a huge horseshoe table in the big boardroom atop the CBC headquarters in Ottawa, a place I would soon come to know all too well. Meeting with us - correspondents, editors, producers, and CBC News management - were Alphonse Ouimet and a clutch of his vice-presidents. As we laid out our case, the president and vice-presidents listened, nodded, and asked questions. Then we went home - and nothing happened. Seven weeks later, we were back in the same boardroom to reinforce our apprehension and to intensify the pressure on senior management to give news a higher priority than it had. At the same horseshoe table, we argued that "The Corporation must establish a clear, new policy in information progamming.... What is mandatory now is a single cohesive information service of the CBC."

Three hours later, President Ouimet summed up our concerns and our proposals, saying, "We hear you," and ended the meeting.

By fall, *Seven Days* had been cancelled and within a year Ouimet had retired as president. New senior management players began responding to the concerns of the News Service. Some of our grievances were met, but there was no basic structural change toward "a single cohesive information service."

While we were lobbying our bosses for more resources and priority for news, I was also involved in a rapprochement attempt with our Current Affairs rivals. A joint News and Current Affairs program was developed; it was a one-hour, once-a-month, prime-time program with Current Affairs broadcaster Warner Troyer and me as co-hosts and René Lévesque as "special interviewer, overseen by News producer Don Cameron and Current Affairs producer Dick Nielsen.

In the fall of 1968, more than two years after that phone call from Cameron and Cunningham and the ensuing campaign for a priority for the television news service, Gene Hallman, the CBC's new vice-president and general manager of English radio and TV networks (the boss of all English-language broadcasting), made me an appealing offer. It wasn't that the money was enticing – it actually meant about a 50 per cent cut in income. But it also meant returning home and, far more important, an opportunity to try to bring about the reforms my news colleagues and I had been advocating for so long.

Gene wanted me to be in charge of all informational programming in English on radio and television. My responsibilities would range from farm broadcasting and children's programs to *The National* itself. The challenge seemed awesome but it also was irresistible.

A whole new world opened up for me as I moved from the front-line trenches of journalism to the management side, which had its own form of warfare, as I would soon discover. But the moment of the change was filled with memories of my frenetic years as a foreign correspondent, the camaraderie of my colleagues, the sense of instant gratification of a good story, and the stimulation of being on-air. An hour before the announcement of my appointment to be head of CBC's informational programming, I strolled with my memories through the television news room on the fifth floor of the TV building in mid-town Toronto, thinking that relationships with my colleagues would never be the same again as I went from being one of the boys to become the boss. In a peculiar way, it saddened me, as I strolled and chatted amid the battered desks, clacking typewriters, ringing phones, and friendly faces. A chapter in my life was ending, and I both did and didn't want it to.

I left the floor to go down in the elevator and across to the neighbouring, grey-painted old brick building known in the CBC as "The Kremlin." A Georgian-style, three-storey building, it had been built by one of the Fathers of Confederation, Oliver Mowat; in Mowat's old living room, now converted to an almost Dickensian office, I was to meet some of my new colleagues. My newsroom nostalgia faded and my excitement rose at the nearly impossible challenge but tantalizing opportunity to try to make happen all the things my colleagues and I had been fighting for over so many years.

The first thing I did in accepting the job as director of CBC News and

Current Affairs programming was to set down a list of objectives. My agenda put particular emphasis on news. I wanted to put *The National* on at 10:00 p.m. and put it in colour, make it longer, establish special correspondents in such areas as science, medicine, labour, and business, and have full-time *National* reporters in all provinces. I also wanted to have the 10:00 to 11:00 p.m. prime-time period exclusively for journalistic programming. Other items on my list included developing an integrated one-hour news and information program at the supper hour on all local CBC stations; having our journalists take over responsibility for special events coverage, such as the opening of Parliament, royal visits, and other major events that hitherto had been done by the Features department; and having live coverage of Parliament. One strong non-journalistic objective I had was to put special emphasis on Canadian historical documentaries.

It was a big agenda, but some of those objectives, such as putting the news in colour, we were able to achieve fairly quickly. I did that quite simply by stealing and lying. Senior CBC management was against the idea (the new president, George Davidson, didn't even have a colour set in his home) and had brusquely rejected all pleas to allow News to use colour film on the grounds that it would be too expensive. "Besides," one of my bosses told me, "colour might distort the news." He didn't say how. As president of the CBC Correspondents Association, I, along with my fellow journalists, had waged a never-ending battle to put the news in colour. At one meeting with management, my Washington colleague James M. Minifie slammed the table and emotionally pleaded for colour on *The National*, shouting, "Blood is red, damn it!" But management had been unmoved.

Now, as I settled into my new job, I decided to ignore the argument about colour "distorting" the news because it was clearly ludicrous, and I concentrated on overcoming the cost objection. First, we hi-jacked a couple of colour cameras from CBC Ottawa and put them into the news studio so at least our studio production was in colour. Then I asked our news people to begin shooting "archival material" in colour, which turned up increasingly on *The National*. Finally, breaking the limits of veracity, I wrote a memo to my bosses saying we'd found a way to avoid any cost increase whatever by shooting news stories in colour. I had instructed our news people, I explained, to reduce the "use ratio" to four to one - four feet shot for every one used. That was significantly under what we had been doing and it would save more than enough to cover any extra cost of colour shooting. In fact, I said with deliberate terminological inexactitude, "We might even get a budget surplus." Never was a less accurate word written because, of course, the ratio was not maintained and the costs were higher. But I shrouded them in the mists of my overall budget so the net financial impact was nil. And that's how the news got into colour.

I found that in juggling budgets, while you can always use more money, you can also accomplish a great deal by redirecting money from long dead or dying priorities to new ones. I learned, too, it's money on the screen that really counts in broadcasting, not money in the office, and came to believe firmly that a budget is the single most important statement an executive will ever make. It's exactly what you are going to do and not just what you say you're going to do.

Finessing budget figures was something totally new to me. Instead of worrying about my monthly expense account of a couple hundred dollars for papers, books, lunches, and taxicabs, as I had been as a correspondent, I was suddenly propelled into a world of multimillion-dollar budgets. I vividly remember, just after I started my new job, finishing off an old Washington expense account for $78.50 and then going into a budget meeting where the arguments were over tens of millions of dollars. It took my breath away. My breath was also taken away by some of the more creative expense accounts of my former colleagues, which I now saw. One item labelled "PACAR" I noticed turned up not infrequently in one correspondent's account. I subsequently learned he used this as a short form for "Pissed Away, Can't Remember."

Besides getting *The National* in colour, I wanted it longer, too. In seeking this I ran into some CBC management opposition as well as some from the CBC's private affiliates, who didn't like the idea of losing any of their local, revenue-producing time to *The National*. But after spirited debate I got an extra two minutes that extended *The National* to twenty minutes. This may not seem like much, but to me it seemed like an enormous achievement at the time. And it took more than a decade before we achieved the most important goal of all - a nightly hour of prime-time journalism.

I was also able to improve *The National* by quickly establishing the "electronic highway" that was critical in moving us out of the dark ages of communication. The electronic highway used telephone company lines to carry news reports from our TV stations across the country to the network newsroom at set times every day. It gave us instant access to news stories from all parts of the country. Before this, stories generally were air-freighted to Toronto - getting a late-breaking story into *The National* meant buying a special line into Toronto, which was expensive, and editors were reluctant to spend the money. With a line available every night and paid for on an annual basis, we began taking in many more stories from across the country, hence providing a better reflection of the nation on *The National*.

The biggest single challenge was to achieve credibility for our journalists within the CBC itself. Outside the CBC, our journalists were generally highly regarded, but inside many in senior management viewed us as mostly sophomoric juveniles: loud, irresponsible, undisciplined, defiant of authority, and bureaucratically anarchistic. To get approval for any of the changes I wanted, that image had to be overcome, and the place to start was with my head of TV News. I had three failures before I found the right man to provide the credibility needed for TV News. First I tried Joe Schlesinger in the job. Joe had worked for the Associated Press in his native Czechoslovakia, the Paris edition of the *New York Herald Tribune*, *The Toronto Star*, and finally, the CBC. While he had an impeccable journalistic pedigree, he also had a hair-trigger temper and hated bureaucratic procedures and union rules that inhibited his not infrequent desire to fire on the spot those numerous individuals he called "idiots." When one too many attempted firings sputtered yet again into what Joe perceived to be a humiliating backtracking by senior management, he wanted out. The Hong Kong bureau was open, so he became our Far Eastern correspondent. As things have turned out nearly twenty years later, Joe became Canada's number-one foreign correspondent.

With Joe off to Hong Kong, I put into Joe's job Peter Trueman, who was *The National*'s executive producer, an old friend, and a former *Montreal Star* reporter in New York and Washington. That, however, turned out to be another mistake. Like Schlesinger, Trueman had superb journalistic skills but no skill at all in managing. And, increasingly, Peter drank. Peter has written extensively about being a drunk, although I never accepted this self-characterization. But he still insists he often drank himself into oblivion to escape the frustrations of his job. He simply didn't like and couldn't cope with a management job. His heart was out in the field, not behind a desk, and he quit after less than a year in the job.

Next I turned to Bill Cunningham, battle-scarred veteran of many CBC wars, a long-time friend and former *National* executive producer. He was a con man's con man, instigator of the rebellion that had put me into my job as director of News and Current Affairs. At the time I approached him in mid-August, 1971, Bill was the CBC correspondent in London. But he had a lot of enemies both at the working level and, more worryingly, at the higher levels of the CBC. He was accused of being erratic, unconventional, boastful, juvenile, and unreliable. He also was a dynamite journalist – aggressive, determined, far-sighted – and he knew exactly what the News Service needed.

He needed some persuading, but Bill took the job as chief news editor and immediately brought in as a special consultant Brian Nolan, a long-time ABC-TV news producer in Europe and New York and an articulate and passionate advocate of an expanded CBC-TV News Service. Prior to working for ABC, he'd worked on CBC's *This Hour Has Seven Days* and for CTV news.

In the spring of 1972, Nolan produced what became known as "the Nolan Report," laying out the details of how to make the CBC News Service a truly first-class operation with enough money for satellite feeds, more producers, more editors, more specialist reporters, more cameramen, more money for travel, and a new weekly news program. The cost would be about $2.5 million.

While I began "massaging the bureaucracy," seeking support for the Nolan Report recommendations from my senior colleagues, suddenly, another problem confronted me. Bill felt strongly that, having prepared his recommendations, the value of which he felt was self-evident, they should be immediately implemented. As a couple of weeks went by without senior management approval, he grew angry, resentful, and discouraged. Finally he quit. I was angry with Bill's resignation because it now made the battle for the Nolan recommendations more difficult, and I accused him of being more excited by the thunder of his own rhetoric than by the persistent, insistent, pragmatic necessities of accomplishment. Bill, in turn, felt I'd failed him in not getting quick approval.

With three flops in my efforts to get the leadership and credibility I needed for News, I was getting discouraged. But my luck was about to change. After an intense, nation-wide talent hunt, we found exactly the right man.

His name was Denis Harvey, the forty-three-year-old executive editor of the *Montreal Gazette* and a life-long journalist who started as a copy boy of seventeen at the *Hamilton Spectator* and rose to be managing editor. As I was researching his background, I was especially struck by a comment columnist Jack Miller made, quoting his old colleague on the *Hamilton Spectator*: "I don't care what game I go into, or how much bigger or better that other man is, I know, I always know deep down, that I'm going to win."

Over a couple of roast beef dinners in a downtown Montreal hotel, Denny was persuaded to accept the job, mostly by the challenge of the exciting world of television to a man who'd spent his whole professional life in a print medium. What made it exciting for me, too, was the fact that after months of coaxing and cajoling, we'd finally gotten senior management approval for most of the improvements recommended by the Nolan Report.

While I was preoccupied by television, radio information programming was also part of my empire, and my agenda of objectives also included making some changes in our local radio programming. The radio network was developing *As It Happens*, which became one of the most successful radio programs Canada has ever had. I felt we needed the same kind of dramatic change for local radio and encouraged an experiment in Winnipeg. Borrowing from some American ideas, our innovative Winnipeg producers put together a 6:00 to 8:30 a.m. program combining news reports, excerpts from City Council, reports from the legislature, traffic reports, sports, and weather. The concept then represented a radio revolution, and it was endorsed by a special study on the future of CBC Radio. With its success in Winnipeg, other stations across the country began developing the idea. Later, a similar kind of radio program was developed for late afternoon to precede the network news at 6:00 p.m. That, too, became standard over the years.

By 1970 the direct responsibility for both radio and television information programming was proving to be an excessively heavy load and my boss, Gene Hallman, decided to split the management of radio and TV so each medium would have its own management team, thus providing a sharper focus. Now the main focus of my attention was on television. I asked all producers, editors, managers, and others to think ahead to the kind of information programming they wanted to see in 1975. It seemed so far away, but out of several trees worth of memos I fashioned a ten-page statement under the banner "Objectives 1975 – CBC TV Information Programming." It was to be the first of a series of philosophical statements that I would put together over the next eight years.

Flowing out of my look ahead to 1975, I plunged into a major revision of the whole TV schedule. Weeks of intense meetings, arguments, and compromises produced a twenty-page document called "The Strips," which envisaged three journalistic programming "strips" of one hour in length in the TV schedule Monday through Friday. One was in mid-afternoon, one at the dinner hour, and one from 10:00 to 11:00 p.m.

Months of argument followed. The finance people said it would cost too much. The facilities people said it would take more facilities than we had. The commercial people said the CBC would lose needed commercial revenue. In the end, we went ahead with one strip, expanding and integrating the local dinner-hour program across the country and adding new journalistic programming to the prime-time schedule, but not as a "strip."

Little did I imagine that the battle for the strips would last for another decade as the fight for prime-time news continued. Still, with Denis Harvey as chief news editor and many of my original objectives in place, we were beginning to achieve the internal and external credibility needed for that breakthrough into prime time. There was progress, too, in current affairs with the birth of such programs as *Marketplace*, political documentaries on the Diefenbaker-Pearson era and on the times of Mackenzie King, and the production of the landmark docudrama *The National Dream*. By 1976, the firestorm of publicity over Lloyd Robertson's switch from CBC to CTV demonstrated both public fascination and internal preoccupation with news, a far cry from the senior management disinterest that had hamstrung us in earlier years.

With Lloyd gone, the search was on once again for someone to sit in the hottest on-air chair in Canadian broadcast journalism. At one point in the search, Denny Harvey asked me why I didn't apply for the job. It was the second time in my career that the subject had been raised. I even auditioned in 1966 before deciding against applying. This time, I paused for a couple of heartbeats before saying "No." The prospect of more money and an end to bureaucratic infighting made the idea momentarily tempting, but there were still some battles I wanted to fight. In fact, even as CTV had lured Lloyd away and I'd been locked into the preparation of the fall 1976 TV lineup, offstage thunder could be heard from Peter Herrndorf, whom I had brought in to run the Current Affairs area of programming. The noise was being made by the internal struggle over *Ninety Minutes Live*.

2 TROUBLE IN NINETY MINUTES

In the fall of 1976, amid all the hullabaloo about Lloyd Robertson's departure, *Ninety Minutes Live* was struggling toward birth and short-lived critical acclaim. Our eclectic hour and a half talk-show mix of irreverence, controversy, interviews, and song and dance had been gestating for more than two years. With headline and magazine-cover adulation, expectations were high, hype was out of sight, and millions of dollars and many a reputation were riding on its success. Every late-night talk show tried in Canada, going back to the nightly *Better Late* with host Rick Campbell fifteen years earlier on Toronto's CFTO-TV, had failed because audiences switched off or switched to an American channel. But we were determined this was going to be different. It was to be no pale northern replica of Johnny Carson, but a uniquely Canadian blend of journalism and entertainment.

In spite of host Peter Gzowski's pre-show jitters, nervous walking to and fro, and apprehension about the critics, at 11:35 p.m. Monday, November 29, 1976, *Ninety Minutes Live* hit the TV screens of the nation as a howling success. "A knock out!" said the *Globe and Mail*. "Near perfect," said *The Toronto Star*.

And it was. As director of News and Current Affairs, I was on a swing through St. John's, Halifax, Moncton, and Charlottetown meeting with producers and station executives and missed the opening night excitement back in the Toronto network studio. But as I watched Gzowski make his debut on my Charlottetown hotel room TV set, I saw he'd shed a lot more than his accustomed blue jeans, sports shirt, and shaggy hair for a tailored suit, tie, and neatly trimmed hair and moustache; he seemed quite at ease for an opening night. One of his remarks a few days before the show began had set the perfect Canadian tone – "We're not going to have Zsa Zsa Gabor on at all," Gzowski had said.

Instead of Zsa Zsa, I saw Canada's Grande Dame of the opera world, Maureen Forrester, singing in her rich contralto voice, guffawing when Peter revealed she told dirty jokes backstage, and admitting she had switched from Scotch to vodka to clear her throat. There, too, on my 19-inch screen, I saw Peter and Lise Payette, an old broadcast friend of his and now a cabinet member in René Lévesque's just-elected separatist government, anguishing about whether Canada could or should stay united. Peter was poignant in his pleadingly hopeful belief in Canada as a single nation, while Lise passionately expressed her own dream of a separate Quebec.

Gzowski enthusiastically talked football with Ottawa gridiron star Tony Gabriel, worried about genetic engineering with Canadian scientist David Suzuki, listened intently to American author Alex Haley speak about his book *Roots*, and applauded lustily at the legendary jazz trumpeting of Dizzy Gillespie. Completing this remarkable opening night were the high-flying antics of a comic trampoline team called The Rebounders, followed by a demonstration of Japanese pressure-point massage.

As I switched the set off in my Charlottetown hotel room, I sat back on the couch and breathed a huge and happy sigh of relief. It had worked! It had worked in spite of violent internal opposition from our own local station program directors who hated giving up their local time in the TV schedule for what one called "This network turkey foisted on us," from the envious CBC network Variety area responsible for light entertainment programming, which felt shunted aside because it wanted to produce its own late-night talk show, from the alarmed and apprehensive CBC commercial salesmen who feared a loss of audience share and commercial revenue by airing a Canadian talk show instead of old American movies. There had been loud opposition, too, from the private stations affiliated with the CBC, who simply hated the whole idea and most of whom refused to carry the program. This meant that some parts of the country would not see it at all. While the CBC local stations had to carry the program, the affiliates had no such obligation.

My happiness at the show's successful debut, however, had a painfully short life. Within weeks, the initial critical cheers for our high-priced, high-risk program adventure turned into jeers as the whole thing began going off the rails: "a perfectly disastrous production . . . a perfectly disastrous host," said *Toronto Sun* TV critic Bob Blackburn, and his comments were echoed from coast to coast.

What had happened? Never before had a show been so thoroughly researched, planned, and tested. Never before had a host gone through so much preparation, coaching, and rehearsal. So what had we done wrong?

IT HAD ALL BEGUN at lunch one late spring day in 1974 shortly after I'd appointed Peter Herrndorf as head of TV Current Affairs.

"Do you know Peter Gzowski?" Peter asked me.

"Sure," I'd said. "I've known him since he was writing at *Maclean's* and I was trying to sell free-lance articles to them years ago."

"I'd like to meet him," Herrndorf smiled earnestly. "There's an idea I'd like to explore with him."

That idea was the beginning of *Ninety Minutes Live*.

A few days later, Herrndorf had lunch with a sceptical Gzowski and with radio producer Alex Frame. Together they had been responsible for the phenomenal success of CBC Radio's *This Country in the Morning*. Neither had much television experience or much interest in the medium, although Frame had been a producer on a prime-time Current Affairs program for a couple of years. The Scottish-born Frame had first met the Amsterdam-born Herrndorf when they were both working in Edmonton, but he really didn't trust him at first, partly because Herrndorf was a Harvard Business School graduate with a reputation as a shadowy backroom CBC power broker and partly because he felt Herrndorf had once tried to move in on a Viennese blonde in an Edmonton art gallery of whom Frame was particularly, if only momentarily, fond. "Then this tomcat came along," he later mused. But such suspicions were quickly overcome and they agreed to develop Herrndorf's late-night show idea.

Typically, I heard nothing more from Herrndorf about this for months except for an occasional passing reference to research he was gathering. In fact, Gzowski, Frame, and a couple of colleagues were hard at work preparing a massive case in support of the show. More than a year later, in mid-1975, Herrndorf loped into my office in his characteristic offhand way and plopped himself down on the couch. As usual he was tieless, wore a loose sweater over one of his favourite blue Brooks Brothers button-down shirts, and was holding a mug of coffee. He smiled in wary affability from behind his droopy black walrus moustache and began to talk. I thought, not for the first time since I'd known him, that this lanky, shambling fellow with his disarmingly casual manner was in fact one of the sharpest up-and-comers at the CBC. I'd hired him to run Current Affairs but I was sure it wouldn't be too long before he was giving me orders.

I vividly remembered the savvy he'd shown about six months earlier when I'd asked him to take on the job as head of Current Affairs programming. He then was a special assistant to the vice-president in charge of English radio and TV, but programming was his first love. However, he was leery of my offer. First, he wanted me to guarantee more program money for the department. Second, he wanted clout with the TV schedule makers to ensure a fast start. Like General Montgomery, he wanted all the resources he could muster so he could attack like General Patton. I soon discovered this was typical of his approach. More often than not it worked.

It's difficult to say where he got the drive for his long, high-intensity hours of work, where he acquired his fascination with power. Maybe it had something to do with the fact his family had to start a new life in Canada at the end of World War II. The thirty-three-year-old Herrndorf had emigrated to Canada with his parents from the Netherlands shortly after the war ended and had grown up in Winnipeg. Later he went to Halifax to earn a Dalhousie University law degree, and, later still, he graduated from the Harvard Business School. He also had an armful of journalistic credentials. He'd been a reporter for the *Brandon Sun* and *Winnipeg Tribune*, an editor at CBC News Winnipeg covering City Hall and the legislature, and a producer at CBC Public Affairs Edmonton, where at one point he'd hired as a program host a politically ambitious young man named Joe Clark. He had also been a Public Affairs network producer in Toronto.

Herrndorf was a political junkie, especially fascinated by American politics. If Peter had a hero, Bobby Kennedy would be his, as he is mine. I remember once being with Peter in St. John's on the night of the 1972 U.S. election, watching the CBC news special reporting the results. As time went on and the conclusion became clear, I called the TV control room at CBC Toronto to ask the producer to end the special and go back to regular network programming, which they did a few minutes later. Peter was aghast. "You're not cutting it off!" he exclaimed. While he admitted the principal results were in, he still wanted to know what was happening in various obscure Congressional races and how candidates had done in specific counties. Since U.S. stations at the time weren't seen in St. John's, he wanted to see more results on CBC. He pouted for a while at my apparent affront to his desires, and then he went off to phone a friend in Toronto, who held the receiver up to a TV set tuned to an American station and Herrndorf happily listened to the political minutiae as the phone bill mounted.

I'd first gotten to know Peter Herrndorf about 1970 when he was special assistant to Gene Hallman, then CBC vice-president and general manager of English radio and TV services. In that job Herrndorf had been a key member of the groups planning the revitalization of TV news and of the Drama and Variety areas. I'd seen him in action during this period and I knew how good he was at exercising power behind the scenes. He was very young, but he looked older with his prematurely bald head and intense style. His talent and driving ambition had led associates to characterize him behind his back as a bald eagle "wunderkind."

He had a passionate commitment to current affairs programming and I counted on that when I wooed him to run that department. I needed someone with his verve to take over what had become a creatively listless program area. I thought he could provide the same kind of leadership in Current Affairs that Denny Harvey had brought to News a couple of years earlier. As with Harvey, my bosses were persuaded to provide a priority for Current Affairs programming, which gave us the resources and clout we needed to get Herrndorf to take my job offer and which would provide a foundation for exciting new program ventures.

As we began working more closely together I found my admiration and liking for him grew, although in spite of a seeming openness he kept a self-protective shell around himself, especially around his personal life. I sometimes found this frustrating when he played his bureaucratic cards close to his vest, and at times I fumed at his unwillingness to share information with me on exactly what was going on in his area of programming. He didn't like me talking program details with his producers. "Generalities, policy and direction, sure," he told me, "but they must know that I, not you, am their immediate boss."

But now, in my office, he was selling his talk-show program idea and he was earnestness and sweetness personified. "The CBC audience is stodgy and old, but we can get a whole new youthful audience," he enthused. "We can bring in a new generation of CBC viewers who aren't watching now. They're available if we only can reach them. The show will be consciously populist . . . heavily Canadian . . . people-oriented, personal, and put some fun in current affairs."

As usual, Peter had done his homework, with every detail from financing to scheduling elaborately examined. He'd also sent out scouting trips to New York, London, and Los Angeles for information on how to run such a show. As I listened to him weave his spell, I became both excited and increasingly uneasy. I was excited at the prospect of the program triumph he envisaged. His confidence was infectious, and so was the thought of translating the popularity of Gzowski and *This Country in the Morning* to late-night television. Maybe Frame, Gzowski, and Herrndorf could actually pull it off. But other thoughts nagged at me. The project would be costly (in the millions), would soak up an enormous amount of time and energy, and would inevitably set off a political war inside the CBC. The program would be as much entertainment as it would be journalism and that would pit Variety, which produces light entertainment programming, against Current Affairs. But Peter, as always, was adamant and enthusiastic, and my doubts washed away in his exuberance.

As I suspected, the Variety area, the Sales department, the local CBC stations, and the private stations affiliated with the CBC were all against the idea. So the battle to win approval for the show would certainly be tough and bloody. Selling me on the idea was only Herrndorf's first stop. Not only did I have to be convinced but so did my key colleagues at "Vatican North," as the network headquarters in Toronto was labelled. (Corporate headquarters are in Ottawa.) We and our key network staff were on five floors of a downtown Toronto building, one of a couple dozen CBC buildings scattered around the city. Our offices got that nickname after we moved to Bay Street from our original location, "The Kremlin," beside the Jarvis Street main studios. My network colleagues included my counterpart program director, Jack Craine, who was in charge of all drama, sports, music, and light entertainment programming, Norn Garriock, the TV managing director and our immediate boss, and Norn's bosses, Don Mac-Pherson and Denis Harvey. MacPherson was the vice-president in charge of all CBC radio and TV English broadcasting who had succeeded Gene Hallman, and Harvey had been promoted from chief news editor to be MacPherson's deputy.

Since Peter had formerly been Hallman's special assistant, he knew exactly the kind of information MacPherson and Harvey would need to make their final decision and he also knew how to tailor his sales pitch to get the best reaction.

Some months after the conversation in my office with Herrndorf, he, Gzowski, Frame, and a couple of colleagues arrived at 2:00 p.m. in the modernistic sixth-floor boardroom of Vatican North for Herrndorf's first major sales pitch to the full network brass. Herrndorf and company were all on edge, especially because the projector for a slide presentation they'd planned was late in arriving and then they found their slides had been made in the wrong size and couldn't be used. Frame nervously toyed with the glasses on his chubby-cheeked face, smiling hesitantly; Gzowski stroked his moustache and fiddled with papers; and Herrndorf kept pulling at the fringe of black hair at the side of his freckled, bald head. Then MacPherson announced he had to leave by four o'clock to catch a plane to Ottawa, and throughout the presentation he made paper airplanes as he listened. But at least he and Harvey were listening.

Herrndorf, Gzowski, and Frame had polished the substance of their presentation for weeks, even resorting to late-night rehearsals and role-playing of the boardroom scenario now unfolding. They knew their primary targets were Don and Denny. Once those two had been persuaded, CBC president Al Johnson still had to be won over. But if and when MacPherson and Harvey were on side, the president's blessing likely could be won without too much difficulty.

Peter opened the talk by slapping down a thick, slick, forty-five-page report Gzowski had written. It was full of coloured charts and diagrams and overflowing with hype and sociological jargon. "This is a proposal modelled on nothing else that has gone before or is now appearing anywhere else," the report said, unhindered by modesty. "The program is not a 'talk' show. Neither is it 'variety.' It is 'public affairs.' But 'public affairs' as never seen before."

"We're after the younger, more sophisticated, better educated audience," Herrndorf said. "It'll bring new people not only to late-night viewing, but, in time, to all CBC programming. We'll give the CBC a whole new image."

As the presentation drew to a close I looked around the long boardroom table. Jack Craine and Norn Garriock were frowning, their deep scepticism written all over their faces. Jack, known among us behind his back as "The Philosopher," gazed up at the ceiling, smiled from time to time, rubbed his tubby stomach, and sometimes thoughtfully fingered his brown and grey beard. He knew the trouble this project would bring him with his grumpy and jealous Variety area. Norn, a tall, hearty wartime Navy officer nicknamed "Guns" by his shipmates, sat erect, his crinkly, grey-haired head cocked to one side, listening warily. He was keenly sensitive to the objections from the private station affiliates of the CBC and our own commercial sales people. Don was waving a big cigar, blowing huge clouds of smoke, and playing with his paper airplanes. Denny was nodding with a concentrated look on his face, if not in agreement at least in understanding. MacPherson's offhand, almost detached style suggested, I felt, that he was interested. I knew him well enough to realize that otherwise he'd be grilling Herrndorf more intently. Denny's nod was another hopeful signal.

The decision at the boardroom table was a cautious "Let's go to the next stage" judgement, meaning not a "Yes" just yet, but a "Positive Maybe," a typically careful bureaucratic approach. Even so, it was another step forward in the continuing effort to put information programming front and centre in our TV schedule. The "next stage" would be preparation for some pilot runs.

Herrndorf's late-night talk show had suddenly moved from being a long shot to a real possibility. Over the next few months I watched with admiration as Peter went into action. Outwardly nothing had changed. He still ambled about the CBC corridors puffing away on his Rothmans as he chatted up secretaries and executives, smoking, gossipping, and downing coffee by the gallon. But now his friendly, eager approach had one overriding purpose. Behind the scenes the Herrndorf juggernaut surged on as he lunched and lobbied, stroked and soothed anyone who would have an impact on the "Go or No Go" decision, from the president on down to a facilities co-ordinator. He infected most of them with his own confident, even arrogant, assumption of a "Go." He even gave Al Johnson a T-shirt with "The Prez" on the back and "Ninety Minutes Live" on the front.

I knew as well the other side of Herrndorf – the cold, smoking anger when he didn't get what he wanted. What he wanted in this daring gamble was nothing short of the best in resources, financing, and talent, and when he didn't get it a tight-lipped, narrow-eyed wrath erupted, leaving in his wake many a bruised and bitter bureaucrat.

And the opposition inside the CBC was also busy. Variety head Jack McAndrew, a black-bearded, balding, hard-driving Maritimer, argued it was "crazy" for Current Affairs to produce a late-night talk show when, he said, "It should be show business, not journalism, for Christ's sake!" There was opposition, too, from Mike Daigneault, my chief news editor, who felt his dream and mine of a *National* longer than the current twenty minutes would be jeopardized. He didn't mind the show itself, but he wanted it to start later so he could have a full half-hour *National*. Herrndorf. of course, would have liked *Ninety Minutes Live* to start at 11:00 p.m., with *The National* moving to 10:00 p.m. A 10:00 p.m. *National* was something I'd been seeking since before I'd arrived back in Toronto from Washington, but that was another battle still to come and it wasn't going to happen just yet. So the start time of *Ninety Minutes Live* would have to be sometime after our 11:00 p.m. newscast.

That presented two more problems. Right after *The National* was a five-minute commentary called *Viewpoint*, an electronic soap box for citizen opinion on everything from geo-political strategy to the value of Santa Claus. This was followed by local news, usually thirty to forty-five minutes long, on our local CBC stations across the country. Herrndorf was spooked by Johnny Carson and demanded that his talk show start immediately after a twenty-minute *National*; this would put him on the air at 11:20, ten minutes before Carson. But it would mean killing *Viewpoint* and incorporating a brief local news report at midnight within *Ninety Minutes Live*. And it would also mean *The National* would stay at twenty minutes.

I had a different agenda: to extend *The National* to twenty-five minutes, or ideally half an hour, and then go to a fifteen-minute local newscast by the local CBC stations, and finally to *Ninety Minutes Live*. Herrndorf was angry at me whenever I discussed this scenario with him because it would delay his talk show until 11:40 or 11:45, ten or fifteen minutes after Carson started. He was also convinced he'd inherit a much smaller audience from local news than from *The National*.

The CBC local stations were angry at me because my scenario would cut back substantially on their local news time; they wanted to start their local news immediately after a twenty-minute *National*. The Sales department was angry at me because my schedule format would eliminate a one-minute commercial between *The National* and *Viewpoint* that earned one million dollars a year for the CBC. They were also mad because the new show would kill the late-night reruns of old American movies, which produced a lot of money in commercials – much more than could be earned in a Canadian talk show. Finally, the private stations affiliated with the CBC were angry at me: in no way would they accept a longer *National* since it would cut into their local time, supplanting some local commercials.

Amid this minefield, the last thing I expected was a public outcry about the possibility of killing *Viewpoint*. For eighteen years, *Viewpoint* had provided a TV platform for what was often clumsy and sometimes inarticulate opinion, but it was opinion expressed by average citizens. Although in its heyday it had been a valuable program, I felt it had become less an effective soap box and more a numbing chatterbox and I'd had surveys taken that showed it was a turn-off for most viewers.

Suddenly, however, everybody – from John Diefenbaker to Foster Hewitt, and from Farley Mowat to Juliette – was publicly castigating us for the program's impending death. Irving Layton wrote a poem pleading for *Viewpoint* to continue. Barbara Frum on *As It Happens* campaigned to preserve this electronic version of Hyde Park corner. I was characterized by a columnist as "The Lord High Executioner" of the public's right of expression. In retrospect, I think I shouldn't have killed it but moved it to a different time and given it a more focused format.

While I was facing all this distress inside and outside the CBC with my scheduling scenario, late one January afternoon in 1976 my immediate boss, TV managing director Norn Garriock, called me into his office. He was upset at my plans to extend *The National* as well as airing *Ninety Minutes Live*.

"You're just not going to get it all," Norn barked as I entered the room. "There's just too much opposition inside and out."

"But we can do it," I said. "The News people can do it; Herrndorf can do it; the plant can do it; the surveys show it'll be popular; and," I said, as my voice rose and I went into one of my favourite fervent pitches, "the CBC is a public broadcaster and has a mandate to do this. It's why we exist. We're not just some commercial venture."

Garriock sighed, having heard this argument from me so many times before, and said, "Well, it just isn't going to fly this time. Run it up the flagpole as much as you like, nobody's gonna salute. When the rubber hits the road, nothin's gonna happen." Normally I would have been privately amused by Norn's excessive fondness for those kinds of phrases, but this time I was too angry to notice.

I thundered out of his office, strode down the hall and into my own, and started scribbling thoughts until midnight. I was desperately look-ing for a way to preserve *Ninety Minutes Live* along with my plan for a longer *National*. There was no damn way I was going to give in. Norn may have thought I was bull-headed, but I called it persistence.

Rather than trying to get everything at once, I decided to try to achieve my late-night objectives one by one. First I won approval, in spite of all the public criticism, to kill *Viewpoint*. In its place we put a news backgrounder called *Special Assignment* produced by the staff of *The National*. It was, in effect, a stalking horse for a longer newscast – the next step in my plan was to incorporate it into a lengthened *National*. But that would be a fight I'd have later with the private affiliates.

While I was battling behind the closed doors of Vatican North, other internal CBC sharpshooters were targeting on *Ninety Minutes Live* and on Herrndorf, Frame, and Gzowski. Sharp criticism came from Ross McLean, program director of Toronto's CBLT. Ross was a highly articulate and talented producer in the early years of TV, and a man who had produced his own late-night TV shows with indifferent success, including the first one in Canada, called *Midnight Zone*, which had aired once a week. The whole project, he said, was "distressingly derivative," "dreary," a "blend of gaucherie and gangling hostmanship," and "sub par and warmed over." If allowed to go ahead, "it will confirm my bleakest view of this company's infinite capacity for self and public torment." But Herrndorf and I were not swayed. Neither were our bosses on the sixth floor of Vatican North.

But we were troubled by the problem of money. It was going to cost at least a couple of million dollars a year, relatively inexpensive for an hour and a half of programming five times a week, but still a lot of money that could have gone to other programs. Some of that two million would come from what was already being spent on the American movies we now wouldn't be carrying, some from budget pruning in Herrndorf's own programming area, some from my overall budget for the whole journalistic area, and some from Don MacPherson and Denny Harvey's budget for running all English-language radio and TV. All of that meant taking money away from other programs. This, in turn, created more enemies for *Ninety Minutes Live*, especially producers whose budgets would be cut or who wouldn't get hoped-for program budget increases. In the end, Herrndorf didn't get as much money as he wanted, but I felt it was enough.

But none of this deterred Peter's enthusiasm. He rejected arguments about spending so much money for the relatively small number of people watching late-night television by citing audience research figures and projections, repeating endlessly, "We're after a young, sophisticated, educated audience which will bring new people not only to *Ninety Minutes Live*, but, in time, to all CBC programming. We'll give the CBC a whole new image to everybody's benefit."

Impressed as much by Herrndorf's dynamism and commitment as by the program itself, CBC senior management began slowly moving toward approval of the show. Finally, in early 1976, about a year and a half after Herrndorf first sold me on his talk-show idea, MacPherson and Harvey agreed to a mid-winter two-week trial run in Halifax to be seen only locally, and a two-week spring run in Vancouver that was also planned to run locally but which we later decided to put on the network.

Now the focus shifted from the battle of the boardroom and the internal memoranda to the man who would host *Ninety Minutes Live*, Peter Gzowski.

Peter had been a boy wonder of Canadian journalism: youngest managing editor in history, at the *Chatham Daily News*; writer for and then editor of *Maclean's*; editor of the *Toronto Star Weekly*; and popular host of *This Country in the Morning*.

Like many of us in the business of journalism, Peter is a shy egomaniac. In his case a healthy ego is cloaked in a "Golly gee, aw shucks" diffidence. Ever since I'd first met him at *Maclean's* in the days when I was still covering the Washington beat, he'd had that same surface boyishness, that smiling enthusiasm concealing an aggressive, competitive core. He knew what he wanted and he knew how to get it. He'd conquered the print world and radio, but television was yet to be won.

While Gzowski had been successful with his radio work, TV still worried him. "My failures have taught me a lot," he told a Toronto critic. "Now if I can't be a successful TV host, it's gonna hurt, but it won't be the end. There'll be other things to do." But even with these self-protective musings, Gzowski was just as determined as Herrndorf and Alex Frame to make the show a huge success.

But if Herrndorf exuded confidence about *Ninety Minutes Live*, Gzowski exuded apprehension, almost as if he were setting himself up for a fall. He was haunted by the critical attacks from his previous TV experience when he had awkwardly and briefly hosted a late-night talk show for, of all people, Ross McLean, now one of his most acerbic critics. One of the reasons he wanted the show tested outside Toronto was to get away from what he called "the torpedo tubes" of Toronto critics.

The first real test was in Halifax, where on a Monday night in late February, instead of local news and an American science fiction film called *Space 1999*, there on the screen right after *The National* was a nervously smiling, bespectacled Peter Gzowski and a parade of guests ranging from former South Vietnam leader Nguyen Cao Ky to eleven-year-old Toronto gymnast Elfi Schlegel. The show began with tears that dripped down the face of undulating U.S. pop singer Freda Payne. Everyone was touched, but the moisture was actually the result of an allergy to the paint on her microphone. Gordon Pinsent sang and talked, then Peter's old pal, radio legend Max Ferguson, imitated Pierre Trudeau in a congratulatory phone call.

One of the highlights of that first show was a flame-haired, exceedingly well-endowed young woman named Cherry Vanilla who called herself "the world's greatest groupie" and who displayed a distracting penchant for pulling down her blouse to reveal more of her ample bosom. When asked on air by Gzowski, "What does a groupie do?," Cherry replied cheerily to the aghast host, "Basically, you go to bed with rock stars."

58

After the opening show, 115 Haligonians called in to complain about *Space 1999* being pre-empted, and there were complaints about the local news being delayed until midnight when it ran as an insert into *Ninety Minutes Live*. But more important to me and Herrndorf, the reviews were favourable. "Gzowski Show Has Big League Aura" headlined the *Globe and Mail* (whose reviewer had gone to Halifax for the trial run) to my relief and Herrndorf's exultation. Even more significant were the audience figures, which showed a big jump in viewers for the Halifax station when the program aired.

Back at network headquarters as we assessed the trial run, it looked to me like a success both in program content and in audience appeal. It blended journalism, gossip, and entertainment in what I felt was a uniquely Canadian mix. Surveys showed a whopping 70 per cent of the Halifax viewers watching TV at 12:30 a.m. were tuned into *Ninety Minutes Live*. (Normally Johnny Carson at that time in Halifax got only 15 per cent of the viewing audience.) It also had been a good shakedown cruise for Gzowski and Frame, who both learned more about TV pacing, guest peccadilloes, audience preferences, and the art of working with local station technical crews. This last was important because the plan was to produce the show outside Toronto one week out of three.

As we were bathing ourselves in self-congratulatory assessments, a government-imposed budget cut suddenly descended on the network and I found myself slashing here, pruning there, and, along with Herrndorf, imploring my bosses to save our baby before it had even been born. They finally did, and by spring of 1976 not only were MacPherson and Harvey committed to the show, so, too, was Al Johnson. Herrndorf's pie in the sky of two years earlier had now become a probable starter for the 1976-77 TV season. The final "Go" and precise air time were still to be worked out after the second trial run in Vancouver.

For the Vancouver run, the audience figures were almost as good as in Halifax, and the critics were mixed but generally positive, including a rave from the *Calgary Herald*'s Bill Musselwhite: "Ninety Minutes Live . . . YAA HOO!! . . . It's great," he wrote. Much as politicians follow intently the columns of political pundits, broadcast executives pay close attention to TV critics. What they have to say is important since they set a mood in the industry even if the public at large isn't much swayed by their comments. And given his years of experience and reputation, we judged Musselwhite as one of the most influential critics in the country.

An extraordinarily high 2,500 phone calls came in to CBC stations across Canada during the network trial run, demonstrating that if nothing else, *Ninety Minutes Live* certainly affected people. In Vancouver alone, there were 528 positive phone calls from the public and only 58 negative ones.

It seemed we were on a roll, and a few weeks later we did a June trial run in Winnipeg. By now, tension had seized Herrndorf, Gzowski, Frame, and their *Ninety Minutes Live* colleagues as they waited anxiously for a "Go or No Go" decision on the show. Reacting to the stress, Gzowski's back went bad on him as the Winnipeg trial run began and he was in such pain he could hardly move. Herrndorf drank more coffee and smoked more Rothmans than ever before, his nerves increasingly taut as days went by with no word on whether his show would be approved. At mid-week of the June trial run in Winnipeg, Don MacPherson called Alex Frame, reaching him when he was in the make-up room with Gzowski. Frame recalls trembling as he picked up the phone to hear Don say, "I just wanted you to know you'll be delayed tonight for half to three-quarters of an hour because of a special."

"Son of a bitch!" said Alex. "You call me to tell me we're going to be late! I want to know whether we've got a Go."

"Oh," said Don, adding that Norn Garriock would in due course let him know the answer.

In fact, the answer came from Don himself a couple of days later on the last night of that week-long Winnipeg run. Herrndorf, who was with the production team, got the phone call from MacPherson about 5:30 p.m. "It's a Go," said MacPherson. The always sternly self-controlled Herrndorf burst into tears, went down to the cafeteria in the basement of the CBC Winnipeg building to tell the production group, and all of them sat around crying with joy and relief that they'd won approval. "It was one of the most memorable moments of my life," Herrndorf later told me.

There remained, however, a couple of gnawing problems. For one thing, critics inside and outside the CBC were deeply split on Gzowski. Some said he looked uncomfortable, had distracting on-air mannerisms, and was inattentive and dull. I for one felt his casual, low-key manner and sleepy voice, his natural curiosity, and his gentle charm overwhelmed any TV inexperience. In time, I thought, polish would come as well.

The second problem with the show was the still unresolved matter of the precise time it would start. On the trial run, we had started the show right after *The National* with local news inserted at midnight. But I was in conflict. I wanted a longer *National*, and I wanted the local news to follow it. But I also wanted *Ninety Minutes Live* to inherit as big an audience as possible from its preceding program – and that would come from *The National* not from local news. Herrndorf kept up intense pressure for the slot immediately following *The National*. Both sides in the dispute raged more loudly as the inevitable day of decision approached.

I anguished for days, wrestling with these conflicting demands. I sought advice from my network headquarters colleagues and finally decided to put on hold my own desire, and Mike Daigneault's, for a longer *National*. We would keep the newscast at its current length of twenty minutes. In a year or two, after *Ninety Minutes Live* was well established, I could move it five or ten minutes later and then extend *The National*. To pacify the CBC local stations I decided to kill the five-minute news backgrounder *Special Assignment* and put the local news on right after *The National*. But I reduced the local news in length to fifteen minutes. That meant the start time of *Ninety Minutes Live* would be 11:35 p.m., five minutes after Carson began.

As I expected, this compromise pleased no one. Daigneault was livid; Herrndorf was apoplectic; and the local CBC stations were outraged. They all appealed to the bosses over my head, but in the end that was the schedule we followed and by mid-summer of 1976 the anger had subsided. The knives were at least temporarily sheathed, but I knew they were waiting to be pulled out again as soon as something went wrong.

That late November night in 1976 as I went to bed in my Charlottetown hotel room after seeing the launch of *Ninety Minutes Live*, I felt we had just scored a triumphant breakthrough in Canadian television programming. I thought the show would reach a big audience and help strengthen Canadian unity by significantly increasing awareness and understanding of all the regions and people of Canada. It was a welcome success after the loss of Lloyd Robertson and the attendant search for his replacement.

But as I've already mentioned, my sweet dreams rapidly turned into nightmares. And the critical knives came flashing, slashing out again, ripping into every aspect of the show and particularly into Gzowski. Everywhere I turned, there were attacks from other program areas, and from Jack McAndrew's Variety area in particular. Assaults came from our local CBC stations, our commercial sales people, our private affiliates, and worst of all, from the TV critics. "It was just awful," Frame later recalled of those first few months.

The critics were fed tidbits of malicious gossip from disgruntled insiders who were jealous of the priority given to the show and consequently sought to wound it. "An inexcusable affront to a national audience . . . a monument to CBC incompetence," said *Toronto Sun* columnist Bob Blackburn. "A lacklustre, unsophisticated charade," said *Toronto Star* critic Dennis Braithwaite. Outside Toronto the critics weren't quite so vicious, but its producers and host Peter Gzowski worked mostly in Toronto and thus were reading their own death notices every day.

Nobody suffered more than Gzowski, and even with his $92,000 salary he was an unhappy man in what he later described as his "fishtank life." He resented the scrutiny because he is essentially a very private person and felt uncomfortable being constantly on display. "This is a public act," he said. "You're up there in front of the camera naked every night." In truth, I can't recall any on-air personality being lambasted with such ferocity. "He slouches onto the set like someone looking for a place to hide," said Braithwaite, adding that Gzowski was "a fumbling amateur. . . . How is it possible that for the permanent host of a talk show, the CBC Brass picked a man who can't talk with any facility, who is manifestly insecure, who won't face his audience or the camera, who has no show business background, doesn't project and who lacks wit, grace and any kind of TV personality?"

He was accused of mumbling insecurity on the one hand and of "terminal euphoria" and "incurable infantalism" on the other. "An embarrassing mix of awkwardness and incoherence," said *Maclean's*, but added, "With all his faults, Gzowski is a real person asking – for the most part – questions that matter." I agreed with the latter part of the *Maclean's* assessment and felt Gzowski's awkwardness would disappear in time.

The attacks came, too, at every meeting I attended with the local CBC program directors. From them I faced an unrelenting assault of bilious ridicule: they wanted the late-night air-time back for their local programs, even though in that time period most of them had previously been running American movies or syndicated U.S. shows. At one meeting in Montreal, the intensity of attack and my defence of Gzowski and the show became so heated that the chairman, Norn Garriock, called a fifteen-minute break "so everybody can cool off." At another meeting, in Vancouver, I was subjected to two hours of concentrated vitriol. Attacks also came at every meeting of our private affiliated stations even though most of them refused to carry the program.

But in spite of all the criticism, I was adamant about going into another season with *Ninety Minutes Live* because I felt the idea was good. It was showcasing Canada and Canadian talent and dealt with issues facing the nation in a way that no other show did – and it warranted another chance.

In many ways it was working. Gzowski's own strong sense of nationalism continuously shone through and the program introduced more French-Canadian singers, comics, musicians, writers, and political figures than English Canada had ever seen before. It wasn't just a regurgitation of the vapid American talk-show style. There were guests from Tuktoyaktuk in the Arctic and Heart's Content in Newfoundland, and from every other part of Canada, and more Canadian performers were seen than in all other CBC shows put together. It had begun showing Canadians a rich self-portrait of themselves. To help accomplish this it travelled from coast to coast, originating one week in three in a city other than Toronto. Across the country people lined up to sit in the studio audience – on one bitterly cold night in St. John's, scalpers were selling the free tickets to those shivering in line for five dollars apiece.

Despite what the critics were saying, Peter improved as the season rolled on. He seemed increasingly more comfortable with the complicated, demanding technology of television. In audience terms, the show was not great, but not bad either, and it was achieving the audience targets we'd set for it. It was averaging upwards of 350,000 viewers a night. Over the week, a total of about one million different Canadians tuned in at least once – not bad for a still-evolving experiment in late-night television.

Most important of all, in spite of the critical attacks and internal sniping, Denny Harvey and Don MacPherson shared Herrndorf's and my sense of hope about the show and fully supported a second season. So before *Ninety Minutes Live* went off the air in late May, we were assured of a go-ahead for 1977-78.

Gzowski came off that first season's twenty-six-week killer run of the program a wreck. His marriage was broken; he was physically exhausted and unhappy with his performance skills. Nevertheless, he was damn well determined to make the show work as he headed off to rest and repair his bruised ego.

As *Ninety Minutes Live* ended its first season it suffered its worst blow so far with the departure of Peter Herrndorf to become vice-president of planning at the CBC head office in Ottawa. His new job had been announced months before, but he had insisted on staying with Current Affairs through to June. With his move to Ottawa, I knew we'd lost the show's greatest champion.

From the moment I brought him in as the head of Current Affairs, I knew Herrndorf wouldn't be there long. He was ambitious, upwardly mobile, and wanted power. Now, Al Johnson needed his zesty programming talents at head office to help plan the future of Canadian public television. It seemed to me that Peter was moving from where the excitement and action were to a grey, bureaucratic Ottawa job, even if the title was nice – "that great vice-presidency in the sky," I had told him. But he had his own career agenda. Now he wanted experience working closely with the president. His private hope, I believed, was to come back to Toronto to take over Don MacPherson's job as vice-president and boss of all English radio and TV broadcasting or possibly to run the Variety area, which he had once told me he "had the hots for."

Some weeks before his departure, Peter came along to my office for a five o'clock private "evaluation session," one of a twice-a-year series of hour-long sessions I held with my senior managers. He was juggling his ever-present mug of coffee as he sat down on my office couch and I said to him, "This is probably the last time you'll ever have this kind of evaluation." His eyes narrowed in concentration as I said I thought he was one of the most self-controlled people I'd ever known and wondered if he didn't need to loosen up a bit at times, to relax and do something utterly unplanned. I'd never known Peter to do anything without a detailed plan of action, even playing basketball or tennis.

Peter's management style was to stroke and stimulate those under him but to bluster and cajole at those above or in other departments. I had some bones to pick with him on the way he sometimes used confrontational techniques to get his way, on his efforts to insulate his producers from my office and his reluctance to give me enough feedback on program details and plans. He responded that he was sometimes tough, but not confrontational, and he felt he needed to give his producers considerable creative freedom to get the best out of them. I had to admit that his approach had worked. Current Affairs programming had never been better, and I took considerable pleasure in our big success stories, such as *the fifth estate*, documentaries such as those on the October crisis in Quebec and on organized crime in Canada, and the now well-established series, *Marketplace*, *Ombudsman*, and *Man Alive*.

As the meeting drew to a close, Herrndorf and I talked about the successes of his Current Affairs programs and I thanked him, too, for his help in putting into effect some organizational changes in our local journalistic programming across the country. That had been difficult for him because it meant giving people from News the dominating role in the local dinner-hour news strip. Hitherto, on almost all CBC stations, the hour consisted of two separate half hours, one run by News and the other by Current Affairs, which led to duplication and conflict, aggravating the historical rivalry of the two areas. I had wanted one boss for the whole hour. Basically, my plan had put News people in charge of the full dinner-hour news programs. But while removing Current Affairs authority in these programs, I added new weekly local current affairs programs and documentaries. As a result of his acquiescence to my plans, Peter had been accused by some local current affairs producers of "selling out." But, in truth, that was a bum rap. He felt his producers would be better off in the end. The changeover took a couple of years and a lot of persuasion, but it worked, providing a far better local journalistic service to viewers across the country.

Shortly after our evaluation session, Peter left for Ottawa, but he would come thundering back a couple of years later with more innovative programming ideas.

WITH HERRNDORF GONE and *Ninety Minutes Live* renewed for another season, I sat back to contemplate some of the accomplishments made in current affairs and historical programming since 1969, when I'd arrived from Washington all fired up and ready to try to change the face of Canadian public broadcasting. Although *The National* and the rest of our hard news programs were constantly my top priority, I'd always believed that current affairs programs and historical documentaries were almost as critical.

In the battle I and others had been fighting to give CBC information programming more importance, I'd always seen our strategy as a two-pronged attack. On the one hand, I wanted more and better news seen by more Canadians. On the other, I wanted to develop the CBC's distinguished tradition of magazine-style and documentary programs – television that would show Canadians themselves in a broader context than pure news allows. In a very real sense, *Ninety Minutes Live* was only the latest effort in this direction – and it wasn't even the first time we had trespassed on the territory of entertainment programming. I'd gone through a similar turf battle a couple of years earlier with the drama-documentary *The National Dream*, based on Pierre Berton's magnificent popular history of the opening of the West and the building of the CPR. That fight pitted information programming against the Drama area, but I had an advantage in this battle because, as my internal campaign to get the series on the air began, Drama had just been badly wounded by a multimillion-dollar program disaster called *Jalna*. Thus it had less influence in trying to stop our efforts.

In early 1972, we asked Pierre Berton to prepare an outline for the series. In characteristically exuberant Berton style, he wrote an exciting summary based on his books *The National Dream* and The *Last Spike*. His outline was the centrepiece of my campaign to persuade my bosses to approve the series. But the most important early decision was whether to make the series a pure documentary or to mix in some drama. It was clear to me we had to dramatize large parts of the story to make it entertaining as well as informative for an audience of millions. But I had to tread carefully. Even though wounded by the *Jalna* failure, the Drama area was ever alert to any incursions into its territory. To minimize that sensitivity, I tiptoed into the dramatized parts, initially describing them as a very small element as we sold the project to the CBC top brass.

Not only would the Drama area be upset, but the project was internally controversial because I demanded the primest of prime-time scheduling – 9:00 p.m. Sunday. This would antagonize other program areas, which also wanted that same time. *The National Dream* would cost a lot of money and require enormous production resources, funnelling them away from other areas. Money was the preoccupation of my boss, Norn Garriock, and I said I could squeeze almost all (and maybe all) of the cost out of my own budget. That pleased him, but he was quite properly suspicious. On the basis of my dubious assertion, however, Norn said "Yes" to stage one and in the spring of 1972 we assigned writers Timothy Findley and Bill White-head to begin working on the scripts.

Suddenly everything nearly fell apart. Producer Lister Sinclair, who had guided the project from the beginning, was unexpectedly chosen by the new CBC president, Laurent Picard, who preceded Al Johnson, as his executive vice-president and the second most powerful man at the CBC head office. Our emergency choice to replace Sinclair was Jim Murray, executive producer of the long-running series *The Nature Of Things*. He had a quiet but determined persistence, was particularly good in controlling money, creatively sensitive, and one damn fine gentleman to boot.

The principal actors, Bill Hutt and John Colicos, signed on in January of 1973, as did internationally acclaimed drama director Eric Till. As the scripts came in to me from Tiff Findley and Bill White-head, with Berton adding his comments (mainly in aid of historical accuracy), I'd pass back to the writers my own suggestions. Now we began to cost out the series with more accuracy. And, of course, it began getting more expensive. As I had expected, the drama element began to grow, which again raised the alarm bells in finance and in the Drama area. They, in turn, growled to managing director Norn Garriock and he growled to me.

"Just the initial costing and planning," I said. "Both costs and drama will, of course, be less, so don't worry."

"But I do worry," said Norn. "It's my job to worry about the bottom line. It's all gotta be A-okay."

I gave Norn a financial plan involving some enrichment from him, extra squeezings from my overall budgets, and a scheme to schedule the series over two fiscal years covering the end of one fiscal year in March and the beginning of another in April, thus amortizing the cost over two annual budgets instead of one. (I had learned my budget lessons well.) We also sold the series to the CBC French network and that provided more money for the production. In total, the cost was about two million dollars for the eight hour-long programs.

Pierre Berton was the on-air guide for the program, popping in and out to capsulize the story from time to time during each hour. He did a magnificent job but there were some problems. On one location on the north shore of Lake Superior at mid-winter with the temperature hovering around -25^0F, Pierre did about fourteen takes of one sequence. He damn near froze to death but producer Jim Murray had him do it over and over again until it was perfect. "They had to warm my lips with hot coffee before the words emerged and then the camera froze and then the sound equipment froze," Berton said.

As *The National Dream* took shape it began to attract a lot of internal CBC attention. Nearly 500 people worked on the production over its two and a half years at forty different locations from the Rockies to Parliament Hill. Altogether, 200 hours of colour film were shot. Murray and Berton insisted on authenticity, so our crews, using 1870s tools and clothes, actually laid track with the railway ties cut in the style of the 1870s.

The engine, which we used extensively, was known as "Old 136," a ninety-year-old CPR steam locomotive that had been in service for seventy-seven years and which Jim found in Milton, Ontario, in the possession of a Toronto lawyer. We spent $20,000 refurbishing it to bring it back to 1870s appearance, but even so, we had complaints. When the program was aired a University of Calgary professor wrote, "The cylinders are wrong. It shouldn't have piston valves or extended smoke boxes."

In shooting out West, Jim Murray hired local cowboys and twenty Blackfoot Indians as extras, including Joe Crowfoot, who was the grandson and spitting image of Chief Crowfoot and who acted the part of his grandfather in the saga. There were problems with the Indians, however, because they demanded to be paid more than the $20-a-day union scale. Our production manager, Len d'Agostino, refused and they only grumpily returned to work on the series, forever after calling Len "Chief Short Arms Deep Pockets."

One near financial disaster was the result of an on-the-spot brain wave from drama director Eric Till. He decided it would be wonderful to cap a rousing speech in the House of Commons by Sir John A. Macdonald with Tory backbenchers singing "For He's A Jolly Good Fellow." It was a terrific idea and the singing made the scene one of the most memorable in the entire series. It was only later, however, that we realized with horror that all those mute extras who had been playing the backbenchers had suddenly been transformed into bit players with speaking parts – under union rules they were entitled to be paid as such from first call of the day. That would have cost an extra $40,000. Fortunately, ACTRA, the performers' union, let us off the hook, waiving the additional costs.

Bill Hutt, who was playing Sir John A., got some free advice on authenticity from John Diefenbaker, who watched the filming of one Parliament Hill sequence. "Your lapels are too wide," Diefenbaker growled, adding, "and you're not going to wear those shoes, are you?"

My next big internal battle was in scheduling the series. I wanted 9:00 to 10:00 o'clock Sunday nights. But that was not a usual slot for information programs and it meant taking eight one-hour slots away from Drama, which normally programmed that time period. The opposition to my scheduling proposal was fierce and at our meetings in Norn Garriock's office, I thought it expedient to reverse tactics and instead of downplaying the cost and size of the project, I exploited them. "It would be a monstrous waste of the CBC's money, the public's money, to not put the series in the very best time possible," I argued.

"Maybe," said Thom Benson, the mercurial director of entertainment programming at the time, who was worried about the reaction in his area, "But it'll be dull as hell ... dry documentary and no audience. The time is too valuable for that."

"No, sir," I said. "It'll be immensely popular to millions. Besides, this time we'll have the dramatic sequences, too."

My objective at this moment was not at all to appease Thom or the pleas of his Drama area, nor to soft-pedal the cost to the Finance people, but rather to sell Garriock on the logic of putting the series in the primest of prime time.

"Okay," Norn said finally. "The bottom line is, we'll do it at nine on Sundays."

With this top-priority scheduling, Norn provided a bit more money to sweeten our *National Dream* budget. We also sought to sell the series around the world and recoup some money that way. The BBC eventually bought the series for about $100,000 and it was purchased and shown in countries around the world, from Italy to Australia and Kuwait to Haiti.

When *The National Dream* went on the air on Sunday, March 3, 1974, it was a smash success. The critics raved and audiences were among the biggest ever. The first program got 3.6 million viewers and the average over the whole series was 3.1 million. The audiences were far larger than for any Sunday night dramas and a critical success beyond my wildest dreams. It was a success that gave me a lot of programming clout I could use elsewhere in our informational programming, and I did.

One area where it didn't help, though, was on a project I badly wanted to do on the Klondike, using Pierre Berton's book as the basis for an epic, twelve-part series that would have scenic wonder, high drama, and political tension and show a key part of the development of Canada. I figured it would take four years and at least $3 million to do, and I thought it would be a natural follow-up to *The National Dream*. We sent advance researchers to scout the Yukon and prepare some preliminary arrangements and early costing. Pierre drafted an outline and writers Tiff Findley and Bill Whitehead prepared a "treatment." But by now, the Drama area was under the strong arm of theatrical director John Hirsch, who foresaw such a project invading his territory as *The National Dream* had done and, equally worrisome for him, eating up money he wanted to get his hands on for drama productions.

John had been hired as a saviour for TV drama and performed in that role as a combination of Billy Graham and Jack the Ripper. He was single-mindedly and articulately determined to get the money he wanted for the kind of drama he wanted. I recall once chatting with him about overall CBC budget problems as we rode down an elevator at Vatican North. "Don't tell me what the problems are!" he grimaced. "I don't want to know. If I hear and understand them, that'll weaken my own preoccupation. I care only about drama. Nothing else. That's why I was hired." It was, I suppose, his worry that nothing weakens willpower so much as an effort to understand.

With new budget cuts from Ottawa ripping through the CBC and with Hirsch's shrill opposition, Norn was suddenly alarmed. "Freeze it!" he barked as I came into his office to discuss the project one day. "We've got too much trouble. The bottom line is that we can't afford what we're doing, let alone anything new. Besides, why are you doing drama when you're only supposed to do information?" We argued; we fired memos back and forth until Norn finally sent a memo saying " 'Nuff said!"

Within hours, I shot back a flaming, two-page memo opening with: "Not by a bloody long shot. I am both astonished and utterly appalled. . . ." I assaulted Norn's budget planning, his decision-making, his judgement, and even his patriotism and loyalty to the objectives of the CBC. It was an insolent attack on my boss that might normally have induced a punch in the nose. But it was a losing battle. After that there were no more confrontations, but the project was delayed and watered down. It was kept alive for another few months, but eventually suffocated through lack of money and other priorities.

THE EFFORT TO BRING ALIVE our Canadian past for massive television audiences had been a central objective I'd set when I first took the job as director of News and Current Affairs. It had begun with a series of eight one-hour programs called *The Tenth Decade*. Ottawa producer Cam Graham chronicled the turbulent tenth decade of Confederation from 1957 to 1967, covering the raucous political feud between John Diefenbaker and Mike Pearson.

Even before Cam had finished *The Tenth Decade* we launched him on a new series of programs on the period from Laurier's rise to power through Borden, Meighen, King, Bennett, and St. Laurent to the collapse of the all-powerful Liberals in 1957. It was called *The Days Before Yesterday*. Mining the same rich motherlode of archival material mixed with contemporary reflections by many of the participants, Cam also did two separate series on Mike Pearson and John Diefenbaker, capturing the personal flavour of each man.

Over the two years of shooting and editing, Cam fell in love with Mike, as did most people who knew him, and that feeling is reflected in the sensitive portrayal of Canada's best-loved Prime Minister, an honest man in a cynical age. Before we could air the series Pearson died. On the last day of 1972 we televised his state funeral in Ottawa, interrupting a football game between Washington and Dallas. To my horror and chagrin, more than 1,000 Canadians jammed the CBC switchboard to complain.

"Who the hell wants to watch a funeral," one caller complained as recorded in the CBC's phone log.

"Seven curses on you damn asses," said another.

Reading the telephoned comments was a sour way to begin a new year, but there was sweet revenge as the reaction came in when the Pearson series was launched on Sunday nights at 10:00 p.m. in the spring. It was universally acclaimed.

The Diefenbaker series was a thirteen-parter by Graham on the life and times of Canada's greatest twentieth-century genius for political theatricality, a man whose colour and charisma made him the best Opposition Leader in Canadian history and one of the worst prime ministers. In the interviews for the programs, Dief amply demonstrated his spell-binding impact as he flamboyantly projected his self-image as a poor, lonely, but highly principled Prairie boy fighting off the rich Ontario scoundrels out to destroy him.

The Pearson and Diefenbaker series completed my objective of a television political history of Canada that covered our prime ministers up to 1968. Now, I wanted to start work on a series called "The Trudeau Years." Cam Graham had numerous conversations with people in Trudeau's office seeking their support. Peter Herrndorf and I had lunch with Senator Keith Davey to see if he would use his considerable influence with Trudeau to try to persuade him. We laid out an elaborate plan developed by Cam for behind-the-scenes shooting and interviewing over a period of years. We were willing to delay airing the series until Trudeau had stepped down as Prime Minister. "It'll be living history," I told Keith at lunch, "a chance for Canadians to see their Prime Minister at work and in private."

"Sounds great," said Keith. But a month later he came back to us to say he'd had a "rather extended conversation with the Prime Minister" but Trudeau had said "No."

"I still think it's a good idea," Keith told me. "I'll try him again later. But don't hold your breath."

We didn't and he still wouldn't agree in response to later requests. As a result, present and future Canadians have lost a chance for a memorable history lesson and glimpse at Prime Minister Trudeau in action.

We not only used the TV screen to portray our political history, but I felt we should also use TV to focus on the social foundations of Canada. Eight one-hour programs in a series called *Images of Canada* were prepared over several years by executive producer Vincent Tovell. The programs were deftly woven tapestries of landscape, seascape, paintings, architecture, social history – touchstones of Canada from our Indian and explorer days to the Centennial celebrations of 1967.

In parallel with the effort to popularize Canadian history and use television as a tool of mass education, we also sought to portray contemporary Canada. This was the preserve of Current Affairs, which later enjoyed such success under Peter Herrndorf's tutelage. The roots of our current affairs programming went back to the early days of television with *Tabloid*, *Close-Up*, and later the legendary *This Hour Has Seven Days*. But much of the current affairs programming had become listless and I wanted to inject some vitality. Unhappily, my initial efforts were not as successful as the historical shows. The first such effort when I'd come up from Washington in 1969 was something called *Weekend*. It is a case study in the pitfalls faced by anyone seeking to change things at Mother Corporation and, in particular in those days, of trying to get the News and Current Affairs areas working together. *Weekend* was to be the program that would finally bury the nostalgia for *This Hour Has Seven Days* and also put News and Current Affairs on a less war-like footing because they would be working together on the project. Most simply stated, it was to meld both news and current affairs in a prime-time magazine program that would run on Saturday and Sunday nights. The Saturday program, seen live coast-to-coast right after the hockey game, would be zippier, brighter, and faster-paced than the Sunday program, but both would be solidly journalistic. It was an innovative and daring concept that was going to revolutionize TV viewing, we thought. And after a couple of years of success on Saturday and Sunday, I planned to push hard for a "strip" of 10:00 to 11:00 p.m. journalistic programming Monday through Friday as well as on the weekend. But I failed to gauge the depth of the animosities still lingering between News and Current Affairs.

On this occasion I won management appproval fairly early, even getting permission to have *Weekend* in colour, still a relative novelty for CBC informational programs in 1969. Then I started to trumpet the program concept to anyone who'd listen. "We're pioneers on the leading edge of programming," I boasted.

After much arm-twisting, I'd persuaded Michael Maclear to leave his job as a CBC roving foreign correspondent based in London to become executive producer in charge of all the news segments in the two programs. He had been impressively successful in getting interviews with world leaders and was particularly talented in translating complicated issues and events into easily understood picture stories. He was also a good friend from my foreign correspondent days. Maclear would work with Neil Andrews, who became executive producer of the Saturday program and who had been producing popular programs on current issues for teenagers, and with Dick Nielsen, a veteran Current Affairs producer who was named executive producer of the Sunday program. In overall charge of the two shows and reporting directly to me was Ray Hazzan, a short man with a black beard and strong principles . He was a former head of TV News so that meant a newsman was in charge.

To my chagrin, this turned out to be as combustible a group of talents as one could imagine, and the trouble began at once. Nielsen was stubbornly determined to be the strong man; Maclear demanded more air time and control for News; Andrews ignored the others to march to his own drummer; and Hazzan raged as he tried to keep his three obstreperous executive producers in line.

The first blowup came between Maclear and Nielsen over the length of the hard news part of the program. Maclear lost the fight, resigned, and went back to London to resume a spectacularly successful career as a foreign correspondent. He was replaced by Ian Murray, a news assignment editor and son of the first general manager of the CBC.

While the Nielsen-Maclear battle was going on, my heart sank at a meeting in my office as I listened to the young, up-and-at-'em, razzmatazz producers Andrews had hired for the Saturday program. Discussing the lighter tone we wanted for the Saturday *Weekend* program, I suggested we might try to interview a spiritualist used by Mackenzie King.

"Who's King?" piped up one producer.

"Some politician," said another.

"The late Prime Minister," I said.

"Oh," they all said.

Neil Andrews winced at this painful example of the inexperience and lack of political awareness of his youthful colleagues, but most of them seemed to find the information a revelation.

Andrews and his young Saturday producers were filled with exuberant ideas and innovative, not to say, joyously innocent, approaches to the program and its mandate. Most had come with Andrews from children's programming, and while bright and creatively daring, their lack of political sensitivity was to prove embarrassing. They felt politics and issues like Quebec separatism needed to be jazzed up with music and jokes in order to reach the mass of Canadians, especially those watching after the hockey game on Saturday nights.

Hazzan not only had his hands full trying to rein in the puzzlingly eclectic Saturday producers, but he also was into trench warfare with Sunday executive producer Dick Nielsen, who wanted to "out Seven

Days Seven Days" in controversial programming. Hazzan and Niel-sen argued over how much time should be devoted to news as opposed to public affairs items. Nielsen felt Hazzan had a "news bias" and interfered too much.

The antagonism between Hazzan and Nielsen was echoed by the News and Current Affairs people who were supposed to be working together. Current Affairs producers could be overheard muttering not so privately that News people were "boozy ignoramuses." News peo-ple complained bitterly about the "airy fairy" Current Affairs pro-ducers. It was, to say the least, not a happy ship.

As we neared the opening of the 1969-70 season and the bright new TV programming world I'd been boasting about, we had two disastrous dry runs. Everything went wrong technically, editorially, and in production. Even an ironing board-like contraption that slid out of a wall and acted as host Lloyd Robertson's "desk" got stuck. "Oh well," Lloyd said with the same calm, smiling optimism he later brought to *The National*. "You know the old saying 'bad rehearsal means a good show.' "

I took faint hope from that. But Hazzan worked desperately to calm the animosities and enliven the program. I continued to exude confi-dence in public, was reassuring to the staff, and was scared as hell in private. This was, after all, my first major foray into new program-ming and I desperately wanted it to work.

On October 11-12, 1969, *Weekend* was launched to a critical response ranging from yawns to yelps. "Saturday's edition was an unmitigated disaster.... The [Sunday] show has some potential," *Winnipeg Tribune* critic Bob Shiels commented in one of the kinder re-views of the opening weekend. Each week I kept saying, "Wait until next week!"

But I was fighting a losing battle. The infighting went up as the ratings went down. "We must develop a team approach," I'd said to Hazzan months before. "There must be the fullest co-ordination, co-operation, and melding of effort for the programs." My own words came back to haunt me. We'd only been on air a week when Hazzan, Nielsen, and Andrews were marching separately and occasionally together in and out of my office threatening resignations and shouting imprecations about each other. Something had to give.

First to self-destruct was the Saturday program over something called "Schmockey Night." Andrews, whom Hazzan was already itching to fire, insisted on devoting most of the program for Saturday, January 24, 1970, to this unique event, a "fun evening" in a Winnipeg hockey rink. Hazzan, the old newsman, insisted that a story on

Quebec politics took precedence. There was a good deal of shouting and name-calling as Saturday approached.

For one last time I looked at the lousy ratings, the complaints piling up on my desk from CBC executives, and my own increasingly questioning memoranda on the Saturday program. Finally I faced the obvious conclusion. The Saturday program simply wouldn't work. Its timing problems in starting after the hockey game meant we never knew exactly how long the program would be and thus we had to suddenly dump items or scramble to add them. This was compounded by a mixture of personal incompatibility and journalistic immaturity among the producers. Reluctantly, I decided to kill it before more damage was done. It meant eating a lot of crow, but that's life.

The final Saturday edition of *Weekend* aired January 24, including the "Schmockey Night" item. "An embarrassingly childish time-waster," said Jack Miller in the *Hamilton Spectator*. I had to agree that it was.

Neil Andrews left, complaining about being misunderstood and confused. "It was never made clear to me or anyone on my staff which kind of focus Knowlton wanted for the Saturday show," Neil told reporters. "Every time I put entertainment in, he said it was too frivolous. I wanted to do things like a national live pub crawl. I think that's an interesting thing to show Canada to Canadians. But whenever ideas like that came up, Knowlton said we should have more information."

The cancellation of the Saturday edition of *Weekend* claimed another victim. Hazzan, while wanting to get rid of Andrews, did not want to lose the show itself, and when I killed it he resigned in protest.

Less than four months after we'd launched the program with such fanfare only Dick Nielsen was left among the program executives, and he continued with the Sunday version of *Weekend* until he left CBC to set up his own production organization a few years later.

One sidelight of the killing of the Saturday *Weekend* show was that in all the frenzied activity of announcing the cancellation, we'd forgotten to tell the president, George Davidson. Just after announcing the cancellation I was in a "think tank" meeting at the Guild Inn outside Toronto, conferring with my colleagues and bosses on future program plans, when a call came in from CBC Ottawa headquarters with a hot, angry, and loud president on the line.

"What the hell are you guys doing down there?" he demanded of my boss, vice-president Gene Hallman. "You never told me a thing about the *Weekend* cancellation, for God's sake! Do you think I'm some office boy! You guys don't tell me anything!"

With only a few words, Hallman thrust the phone over to me as an outraged president continued his tirade in a five-minute, non-stop, explicitly expletive presidential storm. Then Davidson slammed down the phone in my ear and we all looked guiltily at one another. The president, of course, was right. We should have advised him before making any announcement, but we simply forgot in the rush of things. His anger was fortified, I suspect, by a feeling of most CBC presidents that the organization puts them too remote from the program decision-making process. I've always thought that, in many ways, a producer is far more powerful than a president at the CBC since a president may suggest a direction for programming, but it's the producer who actually makes the program happen.

The remaining Sunday edition of *Weekend* struggled on, but despite valiant creative efforts to enliven its deteriorating carcass, after four years I ordered a merciful euthanasia.

STILL SEEKING THE MAGIC FORMULA to rejuvenate our Current Affairs programming, we launched in the fall of 1973 what I described to the TV critics as a "cheeky . . . irreverent . . . impertinent and iconoclastic" program called *Up Canada*.

As a Sunday night replacement for *Weekend*, it was underwhelming, although it did have its moments. One involved a sketch about an allegedly fictional, fun-loving Member of Parliament who left his wife to mind their home and children in British Columbia while he lived in a ritzy Ottawa bachelor pad, frolicking in and out of bed with his secretary through the cold Parliament Hill nights. "Cheeky" it certainly was, and "irreverent," too, meant to poke fun at the supposedly dull, grey lives of our hard-working parliamentarians. The trouble, I discovered to my horror the morning after the sketch aired, was that the name used for the MP was uncannily close to the name of a real MP and uncannily close, too, was the address used, as well as a few other identifiable elements. It was a folly that quickly turned into a disaster – "hell to pay" is an understatement of what followed.

Intensive investigations were launched, libel suits threatened, denunciation was everywhere, and ridicule for the poor innocent MP was intense, especially when he came into the House of Commons the next day, hooted and hollered at as "lover boy." The MP, John Fraser (who became Speaker of the House of Commons a dozen years later), bore no relation to our fictional MP "George Fraser." The real Fraser lived at 1200 Rideau Terrace, our fictional Fraser at 22 Rideau Terrace. The real Fraser represented the West Coast riding of Vancouver South; our fictional Fraser represented the West Coast riding of "Nookie in the

Islands." The real Fraser's wife lived in B.C., and so did our fictional Mrs. Fraser. The real Mrs. Fraser was not amused. As soon as she saw the sketch, she called the real Mr. Fraser, who quite quickly called the CBC. "I'm pretty damned angry," he said in the understatement of the year. "Get my name off that program." The real Mr. Fraser had other more vivid things to say, as did the real Mrs. Fraser, whom he quoted frequently.

Up Canada had planned three episodes of the "lover boy" tribulations of the fictional Mr. Fraser, MP, but I felt one was rather more than enough. "It'll never happen again," I shamefacedly announced. "The Corporation regrets any distress it may have caused by presenting a skit about a fictional Member of Parliament.... Additional segments in this fictionalized skit ... have been discontinued." And after only a short run, the show itself was discontinued; only to a degree did I differ with *Calgary Herald* TV critic Bill Musselwhite, who had written, "*Up Canada* is the worst tragedy since Shakespeare wrote Hamlet." Another Current Affairs effort called *In the Present Tense* was a similarly doomed effort and was booed off the screen.

Fortunately, not all our attempts in those early years to improve our informational programming met the same fate. Signal successes included *Marketplace*, which made Joan Watson Canada's leading consumer advocate, and *Ombudsman*, which with the combative Robert Cooper at the helm became one of the hits of Canadian television during its seven-year lifespan.

Cooper, a feisty twenty-eight-year-old chock-a-block with impatience and a crusading sense of righting wrongs, was known as "the squeak that roars" because of his light voice. But no one questioned his program's integrity. On one occasion Cooper, who had been a storefront lawyer, received a complaint from a CBC cameraman about unfair treatment in being denied some work benefits and overtime pay, and we persuaded CBC president Laurent Picard to appear on the program to answer the charges. As usual, Picard had done his homework, knew the case inside out, and admitted to Cooper that an injustice had been done. Before a million and a half viewers, Picard promised the injustice would be rectified. "When?" asked the dogged ombudsman. "As soon as possible," replied the Corporation president. Although the experience made Picard wince, I thought it was a triumph of journalistic integrity, not only for the program but for the CBC, too.

We were beginning to have some success with our Current Affairs programming, but the corner was finally turned when I brought Peter Herrndorf in to head the department in mid-1974. Typically, he arrived with a fistful of projects, but none of the others proved as troublesome as *Ninety Minutes Live*. One of his first plans was a slick, hard-hitting, globetrotting documentary newsmagazine called *the fifth estate*, which borrowed its production style from the CBS show *60 Minutes* and its editorial approach from the programs of CBS broadcast journalist and icon Edward R. Murrow. By far the most critical element in *the fifth estate* was the unusually heavy funding for research, a vital necessity for its investigative reportage. Without the extra money for research staff, the program might well have ended up like most of its predecessors. The show was produced by Glenn Sarty and co-hosted by the elegant, tough-minded Adrienne Clarkson. Sarty had worked closely with her when she was host of *Take Thirty*, of which he'd been executive producer, and more recently on the prime-time show called *Adrienne At Large*. Her on-air partners included the electric Peter Reilly, formerly one of the CBC's best foreign correspondents, and the rumpled and prickly veteran current affairs reporter and producer Warner Troyer. To this mix, Herrndorf added Ron Haggart, whom he wooed away from CITY-TV in Toronto where Haggart had run one of the best local newsrooms in Canada. Before that, Haggart had been a controversial and highly popular columnist with *The Toronto Star*.

With credit in the bank by having some impressive program success stories such as our historical documentaries, *Marketplace*, and *Ombudsman* and with the new priority given by the Corporation to Current Affairs programming, Herrndorf and I were able to make sure *the fifth estate* got off to a good start. We were able to have it scheduled in the heart of prime time, "sandwiched" between two highly popular entertainment shows. We persuaded the schedulers to put the program right after *M*A*S*H* and just before *Barney Miller*, thereby benefiting from the audience flow out of one and waiting for the other. But the real success would depend on the program itself.

Executive producer Glenn Sarty and his three stars of *the fifth estate* launched their new program in the fall of 1975 with an explosive investigative report on an Arctic plane crash that killed thirty-two people. At last, I knew we had the hard-hitting Current Affairs program we'd been looking for. In fact, *the fifth estate* has become the longest-running flagship Current Affairs show in CBC television history. Goaded and guided by the editorial demands of senior producer Ron Haggart and polished and produced first by Glenn Sarty and later by executive producer Robin Taylor, the program has never lost its lustre or its audience.

One reason for its success is that it's a ship that doesn't rock, unlike its predecessors, especially *Weekend*. While Sarty, Haggart, and senior producer Robin Taylor often held different opinions, they never had a row, concentrating their energies on the program, not on infighting. Much of the credit for that goes to Sarty, whose passionate attention to detail and style ensured the success of the program's brand of popular journalism.

The impressive staff of *the fifth estate* was the result of a Herrndorf talent raid on newspapers, radio, and TV stations, and they came sensing a new vitality in CBC-TV Current Affairs. They went to work on *the fifth estate* and on other program projects Herrndorf was planning, including two blockbuster documentaries, one a two-and-a-half-hour extravaganza called *The October Crisis*, marking the fifth anniversary of the FLQ kidnapping of British diplomat James Cross and kidnapping and murder of Quebec cabinet minister Pierre Laporte, the other an exhaustive, revealing examination of organized crime in Canada called *Connections*. He had a basketful of other projects, too: a documentary series on Canadian culture; one on divorce; several on international subjects.

A good example of Herrndorf's success as head of Current Affairs was *Connections*, an expensive (upwards of $300,000) two-part documentary on organized crime in Canada that aired just about the time he was leaving me and *Ninety Minutes Live* for Ottawa. For nearly two years Peter had encouraged a small group of his producers, sometimes using hidden cameras and microphones, to investigate the Mafia in Canada.

Something like 2,000 people in sixteen cities in the U.S. and Canada were interviewed. The producers, led by Bill Macadam and Martyn Burke and research director Jim Dubro, accumulated nearly 30,000 cards in a cross-indexed reference system. They haunted libraries, prisons, Mafia hangouts, and a score of police stations, gleaning bits and pieces of information and doing interviews. "There was one point during the investigation," Macadam said, "when every time I turned the key to start my car, my heart would skip a beat."

The result was a shattering portrayal of murder, narcotics, corruption, loan-sharking, and money-laundering that made banner headlines across the country, as well as breathtaking television. The program named names and showed faces to prove the Mafia was operating in Canada in spite of many official claims to the contrary. "The CBC has just shot a series on the Mafia that makes the Godfather look like a comic strip," said *The Toronto Star*.

Herrndorf also gave rein to a number of documentary filmmakers, including Donald Brittain. This shambling fellow, barking instructions in his whisky voice, a cigarette forever dangling on his lips with ashes falling on his sports shirt and jeans, gave new meaning to the word "disorganized" in his personal style. But he was one of Canada's finest filmmakers. He worked on joint productions for the National Film Board and the CBC and won awards galore, including an international Emmy, the first Canada had ever won, for his *Henry Ford's America*. One of his most remarkable documentaries done for us, however, was *The Champions*, his two-part portrait of Pierre Trudeau and René Lévesque. Brittain said he was the ideal unbiased Canadian to produce the documentary since he was "one quarter French Huguenot, one quarter American, one half United Empire Loyalist and, according to my Aunt Louise, there's also a splash of Indian blood – Huron." But some accused us of being "Trudeau toadies" for airing the program while others said we were simply showing "more separatist propaganda." In fact, we were putting a personal face on the national unity debate and its two key players. As far as I'm concerned the documentary enriched English-speaking Canadians' awareness of the issues involved better than any other mass media undertaking.

While Herrndorf orchestrated the new Current Affairs series and documentaries, I got involved in developing co-productions with foreign networks, including a series with the BBC called *The Age of Uncertainty* with Canadian-born, world-renowned economist John Kenneth Galbraith. The 6′ 8″ farm boy from southwestern Ontario, who grew up to be a distinguished Harvard professor and high-ranking U.S. government official, best-selling author, and close adviser and friend of President John F. Kennedy, was always a delight with his cutting, self-deprecatory humour and courtly manners. He told me his manners had once been tested severely, however, by President Lyndon Johnson, who called him to the White House once to write an economic speech for him. "Johnson hated economic speeches," Galbraith said. He quoted Johnson as snarling at him, "An economic speech is like pissing down your pant leg. It may feel nice and warm to you, but it don't mean a goddamn thing to anybody else."

The most enjoyable part of the production had been in mid-July, 1976, when we were shooting the final program in the series and had gathered under the maple trees of Galbraith's Vermont farm. It was a "talking heads" finale with Galbraith moderating and the talking coming from such people as U.S. Secretary of State Henry Kissinger, former British Prime Minister Edward Heath, British Labour cabinet minister Shirley Williams, British trade union leader Jack Jones, Katharine Graham, publisher of the *Washington Post*, historian Arthur Schlesinger, and the Prime Minister of Singapore, Lee Kuan Yew.

The first afternoon, we gathered in Galbraith's sunlit garden and as people sat down to chat, no one sat beside Kissinger. In a wounded voice, Henry muttered, "Won't anyone sit beside me? I'm paranoid enough without being left alone like this." Later that night at a gourmet dinner in a hotel in nearby Newfane, Vermont, Kissinger was constantly on the run between the table and the telephone. There was a crisis in the Middle East and he was masterminding the U.S. actions from his dinner. At one point, he came back to the table red of face and bursting with indignation. "Do you know what that idiot ambassador now wants to do?" he screamed at us. "You wouldn't believe it! How can he be so stupid! . . . Oh well, what's for dessert." We never did find out what the "idiot ambassador" wanted to do.

Probably the most exciting co-production I got involved in was *The Second World War* with Thames TV in London. There were several partners and I primarily shepherded through the material on Canada's wartime role, as well as reviewing the whole project, reading scripts, and screening rough cuts when I'd be in London working with an old associate from Thames, producer Jeremy Isaacs. It was a twenty-six-part series that turned out to be the most successful TV portrayal of the war ever made. But I had a hard time getting a CBC prime-time network scheduling. My boss, Norn Garriock, was lukewarm and I resorted to sneaking into his office at night to pin advertising posters over his walls and sending notes about the naval actions being shown, hoping to trigger enthusiastic reminders of his own wartime Navy days. I was only partially successful, however, because while I got the prime-time scheduling I wanted for the series, I only got part of the network. It was seen on CBC stations only, not on our private affiliates.

But the real key to success in the battle for more and better journalism on CBC television was not in our foreign co-productions but in what we produced ourselves in CBC News and Current Affairs. In the spring of 1977, with Peter Herrndorf going to Ottawa, I knew replacing him would be a tough job. After weeks of consultations with producers and others in and out of the Current Affairs area, I settled on a producer who was playing a key role in the success of *the fifth estate*. He was forty-four-year-old, English-born Robin Taylor, a chunky, good-natured graduate of the University of British Columbia and Stanford University who had been a *Winnipeg Free Press* reporter and a radio and TV producer and director of television in St. John's, Newfoundland. While he was thoroughly happy working on *the fifth estate*, I persuaded him to take on the job as head of Current Affairs.

That summer of 1977 his first challenge was *Ninety Minutes Live*, which had become one of the walking wounded. Executive producer

Alex Frame was so gloomy about his failure to make the program a success that he had offered to resign. "We'd been so phenomenally successful on radio and then to get into this!" he reflected a decade later. "Holy smokes! It was definitely a maturing process."

Taylor and I didn't want Frame to quit but we did want some changes to make *Ninety Minutes* more comfortable for Gzowski and more of a unified whole for the viewer, with fewer jarring moments such as going directly from a rock band to a discussion on Quebec separatism. We agreed that it was necessary to change the approach. In fact, before he left Herrndorf had Gzowski, Frame, and their colleagues re-examining the program and new ideas were already percolating. We decided to bring in new people to help Gzowski: Carole Taylor, Keith Spicer, Patrick Watson, Paul Soles, and others as occasional guest hosts and contributors. Our concept was to make it more of a magazine show in which Gzowski would no longer have to do almost everything. We also decided to bring in Winnipeg newsman John Harvard to do hard-edged interviews that would provide a change of pace and ease Gzowski's load. (Peter had never been comfortable with the more confrontational style of interviewing.) Harvard had won the 1976 ACTRA Award for best public affairs broadcaster in TV for bringing a refreshing irreverence to the CBC local Winnipeg dinner-hour news program with his aggressive hot-seat interviewing style and we hoped he would do the same thing for *Ninety Minutes Live*.

As the 1977-78 season got under way in September, the changes seemed to be working. The program had a sharper edge, aided by more short film documentaries, tighter interviews, and faster pacing. And to me at least, Gzowski appeared more comfortable, especially now that his desk was taken away – in another summer decision. Now he didn't seem to be hiding as in the past season. "He's beginning to look like a star," said *Ottawa Citizen* critic Keith Ashford. And at first, many others agreed. But within a few weeks I would begin to have my own doubts.

Meanwhile, CTV was having its own problems with a new prime-time journalistic program that had generated almost as much publicity as *Ninety Minutes Live*. CTV had matched the previous year's snatch of Lloyd Robertson by taking Peter Trueman away from his Global network news anchor job, where he'd gone after leaving the CBC, and making him host of a new Sunday night public affairs hour. The producer was Michael Maclear, who had moved from being a CBC correspondent to CTV and who ought to have known better after his experience with *Weekend*. The show, however, sounded worrisomely impressive at first with lots of money, satellite feeds from everywhere, live reports, producers, cameramen, studios, and hosts galore. Backing up Trueman would be such impressive co-hosts as Bruce Phillips, CTV's Ottawa bureau chief at the time, writer Barbara Amiel, former CBC foreign correspondent Bill Stephenson, well-known Quebec TV journalist André Payette, and Maclear himself. As Trueman later joked, "The end result was a horrendous traffic jam at the make-up room."

The new program launched that fall was called *CTV Reports*. *W-5*, a successful veteran TV news program, was killed to make room for it. Unfortunately (for CTV), *CTV Reports* was an unmitigated disaster from day one. Technically and editorially things just didn't come together on air, with satellite reports popping up in the wrong places, the hosts unsure of what they were supposed to do, and behind-the-scenes wrangling that soon became ferocious. Within weeks, Maclear flamed out as executive producer, being shifted to a half-hour program on Thursday night and grouching as he went, "I refuse to commit suicide on air." For him, it seemed to be *Weekend* all over again. As I heard and read about the CTV troubles, I could only reflect that it sounded all too familiar.

Shortly after Maclear left, and following battles with him, his boss, Don Cameron, and much of the program staff, Trueman quit in a rage that was at least mutual. The chaos on and off the screen resulted in audience apathy and an anaemic rating of less than half a million for the early programs. In short order the program was cancelled.

"The format wasn't working," said CTV president Murray Chercover. "Ratings had nothing to do with it." He was right that the format certainly wasn't working, but ratings had everything to do with its failure as it got clobbered by the CBC's *Marketplace* and *Ombudsman* programs seen at the same time Sunday night.

Somewhat piously, I told inquiring reporters, "It's a new show and it should have been given a chance to prove itself." From a competitive point of view, given its audience ratings, I'd have been delighted if it had stayed on forever. But personally, I was sorry to see the CTV collapse because it would be used as an example by those who argued that journalism in prime time would never be a ratings winner.

I had little time to ponder on this, however, for as the season progressed it became clear that splitting off Gzowski from much of the hard-story interviewing was not working as well as we'd hoped and Harvard's abrasive style began to alienate viewers, anger guests, and irritate his fellow workers. As a result, he began to feel isolated and lonely. His style had worked well for the Winnipeg local newshour, but not on *Ninety Minutes*, and by January we had taken him off the show and moved him to CBC Vancouver to work on the regional Current Affairs program *Pacific Report*. "I was unhappy the way things had turned out in Toronto," he said. "I felt I was never accepted there."

With Harvard gone, Gzowski resumed a more prominent role and my hopes soared yet again as he began to get uncharacteristically, if only briefly, favourable reviews. But the audience wasn't showing much enthusiasm. In fact, as the local CBC program directors, the Sales department, and the affiliates kept loudly pointing out to me, the ratings were falling from the first year and were running under 200,000 a night – even under 150,000 at times, which was less than half of what we'd been getting the year before – and the so-called "cume," the weekly accumulation of unduplicated viewers, had fallen to about 800,000. We were now getting a smaller audience than our local stations used to get with reruns of old Hollywood movies.

Some fundamental changes were clearly needed, and I launched a segment-by-segment, show-by-show examination of the program to get at the creative problems while executive producer Alex Frame and Current Affairs head Robin Taylor were doing the same thing. I promised my bosses I would get back to them with firm recommendations on the future of the show by early spring of 1978. I said my options included keeping the show as is; changing the host; a different time; a different length; making it more newsy and less song and dance; or the reverse.

Some of my colleagues weren't as sure as I was that the show was worth trying to salvage. Norn Garriock, bedeviled by budget cuts and now a scowl replacing his usual smile, called me into his office one evening for another long discussion about *Ninety Minutes Live*. "Look, it's costing us a couple of million a year. For that kind of money we gotta do one bejesus lot better. We'd do better with Hollywood stuff."

"There is no way in hell," I retorted, "that we'll do that. There is no way we'll go back to those tired old American movies."

The movies might have been better, however, than the appearance by Irving Layton about that time reading one of his more exotic poems. It was inelegantly called "The Farting Jesus" and even for late-night television it was a bit ahead of its time. Layton said Jesus was human and therefore "went to the bathroom, excreted and farted." After an uproar in Parliament, CBC president Al Johnson told the MPs that we'd made a mistake in airing the item and added, "it was in bad taste." I could hardly disagree, although Layton could and did. He said bad taste has its place on television, but in any event, he claimed his poem was "a discreet poem . . . I didn't use offensive language . . . I just said that Jesus must have broken wind."

A few months earlier there had been a similar problem in an interview with artist Don Arioli. Peter had intended to talk about sex education for children but the interview degenerated into a salacious, double-entendre-filled conversation as Arioli showed his cartoon characters Jimmy Penis and Victoria Vagina. A defensive Gzowski said scatology was educational, but he convinced no one.

Layton and Arioli were minor problems, however, compared to Gzowski. The eighteen-hour work days, the critics, the internal CBC backbiting, the insatiable demands of television, and the constant travel were getting to him. He was more nervous, losing his on-air confidence, and feeling a lot older than his forty-three years. "We haven't been renewed for next year," he told an *Edmonton Journal* reporter. "But nobody has." Criticism of the show has "driven me crazy," he added. "I'm probably the world's worst TV performer, which I guess is also my strong point. I hope it is." There was increasing agreement about the first part of his statement but not the latter. Alex Frame said years later, "he and the rest of us couldn't look our colleagues in the eye."

There was now a full-scale revolution against Peter by the local program directors, and Garriock shared their distress. I also had a distinct feeling that "upstairs" was getting impatient with the criticism and with Peter's lack of progress as a polished host, and they began distancing themselves from the show. Most of the columnists continued their barrage, coming down from the hills to shoot the wounded of *Ninety Minutes Live* by labelling it "Ninety Minutes Dead." Worse still, the ratings continued to fall.

Gzowski wasn't Johnny Carson or Fred Davis, but he was never supposed to be and he was never going to be. You can't attack a cat for not being a dog, yet people were assaulting Peter for not measuring up to their preconceived idea of what he should be doing.

One evening in March a worried Robin Taylor, whose curly dark hair seemed to be turning grey before my eyes, came over to my office and we talked far into the night about Gzowski, the show, and the future. Peter had a contract for another year, but either he or the CBC could get out of it on relatively short notice. We laid out all the options of killing the show, firing Peter, changing producers, letting the lusting Variety area take it over, and a myriad of show changes and improvement possibilities.

"Whatever we do," I finally told Robin, "we simply can't go on as we now are." Both of us were worn down by all the assaults and agreed if we didn't make some changes, the network would simply cancel the show for next season. Robin wearily went off to talk to Gzowski and to Alex Frame; Gzowski's departure seemed the most likely option.

After listening to them, Gzowski did his own agonizing and finally quit. "The show needs a performer, which I am not," he said. "I need journalism, which the show does not."

It was a painful business for all of us, but especially for Peter, who had tried so hard for so long to make this dream of a uniquely Canadian late-night show a success. "I feel sad about it in a way," he later told a reporter. "There's been a lot of solid friendship among us over the years." Ruminating about the show, he had remarked, "When it was good there was a feeling of elation, but when it was bad I don't think there was anyone who got as depressed as I did." Now he was going to take time out for the peace and quiet of a little farm home he'd bought sixty-five miles out of Toronto. As Thomas Schnurmacher said in his *Montreal Gazette* column, "We won't have Peter Gzowski to kick around next season." Sometime earlier, Peter had mused to several of us one night, "I've had enough failure so that I'm not scared of it anymore." Scared he wasn't, but wounded he was.

In his final show, which was for the first time not live but taped to avoid emotion-induced gaffes, Peter did just about the best job ever, saying, "You are looking at a happy man, like a schoolboy at the end of term." Becoming more subdued and forgivably maudlin, he said, "I want to belong to myself for a while. I think I'll read some books by dead authors who can't be interviewed on TV. I'm going to get to know my kids again. I'm going to watch some prime-time TV. I want to see how Starsky and Hutch are doing. You see, I have taste." It was a brave face, but Peter was devastated and he went off to lick his wounds and stoke up his ego before making a brilliant radio comeback.

With Peter gone, some of the intensity of the internal and external criticism of the show was also gone. But not all. Bob Blackburn of the *Toronto Sun* noted that Gzowski didn't deserve "all the brickbats," although nobody had thrown more than Bob. About a year before he'd written, "Gzowski is gauche, erratic, inattentive, irrelevant, often rude, often sycophantic, coy, dull." But now the tune changed. "He has been grotesquely misunderstood by the CBC. (The show) has been an expensive national embarrassment."

There was, I think, at least a slight sense of guilt among many of the critics that they had hounded Peter out of the job. This was true only in part. Certainly Peter himself had been leery from the start about his on-air smoothness and had never really overcome his initial unfamiliarity with the techniques of television. Maybe he had a death wish about the show. However accurate or inaccurate, the internal and external critical barrage had deeply wounded and confused him, as it had confused Frame and his production staff, who began in the second season, almost erratically at times, to try different things to assuage the attackers. The result was a fuzzier program focus, leaving the audience unsure of what to expect.

But with Gzowski gone the show was renewed for another year, and Alex Frame began the search for a new host for the 1978-79 season. "What we want," he told reporters, "is someone who enjoys being in front of the camera, someone with lots of curiosity who can keep the show happy. I don't think late night is a time for intensity. *Ninety Minutes* isn't the place where cabinet ministers, for instance, should have to account for their deeds."

His comments angered me since they fundamentally were at odds with my and Herrndorf's original intentions for the show. I still thought the original concept of a vibrant mix of journalism and entertainment was workable. But I sensed things were slipping away from me, and I met long silences and shrugging shoulders from my boss, Garriock, and sometimes from my "sixth-floor" bosses whenever the subject came up. To make matters worse, the ambitious and short-fused Variety head, Jack McAndrew, cast increasingly lustful eyes at our ninety minutes.

With that subtextual bureaucratic infighting in the background, we sought a new host for the program. Names floated across our desks, including Patrick Watson, Carole Taylor, Keith Spicer, Don Harron, Adrienne Clarkson, Bob McLean, Bruno Gerussi, Barbara Frum, and Paul Soles. Some fell off the list because they were deemed "too serious," some because they were "too light," and some because they wouldn't touch the job with several ten-foot poles. From the start Frame leaned to Soles, as did Robin Taylor and I. Soles combined both a current affairs interest with his own distinctive light touch.

His performing skills had been apparent when he was a relaxed stand-in host of *Ninety Minutes* earlier in the season. Paul had been co-host of *Take Thirty* for sixteen years and had also hosted a short-lived prime-time series called *This Is the Law*. At forty-seven, he was getting itchy to move on. Still, he knew what kind of killer job hosting *Ninety Minutes* would be and he was well aware of the critical pasting Gzowski had taken. In fact, he'd had a taste of the precarious nature of late-night talk-show hosting when producer Ross McLean hired him to front Canada's first late-night talk show, the weekly *Midnight Zone*, nearly two decades earlier. He lasted only a month.

While the negotiations were handled by Frame, I privately urged Paul to take the plunge. Finally he said "yes," unable to resist the challenge. "He has the kind of qualities we require," said Frame on announcing his new host. "And that means someone who can entertain through the conversational process rather than inform as a journalist does."

Although I didn't yet know it, Alex's comments reflected his increasing flirtation with Jack McAndrew and the Variety area. Also unbeknownst to me, Norn Garriock had been persuaded by McAndrew to give him the show. Garriock agreed with Jack that the show had to shift its balance away from journalism to entertainment. It was a bureaucratic war of attrition in which Current Affairs was the loser, although some of the more traditional Current Affairs producers were just as glad to see *Ninety Minutes* go. But I didn't like it one bit and wasn't going to give up without one last fight. So one warm Sunday in early June, Robin Taylor, Alex Frame, and I drove out the twenty miles to Norn's countryside home north of Toronto and sat by his swimming pool looking out over his fifty acres of hills and bush, arguing about the future of the show. Norn wanted a much lighter show and Alex agreed.

"It'll become Johnny Carson North," I sneered.

"With any luck!" said Norn.

"No!" I responded. "You're destroying the whole concept of an informational program helping this country to understand itself."

"Bullshit!" was his smiling response. "The show's a disaster area, the audience is falling, and our regional people are ridiculing it. If it's going to live at all, this is the only way it has a chance."

Norn heard out my arguments and Robin's, listened to Alex's position, refilled our glasses, and stuck to his judgement. Robin and I drove home in silence. The battle was over, and Alex and Jack began to revamp the show, taping it instead of going live, cutting it from ninety minutes to one hour, and renaming it *Canada After Dark*. Some had suggested the title "Thirty Minutes Less."

There was nothing to be gained by crying over the lost *Ninety Minutes Live* battle, and I was determined to salvage at least something out of the debris, especially since I knew Norn was sensitive to my obvious chagrin. So I intensified my campaign for a longer *National*, temporarily shelved in the push for *Ninety Minutes*, and I also proposed an extra five minutes for late-night local news. The latter proposal, I knew, would please the local program directors and, for a change, bring their support for my idea.

When Norn Garriock finally agreed to a twenty-five minute *National* and twenty minutes for late-night local news, Jack McAndrew reluctantly acquiesced. It would mean a delay of *Canada After Dark* until 11:45 p.m., but Jack and Alex would have to live with it.

But there was a hitch. The private affiliated stations didn't want to carry the extra five minutes of *The National* because it would deprive them of five minutes of money-making local commercial time and delay their own local news. Once again the intricacies of late-night scheduling seemed to threaten my plans. But this time I was determined not to be stymied by their opposition, which would have rekindled some internal CBC opposition to the longer newscast, so I devised a format whereby at about the twenty-minute mark into *The National*, we would take a wide shot of the news set between items and those private affiliates who wanted to could get out and begin their local commercials and news.

As it turned out, only a handful of the affiliates did cut away. It was a producer's nightmare, however, making *The National* lineup more difficult and sometimes leading to a sloppy cutting away for the local stations. I had calculated that after a while the renegade affiliates would get fed up with the technical sloppiness and with complaints from viewers at being deprived of the longer *National* (which I quietly encouraged) and take the whole program. In time, that's exactly what did happen, and *The National* became a twenty-five-minute program across the nation on CBC stations and our affiliates.

Even with McAndrew's enthusiastic efforts and a more entertaining style, *Canada After Dark*, née *Ninety Minutes Live*, still wasn't working, and Alex Frame was plunged into gloomy frustration. Before the season was over he asked that it be killed. "We just didn't have the strength any more to rebuild and make it go," he later said. "God knows we tried."

Garriock quickly agreed to cancel and switched the CBC back to reruns of old Hollywood movies while Paul Soles left TV and went back into acting, his first love. Alex Frame took his creative talents into CBC management, first running CBC television in Vancouver and later taking over the CBC station in Toronto, where he recaptured for local TV programming the kind of success he'd had with *This Country in the Morning* and became an ardent champion of more Canadian programming on CBC. In September, 1987, he rejoined CBC Radio as head of Current Affairs.

"With what I know now," Frame told me a decade after *Ninety*

Minutes, "I could really make it work! Our first mistake was not building the show around Peter. We built it in opposition to him in many ways. We had a band on one side of him and a studio audience on the other, which was totally antithetical to Peter." To this day, I'm unrepentant in my belief that it could have worked as an informational vehicle even with all the odds stacked against it. It could have been something uniquely Canadian if we'd persevered. As it was, it was an audacious failure. In fact, maybe it wouldn't be such a bad idea to give it a try once again.

Peter Herrndorf shares my evaluation and told me years later, "If it had gone into a third year, it would have become as much of an institution as *The National* and *The Journal* have become." Maybe, but it needed a much sharper focus, too. It failed because there was no rhythm, no consistency, and it misused Gzowski, trying to make him into some kind of carnival barker for everything from rock musicians to gymnasts instead of exploiting his talents as an intimate, intelligent conversationalist.

Of course, the trouble with *Ninety Minutes Live* was only one relatively small part of my bureaucratic travails in the late 1970s. *The National* remained a trouble spot, and when Lloyd Robertson went off to CTV my adventures had only begun.

3 ANOTHER PETER PROBLEM

That fall of 1976 when Lloyd Robertson was wooed from *The National* to *CTV News*, it was a front-page story across the country, and everyone seemed to want his old job. Within twenty-four hours of the announcement of Lloyd's departure, I had twenty-five applications sitting on my desk. Within a couple of weeks, I had 125.

Barbara Frum and her *As It Happens* radio crew decided to help us out by holding a week-long series of on-air auditions. With her tongue firmly planted in her cheek, Barbara tried out an extraordinary range of people who claimed interest in the anchoring job. Each one was required to say: "Good evening. This is .... for *The National*," and then read a news item. Then Barbara interviewed them on-air and asked them why they wanted the job. One of the first who volunteered was the Prime Minister's wife. So listeners were treated to, "Good evening. This is Margaret Trudeau for *The National*." Margaret told Barbara she wanted the position because "I think I certainly would bring honesty to the job. I would very much try to tell it like it is." If she were chosen, she said, she would inject more humour into *The National* and canvass more opinions of individual Canadians, although she added, "every night having to criticize my husband and the government would really be more than I could bear." Still, at the end of the interview, she asked, "Have I got the job?"

Others who said they wanted to anchor *The National* and who took the *As It Happens* audition included iconoclastic radio commentator and TV personality Gordon Sinclair, Harold Ballard, the controversial owner of the Toronto Maple Leafs, veteran hockey star and sports commentator Howie Meeker, the Cookie Monster of *Sesame Street*, best-selling author Farley Mowat, Liberal cabinet minister Bryce Mackasey, Conservative Party leader Robert Stanfield, and a recently defeated would-be politician named Brian Mulroney. In the end, Barbara and her editors chose Robert Stanfield. In his on-air response, he said, "Please give me the job ... I'll add energy, vitality, and excitement ..." Barbara and her producer, the emerging enfant terrible of CBC Radio, Mark Starowicz, put me on the air with Stanfield to evaluate his performance. "Well," I joked to him, "Don't call us ... We'll call you."

Ten years later, when I visited Stanfield's Ottawa office to discuss broadcasting policy, he chided me for rejecting him as anchor of *The National*. "You didn't want me. You, aah, aah, aah, did me out of a job," he pouted in his sometimes agonizingly slow way of speaking. "Yes, you're the one who wouldn't let me, aah, aah, be, aah, the anchorman of *The National*." Until he cackled, I thought he was serious.

The waggish *As It Happens* auditions underlined the intense public focus on who would succeed Lloyd Robertson. Among those considered were Peter Jennings, then ABC's principal European correspondent, a former Canadian newscaster and an old personal friend. Also on the list were Peter Trueman, the news anchor at Global; Keith Morrison, who anchored the weekend news at CTV; CBC announcer Jan Tennant, who a few years later went over to Global to anchor the news; veteran *National* back-up George McLean; former Moscow correspondent Ab Douglas, who was now anchoring the local news at CBC Ottawa; and roving correspondent Peter Kent, who had been co-anchoring news specials and *Newsmagazine* with Robertson. It was an impressive field of possibilities.

By mid-October, just as Lloyd and Harvey Kirck launched their CTV duet, the list had been narrowed and auditions were conducted by chief news editor Cliff Lonsdale and Trina McQueen, executive producer of *The National*. Lonsdale's predecessor, Mike Daigneault, had gone to Montreal as head of CBC English-language broadcasting in Quebec. I screened the taped auditions of the finalists and shared their enthusiasm for the handsome, thirty-three-year-old Kent, whose coverage of wars in Vietnam and Cambodia, racism in South Africa, revolutions in Latin America, and the rise of separatism in Quebec had, the year before, won him an ACTRA award as best news broadcaster. From day one Trina and Cliff had leaned toward him, and I now accepted their recommendation that Peter Kent be the new anchor of *The National*.

I knew Peter to be a serious journalist who hated to let his emotions show through in his reports. In Cambodia once he had been doing a "stand-up" report for *The National* in front of a home that had been destroyed in a battle, the family who lived there all but wiped out. Stunned by the mutilated bodies and the scene of destruction around him, Peter's voice cracked and he choked back tears in delivering his report. This wouldn't do. So he insisted on standing there and doing his piece several times before he was satisfied that on the last take he'd eliminated any trace of his emotional reaction. But when the film arrived in Toronto, his editors were overwhelmed with the searing impact of Peter's emotion-choked delivery in his first take, and they used that one. Peter was deeply embarrassed. "They shouldn't have done it," he later told me. "It's not professional."

He'd wanted to stay in Cambodia's capital, Phnom Penh, to watch it fall to the Communists, but his editors, fearing he might be killed in any bloodbath that followed the city's capture, ordered him out the day before. He then flew to Saigon to cover the last days of that city's non-Communist life. That wasn't much better and he narrowly escaped with his life when he was trapped on a bridge just outside Saigon in crossfire between Viet Cong commandoes firing machine guns and mortars at defending South Vietnamese soldiers. "It was rough out there," Peter later said laconically.

Kent was the British-born son of a newspaper editor. He had grown up in Calgary, worked with CTV and Global, and spent in total thirteen years in broadcast journalism. With his cool, competent, and quietly aggressive manner, this tall, lean journalist with the disarmingly gentle smile had a contemporary appeal and was a thoroughly eligible bachelor to boot.

"He does sort of bring out motherly instincts in people," Trina commented to reporters when Kent's appointment was announced at a mid-afternoon news conference in late October.

With his recent co-hosting of *Newsmagazine* and news specials, Peter was familiar with the studio as well as the field. Given his reportorial experience, there was no way the Guild could question his journalistic credentials, as it had with Lloyd, and we intended that Kent would report from time to time on major stories even though, as anchor of *The National*, he had to join the announcers' union.

But Peter wasn't going to push it. "I've been on the road for two years," he said, "and I'm looking forward to a change of pace. Besides, I was beginning to feel burned out." He had slept at home only seven nights in a recent three-month period and when we announced he was coming out of the field and surrendering his safari jacket he didn't even own a suit. So one of his first tasks was to go out to buy a three-piece anchorman's uniform. He also trimmed his hair and put on glasses so he could better see the autocue that unrolled his script in front of him in the studio.

With all the recent fuss about what CTV paid Lloyd to lure him away, reporters wanted to know what Kent was making. "$60,000," he said to the astonishment of the assembled reporters at the news conference. They weren't used to such straight talk. "And $65,000 in the second year." It was $20,000 more than he'd been earning as a correspondent but it still couldn't compete with what Lloyd was now earning at CTV. This didn't bother Peter, who grinned and said, "I'm embarrassed it's so much. They could have had me for less." After the announcement of his appointment the critics cautiously welcomed him as "personable," "energetic," "experienced."

What I'd particularly wanted from Peter was a five-year commitment to the anchor job since I felt strongly *The National* must have continuity to build consistency and audience loyalty. However, he was reluctant to commit himself for more than two years, a reluctance that turned into headaches for me even before his two-year contract was up.

To have the biggest impact, we scheduled Peter's *National* debut for Monday, November 15, 1976, the night of the Quebec election, which again pitted René Lévesque and the Parti Québécois against Premier Robert Bourassa and the Liberals. It turned out to be a chaotic first night with the breaking story of Lévesque's history-making separatist triumph, which meant many last-second changes before and even during the newscasts. Peter's floor director, Art Bouchard, kept slinking up to Peter's desk just out of camera range to hand him hastily rewritten script pages and yank the outdated ones away. Peter, ever cool under fire, didn't bat an eye.

"THERE ARE TWO THINGS about Peter Kent you have to understand," Trina McQueen said. "First, he's the most controlled person I've ever known. He really doesn't care that much about anything. That's why, when he's ready to leave, he'll just leave."

As the first months went by, he seemed to get more relaxed and comfortable in the anchor chair, appearing in his neat shirt and tie and conservative jacket. What viewers didn't know was that, out of the camera's eye, he wore faded blue jeans and desert boots. Perhaps I should have realized this was a sign he hadn't really left his other life. Always a study in contrasts, Peter was sober, earnest, and well-combed, but when the camera lights blinked off, off, too, came his glasses, jacket, and tie as he reverted to being a happy-go-lucky vagabond. After *The National* was over he loved nothing more than strumming his guitar at midnight in his small Victorian home in the Toronto Beach area. In the mornings he could often be found scraping down the bottom of his treasured forty-foot tugboat *Sagamore*.

There was a brief leave-taking for Peter about a year after he began anchoring when the announcers got fed up with the slow progress of their contract negotiations with the CBC and Peter joined his fellow union members in a twenty-four-hour strike. Along with George McLean, Jan Tennant, Harry Brown, Alan Maitland, Rex Loring, David Schatsky, and others, Peter marched in the picket line holding on a leash his dog. He took a lot of kidding as "the highest paid striker in the country's history," as *Toronto Star* columnist Gary Lautens described him.

Unlike the strike of 1972, the one-day walkout by Kent and his colleagues was not a serious disruption in programming. As in 1972, it gave me another taste of sitting in *The National*'s anchor chair, a welcome brief respite from my managerial chores. Although I was a bit nervous at first, I enjoyed myself and was impressed with the professionalism of the desk editors and producers. It was a good opportunity to work with them directly and I told Trina McQueen, "They're a damn good group."

While watching Peter's progress in the anchor chair, I was also warily watching the news ratings war with CTV. So I was comforted by the fact that Lloyd and Harvey had boosted the audience to *CTV News* by less than 100,000 to just over one million; *The National* still was ahead by about a three-to-two margin. How much of that lead was caused by Peter and how much by our better journalistic bench strength, I wasn't sure.

Two stories dominated Peter Kent's first year on *The National*: the Parti Québécois transformation of Quebec and accompanying soul-searching in the rest of the nation, and the RCMP scandals. For a while it seemed that every day brought new revelations of illegal mail openings, office break-ins, barn burnings, phones being tapped, and other misdeeds by the RCMP.

The RCMP story, since it went to the centre of power, got us in hot water with the government and we were under pressure to stop the stories. In late 1977, as Peter marked his first year as *The National*'s anchorman, Solicitor General Francis Fox attacked us for our investigative reportage, telling a Liberal political meeting in Montreal, "I think their (CBC News) activities are very irresponsible." It was not the first time public broadcasting had been under this kind of pressure.

In fact, our activities were the height of journalistic responsibility and the system of double- and triple-checking of facts on the RCMP story was a model of professionalism. The strength of our reporting was a product of some superb journalists who had been coming aboard in recent years. One of this new breed of journalists was Ottawa reporter Brian Stewart, who took the lead in breaking the RCMP story. Nothing was reported by Stewart or his colleagues that didn't have at least two and sometimes three direct verifications from witnesses. Orchestrating this effort was Ottawa assignment editor Elly Alboim, an intense, articulate, scoop-searching newsman.

The touchy political situation put Trina McQueen on the firing line. She set up a special team, even borrowing *the fifth estate*'s Mounties expert Joe McAnthony to help with *The National*'s research on a daily basis. There was no way we were going to be caught with our facts down.

Behind her smile and soft voice was a steely determination not to make a mistake that would damage our credibility, and she didn't. "A gutsy lady," as an *Ottawa Today* columnist noted at the time. Described in a Canadian Press interview as being "a hard-boiled, hard-driving newswoman," she commented, "What I have going for me is a very large go-to-hell factor." Trina had been one of our best TV reporters and I'd always thought she would have made an ideal program host with her potent combination of brains and beauty. But in her mid-thirties she went into the executive ranks of the CBC and never looked back.

Solicitor General Fox eventually admitted the CBC revelations were "substantially correct," but he said CBC was wasting public money on an unnecessary probe. "I think they have too much money," he said, adding that perhaps money should be taken away from the CBC and given to the RCMP. A storm of protest broke over that threat and he later said, "My statement was more rhetorical than one of trying to intimidate anyone. . . . I had no intention of making any threats."

I was proud of what McQueen, Stewart, and our Ottawa bureau had done on the story and felt they deserved accolades for their first-rate journalism. So did most columnists and newspaper editorials, and the written press followed our lead, including *Maclean's*, which headed a cover story, "The Gang That Couldn't Spook Straight."

As irritating as I and my colleagues found the government attacks against us, they paled in comparison to the political assault over the other big story during Kent's first year: separatism. The night of Monday, November 15, 1976, was not only the start of Peter Kent's anchoring of *The National*. It was also the start of a dramatic, con-

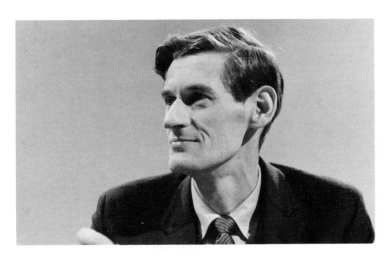

Pioneering TV correspondents James M. Minifie, Stanley Burke, and Michael Maclear. *(CBC photos by Robert C. Ragsdale (Maclear) and Herb Nott)*

ABOVE In conversation with the anchorman's anchorman, Walter Cronkite of CBS News, on the occasion of his 1981 retirement. *(CBC photo by Fred Phipps)*

LEFT Denis Harvey, former CBC chief news editor and now vice-president of CBC English television. *(CBC photo)*

BELOW *The National* anchormen's club. From left to right, Larry Henderson, 1954–59; Earl Cameron, 1959–66; Stanley Burke, 1966–69; Lloyd Robertson, 1970–76; and Peter Kent, 1976–78. The only one missing is Warren Davis, 1969–70. *(CBC photo)*

THE NATIONAL

ABOVE Celebrating my first night on *The National* with executive producer Trina McQueen, November 20, 1978. *(CBC photo)*

BELOW, LEFT The prime-time *National*'s executive producer, Tony Burman, 1980-82.

BELOW, RIGHT *The National*'s director, Fred Parker. *(CBC photo)*

The CBC-TV News 1979 election campaign team. From left to right: David Bazay, David Halton, Mark Phillips, author, Frank Hilliard, Don McNeill, Peter Mansbridge, Mike Duffy. *(CBC photo)*

The annual CBC correspondents gathering in 1987. Standing left to right: Sheila MacVicar, London; Michael McIvor, Moscow; Don Murray, Paris; Terry Milewski, Jerusalem; David Halton, Ottawa; Tom Kennedy, Beijing; Hal Jones, Washington; Patrick Brown, London. Seated: Joe Schlesinger, Washington; author; Ann Medina. *(CBC photo)*

At the CBC televised New Year's Eve extravaganza to welcome the 1980s with co-host Barbara Frum. *(CBC photo by Fred Phipps)*

Interviewing Joe Clark in December, 1978, with CBC Ottawa reporter Mike Duffy. *(CBC photo by Fred Phipps)*

Covering the 1984 Liberal leadership convention with Peter Mansbridge and David Halton. *(CBC photo)*

ABOVE Executive producer Mark Starowicz in *The Journal*'s newsroom. *(CBC photo)*

The Journal's Mary Lou Finlay. *(CBC photo)*

Peter Herrndorf. *(CBC photo)*

The National's newsroom staff in the fall of 1982.   (*CBC photo*)

The Prime Minister explains a position to Lorraine and me at a private
dinner at 24 Sussex Drive in December, 1984.

A social moment in Ottawa in spring, 1987, with Nancy Reagan and
Mila Mulroney.

Choosing a red tie for *The National* with the help of Lorraine and
grandsons Jesse (left) and Robert (right).

certed, high-level political attack on the CBC that rumbled throughout the nation for months. Starting in January, 1977, just two months after René Lévesque's victory in Quebec, the Liberals began charging that the CBC in Quebec was riddled with separatists who were using CBC programs to destroy the nation. "Every night," said Urban Affairs Minister André Ouellet, "there's bias, and every night it's in favour of the separatists. It's done by the guys who do the lineup every night and by the producers." He went on to urge Al Johnson to "fire the bloody guys who are working separatists." Ouellet's comments were reinforced by former cabinet minister Jean Marchand, an old Trudeau personal friend, who said in January in his first speech after he was appointed to the Senate, "... if this country is ever destroyed it will be in large measure because of one crown corporation ... Radio Canada."

Within hours of Marchand's speech, one Quebec cabinet minister after another joined the escalating clamour. Federal Industry Minister Jean Chrétien said CBC seems to have "forgotten its raison d'être in Quebec to promote national unity." He added, "I am frustrated every night by it. But what the hell can you do?" Shortly thereafter Mitchell Sharp, just retired as a cabinet minister, chimed in: "and may I ask what is the CBC, owned and paid for by Canadian taxpayers, doing to help ... to promote harmony and understanding? My observation is bloody little, and I include both the English and French networks." Even the Liberal government leader in the Senate, Ray Perrault, got into the act, warning in a TV interview that if the CBC didn't fulfil its mandate, "then we as parliamentarians must be prepared to step in." These kinds of threats had been made in the past, but seldom had such a concerted public attack been made on the CBC by government officials.

The accusations not only alarmed those who cared about the CBC as a national institution, they also infuriated Peter Kent, who began to fear that the government might be seeking to manipulate CBC news programming to suit its own policies. He was also increasingly concerned about the technologically antiquated news studio and control room, the frequent delays of the newscasts caused by sports events, the lateness of the 11:00 p.m. start, and the shortness of *The National* – we had temporarily lost the battle for a longer newscast to *Ninety Minutes Live*, then still limping along.

Kent grew grumpily discontented and as he moved into his second year he complained to reporters, "If a couple of improvements aren't made in *The National*, which I anticipated when I signed the contract, then I don't think that I'd be interested in staying on." He added, somewhat petulantly I thought, that he wasn't sure he'd stay beyond his November 15, 1978, renewal date in any event.

His complaints, if overstated, were largely justified. Peter's complaint about sports was an old and legitimate one: delays were frequently caused by live coverage of hockey, baseball, and football roaring like a cannonball freight train through the prime-time schedule. They earned a lot of commercial revenue but gobbled up enormous amounts of prime-time – more than on any other major network in the world. I and my colleagues had persuaded CBC president Al Johnson to set down a policy of limiting these prime-time intrusions, especially in the spring when baseball and the Stanley Cup playoffs coincided, sometimes delaying *The National* as often as four nights a week. Johnson made a commitment not to carry prime-time baseball until after the Stanley Cup finals and we were able to get agreement to tape and delay baseball games to the West so they would not delay the local dinner-hour news programs. We also began inserting a short newscast at halftime in football games or in other events that delayed *The National*. Nonetheless, sports events still delayed the news too often for Peter and at one point he told me, "*The National* is still taking a back seat to sports and beer commercials."

God knows his complaints about technical inadequacies were valid. *The National* operated with ancient studio cameras, an audio board of considerable archeological interest, and a vintage switcher (the machine that punched up the pictures from cameras and tape machines) that more than occasionally broke down. "It's an electronic slum," Peter said.

"One night," Trina McQueen told a meeting of CBC executives, "*The National* will simply go off the air. We can't go on this way." Indeed, we couldn't, and by mid-winter 1978 new equipment was promised for the following fall. But the promises came too late for Peter.

The more I talked with him, the more I was convinced he was looking for a way out of *The National*. Not that his concerns about the program weren't genuine, but he seemed to be using them to buttress his sense that it was time to move on.

Looking back at his career pattern, I could see he'd always had a relatively short attention span in one job. "I think you lose your vitality if you don't constantly have a new challenge of sorts," he once reflected. Now he began getting out of the studio on assignments around the world. In fact, during the last half of his second year, weekend anchor George McLean had filled in for Peter almost as many times as

Peter himself was there. That worried me because I felt strongly that we needed Kent's consistent presence in the anchor chair. So as he got more itchy to spend time away from the studio, I pleaded with his friends and colleagues to talk him into staying, even indicating we could handsomely increase his salary. But money didn't really interest him, as it never had. Then, in the early summer of 1978, Peter talked to reporters and said he was planning to leave in November, although he added somewhat coyly, "I might be talked out of it."

So again in June we tried to change Peter's mind. But even if we'd been able to get him everything he wanted, from a new studio and control room to an earlier time and a longer *National* with no sports-caused delays, I think he still would have gone. His heart simply wasn't in the job any more. He didn't, however, have any animosity toward CBC management. "My personal bitches aside," he told me, "I still think the CBC News Service is the best in the country. It just isn't as good as it could be." He said he didn't have any specific plans and talked about going back to radio, working for a newspaper, or "maybe doing something else for TV news." He was interested, too, in the possibility of spending more time covering stories in Africa.

His criticism focused on what he perceived as the CBC's corporate split personality. "We are a compromise public broadcasting corporation," he told a Toronto columnist. "We have not decided whether we are public or commercial." In truth, of course, the CBC was and is a compromise of both public and commercial broadcasting since it carries commercials and is highly conscious of ratings as well as being a tax-supported public broadcaster. I've never found that mix offensive in principle as long as public interest always remains supreme over commercial concern. It was the fight to maintain that supremacy in day-to-day operations of the CBC that preoccupied so much of my own bureaucratic career. But for Peter the compromise was unacceptable, and he now wanted out of the anchor chair when his contract ran out in mid-November.

He was ready to resume the role of world-roving correspondent and suggested that he open a CBC African bureau even though he knew it would mean a $20,000 cut in his pay. Chief news editor Cliff Lonsdale, a former Rhodesian journalist, was enthusiastic about the idea and I agreed. It was a part of the world we were not then covering adequately. So in late August we announced that when he left *The National* in November, Kent was going to open the CBC's first African bureau, probably headquartered in Nairobi or Johannesburg.

About 7:00 p.m., a few days after the announcement, I was sitting in my office working on a speech I had to deliver the next day and listening with half an ear to Barbara Frum on *As It Happens*. "We've got the scoop," I heard her say, and as both ears perked up I was stunned to hear her describe a letter Peter Kent had sent to the broadcast regulatory agency, the Canadian Radio-Television and Telecommunications Commission (CRTC), which would be holding a public hearing in a month and a half to consider the renewal of the CBC broadcast licences. The scoop that Frum reported to her radio audience was Kent's charge that the government had interfered with CBC news programs, citing specific instances where he felt decisions in covering events had been influenced by telephone calls from the Prime Minister's Office.

The *As It Happens* "scoop" was reported on air by Toronto *Globe and Mail* reporter Jeff Carruthers. Peter's "bomb," as Carruthers described it, was a list of four times when Peter said CBC changed coverage decisions because of calls from the PMO. One was coverage of the PM's speech to the Canadian Association of Broadcasters in April, 1977; a second was Trudeau's speech to the Economic Club of New York in March, 1978; third was our coverage of the First Ministers Conference in February of 1978; and fourth was a Trudeau speech on the economy in August, 1978. These instances, Peter wrote, demonstrated the CBC had allowed itself to be manipulated or intimidated by the Prime Minister's Office, and he felt they raised the possibility of future interference in more serious circumstances by the government of Canada. His comments echoed his fears expressed earlier in the year following attacks by government leaders on our news coverage of the RCMP "dirty tricks" and separatism in Quebec.

I quickly got a copy of Peter's letter and discovered that its seven pages were mostly devoted to subjects such as his worries over creeping commercialism and the number of American programs. It was only near the end that he made the accusation of prime ministerial interference.

The four events Peter cited were all decisions that involved me, although Peter directed his unhappiness at the president and "management," not specifically at me or the News Service. And I knew all four accusations were unjustified. In the first two instances, I was simply conned by the Prime Minister's special media adviser, my old friend Dick O'Hagan. Dick had called to tell me that Trudeau would be making major policy statements. I knew Dick as a reliable and helpful official, so I made a few other calls that confirmed his sense of their importance, discussed it with my colleagues, and then decided to do live coverage. There was no government pressure, no implied threat that we had better cover the speeches, only advice that they'd be of extreme importance. The decision was, of course, up to the CBC and had been made by us. As it turned out in both cases, I made the wrong decision based on hyped information. It was simply bad journalistic judgement. In the case of Trudeau's economic speech in August, 1978, I had been on vacation at the time, but I had no doubt the decision to carry the speech was the right one. It was indeed an extremely important news event with Trudeau announcing major cuts in government spending.

The case of the First Ministers Conference was somewhat more complicated. We had planned live coverage of the opening day, a half-hour prime-time wrap-up on Monday night, and a one-hour prime-time wrap-up special on Wednesday, the final night. In addition, my deputy, Don Ferguson, and I had planned some options, including the possibility of doing a prime-time special Tuesday night and going live on the final day. It all depended on the newsworthiness of the meeting.

The trouble began shortly after the conference opened in February, 1978. Alberta Premier Peter Lougheed complained about the CBC not carrying the entire conference live, charging that Canadians would not be getting a chance to hear what all the premiers had to say. Several other premiers joined in the complaint. The Prime Minister laughingly told them, "I guess the CBC found that you weren't newsworthy but that Lévesque and I were." Trudeau's principal secretary, the cherubic, backroom power broker Jim Coutts, slipped out of the conference room on his own to phone the CBC president to, as he put it, "convey complaints" from the premiers. It was a phone call I wish he'd never made. It became a cause célèbre at the time when it leaked out to the media. Now it had returned to haunt us.

In fact, it was nothing more than a damn nuisance that inevitably coloured the perception of whatever we did. Several hours before the Coutts phone call, Don Ferguson and I had decided to carry a news special that night wrapping up the day's events at the conference, but that decision was now tainted in that it would appear to have been made after and not before the call from Coutts. But the situation got worse. After the call, of which I was advised by the president's office shortly after it was made, I decided we would continue with our original plan not to carry the second day of the conference live. In my judgement, the agenda did not look sufficiently newsworthy to warrant all-day coverage. Besides, we now planned to carry a prime-time evening special.

As the conference progressed, however, we had to reconsider that initial judgement. The conference became more newsworthy as the arguments among the premiers and the Prime Minister heated up, so we began to consider the options we'd kept open, including going live for the whole final day. Ferguson and I had to try to evaluate the conference on the basis of its news value and to ignore the implications of the phone call from Coutts. Finally we decided to go live on the final day, recognizing full well we might now appear to be caving in to the Coutts call. Sure enough, the newspapers and politicians denounced us for doing the bidding of the Prime Minister's Office, and even some of our own news people agreed. Among them was Peter Kent, who was anchoring the coverage in Ottawa and was unaware of all the facts of the matter. Trudeau didn't help things when he told the conference of our plans, adding, "I wish I had the influence with the CBC that the Premier of Alberta has." Later, talking to a dubious reporter, I sighed, "We live in a pretty warm kitchen. We use our best judgement and go with that." CBC now carries gavel-to-gavel coverage of these conferences and thus avoids this kind of problem.

The same kind of pressures came two months later in mid-April with the Liberal Party convention in Quebec, which chose newspaper editor Claude Ryan as the provincial leader. The vote was early Saturday night and we scheduled full network coverage from 6:00 to 7:00 p.m. Wanting as much prime-time exposure as possible, the party deliberately delayed announcing the vote results until 7:30 p.m. We'd stayed with it until the result of Ryan's easy win was announced. Then I was confronted with the decision whether to wait even longer for Ryan's acceptance speech and run smack into a confrontation with the hockey game beginning at eight, or to get out before he began to speak. I was also under intense pressure from my boss, TV managing director Norn Garriock, who was worried about the commercial revenue we were losing because of news specials. On this occasion he was particularly concerned about having the hockey game start right on time at eight. I knew Ryan was partial to long and often boring speeches, and I made an educated guess that he would spend most of the time thanking his associates and wouldn't enunciate new policy. So I decided to get out before he started to speak. As it turned out, I was right that his speech was long, dull, devoid of news, and ran well past eight o'clock. CTV did not carry the event at all, but CTV affiliates CFTO in Toronto and CFCF in Montreal did, including the start of Ryan's speech, but then cut him off and went back to regular programming at eight.

We got dozens of complaints about our cut away after the vote, but there would have been thousands if we'd delayed the game. Clearly, the audience was on our side but the critics were not. My argument, that we already had the result and Ryan's "thank you's" were not vital to the national interest, was dismissed by some editorial writers as a surrender to commercialism and hockey. "Nash should be hanging his head in shame," said the *Ottawa Citizen*.

Over the years as director of CBC-TV News and Current Affairs, I got scores of calls from politicians and their aides and private-sector groups, all seeking coverage of their activities, and I never felt that this was in any way improper. I simply had to consider what the news value was and make a decision on that basis. What would have been improper would be to make a judgement because of political pressure or personal friendship instead of journalistic evaluation.

But Peter Kent's letter to the CRTC that September of 1978 was a newspaper bombshell. Front-page banner headlines met me the morning after the *As It Happens* "scoop." "Kent Attacks P.M. Pressure For CBC Time," said the *Toronto Sun*. "P.M.'s Office Slants CBC News – Kent," said the *Ottawa Journal*. "CBC Bowing To P.M.O. Kent Says," echoed the *Globe and Mail*.

Combining Kent's criticism to the CRTC with his just announced appointment to Africa, the newspapers had a field day. His new job was characterized as "banishment to the dark continent," imagining, as *Toronto Star* columnist Gary Lautens did, that Kent would be getting assignments to "go over Victoria Falls in a barrel" or enter a "swimming race with crocodiles" or "debunk the old wives' tale that it is impossible to safely put your head inside the mouth of a bull elephant during the mating season."

Kent himself was furious and embarrassed at all the publicity. He had never thought his letter to the CRTC would be made public. "I think the CRTC is unwise in releasing a presentation that is neither complete, cautioned or fully considered," he said. "It's unfair to the CBC and to me," and is "mischievous, irresponsible and sensational." He even accused *As It Happens* and Carruthers of distorting what he'd written to the CRTC: "He kissed off the prime concern," Kent complained. It was an ironic example of a journalist making the kind of criticism politicians make every day about the media.

Peter's prime concern in his letter was that "news and public affairs, which is supposed to be the central service of the CBC, is being compromised by total domination of the broadcast day by commercial interests." But even that charge was not true. News and public affairs programming had increased dramatically on the CBC in the past eight or nine years, especially in prime time. Peter also began backing away from his assertions of prime ministerial interference with CBC news programming. He said as the storm broke around him that the Prime

Minister's Office had not "tampered with or controlled the CBC's action. . . . The CBC, in the coverage of these events, has not been compromised at all. But it's my feeling that if I'm wrong and we haven't been vulnerable, then there is still the appearance of vulnerability."

Since Peter was suddenly at the centre of a major controversy, the Friday night the story broke we took him off *The National* and he spent the night in shirtsleeves and jeans in his office answering phone calls from reporters. The next day, Al Johnson joined the fray, saying, "Any allegation that CBC News decisions are affected by political interference is completely untrue. At no time ever in all the time I have been with the CBC has any editorial decision been altered as a result of political pressure."

But, denials or not, newspaper columnists and editorial writers across the country demanded an investigation into the Kent letter and the Radio and TV News Directors Association urged an inquiry, as did Opposition members in the House of Commons.

Even with his publicly expressed distress with the "sensationalizing" of his letter, there were bitter recriminations against Peter within CBC senior executive ranks. The immediate reaction was to fire Kent, or at least severely reprimand him. "Fire the bastard," one of my bosses told me. There was no way I was going to do that because, while Peter was wrong in his specific accusations and had embarrassed the CBC, he surely had a right to express his general concern about the CBC's fulfilment of its mandate. Beyond that, Kent was a fine journalist and I had no intention of losing him.

But I felt Peter had to correct the impression of government manipulation of CBC News that had been left by the media stories. I also hoped this act of contrition would lessen my bosses' insistence on firing him. Sunday afternoon, two days after the story broke, I went over to his house to help him work out a letter to the CRTC moderating his accusations. While his bloodhound Sagamore and his cat Rocky sniffed and stretched around him, Peter munched popcorn and tapped out a letter that modified his assertions of prime ministerial interference.

Meanwhile, Trina McQueen and others were also urging that Kent not be fired, and with their efforts and the new letter, "upstairs" somewhat grumpily relented. By Monday, with the story ebbing at least temporarily, Peter was back at *The National* anchor desk.

PETER KENT'S ORIGINAL LETTER and the violent reaction to it was only the latest in a long history of uneasy relations between the CBC and the federal government. In the war year of 1942, heated national debate swirled around a nation-wide plebiscite on the issue of conscription, and here, too, Quebec was the focus of the dispute. In allocating air time for speeches on the issue, the CBC obediently sided with the government and the "Yes" side of the question of conscription, squeezing out those from Quebec who wanted network radio time to speak against mandatory military service. In rejecting pleas for network air time from the Quebec anti-conscriptionists, CBC associate chairman Augustin Frignon wrote of the need to be "in conformity with instructions received from the federal government." At the time, the CBC also carried only muted news coverage of anti-conscription demonstrations in Quebec.

The CBC had simply done what Prime Minister Mackenzie King expected it to do and, indeed, directed it to do. During his long tenure King fired many a private rocket at the CBC; even his relatively mild-mannered successor, Prime Minister St. Laurent, once complained about the CBC being unfair in reporting on government policy, although he claimed he spoke only as a private citizen – and St. Laurent was told by then CBC head Davidson Dunton that his comments would be treated exactly the same way as those of any citizen.

A few years later, Prime Minister Diefenbaker became enraged at a CBC radio program called *Preview Commentary*. It had carried commentators critical of, among other things, the Diefenbaker government, and Dief wanted it removed from the air. "Heads will roll," said CBC acting president Ernie Bushnell, essentially meaning his own if the program weren't killed at the Prime Minister's whim. Instead of rolling over, however, thirty-four senior CBC programmers tendered their resignations. The CBC Board of Directors quickly assembled, overturned the decision, and the program was brought back. So were the programmers.

The occasionally stormy relations between CBC and the government had reached a new intensity in 1970 during the October Crisis, but complaints about CBC coverage of the FLQ, which sought separation through revolution, and of René Lévesque's Parti Québécois, which sought it peacefully through the political process, had been heard for years. In 1964, a then little-known author by the name of Pierre Trudeau, writing in Montreal's *Cité libre*, said of separatists, "they want to abolish freedom and impose a dictatorship of their minority.... There are numbers of them in the editorial rooms of our newspapers – they swarm at the CBC and the National Film Board – they press with all their weight in the mass media. . . ."

Four years after writing that, Trudeau was Prime Minister and the "swarm" was ever present in his mind and growing more ominous. After little more than a year in office, he complained bitterly about separatists working at the CBC and warned that if CBC president George Davidson did not root them out, "We, the federal government, will assume our responsibilities. We will put a lid on the place. No one should think that we will not do it. If necessary, we can produce programs and, if we can't, we will show Chinese and Japanese vases." Davidson responded two days later, saying, "It has never been and is not the practice of the CBC to investigate the political sympathies of the people being hired." He would not, he said, conduct "a witch hunt."

A year after that outburst, it seemed as though Trudeau's worst nightmare had come true with the early October FLQ kidnappings of British diplomat James Cross and Quebec cabinet minister Pierre Laporte.

On Thursday, October 15, I was in the middle of a late-afternoon meeting in the top-floor boardroom in Ottawa with CBC colleagues and representatives of the CBC private affiliated stations when a note was slipped across the table to me: "See me plse. GFD." It was a presidential summons. When the meeting broke up about 6:00 p.m., I went down the hall a few steps to Davidson's spacious but austere office. Sitting at the far end behind a big desk, the tall, thin CBC president looked more like a worried accountant pouring over a questionable tax return than the head of Canada's most important cultural institution. A long-time Ottawa civil servant, Davidson was a tough, efficient, and shrewd administrator who had been brought in from the Treasury Board after the *This Hour Has Seven Days* hulla-baloo.

It was getting dark as I entered his office and he got up to flick on the lights while motioning me to sit down. We chatted for a moment about news coverage of the FLQ crisis, which he worried might be "inflaming" the situation, and in mid-sentence one of the two phones on his desk rang.

"Yes, Minister," said Davidson. Assuming Davidson would want some privacy in a conversation with a cabinet minister, I got up and started to slide out of the office. But he waved at me to stay so I sat down and eavesdropped on his end of the conversation. There wasn't much to hear: "Yes, Minister . . . Yes . . . I see . . . Yes . . . I agree with you . . . Indeed . . . Yes. They did, eh? . . . Really . . . Yes . . . I see." It went on like this for about ten minutes.

It turned out Davidson was talking to Secretary of State Gérard Pelletier. When he hung up, he thoughtfully rubbed his big, elongated right ear. His mournfully long face looked even longer than usual. "It's bad," he sighed. "The next forty-eight hours are absolutely critical. We're on the edge. There could be disastrous consequences."

With his face grim, he talked of FLQ plans for revolution, murder, destruction, and terror. In recent years about 100 bombs blamed on separatist extremists had gone off in Montreal, killing or maiming dozens of people. As Davidson described his conversation with Pelletier, it was clear they were two very shaken men. To them at that moment, an insurrection was a real possibility. As he spoke I was swept up by the tension, fear, and sense that the country was indeed on the edge of great danger. There had been police reports of large quantities of dynamite and weapons stolen from armouries, bomb scares throughout Montreal and elsewhere, and student demonstrations in Quebec in support of the FLQ, and the federal cabinet had ordered armed troops to guard cabinet ministers, members of Parliament, and public buildings. Quebec Premier Robert Bourassa had requested the military be sent in to help Quebec police in the search for the FLQ kidnappers. A group of Quebec leading citizens, including Claude Ryan, who was then editor of *Le Devoir*, René Lévesque, and prominent leaders of labour bodies and teachers urged the government to exchange the FLQ-held hostages Cross and Laporte for "political prisoners" jailed for acts of terrorism. That very Thursday, just before Pelletier called Davidson, the cabinet talked of imposing the War Measures Act and of the possibility of censorship as it, and especially Prime Minister Trudeau, began to fear the will to resist the FLQ demands was crumbling as tensions rose in Quebec. When he phoned, Pelletier told Davidson of the possibility of FLQ plans for escalating terror, and he added ominously that while some extreme action might not occur that particular night, it might well occur within the next forty-eight hours. The idea that it "can't happen here" was suddenly very fragile.

In retrospect I know I should have questioned Davidson more fully about the evidence for the assertions made by Pelletier, but the atmosphere so crackled with fear that I accepted the thesis that the country was in mortal danger. As Davidson saw it, the whole future of the nation was now at stake and CBC had to do its part to "help diffuse things." Later it became known that government fears were propelled by much wrong and exaggerated information about what turned out to be a ragtag collection of self-styled revolutionaries. At the time, however, all we had to go on were the police and military reports and what the government was saying.

Pelletier was calling the heads of all news organizations, clearly hoping they would refrain from what he called "speculative stories and inflammatory commentary on what was a matter of national security." Davidson was willing to co-operate. "I don't care what the others do," he told me, "I'm concerned about the future of this country and, by God, that's paramount."

He felt it was "in the national interest" to be guided by Pelletier's concerns and to "minimize the commentaries" and "eliminate the speculation" that might "jeopardize the very delicate balance." He said, "We can carry factual information on what's happening but not speculative discussions." As the meeting drew to a close he directed me, as director of TV News and Current Affairs, to implement these constraints and to call my colleagues in both the English and French networks. Around 6:30 p.m., as I slowly walked out of his office and into a neighbouring room to make my phone calls, I was now almost overwhelmed with a sense of foreboding. I knew that I was deserting some fundamental principles of free and unrestricted journalism, but believing bloody revolution was just around the corner, I rationalized that the nation was more important than a headline, more precious than unverified speculation or inflammatory commentary. If our actual national interests were at stake, if we were teetering on the edge of insurrection, then journalistic restraint could indeed help preserve the nation.

In my first phone conversations with key producers and management colleagues I retained that sense of urgency and fear about our national security. I met some initial resistence, but the tension in my voice and the few details I offered quickly persuaded them to agree. My deputy at the time, John Kerr, was in Toronto and under his and my name, he sent out a telex to all our news bureaus and to other journalistic programming areas, urging "special restraints be applied to all News and Current Affairs programs dealing with these events and their implications.

"We cannot overemphasize the need for responsible editorial judgement at this time," the telex added. "If we have reservations about any story or commentary or analysis or discussion, we must be prepared to kill it." I later talked with John Dauphinee, general manager of Canadian Press, who had also received a phone call from Pelletier. He told me he'd responded much as we had and had put out a similar guideline to CP news bureaus across the country.

No news story was killed by the CBC as a result of the telex, although a lot of double- and triple-checking of stories went on, and some Current Affairs discussion programs and a couple of documentaries were delayed or cancelled.

One of my first phone calls after leaving Davidson's office was to Ottawa Current Affairs producer George Robertson, who had a discussion program that night at seven, less than half an hour away. "Okay, it really sounds serious," he said. "I'll change our program subject from the FLQ. But later, when the smoke clears and we have more time, I'd like to discuss this with you because what you're doing is damn serious." It was, of course, and his comment gave me pause. I continued phoning colleagues in Toronto and Montreal to convey the essence of Davidson's concerns, but Robertson's comments nagged at me. There was no doubt in my mind that the cabinet's fear was real, but about an hour and a half after Pelletier's phone call, as I paused between calls, the tension began to wear off and I began to wonder about the evidence on which the fear was based. What was it? Where did it come from? How reliable was it?

I recalled that the Prime Minister had spoken out earlier against media coverage of separatists and the FLQ. "The main thing that the FLQ is trying to gain from this is a hell of a lot of publicity for the movement," he had said, "and I am suggesting that the more recognition you give to them, the greater their victory is, and I'm not interested in giving them a victory." As I reflected on that and my own doubts about what we were doing, I realized there was far more assertion than evidence for the insurrection fears. I began to suspect the nation might not be teetering quite so close to insurrection as I had at first believed. With that realization and without consulting Davidson in his office next door, I talked with my colleagues in Toronto and another telex was sent out, modifying the earlier one by urging simple responsible journalistic professionalism.

About nine o'clock, having finished my phone calls for the time being, I walked over to the president's office, where he again made it clear that he shared the government's apprehensions. I didn't tell him of the second moderating telex being sent out, but simply reassured him our journalistic programs would be "prudent." Then he drove me over to the Ottawa CBC station. I wanted to be there in case the Prime Minister suddenly wanted to make a television statement that night. He didn't, and around midnight I flew back to Toronto from the highly charged Ottawa and went straight to our newsroom.

When I arrived it was to discover that Davidson had spoken to the Canadian Press, publicly criticizing CBC coverage of the FLQ crisis, saying a "greater sense of accuracy in news and a greater discipline" were required in the circumstances. It turned out that Canadian Press had heard of our "restraint" telex and from several newsmen whose Ottawa discussion program on the FLQ, produced by George Robertson, had been cancelled. Curiosity pricked, the news agency called Davidson at home. "There had been," CP quoted him as saying, "instances of inaccuracies in CBC coverage as well as other reporting and all sorts of wild rumours and speculation. When you're playing with men's lives it's necessary to be somewhat more serious." Later, to *The Toronto Star*, he said of CBC News, "I told them to cool it," and to the *Toronto Telegram* he said he wanted CBC to "show a greater degree of responsiveness" in our coverage.

I was apoplectic when I saw the interviews. It was one thing for the president to tell me in private of his displeasure at our news coverage, but quite another to make a public statement. In the flood of events since James Cross had been kidnapped, we had made some errors. We had, for instance, misinterpreted a statement by Premier Bourassa, saying he had flatly rejected all demands of the terrorists when, in fact, he had not gone quite that far.

We'd also been criticized for a confrontational interview done the previous Tuesday by Ottawa reporter Tim Ralfe, who had been assigned to stake out Prime Minister Trudeau and seek any comment he might make on the crisis. In the afternoon, Trudeau arrived at his Parliament Hill office and on the steps just outside the East Block he ran into the waiting Ralfe, an emotionally volatile anti-Trudeauite who, in this instance, let his personal feelings overwhelm his professional standards. "Sir, what is it with all these men with guns around here?" Ralfe demanded in reference to armed soldiers ostentatiously guarding Parliament Hill.

Trudeau baited Ralfe, deliberately provoking him into losing his professional cool and turning the reporter's highly charged questions into adversarial statements. At one point, when Ralfe asked him how far he was willing to go to deal with the crisis, Trudeau said, "Just watch me!" It was a brilliant example of Trudeau's ability to convert a hostile interview into exactly what he wanted to say. In fact, the Prime Minister and his aides were so impressed with what he said about "weak-kneed bleeding hearts" who are afraid to take tough measures against "outlaw bandits" that they immediately mimeographed a transcript of the interview. It would, they knew, strike a responsive chord in most Canadians at the time. It was rushed to the Parliamentary Press Gallery while CBC News was frantically editing it to cleanse the interview of Ralfe's emotionalism.

Peter Trueman, then running *The National*, was furious at what he felt was Ralfe's defiance of "every journalistic standard I had ever heard of" in his harangue of the Prime Minister. True enough, Ralfe had overstepped the bounds, but in the process he'd obtained a rare look at Trudeau's inner thinking. Trueman, however, was in a rage and openly reprimanded Ralfe. In the end, Ralfe quit, first to go to CTV and then into the backrooms of the Conservative Party to continue his vendetta against Trudeau.

Outside the Corporation there had been heavy criticism of Ralfe for being "irresponsible" and also attacks on Trueman for censoring Ralfe's questions. But with few exceptions our news coverage had been good, comprehensive, and thorough. I was proud of it and Trueman, who was directing the daily news coverage, deserved credit for that.

As I stood in the newsroom about 2:00 a.m. contemplating Davidson's swipe at our news coverage, I became aware of just how dog-tired I was from the emotions of the past eight hours. It had been non-stop tension since I'd first walked into his office. Now I was worn out from the travelling from Ottawa and incensed at what I felt was an unfair public attack by the president on his own journalistic staff. I continued to steam in the newsroom and called several of my colleagues, including my French network counterpart, Marc Thibault, who was aghast at the president's comment. Neither of us were able to reach Davidson, who a few hours earlier had refused to be interviewed by a CBC news crew about what he'd said to Canadian Press. What none of us knew at the time was that while we were stewing about the president's comments to CP, the cabinet had once again been discussing imposition of the War Measures Act. And at 4:00 a.m. the Act had been promulgated.

About 5:00 a.m. I tumbled into bed exhausted; three hours later I groggily awoke to find the War Measures Act in effect and to be caught in the middle of another day of national and CBC internal crisis. All day that Friday I was inundated with complaints from Trueman, the news union, and others about the president's attack on our News Service. "A stab in the back," the news union said. "Wrong, wrong, wrong," Trueman said. There were threats of resignation, letters of protest, and many loud arguments. Down the line with the News people, I sought to minimize the criticism, suggesting it had been taken out of context and emphasizing the pride I felt in what we had been doing. Up the line, I expressed outrage and demanded a clarifying statement. (Nothing came that day, although three days later Davidson told the news union in a telex that there had been a "misunderstanding" of his remarks, that he was referring to all the media, not just the CBC, and that "I am keenly aware of the long hours and strain under which all concerned are working during this period. I believe that CBC has done and is doing a creditable job if the totality of our efforts is seen in the proper perspective.")

The feud with Davidson began to fade by Friday night, as an icily controlled Prime Minister Trudeau, wearing a dark suit and his face seeming more chiselled and older, went on television to explain why he had invoked the War Measures Act. Among other things, the Act formalized constraints on news coverage, but those constraints were, in fact, less restrictive than the voluntary restraints Pelletier and Davidson had sought and even less than those ordered in the initial directive from myself and Kerr.

I immediately asked our lawyers to get an official government interpretation of the Act as it affected news coverage. Within a couple of hours they told me that normal news and public affairs coverage could be quite properly carried on, including reporting of newsworthy statements by the FLQ. I was advised that only when the media allow themselves to be used as a propaganda vehicle for the FLQ and are, in effect, communicating statements as an agent for the FLQ would there be an offence. Reporter Larry Zolf talked to then Justice Minister John Turner, who echoed that interpretation, and Defense Minister Donald Macdonald offered a similar comment, saying the War Measures Act "doesn't prevent news reports of the situation in genuine reports and commentary on what is happening."

By Saturday afternoon, two days after my chilling meeting in George Davidson's office, I was in a position to act on this advice. First, I notified my bosses that I was going to modify the Thursday night guidance. An hour or so later, I asked Trueman to send out a notice to the News Service. "From now on," Trueman then told his editors, "the only thing we must avoid is carrying propaganda state-ments by the FLQ. . . . We will, of course, continue to use normal news judgement and restraint in the face of a very delicate, even explosive, news situation. . . . The intent is to avoid presenting ourselves as a vehicle for FLQ propaganda."

While all these arguments swirled around us, we were providing live coverage and extended newscasts on the FLQ kidnappings and threats. It was a pioneering version of the kind of coverage given to the Iran, Beirut, and other hostage crises of the 1980s. Producer Bill Harcourt, who was supervising the special coverage, had gone sleep-less for nearly forty-eight hours, and Montreal reporter Peter Daniel was dragged off to bed after nearly collapsing from lack of sleep.

Late Saturday night the momentary calm was suddenly broken. I received a phone call at the home of a colleague in mid-town Toronto where I'd been going over the week's events with a dozen associates. For the first time in days I was looking forward to something more than three hours' sleep. The call advised me that Pierre Laporte had been murdered. Suddenly I was catapulted back into the middle of the crisis. Immediately, I phoned the newsroom and told them to get a bulletin on the air and then started organizing special live coverage.

I was so utterly preoccupied with the logistics of getting the news out that the enormity of the tragedy had not yet hit me. I broke every speed limit driving down to the newsroom, and suddenly as I sped down Yonge Street tears coursed down my face and I found myself shaking with sobs and saying to myself: "My God, how could this happen here? We're Canadians, we don't do things like this."

As I braked to a stop outside the CBC building on Jarvis Street, I forced my mind to click back to logistics. Even in the midst of a tragedy, journalists are incurably and aggressively competitive, and as the hours of Saturday night rolled on into early Sunday morning, I was pleased to see the CBC far ahead of anyone else on the story. While we were carrying our bulletins and special reports on the FLQ murder of Laporte, one of the biggest stories of the decade, our CTV competitor in Toronto was carrying a Don Knotts movie, interrupted only by commercials. Eventually they got Don Knotts off the air, but long after we'd broken the news. Mind you, a lot of viewers complained to the CBC that night. There were 556 calls of protest in Toronto alone, complaining about the news bulletins interrupting the late-night movie *The Train*. That night *The National* got one of its biggest audiences ever: 2.5 million.

The worst mistake of our entire coverage of the FLQ crisis came that same night in the midst of the Laporte murder crisis. Just before 1:00 a.m. Sunday the French network broadcast a report that Cross also had been killed and his body found in the trunk of a car. A few minutes later we picked up the report on the English network, after being assured by the Montreal newsroom that it was a legitimate police report and had been checked. We carried the story for about an hour before a very tired and harassed anchorman, George Finstad, corrected it. Canadian Press also put out a bulletin, but killed it within minutes. Later there was a suggestion it might have been an FLQ "disinformation" effort to cause panic, but I'm satisfied it was simply a failure to triple-check a piece of raw information and rumour of the sort that always floods in in a time of crisis. One cruelly painful result of our mistake was that Cross himself heard the report of his own death and was sick with worry about what his wife was going through.

But by far the dumbest action we took during the FLQ crisis came a week and a half later. Veteran newsman turned producer Gordon Donaldson had put together an hour-long film on Lenin based on old newsreels, graphics, and great gobs of romanticized footage from an old movie by Sergei Eisenstein. It was a straightforward documentary, a bit plodding, but historically interesting; months before I'd approved it for broadcast. Now, in the context of the paranoia produced by the FLQ crisis, some saw sinister connotations to it.

In the House of Commons, Lloyd Crouse, a Conservative MP from Nova Scotia, rose to denounce the upcoming Lenin program as a danger to society and an incitement to FLQ and Communist revolution in Canada. "A document for revolution," Crouse called it. He demanded the program be cancelled, although he admitted he hadn't seen it. I thought it was a joke when I first heard some of my bosses were nervous about the program. But it was no joke. And our French network colleagues, even more sensitive to the FLQ crisis then we were, expressed exceeding apprehension, even though the program would be seen only in English in Montreal. "You just don't understand how serious all this is," one official told me. "I've had death threats. We're in the heart of it all. Don't make it worse for us."

As sympathetic as I was to these sentiments, I nevertheless vigorously opposed any cancellation or delay in the program because I thought the fears that it would cause revolution in the streets were, quite simply, ridiculous. To prove my point, I had the program screened for the senior CBC officials in Toronto, along with producer Donaldson. "Well, that's surely no inflammatory show," I said after the screening. "If anything, it's dull."

Everyone agreed. But the pressure from our French colleagues intensified. Phone calls flew between Toronto, Montreal, and Ottawa. Finally, a network summit meeting began in vice-president Gene Hallman's first-floor office in "The Kremlin." The fears of our French colleagues were discussed, the program itself evaluated, and the impact of a delay or cancellation considered. "We'll attract ten times the attention to the program if we kill it," I argued. "When people see it, they'll know it's no bloody revolutionary tract ... no incitement to riot." It was clear, however, that Hallman, a deeply sensitive man, was keenly aware of the agonies of our French colleagues. Sensing his concern, I suggested, "If worst comes to worst, why don't we just cut out Montreal and show it as we normally would to the rest of the country?"

But after more phone calls from CBC Montreal and Ottawa, Gene decided to delay Lenin for a few weeks. The French were grateful and relieved, but a flood of critical editorials, columns, and comments swept over us as soon as the decision was announced, attacking us for being "timid," "craven," "mindless," and "idiotic." CBC president George Davidson was the focus for the attacks, but, in fact, he'd had nothing to do with the decision.

To fill the one-hour hole left in the schedule by the last-minute lifting of Lenin, my Current Affairs colleagues hastily reached up to the documentary shelf and grabbed a program on avalanches. Unbeknownst to any of us, it included a full minute of instruction on how to make a home-made bomb designed to prevent avalanches. In fact, it was a useful guide for any would-be bomb-building revolutionaries and far more incendiary than some old historical footage on Lenin. As a result we got a well-deserved national horse laugh. When George Hees raised the matter in the House of Commons after the program had been shown, the only response I could make was that it "was in the context of needing explosives to avoid heavy accumulation of snow which can lead to severe damage caused by avalanches. It was entirely appropriate to the program." Not only politicians must occasionally practise double-speak.

Aside from the media criticism there were 1,000 phone calls to the CBC switchboards across the country about the Lenin cancellation, only twenty-five of which supported our action. Our producers, too, were up in arms about the issue. I've always found it painful to defend the indefensible publicly, but defend it I did in this case, although not with much enthusiasm.

On December 8, a few days after Cross had been released, we showed the Lenin program and a Toronto *Globe and Mail* headline said it all: "Lenin Delay Not Worth The Trouble."

But of all the actions we took during the October Crisis, the most significant questionable action was the "restraint" directive growing out of the Davidson-Pelletier telephone conversation. The directive was in force only a couple of hours before being substantially modified, but those two hours saw a degree of self-censorship that, in retrospect, should never have occurred. As a result of it Davidson came in for almost universal media condemnation in the weeks that followed. He was denounced as "craven," "absurd," "confused," and "frightened."

"Frightened" he probably was at the time because he believed there was real danger to the country. But as far as I'm concerned, he did not act as a slavish yes man to Pelletier but rather as a Canadian nationalist deeply worried about the survival of his country and fearful of almost immediate insurrection.

Despite his public comments criticizing CBC coverage, Davidson continued to insist that there had been no self-censorship by the CBC. "There is no reason for self-censorship to exist and it does not exist," he said to reporters. "Can you point to any instance of news that has been kept off radio or television because of censorship or self-censorship?" True enough, no news report had been kept off because of censorship, but certainly some commentaries, discussion programs, and documentaries had been withheld.

In a speech in Toronto a few days after the War Measures Act had been imposed and during the height of the criticism, I said the media as a whole – and I thought the CBC, too – had, over the past couple of years, underplayed rather than overplayed stories on Quebec. "It's our responsibility," I told a United Nations Association conference, "to make the public aware of the living dynamite in our society and not be frightened off by cries from those who do not want to hear about unpleasantness. The media must not be an avenue for propaganda that will inflame any situation, but they must at the same time report what has happened and why, however unpalatable the facts may be to some. We must be extremely wary of allowing ourselves to overreact in the quite proper use of discretion and restraint in reporting these events."

In a way, it was a public criticism of myself for going too far for a couple of hours that night in George Davidson's office. The problem for the media in that kind of a situation is how to evaluate the assertions of those in authority when you can't get at the evidence yourself. The answer for journalists must be to be sceptical but not cynical. I certainly was not sceptical enough about what Pelletier had said to Davidson and let my nationalism override my journalistic values. There are times when that is necessary, but this wasn't one of them and I was wrong.

HAVING LEARNED SOME LESSONS from the October Crisis, we had been better prepared for the government onslaught against the CBC in the winter of 1977, which so worried Peter Kent during his first year at *The National*'s anchor desk.

There were McCarthyesque overtones that had unpleasant echoes for me – I'd covered Senator Joe McCarthy in his heyday in Washington in the 1950s. Urban Affairs Minister André Ouellet, who had been a leader in the attack, was quoted as saying he had "a list" of CBC French network employees who were out "to destroy the country." Maurice Dupras, a Quebec Liberal MP, demanded loyalty oaths of all CBC employees. Simma Holt, a Liberal MP from Vancouver, yelped,

"The CBC has divided Canada. . . . If we don't clean it up, our country is going to go to pieces." At one point in the House of Commons, Prime Minister Trudeau said, "When the taxpayer picks up half a billion dollars a year to have a public broadcasting system, he is justified in ascertaining that the system does not set out to destroy the country."

That winter of 1977, as I read and heard these words, I remembered something my first network boss, Gene Hallman, had said eight years earlier to the CRTC investigation into a controversial program on the environment called "Air of Death": "One of the tests of a healthy democracy," he told our country's broadcast regulator, "is the tolerance of unpopular minority opinions. . . . The CBC has a responsibility to see that seriously held minority views ... find a place in its programs along with the more conventional, despite the discomfort and criticism this may provoke among some section of our audience." These most recent screams of federal rage, however, made me begin to doubt whether this government was prepared to meet that "test of a healthy democracy."

It was, I reflected, the old Cleopatra syndrome: killing the messenger who bears bad tidings. In Shakespeare's *Antony and Cleopatra*, a messenger arrives to advise the Egyptian queen that back in Rome Marc Antony has married Octavia. Cleopatra's anger at this news of betrayal by her lover is taken out on the innocent messenger. She calls him an "infectious pestilence" and suggests he be "whipped by wire," "stewed in brine" and "smart in lingering pickle" before being scalped and finally killed. As she ends her tirade, Cleopatra then says, "Though it be honest, it is never good to bring bad news."

Through all the reckless charges and countercharges in the wake of the PQ election victory, there was little evidence offered to support the assertions. Despite Ouellet's "list" no names were offered, no programs identified, and the government watchdog of the airwaves, the CRTC, received only a tiny handful of complaints.

As the crescendo rose in decibel level, CBC president Al Johnson, who had been in the job a couple of years, became furious and counterattacked in every public forum he could find. "We have never engaged people on the basis of a political blood test," he told an Ottawa Kiwanis Club meeting. "And we are not going to start now." Like most of us, he assumed there were separatists working for the CBC in Quebec just as there were separatists working for newspapers, performing on stage, working in libraries, teaching in schools, and working in business and the civil service. There was nothing illegal about being a separatist. It was a philosophy Johnson abhorred as much as Davidson had, but he took the position that he would not act against anybody unless they allowed their personal bias to influence a program decision.

Johnson did have concerns, however. He felt both the English and French networks were failing to reflect adequately Canada's two cultures to each other. In Canadian news, the French network primarily carried stories about Quebec in its newscasts and documentaries, arguing that 90 per cent of its audience lived in Quebec. But Johnson felt Radio Canada had to cover the rest of Canada much more fully. Similarly, he felt the English network was not reflecting Quebec society as effectively as it should. That was my responsibility and I agreed with him. We had failed, for instance, to make English-speaking Canadians fully aware of the incredible social and political changes taking place in Quebec and of the impact Lévesque and his supporters were having. To most of our viewers, the PQ victory must have seemed an incomprehensible surprise.

But my French network counterpart, Mark Thibault, and I told Al we were running an independent News and Current Affairs service, and that to maintain our journalistic credibility we could not and would not become propagandists for any point of view. Our fear was that the federal government wanted to transform CBC journalistic programming from the role of public watchdog into that of the Prime Minister's lapdog. Reflecting the reality of the country, including the actions and attitudes of Quebec separatism, we argued, was necessary for a full understanding of the issues before the country.

Thibault and I insisted that our journalism must not be used in the battle for national unity, except as a trustworthy, honest reflection of what was actually happening in the different parts of the country, with reportorial decisions based only on the highest journalistic professionalism. Al Johnson agreed with that attitude and supported us publicly as well as privately.

The political attack on the CBC was based on a wholly false assumption that the Broadcast Act said the CBC was legally committed to "promote" national unity. In fact, the Broadcast Act said no such thing. It said the CBC must "contribute to the development of national unity and provide for a continuing expression of Canadian identity." It may sound like splitting hairs, but the hairs are important in this instance, and there was a world of difference between "promoting" national unity, as everyone from the Prime Minister on down seemed to think was the law, and the mandate to "contribute to the development of national unity," which is what the law actually said.

Indeed, the terminology had been a key issue when the legislation had been passed in 1968. At the time an effort was made to substitute the word "promote" for "contribute," but the effort was defeated because Parliament felt the word had a propaganda flavour to it. Secretary of State Judy LaMarsh, when she was asked how the CBC was to "contribute" to national unity, told the House of Commons, "It is not for the government to define." LaMarsh was absolutely right.

I so resented the attacks on the CBC that I probably spoke out more than my bosses would have liked. In speeches in Sydney, N.S., Brandon, Man., Edmonton, Winnipeg, Regina, Toronto, and Saskatoon, and in interviews as I travelled across the country on other CBC business, I reiterated the theme of the absolute necessity for journalistic professionalism and integrity to prevent CBC journalism from becoming a propaganda tool. I also peppered the News Service staff with memos urging our reporters and editors not to feel intimidated by the political jack-hammering we were taking.

As spring of 1977 arrived and this crisis passed from boiling hot to merely simmering, I reflected on why it all happened. It seemed to me that while it's now traditional for politicians to blame the media when they lose elections, this example had surpassed anything ever before experienced in Canada. It even surpassed the campaign of U.S. Vice-President Spiro Agnew, who had attacked the media as "demagogues of divisiveness" and "nattering nabobs of negativism." The intensity of Trudeau's and the Quebec Liberals' attack reflected not just their deep wounds after losing the Quebec election to Lévesque but a genuine if hyperventilated fear that Canada was in danger of breaking up because of separatist influences. They could see everything they had ever stood for endangered and they lashed out at the most visible and available target, which happened to be the CBC.

But things suddenly heated up again in July, 1977. Trudeau had asked CRTC chairman Harry Boyle to investigate the accusations of separatism in the CBC, and after four months of hearing testimony and reading documents the CRTC rendered its verdict: "Guilty," though not guilty as charged in regard to separatists influencing programs. In fact, the CRTC research showed only 13 per cent of Quebecers thought CBC was biased in favour of separatists while 12 per cent thought CBC was biased in favour of the federal Liberals. But the CBC was "guilty" nevertheless of failing to contribute to the development of national unity, said Boyle, and, he added, it was "biased to the point of subversiveness."

"The failure of the CBC to provide adequate communication among the various groups and regions within Canada is a form of bias," the CRTC said. "Bias in the sense [that] what runs counter to the principle of democratic debate is a form of journalistic malpractice that must be corrected by the CBC."

The impact of those words on us was devastating and incomprehensible. It seemed to me Boyle had simply not watched CBC television, had not seen *The National Dream* and all the historical documentaries, had not seen the reflection of the regions on *Ninety Minutes Live*, and had not seen the reporting of contemporary Canada on *the fifth estate*, *Newsmagazine*, *Man Alive*, *Marketplace*, *Ombudsman*, all in prime time, let alone *The National*. His report was studded with factual inaccuracies and wonky judgements. What particularly raised my blood pressure was the sweeping accusation against all broadcast journalism: "... the electronic news media in Canada, English as well as French, are biased to the point of subversiveness.... They are biased because so far as they are able, they prevent Canadians from getting enough balanced information about Canada to make informed decisions regarding the country's future. They are biased by their assumptions about what is newsworthy and what their audiences want to hear. These assumptions really amount to two. First, only Canadians living along the St. Lawrence axis from Quebec to Hamilton, belong in the news; all others are some kind of Canadian fauna living in the boondocks to be noticed only when they do something picturesque. The second assumption is that English Canadians could not care less about what happens to French Canadians and vice versa. These assumptions are intolerable. They also are extremely stupid."

From my point of view, what, in fact, was "intolerable" and "extremely stupid" was the assertion that those assumptions were in fact held at all. Certainly they were not at the CBC, nor at CTV or Global.

I had known Harry Boyle for a couple of decades, since I did freelance reports and interviews for him from Washington when he was a CBC producer. I knew him to be a rumpled, disorganized, but wily old fox still bearing some ancient private grudges about the way he felt CBC had treated him as an employee. He had, however, an agenda of his own about the CBC and he used the Prime Minister's request to turn the focus away from the accusations of separatism to his own concerns about CBC insufficiently reflecting the regions of Canada. The report was Harry's swan song as chairman of the CRTC and he used it to pour out his long-nurtured philosophy of what he felt the CBC should be. In doing so, he turned the whole inquiry away from the accusations of separatism to focus primarily on the English network and its regional reflections. But by mid-summer of 1977 the participants seemed exhausted by all the arguments, and the CRTC criticism, along with the political accusations, faded away. They had, however, left deep wounds.

ATTACKS ON THE CBC were, of course, nothing new. Whether at CRTC hearings, parliamentary committees, or in the House of Commons, we were under constant assault for a variety of perceived failures: being too tough in our current affairs programming, or too soft; being too anti-American, or too pro-American; presenting not enough programs on science, the elderly, the young, the farmers, the arts; and being anti-business, anti-labour, even anti-Gaelic. I received letters attacking the CBC as obscene for a documentary we had done in which a woman's breast had been bared. For the same program, I also got a letter attacking us for being "goody two shoes" for showing only one breast instead of two. On another occasion, because of some program we had carried, my office was picketed by something called the "Sado-Masochist Society of Toronto."

Nova Scotia MP Pat Nowlan was worried about "lefties" running CBC programming, and he startled the House of Commons with a claim that he had proof showing CBC danced to the Kremlin tune. He said CBC had succumbed to pressure from the Soviet embassy in Ottawa to cancel a Time-Life documentary on former Soviet Premier Nikita Khrushchev. Although he probably didn't know it, I was the one who cancelled the program. The story began two years earlier when Time-Life offered the documentary to me based on Khrushchev's best-selling book of remembrances. It was a good documentary, but too long. I demanded the right to edit it down and the Time-Life sales head said that would be all right. I announced we would show it. A couple of weeks later, the sales head called, full of apologies, to say he had been ordered to tell me the documentary could not be edited. Angry at this turnabout and unable to take the longer version because of the scheduling problems it would cause, I killed the deal. But having announced we were carrying the Khrushchev documentary and then cancelling it raised suspicions among the excessively intensive anti-Communists that it was all a Kremlin plot to prevent Canadians from seeing its revelations. MP Nowlan said he had information from "within the CBC" that Soviet embassy pressure forced the cancellation. It was, of course, nothing of the kind. But ever since, this incident has remained in the minds of the paranoid far right as a proven example of CBC's left-wing treachery.

The litany of criticism had at least momentarily subsided by the fall of 1978, when Peter Kent made his ill-founded accusations. But undoubtedly the attacks by both government and others fuelled Kent's fear of manipulation by those in power in Ottawa. The latest CBC furore, this one surrounding Peter's letter of criticism to the CRTC, died down after only a few days. Throughout that pressure-filled early September weekend after the *As It Happens* "scoop," Peter had remained the calmest of anyone even when he heard of the high-brass threats of dismissal. He was characteristically self-contained and self-assured, genuinely bemused and baffled by all the fuss. "Why should everyone get excited over it. . . . It's just a letter," he told Cliff Lonsdale and me at lunch. "I was never one to get into trouble, except as a kid in Medicine Hat when I started a strike of newspaper delivery boys because we wanted another cent per paper delivered."

By Monday, only four days after the story of Peter's accusations broke, and as all the headlines were receding, he was back on *The National*. But a couple of weeks later, in mid-September, he went on assignment to Africa. That saw him back in the newspaper headlines when he was thrown out of Rhodesia supposedly for "biased" reporting. Peter was now back in the correspondent business, his anchoring of *The National* past history.

A couple of months earlier, when it had become clear that Peter was going to leaving his anchoring role, executive producer Trina McQueen began thinking of who might replace him. There were the "usual suspects" whose talents always brought them forward when an anchor was considered, ranging from Global's Peter Trueman and CBC correspondents David Halton and Don McNeill to Tony Parsons at CHAN in Vancouver and CBC announcers such as Jan Tennant and George McLean. A month or two before Kent had definitely said he was going, Trina casually mentioned to me, "And of course, there's you."

I smiled, said something like "Hmmm," and filed away her comment in my subconscious. But the idea kept popping back into the forefront of my mind as time rolled on, and it sounded increasingly interesting. It was the third time the possibility had come up. On the previous occasions, the time just wasn't ripe because of other things I wanted to do. This time, with many of my objectives achieved in my job as director of News and Current Affairs, I was more open to the possibility of change and I mused out loud about it to a couple of colleagues, including Trina. But I wasn't sure I wanted to be a candidate for the anchor job. A few weeks later in mid-June, over lunch, Trina smilingly asked, "I don't suppose you'd consider it?"

"Well," I said, smiling back, "maybe. Maybe."

"Oh," she said. "That would be terrific," and we then went on to other things.

A week later, Cliff Lonsdale and I were in Vancouver for a Radio and TV News Directors Association meeting and at a cocktail party he, too, raised the question.

"Well, what about it?" he asked.

"I want to think about it some more," I said. "I'll give you an answer when I get back from my holidays in Greece."

4 *THE NATIONAL*

I needed time just to sit down quietly and think, far away from the frenetic crises, constant travel, and program preoccupations of my job as director of CBC-TV News and Current Affairs. It was a job I loved and which had stretched me professionally and enriched me by its challenges, but many things had changed since I took it over nearly a decade earlier.

I thought back to what now seemed the beginning of it all – 1966 – when I was still happily ensconced in my job as CBC Washington correspondent and received that phone call from producers Don Cameron and Bill Cunningham. They'd asked me to help launch a campaign to change the face of TV journalism. In the end, I'd moved into the executive ranks to try to make it happen. Now, as I looked at the current state of TV journalism, many of the reforms we'd sought had been accomplished. Journalism programming had internal priority and clout; *The National* was longer and in colour, its quality better, and it had more reporters, cameramen, and technical facilities. Our Ottawa parliamentary news bureau had expanded fourfold; we had added specialist correspondents and had expanded and significantly enriched our local journalistic programming. Our Current Affairs programs had high impact and popularity and so did our historical documentaries. Altogether we were airing three to four times more information programming than we had been before, and much of it was in prime time. One of our biggest improvements was in technology, replacing telephone lines with satellite transmissions to improve the "electronic highway" that brought reports from all across Canada for our newscasts and other programs. We had also moved from film to electronic news-gathering videotape cameras (ENG) that gave us a speed and an immediacy in getting reports on air that we'd never before dreamed possible. Another technological innovation had been the recent start of a daily satellite feed from the Visnews TV news agency in London (of which I was a member of the Board of Directors representing CBC, a founding partner). For the first time that gave us access to same-day news coverage by the BBC and other European networks. It also provided a less expensive way of satelliting in reports from our own correspondents, since we could tack our reports on the end of the Visnews feed. All this had significantly enhanced *The National's* coverage. Technologically, CBC News had become one of the most advanced broadcast organizations in the world .

There had been failures along the way, too, such as *Ninety Minutes Live*, the loss of Lloyd Robertson, the unsuccessful effort to get *The National* into prime time and to make it a half hour (although I had finally been able to lengthen it to twenty-five minutes), and many traumatic moments such as Peter Kent's stormy departure. But when I summed it up for myself, I felt that in many ways the "revolution" we had brashly talked about in 1966 had happened, although there was still more to be done.

There had been, though, a personal price. The constant travel and professional preoccupation had made a shambles of what little personal life I had. It was a familiar story, which in this respect hadn't changed since my correspondent days. If I wasn't travelling, I was at the office early in the morning to get my dictation done before the phone started ringing and meetings were called. And I was often there until late at night to have more meetings or deal with the latest news or management crisis. Weekends were mostly working days as well. After our return to Toronto in 1969 my wife Sylvia and I did get away for holidays occasionally, but even then I couldn't curtail the obsessive demands of the job, taking my memos and program plans with me. It was impossible and unfair, and I suppose I was a classic workaholic, which strained our marriage: inevitably, we drifted apart.

It was now four years after Sylvia and I had finally parted and I was now sharing my life and future with Lorraine Thomson. We had met at meetings of the Canadian Mental Health Association, where I was chairman of the Toronto branch and Lorraine was a Board member and fund-raiser. She had studied ballet and danced in stage shows and in the big variety shows of the early years of CBC-TV. Later she became a radio and television interviewer and host, and later still she began to produce her own programs as well as being the program coordinator for *Front Page Challenge*. In that role she became friends as well as an associate of people like Gordon Sinclair, Betty Kennedy, Fred Davis, and Pierre Berton. Lorraine had an awareness and sensitivity that would be invaluable in helping me to decide whether or not to move out from behind my executive desk to in front of the camera again. Her judgements, based on her wide experience and her abundance of common sense, would be sorely needed, for I was about to make one of the most difficult personal decisions of my professional life. I'd considered leaving my job before when offers had come my way over the previous ten years, but I had been too fascinated by television to break away from the CBC.

WITH THE PROSPECT of a more enticing and drastic career change dangling before me as anchor of *The National*, Lorraine and I headed off for a month-long holiday in the Greek islands. As we swam around the coral reefs at the island of Skiathos and dipped our toes into the warm sand, we thought and talked endlessly about it. I had no doubt I could give the anchor job the journalistic credibility it needed, but I was less sure about the demands of being on-air night after night. I was also uneasy about the repercussions of moving from the front office as head of News and Current Affairs to being a "Joe Workie," albeit a highly visible one. What about personal relationships? People I'd been boss of would be my bosses now. Would I be accepted by my new colleagues? What about the invasion of privacy that inevitably flows from the high exposure of anchoring *The National*? What about the costs of the topsy-turvy lifestyle, working until midnight or later and having virtually no social life?

As always when considering a career change, I made a list of all the pros and cons and all the professional and personal implications. I knew Cliff and Trina wanted me to be a candidate because they liked the journalistic credentials I could bring to the anchor desk, and I had, in a sense, auditioned on air for the job a number of times when the announcers had walked out. I had, of course, also anchored many a program when I was a correspondent in Washington. In short, they thought I could handle it.

I wasn't so certain.

On the plus side were the obvious challenge, the prospect of the adrenalin-surging excitement of being on camera live every night, the professional and ego gratification. The more I thought about it, I had the growing conviction that I could do it. And Lorraine agreed.

I knew it would be a big, risky jump, but then, it could be no bigger or riskier than when I left Washington as a foreign correspondent and came back to Toronto as director of News and Current Affairs. In a way I would simply be returning to the frontlines of journalism, my first love. The CBC was an exhilarating place to work because if you had the desire and capability you could switch back and forth between the bureaucracy and the creative side, something like a university professor switching between administration and teaching.

In fact, I've always thought of television as the greatest potential teacher the world has ever known, and when I took on the job of running our information programming one of my central objectives had been to try to use television as an educational vehicle in the broadest sense. Aside from doing that through our newscasts and current affairs programs, there were other ways to reach for popular education, such as the historical documentaries and series we'd produced, from *The Tenth Decade*, on the Diefenbaker-Pearson years, and the other political documentaries to *The National Dream*.

Sitting on my hotel balcony watching a stunning Greek sunset over the Aegean and reflecting on our history programming over the past years, I felt pride in what I'd been able to do in another area of using television for education – our children's programming. This, too, had been my responsibility and one of my greatest satisfactions. Programs such as *Mr. Dress-Up* and *The Friendly Giant* rolled along successfully, but I had been impressed with the fast-paced style, high-quality production, carefully woven educational content, and enormous popularity of an American series called *Sesame Street*. My head of our children's programming, the sensitive, white-haired, and bearded Dan McCarthy, who could pass for a rotund brother of the Friendly Giant, recommended that we try to "Canadianize" the series.

We wanted to insert our own segments into *Sesame Street*, which we began to carry in the early 1970s, teaching preschoolers basic French and showing them the lakes and oceans, mountains and prairies, and the fishermen, hunters, city dwellers, and farmers of Canada. But the New York producers were ferociously protective of their successful show. Their apprehension was based on their doubt that we could maintain the same quality of production as in the rest of the program.

"No bloody way," I had been told when I first proposed "Canadianizing" it by adding five to six minutes of Canadian material to the show, replacing material on learning Spanish and on Puerto Ricans and Mexican-Americans, which had no relevance to Canadian children. I also wanted to get rid of the American pronunciation of the last letter of the alphabet as "Zee" instead of the Canadian "Zed." It was a small point but it drove me nuts to think of a nation of Canadian children growing up saying "Zee."

With Dan McCarthy and his producers providing the creative ammunition, I kept firing away at the *Sesame Street* owners, demonstrating our production ability, guaranteeing them a final qualitative veto, and making several visits to the New York producers – The Children's Television Workshop – to demonstrate our production bona fides.

After a couple of years of constant pressure, I was finally given the go-ahead by the American producers to negotiate a deal with Mike Dann, a former CBS program director who represented the show. The final negotiations with Dann went on at, of all places, the Miami Beach Convention Center. It was July, 1972, and the Democratic presidential nominating convention was choosing Senator George McGovern as its candidate. We had to meet there because Dann was co-ordinating all the television coverage for the Democratic Party, and even though he was so busy I was anxious to finish the negotiations and get on with the show. So while the voting for McGovern was going on on the convention floor, Dann and I sat in his mobile truck control room in a parking lot outside the convention hall, surrounded by TV monitors, shouting technicians, and oppressive Miami Beach heat and humidity, negotiating the final details of the agreement to "Canadianize" *Sesame Street*.

That done, Dan McCarthy and his CBC producers set to work. Ever since, they've produced high-quality inserts, seamlessly sewn into the American show, which have immensely enriched the program for Canadian children and brought the CBC bigger audiences of Canadian youngsters than any previous children's program. The first of the Canadian segments rolled onto the screen in January, 1973. I wanted to increase the amount of Canadian segments over the years until we reached fifteen minutes, and today we have more than twenty minutes. Although I clearly felt very strongly about "Canadianizing" *Sesame Street*, it wasn't until a decade and a half later, sitting with my three-and-a-half-year-old grandson watching *Sesame*, that I truly understood how important it was.

A third area of using TV for education of which I was especially proud was getting television cameras into Parliament so Canadians could see their democracy in action. The Speaker of the House of Commons was considering the idea and we and others lobbied hard with the parliamentarians to get TV the same access as the print media. But there were major objections: the TV lights would be too bright for the MPs; some MPs might grandstand in front of the cameras; the gladiator aspects of politics would be emphasized by television; Canadians wouldn't understand what was going on; the Opposition would get too much attention through televising Question Period while the government would look defensive. The list went on, and even within the CBC there was some high-level objection. I recall a CBC president telling me he opposed cameras in the House of Commons because televised proceedings would alienate Quebecers since they would see most of the debates were in English, not in French.

My colleagues and I countered that television would enable Canadians to better understand not only how government works, but the issues themselves. The fight to get TV into Parliament had been going on for years before I got involved, but it intensified at the start of the 1970s. As part of our effort to demonstrate the value of TV showing the debates of our elected representatives, the program *Weekend* went to Manitoba to put on air the first coverage of a debate inside a provincial legislature in early 1970. Produced by Larry Zolf, it stirred enormous interest and we sought permission from other legislatures for coverage. Alberta allowed television in for selected occasions without problem, and the only complaint I heard was from Nova Scotia, where Premier Gerald Regan protested that the overhead camera showed his bald spot. Then we got permission for experimental TV coverage of a Senate committee hearing examining marijuana legislation. Through these demonstrations we were able to dissolve most of the apprehensions of the MPs, and after a total of fifteen years of debate, TV cameras finally arrived in the House of Commons. Live TV coverage began October 17, 1977, with the CBC pre-empting the soap opera *The Edge of Night*.

Conservative Opposition leader Joe Clark popped up with the first question, about unemployment, noting that one million unemployed probably were watching the House of Commons (a gross exaggeration) "because they had nothing else to do." Initially, Canadians were startled by the traditional desk-thumping (which later changed to simple hand-clapping because the politicians thought it looked better) and by the noisy acrimony and heckling. They also were struck by little vignettes, such as on that first day seeing Federal-Provincial Relations Minister Marc Lalonde picking his teeth with his translator earpiece, another MP reading a newspaper, and NDP leader Ed Broadbent scratching his crotch. In time, the MPs learned it was best not to do that sort of thing while on camera.

We carried live most of that first day's Question Period, cutting away a few minutes after three to the consternation of the new parliamentary fans and the relief of old soap opera addicts. CBC switchboards lit up across the country when the MPs came on instead of *The Edge of Night*, with angry comments including, "It made politicians look like a bunch of pom pom idiots" and "MPs clank too much on their desks." One viewer called in to say broadcasting the House of

Commons "will cause revolution," while another asked plaintively, "How long do we have to listen to this crap?"

Even with such complaints, it was a significant milestone in using TV for education. Very few Canadians had ever seen Parliament, and on this first day of TV in the House it seemed like eavesdropping on a private meeting of very powerful people. To watch the Prime Minister and his cabinet ministers being peppered with questions was utterly fascinating and illuminating, even though nowadays it seems quite routine. Almost every night on *The National* we used brief clips from the House of Commons debate, and we began a weekly review of the debates in a program called *This Week In Parliament*. Later, we also began putting out the entire day's proceedings live on a special parliamentary channel.

As I looked back on my managerial career, I reflected that behind all the programming successes and failures, behind the difficulties of dealing with the demands of stars and producers, was always the dreaded and much-maligned CBC bureaucracy, that mass of supposedly grey, faceless souls who make the place run. In 1969 when I'd first arrived at network headquarters in Toronto the bureaucracy seemed impenetrable, but now that I was thinking about leaving my job, I felt I'd learned at last how to manipulate the financial, plant, planning, scheduling, and administrative staff to get what I wanted for my programs.

"The only thing that really matters in broadcasting is programming; all the rest is housekeeping," said the Fowler Report on Broadcasting in 1965. That's true, but there is an awful lot of housekeeping that flows from the programming. In any large, socially activist organization, I suppose, it's realistic to expect the regular confrontation of wills, ambition, and idealism versus scepticism, office politics, occasional stupidity, organizational barracudas, and two-bit Torquemadas. Some I had dealt with had flawless tactics and non-existent strategy; they paid lip service to the principles of public broadcasting but their lips didn't have much to say. There were others with silver tongues and leaden minds. But these few were easily outnumbered, if not entirely silenced, by a majority of dedicated, hard-working, intelligent men and women.

Most of the clashes came because we all had our own agendas, all wanting a larger share of corporate resources in what we believed was a just cause. My boardroom battles were mostly fought in our network headquarters at "Vatican North" and particularly on the fourth floor, which housed the TV executive suite. It was there that I learned the choices were compliance, compromise, or confrontation. And it was intriguing to watch the idealism of some wither at the touch of reality. The challenge, I had always felt, was where to compromise between what you wanted and what you could get. Although there are times when you have to risk what you already have in order to get what you want, for the most part I was not often a confrontationalist, an all-or-nothing boardroom combatant. Persistence and patient insistence seasoned with a few righteous rhetorical outbursts were my preferred weapons. Nonetheless, I used every trick I could muster to squeeze as much as I could out of every meeting, and over time I found much depends on where you set your sights. A low level of expectation is obviously easier to achieve than a high level, but I'd rather get 75 per cent of a lot than 100 per cent of a little.

The battle lines at network headquarters were everywhere. The Entertainment program directors (there were four of them while I was there - Doug Nixon, Thom Benson, Don Goodwin, and Jack Craine) and I often were allies fighting the managers of constraint - the finance and resource people. Just as often we were adversaries fighting each other for air time, money, and resources. The often besieged and ever patient Norn Garriock was, as managing director, the man in the middle, not only trying to balance the budget but also to keep relative peace among his aggressive colleagues while seeking to present a united front to his bosses on the sixth floor. Norn was not a prude, but in some ways he was a bit innocent. Thus I was taken aback at one meeting in a CBC boardroom when Norn and a dozen of us were dissecting a production in which a producer had sprinkled an extraordinary number of four-letter words like a little boy trying to demonstrate his machismo. Finally, after half an hour of heated debate on what should be kept in and what thrown out, I could hardly believe my ears when I saw Norn slam his fist down on the table and shout, "Okay, that's it! I've decided. We'll leave in three fucks and four shits and all the rest have to come out!"

One problem we had was that our program areas were scattered all over town. Current Affairs was in one building about ten blocks away from my office, along with the Arts and Science area; News was in another building a dozen blocks away; Agriculture and Resources in still another; and the Children's area in yet another. The studios were all over the place.

Over the years, all the senior officers got increasingly pulled away from the production areas and pushed into ever more meetings with each other, with head office, with affiliates, with regional senior officers, with the French network, with the CRTC, and with parliamentary committees, individual politicians, and pressure groups of one kind or another. One colleague of mine occasionally carried a fake "beeper" and when he simply couldn't take any more of a particular meeting, he'd escape by setting off the "beeper" himself and leave, muttering, "Must be that phone call from Los Angeles." The whole process seemed to conspire to draw you away from your creative production heart, and you had to fight constantly against creative estrangement. Sometimes it felt like the CBC was simply a series of meetings in search of a program.

Creativity and management always have a hard time living together. As writer Alan Needham, who once tried it himself at the CBC, has said, "Necessity brings the two together as bedfellows, but there is always barbed wire between the sheets."

My most prickly relationships, and at the same time the most rewarding, had been with my immediate boss, Norn Garriock, who orchestrated what the nation saw on television. Norn had been a CBC farm commentator before joining the ranks of management and was a bluff, hearty executive who, faced with head office directives to raise more commercial revenue, constantly worried about revenue shortfalls and the protectively gloomy forecasts of the Sales department and was always aghast at expenditure overruns. Norn's preoccupation was to balance the budget. With all these worries conflicting with his own commitment to public broadcasting, it's a wonder Norn wasn't driven into schizophrenia.

He was squeezed from the top by CBC Ottawa and pushed from the bottom by me. Throughout the years of these twin pressures, he maintained an affable unflappability and we remained professional and personal friends in spite of our differences.

Running the entertainment side of CBC Television when I'd first come up from Washington was Doug Nixon, a CBC veteran who had organized CBC coverage of the founding conference of the United Nations in San Francisco in 1945 and had been regional program director for CBC Vancouver.

I got my introduction to the kind of firestorm that can explode about you in this business when Doug decided in 1969 that he wanted a younger image for Variety programming on the CBC and cancelled the highly popular, country-style music program, *Don Messer and His Islanders*. That set off what to me then was a breathtaking explosion of public protest, parliamentary indignation, marches on Ottawa, and critical newspaper editorials. In spite of the outpouring of national affection and support for Messer, Charlie Chamberlain, Marg Osborne, and the other Islanders, Doug was grim-jaw determined to "kill the geriatric fiddlers," as he descibed them to me, and to bring on the younger generation of musicians and singers. "Goddamnit, they won't stop me!" he said. "That stuff has had its day."

Doug never really recovered from the outcry over that cancellation, losing much of his internal political clout because his action was deemed imprudent and impetuous. But, in fact, that was Doug. He was imprudent some of the time and impetuous most of the time. He clearly hadn't thought out the consequences of such a show cancellation and the whole episode taught me an early lesson in careful planning for such major program changes. Just how deep the loss of Messer was felt was brought home to me when flying to Halifax from Toronto eighteen years later. I was sitting beside a paper company executive who was returning home to the Maritimes, and as we talked about the CBC, he said, "I'm a strong supporter, but you know, I can never forgive the CBC for taking Don Messer off the air."

Doug's love of the contemporary entertainment world and its hyperactive lifestyle, his impetuosity, to say nothing of his appetite for long liquid lunches, continually got him into hot water with his bosses. He was a fervent, almost evangelical programming idealist and his eyes would dance with fiery enthusiasm as he described some new show idea. Hardly a grey, faceless bureaucrat, his heart was on the studio floor more than in the boardroom, and he increasingly ignored the more mundane office routine and management demands. Doug finally blew up one afternoon when he went storming into the office of his boss and quit in a towering rage over some newly perceived bureaucratic indignity.

He was succeeded by an equally flamboyant emotional crusader for entertainment programming, Thom Benson. A veteran CBC programmer and one-time golden-voiced Winnipeg announcer, Benson had the looks of a middle-aged matinee idol and the style of a Sherman tank. At heart, he was a passionate and sensitive programmer, a proud, soul-deep Canadian nationalist. He'd held the job for five stormy years, brilliantly buying exactly the right Hollywood programs and infusing his program areas with enthusiasm. But like his predecessor, he'd been loudly unhappy with the details of planning systems and other bureaucratic processes and was haunted and hounded by the failure of his drama series, *Jalna*, a complicated Canadian production that infuriated the critics and intimidated the audience. He similarly infuriated and intimidated many of his colleagues with his expletive-flavoured, exuberantly passionate style of management. In a sense, Thom and I were network adversaries because we both were seeking the same money and air-time priorities and thus were on a constant collision course. And yet our battles never, or hardly ever, became nasty and we shared the same commitment to public broadcasting and the same abhorrence of the bureaucratic sludges who impeded creativity.

The one man I owed the most to in my bureaucratic career was the cultivated, gentle intellectual, Gene Hallman, who as vice-president of English broadcasting had brought me to Toronto back in January, 1969. It was a thunderbolt from the blue five years later when he was unceremoniously turfed out of the job. CBC president Laurent Picard, who'd succeeded George Davidson, wanted fresh, tough-minded leadership in English broadcasting for the CBC and replaced Hallman with Don MacPherson, who was then running the CBC Toronto region, and chief news editor Denny Harvey, who would be MacPherson's deputy. They were less idealistic than Gene but equally committed to quality programming and much more aggressive managerially. When he left, the silver-haired Hallman, at fifty-five, went back to law school. "I may be the oldest law graduate ever, but I don't give a damn," he smiled.

Picard had brought about a managerial revolution at CBC with his Harvard Business School-style emphasizing efficiency, his internal reorganization, and his relatively quiet lopping off of senior heads almost everywhere in sight. His approach was a mailed fist in a velvet glove. During his three-year-presidency, he had promoted and then demoted an executive vice-president and had overseen the replacement of almost every senior officer in English broadcasting except for Norn Garriock, Jack Craine, and me.

Picard was gone by the summer of 1975 and in his place strode Albert Wesley Johnson, the stubborn, stocky, big-shouldered, wavy-haired son of a Prairie preacher, a savvy long-time mandarin who never lost touch with his roots. He didn't have a moment's experience in radio or television, although he had a powerful passion for the nation and a deep philosophical commitment to public broadcasting.

An associate of mine once said, "The best president of the CBC would be an idealistic son of a bitch, thirty-five years old, perfectly bilingual, willing to wade in blood up to his ankles and with a feeling for the country in his soul."

Al was fifty-one, not thirty-five, and he was struggling to perfect his French. He came to the CBC from the deputy ministership of National Health and Welfare, had previously been Secretary of the Treasury Board, and before that had been one of Tommy Douglas's golden-haired boys in Saskatchewan, pioneering social progress as a senior civil servant. While Picard enjoyed his reputation for having shaken up the CBC administration, Johnson wanted to be remembered for the programs.

NOW, MUNCHING SARDINES and sampling ouzo on Skiathos, I was weighing a move of my own out of my management job, and I reflected that endless travel and meetings were aspects of bureaucracy that I wouldn't miss one bit.

Lorraine and I discussed all the pros and cons and finally decided that, yes, I would be a candidate to anchor *The National*. Once the decision was made, I began getting impatient to start and looked forward to getting back to Toronto from our month in the Greek sun and sea. I knew, however, there was still a selection process to go through and that just wanting the job didn't mean I'd get it.

When I got back, tanned, rested, and eager for the change, Cliff Lonsdale came around to my office and said, "Well, are you or are you not going to be a candidate? Time's getting short."

I thought he was rather brusque and reflected that maybe our relationship was already beginning to change. I looked around my office for half a minute and then at him. "Okay," I said, "I'm a candidate."

"Then you've got to write out an application," he replied with only a slight smile. I wrote him a brief note and the process began.

The first thing I did next was to tell Norn Garriock and Don MacPherson and Denny Harvey that I had declared my candidacy for the job and therefore had to be cut off from discussions about it. Cliff, as chief news editor, would thus bypass me and go directly to Norn, the TV managing director, as he considered me along with others for the job. I was suddenly just one of the applicants for the job as anchor of *The National*. Although Trina and Cliff had sought me out, they had a responsibility to consider others, too. It was an unsettling feeling to find myself in this strange limbo.

The timing for all this was decidedly awkward. A couple of weeks after I'd said yes to Cliff, Peter Kent's letter to the CRTC was revealed and then came the media tempest. In early September, at the launch of the new CBC television schedule (the same event at which two years before I had announced Lloyd Robertson's dramatic departure), the main thing the critics wanted to know was who was going to replace Kent. It was, I said, a decision Cliff Lonsdale and Trina McQueen would be making, then added, somewhat ingenuously, that my name "might be on a list along with a lot of others."

While the selection process was under way, *The Toronto Star* began a campaign to have a woman as anchor. Columnist Dennis Braithwaite wrote, "First of all she must be striking in appearance, not just pleasant or neat. The face has to be fantastic; the eyes extraordinary; the voice compelling – throaty, warm and totally Canadian.... I prefer to look at and listen to a terrific woman than any kind of man." As with Lloyd's leaving, all sorts of people took an interest. One woman called me from Hong Kong to say she wanted the job. Another wrote saying, "I'm suggesting a teenager for the job – me!" Cliff and Trina were flooded with calls. As seemed to happen whenever *The National* was looking for a new anchor, the story became front-page news.

The Star's Braithwaite, hearing rumours that I was a leading candidate for the job, was appalled: "The Word For Knowlton Nash Is Lacklustre" headlined his column in mid-September. "A competent broadcast correspondent for the CBC, notably in Washington, before being elevated to director of News and Current Affairs, he's a horn-rimmed fellow with a stentorian voice who reads the news as one wholly committed to CBC's understanding of life as something real and earnest."

While Cliff and Trina looked over their lists, I was preoccupied going back and forth to Ottawa preparing for the forthcoming CRTC hearing on the CBC licence renewal, writing some of the CBC presentation and writing my own remarks to the Commission.

As the hearing began at Ottawa's Château Laurier in mid-October, Al Johnson was, as always, nervous in the last minutes before he gave his presidential testimony, but he delivered two hours of non-stop passion, schmaltz, and elegance. The critical theme running through all his comments was the need for more Canadian programming, not only on the CBC but on private TV, too.

As usual in these CRTC hearings (this was the third one for the CBC, the others having been in 1970 and 1974), a flotilla of critics at large sailed into the hearing room in person or by brief. For eight days the grinding of axes echoed in the hearing room as they came, 166 of them – politicians, business people, homosexuals, churchmen, scientists, feminists, producers, writers, private broadcasters, performers, advertisers, anti-abortionists, and ordinary citizens.

I was given the role of articulating the English Radio and TV philosophy, output, and process for information programming. As it turned out, it was to be my swan song as director of News and Current Affairs. Lonsdale had flown up to Ottawa the night before I was to testify with a specific offer to be the new anchor of *The National*. After an hour of discussion in my hotel room, I had accepted it. The move

136

would be announced in a couple of weeks, but meanwhile my mind was focused on my statement.

In it I stressed to the CRTC the importance of television journalism – "The most powerful instrument of journalism the world has ever known" – and stated the CBC was Canada's most important and influential source of news. I described the eighteen television production centres in the country producing journalistic programming, the Radio and TV News bureaus in thirty cities across Canada and in London, Washington, Moscow, Hong Kong, New York, and Paris, the 7,500 hours a year of network and local TV journalistic programming we aired and 50,000 hours of radio journalism.

I now realize I was doing more than addressing the CRTC. I was subconsciously trying to sum up my old list of objectives set when I had started my job nearly a decade earlier, and measuring what had and had not been accomplished. But there were some things I felt I couldn't mention, such as the ending at long last of the state of war between News and Current Affairs, which was now down to only an occasional skirmish. Also I didn't mention what I felt to be my biggest accomplishment. Prior to 1969, senior CBC management had, at best, a disdain for most of our journalists, tolerating them as necessary evils, not to be trusted and not to be encouraged. No progress could be made at all for our journalistic programming until that negative attitude was turned around. Thanks to the understanding of some of my early bosses, such as Gene Hallman, and, more importantly, thanks to the hard and brilliant work of the journalists themselves, the turnaround happened. For News, the key person had been Denny Harvey, who had led the revitalization, inspiring a new sense of purpose and excitement in the CBC newsrooms of the nation. *The National* had never looked better than under Denny as chief news editor, for he concentrated on production values and more in-depth stories. He had only one complaint: "The goddamn job is so visible it's incredible!" Denny hadn't realized the focus of attention he'd be getting when he sat down in the hottest editor's seat in Canadian journalism. He'd accomplished his turnaround in CBC News in just over a year when CBC president Laurent Picard saw how good he was and made him the assistant general manager of English broadcasting. The same kind of turnaround occurred in our Current Affairs programming thanks to Peter Herrndorf.

My job had been to get the money, the facilities, and the air time and to try to provide the leadership. Most of what we had done had worked.

But while we had achieved the majority of our early objectives, there still were a couple remaining; as well, new objectives were now needed. It's not good enough just to be a good manager in CBC, you have to continually set new targets, encourage new creative innovations, constantly enriching the program service. Managing the assembly line is important, but not nearly so important as improving what's coming down that assembly line. And, to be honest, for me, there is not that much professional satisfaction in simply being a manager of constraints.

I also didn't tell the CRTC that morning of my failures: most of all my failure to get *The National* on at 10:00 p.m. instead of 11:00. So I was mightily encouraged when my colleague, program director Jack Craine, told the CRTC that eleven o'clock was much too late for *The National*. "It makes no sense at all," he said. Jack's words echoed Al Johnson's opening statement, in which he pledged, "We propose, as funds become available, to lengthen *The National* news on the English network and to bring it to Canadians at an earlier hour. We have known for some time that TV audiences fall off sharply prior to 11:00 p.m., and we believe an earlier *National* would be welcomed by our viewers." It took another three years before the 10:00 p.m. *National* finally happened, but I felt sure on hearing Al and Jack commit themselves before the CRTC that our decade-old campaign for an earlier *National* was finally going to happen.

When Peter Kent finally strode into the CRTC hearing room to testify, it was somewhat anti-climactic. He wore a well-pressed brown-striped suit and behaved like a decorous schoolboy. Not a question was asked about his charges of what he felt was political interference in program decisions. His prepared remarks were concentrated on the need for a policy governing prime ministerial access to the air, the lateness and the shortness of *The National*, and the delays caused by sports. He also softly criticized Al Johnson for not having a programming background and argued that the president's civil service background made him more susceptible to government pressure.

His criticisms were listened to politely, then he slipped quietly out the door. What started out as a bombshell ended in a fizzle. Peter headed off to Africa and I catapulted noisily into *The National*.

ON A CRISP, OCTOBER FRIDAY MORNING a week after my CRTC swan song, the announcement that I would anchor *The National* was made. The locale was the first-floor boardroom of the CBC's Kremlin, its dull brown walls made more sombre than usual by the amount of smoke from the puffing media men and women that curled up toward the elaborate brass chandelier hanging over the centre of the room. The place was jammed with reporters sitting row upon row, a dozen TV news cameras, and blinding lights. All eyes, lenses, and bulbs were focused on chief news editor Cliff Lonsdale, vice-president of English broadcasting Don MacPherson, and me as we entered the room, smiling nervously. A table had been set up in front of the long, narrow window whose drapes had been drawn, and we sat down to face the reporters and cameras. I had faced these people many times before, but this was different. The spotlight would now be on me, not on my programs.

"I won't keep you in suspense," Don said, knowing there was really no suspense at all, given the media speculation that I would get the job and my presence there. "I am announcing today the appointment by the chief news editor of Knowlton Nash as chief correspondent and anchorman of *The National*." Then Lonsdale added, "When Peter Kent indicated that he wanted to leave *The National*, the executive producer, Trina McQueen, and I talked about a number of possible candidates. We were looking for someone with a broad journalistic background as well as on-camera ability. Knowlton's recognized as an authority in journalism and he handles television well. We were delighted when we approached him and found he was interested."

While they spoke I sat there looking over to the ornate fireplace at the side of the room and all the faces in front of me reflected in a big mirror above it and meditated at this sea change in my life. Then, finally it was my turn. "I accepted the offer," I said, "because it provides a whole new set of demands and challenges . . . and I eagerly look forward to resuming my first love of front-line journalism."

With all the rehearsed preliminaries out of the way, the first question naturally zeroed in on money. "How much are you getting paid?" asked Jack Miller of *The Toronto Star*. "That's something I prefer to keep private," I said, adding, "but it's more than adequate." The money question persisted with suggested figures of $75,000, $85,000, and $90,000, and I blithely denied and dodged them all. In fact, I was getting $77,500 in salary and contract but nobody hit on that precise figure. My embarrassment at the question about money was ironic, I recognized, since I was a victim of my own stimulation of curiosity in anchormen's paycheques from the time Lloyd Robertson left the CBC for CTV. Lloyd, I'm sure, would have enjoyed my discomfort.

The long-standing battle between the Canadian Union of Public Employees (CUPE) representing the announcers and the Canadian Wire Service Guild representing the news people, which had so frustrated Robertson when the Guild sought to prevent him from reporting and writing, had been informally resolved with Peter Kent's arrival a couple of years before. I was going to do the same kind of job as Peter, and in recognition of the broader journalistic role that had evolved, I was given the title of chief correspondent.

But union problems still rumbled in the distance as the reporters shot questions at me in my new, more public role. One of them asked whether the announcers' union would object to my appointment. MacPherson and Lonsdale confidently said they couldn't see why there would be an objection since all the proper procedures had been followed. Actually, we weren't as confident as we sounded. Although we had meticulously followed all the union agreement rules about the appointment, we knew there would be objections borne of jealousies, frustrations, and suspicions of some who had hoped to get the job but didn't, and the fact that I was a management officer going back into the ranks. What I didn't realize, but soon would, was the intensity of those objections.

Within half an hour of the end of the news conference, while I was chatting with Cliff Lonsdale in his office, the union complaints started coming in. They said it was unfair and improper to want the anchor of *The National* to have a journalistic background, and some claimed I had appointed myself to the job. For the next month, those themes would become a crescendo. CUPE officials would claim that my appointment – described as "this parachuting of a management guy" – was "an insult" to other announcers and would warn that the union would take "whatever action we can" to kill the appointment.

For me as a journalist, it was a sobering lesson on how an incorrect and unfair accusation can linger long after it has been demonstrated to be wrong. For me as an individual, it was an equally sobering lesson on the need to keep a protective coating over my emotions. Day after day I read the newspaper stories on the union attack and had to parry questions from the press. But above all I felt my public response had to be the quiet assertion that it was valuable for CBC credibility to have an experienced journalist as anchor for *The National*, that all proper hiring procedures had been followed, and that I hadn't "appointed myself" to the job. I did my best to be dignified in public, but I seethed privately at the criticism.

In the first place, to claim that a journalistic background was unnecessary and even undesirable for the anchor of *The National* was the height of neanderthal lunacy. To be credible, to be honest, to be effective, the anchor has to have a journalistic background, not only to communicate understanding and confidence for *The National* itself but for participation in other news programs and off-air speeches, seminars, lectures, and various public activities in which an anchor should be involved to help cement a relationship with the viewing public. In the preparation of the newscast itself, including the editing and consultative process, without journalistic background, the anchor can make no credible contribution. The anchor simply has to have been there. Otherwise, it's fake; it's acting. Even Lloyd Robertson, who had no journalistic roots, had steeped himself in the news business ever since he moved from straight announcing to be a newscaster in the 1960s, covering elections, disasters, and other major events as well as anchoring. The needs and style of broadcast journalism had changed dramatically from the "rip-and-read" days of early broadcasting when announcers simply read whatever was handed them without knowledge of the events or the process of reporting.

While angered at the overall union attitude, I was most hurt by the accusation that I had appointed myself to the job. It was nothing less than an insult. But it was one Trina McQueen had warned weeks before might arise. At the time I had airily dismissed her apprehension with the confident comment, "Well, we can easily handle it if and when it ever comes up since we know it's not true." How naive I was!

When my appointment was announced, George McLean, who had substituted during Peter Kent's frequent absences from the studio and who wanted the job, felt wounded. He didn't agree with the idea that journalistic credentials were necessary or even desirable. CUPE officials took up his cause and launched a formal grievance. One official, Barrie Davis, even told reporters, "Newscasters have never done journalistic work but Nash will." Another official, Kent Marshall, exemplified the union approach, saying, "I really don't know what the appeal of Nash is. He looks like a tired piece of dough."

Even though George McLean had been deeply distressed at not getting the job, we remained on good personal terms. Over a late October lunch a week after my appointment, he wished me luck and gave me some advice on anchoring: "Always read the script two or three times before air. It seems easy, but believe me it's not." I had lunch with Lloyd Robertson, too, a couple of days later and he drew on his long experience of anchoring the news to give me valuable advice on handling the job. Among his tips was the simple but difficult admonition: "Just remember, concentration is everything!"

Then in early November I took off on a week-long cross-country promotion tour. This was a welcome opportunity to chat with columnists and reporters, who were more interested in the kind of job CBC News was doing and my role in it than in a union squabble. But as my November debut drew closer, being in the public spotlight in a way I'd never experienced before began to take its toll, and for a time I even wondered if I'd made a mistake in taking the job. Suddenly there was an intense focus on every personal detail from my ties to my glasses ("a goggle-glassed fellow," said a critic), from the cut of my suits to the length of my hair ("a haircut like it was done by the prison barber," said a reporter), from the fact I sipped five Diet Pepsis a day to my habit of jogging six miles every other day. To some degree, I'd been "in public," as it were, for a couple of decades as a TV correspondent and a somewhat visible head of TV News and Current Affairs, but I never experienced or dreamed of the intensity of curiosity and exposure that now hit almost overnight. "Knowlton Nash is a private person who has just taken on a very public job," said the *Winnipeg Free Press*. How true!

Suddenly I was an object to be poked, probed, prodded, and exposed, and while it was nice to be recognized and often pleasant to be quoted, I found myself sometimes embarrassed, occasionally exasperated, and more than once aghast at things it was claimed I had said or at what was written about me. It was especially astonishing to read thoughts I'd never thought, comments I'd never made, and to discover motivations I'd never had. Being reported on instead of being the reporter gave me second thoughts about and also some insight into some of the more peculiar aspects of my profession of journalism. There were comments that I was given the job to "save Trudeau," as one columnist wrote, or to impose a "managerial imprint" on the news, or as another critic said, to air only "good, clean news." All of it, of course, was nonsense, but I began to have a little taste of what Peter Gzowski had gone through in what he called the fishbowl.

I found a protective coating useful not only in warding off emotional damage from the critics, but also as insulation against an inflated ego. In a way, I had to develop a sense of distance between myself as an individual and that guy who was the new anchor of *The National*, a slight form of self-induced schizophrenia. It was, I found, a necessary piece of equipment in my personal survival kit. The last thing I wanted was to get a "star" complex with all its egocentric trivializations. I'd known a few people whose high profile had beguiled them into becoming demanding boors and I wasn't going to let that happen to me. It was all pretty heady stuff, but I knew it could be fleeting. I had a vivid reminder of that a few years later when I fell in behind a smiling, white-haired old man at the Ottawa airport. It was former Governor General Roland Michener, who had been the highest-ranking citizen in the land, cheered by millions, entertained by the Queen, the Shah of Iran, and royalty the world over, paid homage to by presidents and prime ministers, saluted and guarded by the Army,

Navy, and Air Force, his way cleared by the RCMP and trailed by a coterie of officials. Now, a few years after leaving the Governor General's office, here he was walking alone up to the security gate at the Ottawa airport.

"Where's your ticket?" snapped a security guard who only saw just another elderly traveller. "Oh, right here," said the former Governor General. "Right here in my hand."

"Thank you," said the guard. "Now just go through the gate over there."

"Yes, all right," said Michener.

Nobody, not the guard, not the Air Canada attendants, the ticket takers, or the other passengers, took any notice of the amiable old man, clutching his black fedora and black briefcase and shuffling along in line with everyone else to board the plane. I sat beside him as we flew to Toronto, chatting about politics and history. After we landed he stood up, grabbed his coat from the overhead rack, stuffed a package of uneaten Air Canada cookies into his breast pocket, smiled, and said, "Well, it's been good chatting with you." Then he joined the line waiting to get off the plane.

In mid-November, after I'd returned from the public relations tour, I began to prepare in earnest. There were rehearsals, trial runs on an afternoon newscast to Newfoundland, and the anchoring of *Newsmagazine*. In the rehearsals organized by director Tom Kavanagh we game-played every possible on-air disaster scenario, from equipment breakdown to sudden story changes, and all the last-second chaos that can happen on air. We had to change the lighting to minimize the glare off my glasses and I had to pay attention to the colour of my clothes so they blended well with the set colours. I also got familiar with the studio and control room crew with whom I was sharing this new adventure.

Finally, the launch day, Monday, November 20th, arrived. In the afternoon when I came into my new cubbyhole office (about one-fifth the size of my old office as director of News and Current Affairs and with no secretary), there was a greeting card sitting on my desk that wiped away most of my apprehension and nervousness about my debut. It said, "Welcome . . . It's hard to get used to the atmosphere, but we're sure you'll enjoy the ride." It was such a small thing, but it meant so much. And I've kept the card pinned on my office wall ever since as a kind of good-luck talisman.

That first day I spent the afternoon in the newsroom getting to know my new colleagues better and going over our coverage plans on the news developments of the day. After a brief dinner break alone with

Lorraine, I plunged into my new world of anchoring. In the large, open-spaced newsroom, I sat down across the news desk from the lineup editor, Dennis McVarish, and the producer, Peter Rehak. Rehak was a quiet, gentle fellow who was an award-winning newsman, one-time Bonn, Vienna, and Prague Associated Press bureau chief, and a former Bonn correspondent for *Time*. Behind his quiet demeanour Peter applied his wealth of journalistic experience to *The National* and eased me into the anchor hot seat as tenderly as possible.

As the countdown to air time began, I chatted from time to time with Rehak and McVarish about the program and about how we were handling various stories, glanced through the Associated Press, Reuters, and Canadian Press news agency wires, and read through and edited the script pages tossed over to me by the four writers around the desk. We all were self-conscious because not only was it a first night for me, but a clutch of newspaper and magazine reporters and photographers were crowding around, looking over our shoulders, snapping pictures, and taking notes, a somewhat surrealistic beginning. My new colleagues glanced up from time to time from their typewriters to see how I was doing in getting ready. I found they were wondrously supportive when I needed it most, getting through that first newscast to one and a half million Canadians amid all the media hype and clamour, union pressures, and first-night jitters.

At 9:45 p.m., I scooped up my script and took the old and groaning elevator down five flights to the ground-floor studio for the first edition of *The National* that went out to Atlantic Canada at 10:00 p.m. (11:00 p.m. in the Maritimes and 11:30 p.m. in Newfoundland). I nearly tripped over some of the camera cables snaking across the studio's light-blue tiled floor as I walked over to my anchor desk. With a tight smile to the three cameramen and my floor director, Art Bouchard, I settled into the chair, checked to be sure the pages of my script were in order, and then we were on the air.

"Good evening," I said after Allan McPhee's crisp introduction of *The National*. "A bizarre tale of mass murder and suicide unfolds in Guyana. . . ." It turned out to be one hell of a busy news night with the breaking story of 1,000 dead in the People's Temple of Jonestown, Guyana, where a madman named Jim Jones gave out poison to his suicidal followers. With that kind of a story and others such as the incredible rise in the cost of postage stamps from 14 to 17 cents, the newscast couldn't help but be a memorable beginning for me. In my black-rimmed glasses and light brown suit, with palms perspiring and voice tight, *The National* went off with only one hitch. In a story on a narcotics charge against Keith Richards of the Rolling Stones, I misidentified him as a drummer, spurring sarcastic phone calls and momentary panic in the control room. Lineup editor Dennis McVarish called me between items with a correction. "But, of course," I corrected at the end of *The National*, "he's a guitar player." And then, with hands clasped and a smile of relief, I chirped, "Good night!"

As the camera's red lights blinked out and the studio lights dimmed, I sat there a moment in the quiet semi-darkness, heaved a big sigh of relief, and recalled the words of Bob Dylan: "The times they are a-changin'." They certainly were, and the transition from executive suite to TV hot seat was now complete.

I rose, smilingly shook hands with floor director Art Bouchard, who had worked with Peter Kent for two years, and thanked the cameramen who had been so helpful with little bits of advice and comfort – "Why don't you go over your next introduction while the previous item is running?" "Put a little piece of tape on the desk where your centre position is and you can easily check it to be sure you're centred up on camera." As Art had smiled, "Don't worry, we're all friends here."

That was the one overriding sentiment of the night: we were all friends here. Professional, demanding, stimulating, but, overall, friendly, for we all knew – technicians, journalists, and production staff – that we were together in launching this new adventure. There is no business I know of that demands more split-second collaboration than television news, and one sour soul, from lineup editor to the audio man, can destroy the program. It's a business where nanoseconds and millimetres make the difference.

No one knew that better than Trina McQueen, the thirty-five-year-old executive producer of *The National* who'd got me into all this by suggesting I apply for the job. She was a hard-driving, hard-working journalist, but she also knew when to coddle and stroke the egos of her staff. Tonight, she was stroking. "Terrific," she smiled at me after we all had trooped upstairs from our first-floor studio to the fifth-floor newsroom to guzzle beer, munch cheese, have our pictures taken, gossip, joke, and laugh at the Keith Richards gaffe while congratulating ourselves. It was a wonderful feeling to let all the pent up pressure slowly ease out. After half an hour or so, I drove home and Lorraine popped open a chilled bottle of champagne. All in all, I felt pretty good about the debut and grateful that it was over.

The critics for the most part thought it went well: "... just a little nervous under fire," said the Toronto *Globe and Mail* the next morning, hitting the mark; "... sobriety blending with humanity," said the *Toronto Sun*; "... appears competent, looks authoritative," said the *Edmonton Journal*. "He tends to bob and weave," said the *Windsor*

Star; "... nice suit, well-knotted tie, neatly combed hair," said the *Ottawa Journal*. "A nice new hair do," said a Halifax paper. "Nash reminds me," said Ottawa columnist Douglas Fisher, "of the actor Alec Guinness playing the role each night of the nice Canadian." With hindsight, as I look at a tape of that first *National* today, I think I spoke too fast, moved around more than I should have, and my voice was too tight – a B- rating at best.

Scores of letters, telegrams, and phone calls came in saying my first night had been either terrific or terrible. "You are probably a good egg and maybe knowledgeable, but I for one think your performance is poor," said a woman from Lanark, Ont. A Burlington, Ont., woman was more blunt: "Dear Sir, I do not want you on the National news. It's like having a clam report the news." A Toronto man agreed with that sentiment: "He has neither the appearance nor the voice, nor the personality for this key job. He was a reasonably fair reporter, it is said, and that is what he should still be doing."

Fortunately, most of the mail was on the plus side. Some of the compliments were unexpected, however, such as, "You were scrumptious and delicious and spiffy," from a Toronto woman; "Welcome down from the ivory tower," from an Ottawa man; "I believe you," from a Montreal man; "You're looking good on air, but your jacket collar gaped," from a Vancouver woman; "May the glow worm that first glimmered continue to light up your life," from a Winnipeg telegram; and from Red Deer, Alberta, a man wrote, "You are simply beautiful, so calm, so dignified, so precise, so careful. God bless you."

One somewhat less enthusiastic evaluation came to me via Senator Keith Davey, who quoted Prime Minister Trudeau as saying, "That new guy on the news ... what's his name? ... isn't too bad."

IN THOSE WANING DAYS of 1978 there were many newsworthy new faces coming on the scene: Ayatollah Khomeini in Tehran, Margaret Thatcher in London, John Paul II in the Vatican, and the Sandinistas in Nicaragua, all providing us with many a story, to say nothing of the political story in Canada with Pierre Trudeau still Prime Minister but trailing badly behind Joe Clark in the public opinion polls. This heavy run of news was straining our reportorial staff and although we'd begun making use of the new electronic news-gathering (ENG) cameras, we still relied on film in much of the country.

It was less than a year before that I'd first seen ENG cameras in action after we'd got them into some key areas, such as Ottawa. My first exposure to ENG was at the Liberal Party conference in Ottawa in the winter of 1978 as I watched a reporter doing a piece for *The*

National, recording delegate reaction to a Trudeau address. He came back up to our CBC newsroom on the second floor of the Château Laurier and played back the videotape he'd just recorded. Looking at it, he decided he needed more specific reaction from delegates and went down to the convention hall for further interviews. I reflected that I had just seen a revolution. Before the ENG equipment, in the days of film the reporter would never have been able to see his report and then improve it by getting the needed extra reaction. With film, he would have had to send it by motorcycle courier to a laboratory where it would take half an hour or so to process, and then it would be motorcycled back to an editing room and only then could the reporter see it. By that time, he'd have no chance to improve it because the meeting would be long over.

"God," I said to him, "I sure could have used ENG when I was in Washington. It's a miracle." Indeed, it was a miracle. As we spread the equipment through the system, other program areas wanted to use it, too, and battles began over who had ENG and when. Since we had pioneered it at CBC News, I was able to use that leverage to argue successfully that there must be a CBC-wide policy established that News always had first call on ENG equipment. Now, as a member of the News Service, I could see first-hand the value of this technological breakthrough.

My first year on *The National* was a hectic one with so much breaking news, more travel than I'd bargained for, and the nightly challenge of fronting *The National*. I was still a bit nervous on air – "controlled terror," I'd described it to one colleague – and I asked my anchoring predecessor Peter Kent when he'd stopped being nervous. "I never did stop," he ruefully replied, even though he never showed his nervousness on air. There's no doubt the job is a high-wire act with no net. Even though there is a highly competent team behind you, once the camera's red light blinks on, you're out there all alone. And things, of course, sometimes do go wrong. Warren Davis once fell off his chair in the middle of a newscast. I began one night with no microphone, having forgot to put it on. My fifty-pound TV monitor built into the desk once fell through to the floor and crashed onto my toes while I was on camera. I was able to stifle my scream of pain until we were off the air. The announcer once introduced the newscast by saying: "*The National*, with George McLean." "Oh no it's not," I said as I came on the screen and carried on with the newscast.

Occasionally we misidentified people. Once in later years, we identified journalist-turned politician (briefly) Peter Worthington as a Liberal, which he most decidedly was not. Another time I was reporting on a Russian news development, and as I said "Soviet leader Andropov retaliated against the United States today," suddenly through some technological quirk our TV picture flicked over to a western movie running in another time zone in which, at the precise moment I was speaking of Andropov's retaliation, viewers of *The National* saw a cowboy rear back and slug another, saying "Take that!" Then, just as suddenly, I was back on the screen still talking about Andropov. It made for rather astonishing television viewing.

Perhaps the most embarrassing technical foul-up came during a newscast that featured, among other things, a story on the Canadian hog industry preceded by one on Dr. Henry Morgentaler's abortion clinics. We have what are called "cells," or pictures that appear beside me when I'm introducing the story. In this case those two stories were inexplicably mixed up. When I introduced Dr. Morgentaler's item, a picture of a hog flashed up. Our mistake couldn't have been worse and our phones rang off the hook from either outraged or pleased viewers, depending on their attitude toward abortion. A similar mix-up occurred when we had back-to-back stories on Richard Nixon and an anniversary of the death of Adolf Hitler. The inevitable happened, and up popped Hitler's picture over my shoulder as soon as I started talking about Nixon.

Another less serious mix-up occurred when we miscalculated wildly in transferring the depth of a British snowfall from inches to metric. "One hundred and twenty-three kilometres of snow fell today," I informed an incredulous nation. As a matter of policy, we had decided we would convert everything to metric on *The National*, the result of which was a bogus memorandum someone sent around the News department, signing himself as "Horace Giles Smythely, Counsellor, English Language Usage." Reference to Scotland Yard would no longer be allowed, the memo said. "Henceforth," it added, "it will be Scotland Metre."

As a correspondent I'd anchored hundreds of programs over the years, but before starting on *The National* I'd never used a Teleprompter, or autocue as we call it. Basically, in the autocue system a small camera in the control room focuses on the script as it rolls by on a moving desktop platform. What the camera sees is transmitted to a receiver attached to the big studio cameras in front of me at the anchor desk. By a system of mirrors, the picture is then projected in front of the studio camera lens. So when I look straight into the lens, I'm actually seeing the words of the script.

Reading from an autocue is an art in itself because you can so easily become its slave, mechanically reading the words that roll up in front with no real sense of the story you're talking about. You have to make the autocue work for you, go at your own pace, and turn your reading into conversation. You can't be too casual, however, or ad-lib too freely because cells, pictures, and tape come up at precise, previously determined places in the script, and to deviate throws everything off. Half and quarter seconds are critical in the timing of a television newscast.

In the early days of television, newscasters simply read their scripts, usually head down and glancing up only occasionally. Naturally, producers wanted better eye contact with the audience and one went so far as to try out a Braille system. CBS producer Don Hewitt wanted his anchor, Douglas Edwards, to learn Braille and do the newscast with his fingers flicking across the pages in front of him. It didn't work, however, and some newscasters resorted to printing out the entire newscast on long cardboard sheets that could be held up for them just to the side of the camera. In time, the Teleprompter came along to solve the problems of eye contact with the audience.

Our Teleprompter was far from perfect, however. Occasionally, it would simply stop in the middle of a newscast, or worse, start rolling backwards. Sometimes the wrong page would turn up or the whole page just slip off the screen to the side. During the first years I was doing *The National*, the autocue operator, an erstwhile cartoonist, began sketching comic cartoons at the end of the script that, when they came up as I said "Good night," induced a broad, end-of-program smile. Occasionally he'd draw a picture of a scrawny dog barking "Good night!"

The autocue operator is as critical to the success of a program as is the floor director who stands just out of camera range in front of the anchor desk. He's the boss on the floor, giving cues, directing the anchor to one camera or another, hand-holding any guest interviewees who may turn up, and generally keeping order on the studio floor.

One who worked with me a few times during my first year was Steve Hyde, the most legendary of CBC studio directors. An Australian, Steve as a child performed with his parents on English music hall stages and was one of the few men to enter the British Navy as an Able Seaman and come out ten years later still an Able Seaman (although that included a tour as a prisoner of war in Korea). Steve has floor-directed *The National, The Journal, Front Page Challenge*, and most of the major variety shows over the past couple of decades.

As becomes his Australian inheritance, he is a memorable storyteller and completely unimpressed with authority. During a *Front Page Challenge* show with Indian Prime Minister Indira Gandhi as a guest, he told her to sit in a chair by saying, "Put your little ass over here, dearie." She did. When Prime Minister Pierre Trudeau was on the program, Steve insisted on calling him "Peter." A few years later when Trudeau came back to the program, Steve was admonished to be on his best behaviour, and for once he was. A puzzled and seemingly disappointed Trudeau remarked,"You're behaving yourself tonight, Steve. What's wrong?" More recently, doing a classical music program, Hyde addressed the slightly pudgy world-famous violinist Isaac Stern by saying, "You sit over here for this number, Tubs."

Steve's a master at calming down nervous on-air "talent." He also has seen every trick in the book used by competing TV personalities trying to upstage each other. "One host had a neat trick," he once told me, "of saying to her partner ten seconds before going on air, 'What's that mark on your face?' or, 'Is that a stain on your jacket?' The poor bloody partner would spend the whole show worried about the mark or stain while the other sailed serenely on."

The floor director counts down to air with fingers flailing from five seconds down to zero and ends with a sharp finger pointing to the camera. At that cue, the anchor begins to speak. On one occasion, my over-stimulated floor director flashed his finger down too close to the camera and smacked into it, cutting open his finger and splashing blood over my script just as I said "Good evening." He bit back his pain until we were into the first taped report.

One of the challenges of anchors in Canada is saying the names of some towns, especially those in Newfoundland, and on occasion I've had to be particularly careful with my facial expression in reporting stories on events in such communities as Sheshatshit, Nfld., Virgin Tickle, Nfld., or Dildo, Nfld. After those, Heart's Content and Joe Batt's Arm were easy.

The trick in TV newscasting is to appear relaxed in what is a pressure- and tension-filled environment. But nowhere is the tension greater than in the control room up a flight of stairs from *The National*'s studio. There the director commands a team of technical associates handling the audio and video and controlling the colour, the camera shots used, the time of each item, and half a dozen videotape machines playing back inserts. One director of *The National* got so rattled once she forgot what tape machine a particular insert was on and shouted, "Roll everything!"

Once on the last night of October, to lighten up the end of the newscast, I intended to wish everyone a Happy Hallowe'en, but instead what I said was "And Happy New Year everyone!" I wanly smiled and corrected, "I mean, Happy Hallowe'en."

About a year after I'd begun *The National*, the calm demeanour of director Tom Kavanagh was replaced by the puckish enthusiasm of twenty-five-year-old Fred Parker, who kept his cool in the intimidating intensity of the control room by his effervescent but corny joke-cracking. Fred was the director on one occasion when our timing of the *The National* went askew, and as we neared the end of the program we discovered that, through an addition error, we were two and three-quarters minutes short, which is an eternity in television. I recapitulated almost every story we'd aired, and still there was more than a minute and a half to go, so Fred had the camera move back to take a long shot of the set, and then keep on moving back until the remaining time was eaten up. The cameraman kept going back, back, back ... until he was out the door of the studio and into the hallway, still shooting his now very long shot before the program mercifully ended.

The first year had its harrowing moments, but perhaps the the most intimidating moment in all the time I've been anchoring came on a wintry night in 1981 at precisely 11:00 p.m. as *The National*'s opening animation, which we called "The Bloops," began rolling. Out of the right corner of my eye I suddenly noticed half a dozen people running into the studio through a side door. We had about four seconds to my "Good evening," so I shouted at the intruders, "Hey, stop!" But they kept running toward the cameras so I leapt out of my chair and ran toward them with cameraman Peter Peters at my side. We each grabbed one of them and wrestled them to the ground. I didn't know whether they were terrorists, kidnappers, or just people bent on destruction. Only when I heard one of them, a young woman, screaming in French did it suddenly hit me that they might be journalists from the CBC French network, journalists who had been on strike for months, forcing the French news off the air. Some union members had decided publicity was what they needed and *The National* was their target. While Peter and I were holding a couple of them, our director, Fred Parker, and a couple of other technicians came running into the studio to help. As we were all shouting, pushing, and shoving, one of the invaders started smearing vaseline on a camera lens and sticking on decals saying in French, "We will have the last word."

They had timed their studio invasion for precisely 11:00 p.m., hoping all of this would be seen across the nation. However, they had forgotten about our opening animation. So on this evening as the animation ended, instead of me saying "Good evening," the audience saw a blank screen and heard muffled shouts and grunts and much thrashing about - the microphones had been left open. Lorraine was watching at home and thought I'd had a heart attack. The phone lines suddenly went wild as viewers flooded the CBC switchboards with questions about what was happening. Four of the invaders scampered out of the studio and into the street, but we held on to two others and turned them over to the police, who by now had arrived.

Then we scraped the decals off the camera lens and, thirteen minutes after the invasion began, we went back on the air with my saying "Good evening." With a somewhat sheepish smile, I apologized for our absence and explained about our visitors. One of the "visitors," Rosemary Collins, later commented, "We were only trying to make the point that if it was *The National* off the air there would be a public outcry, while nobody cares about the French news." A few months later I met Rosemary at a party at CBC Montreal. She smiled and told me, "I'm sorry, we didn't mean to cause you trouble, but we just wanted to make our point." "Well, you certainly gave us an adventure!" I replied.

Actually, it had been the second adventure in as many days. The night before the studio invasion, the fire bells suddenly started clanging just minutes before *The National* was to begin as a fire broke out in the basement of our TV building, although we didn't know it at the time. In the basement French studio the sprinkler system went off, dousing our French colleagues. Then thick smoke curled up the corridors and into our studios on the main floor. "Let's go on anyway," I said to our director. "It could be a dramatic sight if it really is a fire." I didn't think it was, though, but the whining sound of fire engines and the sight of firemen in masks, slickers, and helmets carrying hoses and axes through the hallway and at the studio door tempered my enthusiasm to go on. So we ran a tape of *The National* that we'd done an hour earlier to Atlantic Canada. After the firemen left we did an updated version of *The National* for the West.

A few weeks later, again just fifteen minutes before *The National* went on the air, a stink bomb was set off outside the studio. We'd thought it was a gas leak, but it turned out to be noxious fumes pouring out of a six-inch glass vial. Most of the employees in the building fled outside, but a dozen of us stayed behind and, holding our noses, figuratively in my case, we carried on with the newscast.

That first year on *The National* gave me a new appreciation of our space-age communications technology even if we still lacked the kinds of latest electronic gadgetry the U.S. networks had. But over the years I also learned this technology can bring you some unexpected moments. CBC Ottawa correspondent Mike Duffy once found just how embarrassing satellites can be. On a *Sunday Report* program in the

152

mid-1980s, *Globe and Mail* columnist Jeffrey Simpson and I were in the Toronto studio talking to Duffy in Edmonton via satellite. He was there covering a Premiers' Conference, which we were going to discuss with him on our program. As we chatted and joked with each other before taping our discussion, Mike whimsically pretended to be a romantic fiction writer. In his flight of fictitious fancy he graphically described to us a torrid romantic setting in which he was a lustful hero rising from a well-used bed with a busty damsel beside him. His storytelling had both Jeff and me laughing. But it turned out Brian Mulroney and several cronies were also enjoying Mike's performance. They were at the Prime Minister's Harrington Lake vacation retreat outside Ottawa and had been moving their satellite dish around to try to bring in a Sunday football game when they suddenly saw the CBC's Mike Duffy beaming in from Edmonton with a somewhat scatological tale of romance. The Prime Minister thought it was uproariously funny, a sentiment, I was later told, that was not at all shared by Mila. Of course, we didn't know any of this until one of Mulroney's colleagues called Mike to kid him about his amorous storytelling. He and we were dumbfounded, and it brought home to me for the first time that even rehearsals and pre-program chatting with guests and colleagues in other cities are all up there in the sky. Anyone with a dish can watch us if they can find the channel we're using.

Another satellite miscue occurred when I anchored *The National* out of Vancouver on the opening night of Expo '86. The pictures of me in Vancouver were flashed back to Toronto by satellite and "married" there to the rest of the program, and then the whole *National* was sent out on another satellite channel. Opening night saw a torrential spring downpour in Vancouver that pummelled our *National* anchor booth perched high atop a wooden stand with a back window overlooking Expo. The idea was to have the sparkling sight of Expo behind me as I did the news, but the rain blurred that possibility. So whenever I finished an introduction and we went to a report, a man in a yellow rain slicker would rush out to clean off the window behind me with a minute or two of vigorous window-wiping. For some inexplicable technological reason, viewers in Thunder Bay, Ont., saw the satellite feed coming in from Vancouver rather than the "married" program coming out of Toronto. The result was that they saw me introducing the news reports and then saw the man in his yellow slicker bustle out to the window behind me and briskly wipe away for a minute or two. While he was wiping, I'd be going over my next script page, talking to the cameramen, and watching a TV monitor. Then I'd straighten up and introduce another report, and, immediately, out would come the window cleaner again. That went on for the entire program, which gave Thunder Bay viewers a unique perspective of *The National* that night.

We've had other satellite problems, including mix-ups when someone at the network grabbed the wrong tape off a shelf and instead of satelliting to the West Coast a tape of that night's program, he grabbed the tape of a week-old *National*. It's happened a couple of times, making for confused viewers wondering about déjà vu and mortified editors and technicians at network headquarters.

More recently, there was an embarrassing gaffe when a satellite mix-up suddenly replaced Big Bird on *Sesame Street* with several minutes of a porno film showing a stark naked man parading about. The problem resulted from someone punching a wrong button, which brought down off the satellite the U.S. Fantasy channel instead of *Sesame Street*. The kids in Montreal and much of Ontario who saw this unscheduled segment may not have been upset but their parents certainly were. Local station switchboards were besieged with angry calls.

In spite of the occasional technological goof and occasionally awkward moments for the anchor because of the night-after-night TV exposure, I found there was a plus side, too. For one thing, my phone calls tended to get returned more quickly than might otherwise have been the case, and some normally closed doors were opened, all of which are handy for a journalist. Most of the people I would meet on the street, on the subway, or shopping were more helpful and friendlier, sometimes perhaps a little too friendly. Once when walking to work down Jarvis Street in Toronto, a car screeched to a stop across the street and a young woman I've never seen before or since leapt out, ran through the traffic, threw her arms around me, shouting, "I love you!" and then just as quickly ran back to her car and sped off. While such exuberance is rare, complete strangers do say the darndest things. "Oh, you're you!" or "You look just like you." Once you become at least a vaguely recognizable face, you're also subject to a lot of staring as often people try to figure out who you are and where you've met before. "Weren't we at university together?" some people will say. "Don't I know you from somewhere?" or, "I know! I know. I've got it! You're Fred Davis!" One frequent refrain is, "You look younger and thinner," and I explain that's because the studio lights add about fifteen pounds and ten years to your appearance. One of the mixed blessings I found in my first year of anchoring *The National* was the number of invitations to judge things, everything from beauty contests to hog-calling competitions. One such affair, which included both plus a number of other events, was the annual Binder Twine Festival in Kleinberg, Ont., just outside Toronto. The emcee was the Squire of Kleinberg, Pierre Berton, dressed like a top-hatted circus ringmaster. Cartoonist Ben Wicks, an old friend, my wife Lorraine, and I did satisfactorily in judging the hog-calling, the milking, the dancing, and the nail-hammering, but we ran into an arithmetic problem with the beauty contest. The problem, frankly, was Ben. He'd mixed up the scoring, giving low marks to the best and high marks to the least best, the reverse of what it should have been. Our numbers were added up and when Berton announced our choice as the winner, we were all as astonished as Pierre and the audience. Boos and cat-calls greeted our apparent selection, but she gamely came forward and accepted the honours. The verbal abuse and protest at the judges continued interminably, while we puzzled over what had happened and finally discovered Ben's error. In momentary panic, confusion, and embarrassment, it was decided to award two first prizes, one to the real winner and the other to the unfortunate lady we had mistakenly announced. Neither Ben nor Lorraine and I have ever been invited back.

Ben got me into hot water a year later when he asked me to join him after *The National* one night at a downtown Toronto tavern for an event he was emceeing. "Sure," I said, "anything for a friend." So about midnight I turned up to find Ben moderating some kind of contest. He saw me come in and welcomed me from the stage. Then, to my horror, he invited me to join him in judging what turned out to be a "Bad Breath Contest." That was unquestionably the worst-ever appearance for the anchor of *The National*. The following night a "Wet T-Shirt Contest" was held, but I declined Ben's invitation for that.

Part of the job of front man for *The National* is representing CBC at various events (bad breath contests not among them), occasionally being a master of ceremonies and participating in charity fund-raising affairs. Some of it is duty, much of it is fun, and all of it is time-consuming. I have found myself on occasion selling hamburgers for the underprivileged, bicycling for the handicapped, running for heart disease, parading for cancer, breakfasting for kidney disease, brunching for heart diseases, lunching for muscular dystrophy, speaking for community charity campaigns across the country, appearing on tele-thons, and chatting with groups from the indigent elderly to the needy youth. Then there are the celebrity auctions to raise money for a boat for Toronto slum kids, an artificial ice rink in Glenboro, Man., a London, Ont., arthritis research program, telescopic lenses for the nearly blind in Timmins, Ont., and a computer for a Grade 5 class in Fort St. John, B.C. I usually send along a tie I've worn on *The National* to these auctions, and over the years, at last count, I had donated 238 ties to one fund-raising auction or another. There also are "Charity Car Washes," "Charity Chili Cook-Offs," and "Charity Dish Washing," although most of these, frankly, I try to duck.

Charity work even caused me once to dance on the stage of the Royal Alexandra Theatre in downtown Toronto. As a teenager, Lorraine trained in ballet, and she began her professional life as a dancer, including performances at the Canadian National Exhibition Grandstand show, and later on CBC-TV variety programs. As an awkward teenager, I barely survived Arthur Murray dancing lessons in Toronto and had no ambition, let alone the talent, to dance on the stage. Nevertheless, there we were dancing one night at the Royal Alex before 2,000 people. It was a night to raise money for the Famous People Players, a black light group of mentally retarded youngsters from Toronto who perform on stages across North America. Founder Diane Dupuy, in a moment of madness insofar as I was concerned, thought it would attract attention and be a good fund-raiser if she could get me and Lorraine to perform a "Me and My Shadow" number, sung by Gordon Pinsent. In an equal moment of madness, I'd agreed without quite realizing what was involved. I realized soon enough when we stood on the stage behind the footlights and the music began. It was agreed by all that Lorraine was superb as all her old dancing skill flowed back while I was, at best, adequate.

There are scores of requests, too, for so-called "celebrity recipes" from newspapers, magazines, and authors, which, since my cooking talents are confined to warming up things in a microwave, are fulfilled by Lorraine masquerading as me. I've found myself credited with all manner of gastronomic exotica from a "Tahitian Raw Fish Hors d'Oeuvres" to a Bulgarian goulash called "Giuvech." When faced with such recipe requests, broadcaster Bill McVean told me he has different approach: he sends along his recipe for toast.

Mail is another source of constant surprise. An average of 75 to 100 letters a week come in to me expressing outrage over perceived biases, concern about grammar and pronunciation, or effusive compliments. I try to answer them all since their concerns help me understand the audience of *The National*. My sense of the importance of letters as a measurement of public concern over significant issues was jarred, however, in a conversation I once had with advice columnist Ann Landers when she was visiting Toronto. She told me she once got 15,000 letters – far more than Walter Lippmann ever received – on a single column reference she made on the question of whether toilet paper should come off over the top of the roll or hang down from the back. She advised it was fashionable to come over the top.

Aside from major issues involving Ottawa politics and world diplomacy, people write in with the most unusual comments. "I am sending you photographs of my toy poodle, 'Mr. Bo,' who watches your newscast every night," said a viewer from Queen Charlotte City, B.C. "He sure is a great admirer of yours. At the end of the broadcast he always starts barking."

Another dog got confused when we moved *The National* from 11:00 to 10:00 p.m. His owner in Winnipeg wrote in to say his little dog always went to the front door to be let out when he heard my voice say, "Good evening" at 11:00. But the dog got confused when I said it at 10:00 and then came back at eleven with the update. "Well," he wrote, "the confusion you cause this little dog who knows it was out and back, or was it? Did I or didn't I? Do I need to or not?"

Dogs weren't the only pets affected by the new *National*. A woman from Victoria, B.C., complained that the "Coming Up On *The Journal*" promos within *The National* disturbed her bird. "My budgie starts to make such loud, angry noises every time they come on. You wouldn't believe how such a tiny creature can scold . . . but he is such a love I just cannot put him in another room. . . . Thanking you sincerely for your help in this matter."

Some letters are romantic, some erotic, and some mildly threatening. "I'm thinking of switching my love from you to Peter Mansbridge!" wrote one Winnipeg lady.

A fastidious viewer from Medicine Hat had clear advice for me: "Think Yiddish and wear British." An extraordinary number of people are concerned about my ties, complaining, complimenting, or sending in new ones. People also send in everything from cashews and bagels to cans of soft drinks and carrot cakes. They also share their personal joys and pains, as a man in Bracebridge, Ont., did, who catalogued his problems as follows: "Since my retirement the following has happened: 1. Kidney stones removed. 2. Appendix taken out. 3. Gall bladder out. 4. Cancer. Lost large bowel and rectum. I wear a pouch. 5. Small seizure so I no longer drive. 6. Open heart surgery – two valves replaced with pig valves and No. 3 repaired. Other than that, I feel fine."

Many Canadians write in demanding "more good news" and asking me to smile more on *The National*, but a man from Fredericton, N.B., was typical of some letter writers who disagree about smiling. "What the hell is there to smile about in the news today," he said.

"Americanization" of the English language is a sore point with many Canadian viewers, such as man from West Vancouver, B.C., who wrote in to complain about "your adoption of the crude American habit of pronouncing u like oo. . . . I think it was Franklin Roosevelt who invented this absurd way of murdering our beautiful language." From New Hazleton, B.C., a woman wrote, " 'An historic . . .' is American English and a bastardization. Stop it!"

One of the most treasured letters I've received came from a man from Dwight, Ont., who remembered working with my father at the Hamilton Jockey Club where he ran the racetrack betting system, the parimutuels. "I had always thought Mr. Nash was a southern gentleman," he wrote to me. "I was only 19 in 1925, I had to visit the track each day in the morning to pick up copy for the next day's program to be printed . . . and there was Mr. Nash, the tall, but slightly stooped gentleman with his soft speech and gracious manner. He always greeted me with a 'Good Morning, Leonard,' and a 'Thank you for coming in'. . . . His words of thanks put me on cloud nine until I saw him again. When an older person treats an insecure 19 year old as an equal and with courtesy, he sure makes an impression on the kid. Mr. Nash was one of these great men to me. . . . You had a great father! I shall enjoy you on CBC much more now, Mr. Nash's kid!"

One letter took me aback when I was advised of a couple in Windsor, Ont., who had named their second son "Knowlton." "He watches *The National* every night, too," the happy couple told me. A few years after getting the letter, they brought young Knowlton to CBC News and I took him and his family on a tour of the newsroom and the studio and sat him in my chair to his giggling pleasure and the amusement of our technical crew.

I've had a lot of trouble over the years with the name Knowlton in misspellings and mispronunciations. Sometimes it comes out in letters as "Nolan," or "Nowlan," or "Noel," or "Nolton." I had one letter from Calgary addressed to "Mr. Northern Nash," a couple to "Gnolton Gnash," several to "Norton Nash," and many to "Milton Nash."

FROM TIME TO TIME, flipping through letters or sitting in the anchor chair, my mind would race back to my foreign correspondent days, so seemingly free and easy compared to my new job. I began scribbling notes about those days, checking through notebooks, datebooks, clippings, carbon copies of old radio and TV scripts, and a half dozen boxes of memorabilia. Then Jack McClelland of McClelland and Stewart asked me to write a book and I started to get serious about it. I spent two or three hours almost every day for a couple of years sorting out notes, researching, writing, and rewriting in hotel rooms, on airplanes, on beaches, and mostly on our dining-room table. Finally, in the spring of 1984 it was finished.

That fall I flew out to Vancouver to start my cross-country book publicity tour and quickly found that the interviews can kill you. As a reporter talking to another reporter, I inevitably found myself trying to help out the interviewer. When he or she asked a bunch of easy questions, I would find myself saying, "But you should hear the real story!" and then laughingly proceed to tell it, as if I was sharing secrets with a fellow journalist as together we sipped a beer. Or I would make little indiscreet asides about acquaintances, as all reporters and editors do, standing at the Press Club bar. The trouble is, I tended to forget the guy I was gossiping with was not an old pal, but an interviewer carefully making mental notes to include my indiscretions in his story. The next day I would find all my slanderous private gossip under a three-column headline, plus a review of the book bemoaning the fact that I was too chicken to put in the really good stuff.

The phone-in radio shows offered this innocent reporter-author another challenge, responding to questions such as, "What do you know about Pierre Trudeau and the Titled Transvestite?" as I was asked by a Winnipeg radio show caller; or, as a Vancouver listener inquired in a reference to John F. Kennedy's amorous reputation, "Is it true he was known as 'Jack the Zipper'?," a characterization I'd never heard before; or answering a Winnipeg phone-in caller who asked, "What about bigots?" I came out four-square against them, but the listener responded, "Well, I'm a bigot and proud of it!"

A lot of callers wanted to talk about *The National*, not the book, and one woman in Edmonton giggled to me and the radio audience that "You're in my bedroom every night and I watch you between my toes." A man in Winnipeg said, "Tell Barbara Frum I love her." On an Owen Sound, Ont., phone-in show, a man asked, "Are you married to Barbara Frum?"

"No," I said.

"Well, I've got a bet on this," he responded. "Are you sure you're not married to Barbara Frum?"

THERE IS ONE NIGHT of the broadcast year when things are less formal than any other on *The National*, as I discovered on December 31, 1978, a little over a month after first occupying the anchor chair. Colleagues brought down cakes and cookies to the newsroom and studio and I brought along a dozen or so bottles of champagne. It was a custom to end *The National* on a light note on New Year's Eve and we gathered as many of the editors, copy clerks, and technicians as we could around my anchor desk to wish the country "Happy New Year." For this we allocated about ten or fifteen seconds and it went off without a hitch.

On a particularly memorable 1982 New Year's Eve, however, as we began this festive salutation, to my horror I heard the script assistant say, "Oh shit! It's two minutes and fifteen seconds." At that point I could think of nothing to fill the unexpected and unwanted extra time with all my colleagues standing there grinning beside and behind me, except to break into "Auld Lang Syne." The trouble was, I was the only person with a microphone. The result was an exhibition of unquestionably the worst vocalizing ever inflicted on an unsuspecting nation. In the days that followed, letters flooded in, including one from a lady in Winnipeg who enclosed an article entitled "For The Singing Impaired." A letter writer from Qualicum Beach, B.C., said her husband used to say she had the worst singing voice in the world, but "when you broke into song, my husband paid me a compliment by commending my voice in comparison with yours. Thank you."

But the most impressive New Year's Eve I've ever had on-air was at the end of my first full year as anchorman. It was December 31, 1979, and executive producer Trina McQueen wanted a news review of the 1970s mixed with music, comedy, and a big celebrity-filled party. She invited a couple of hundred of the elite from show business, the arts, politics, and the media, everyone from Lieutenant-Governor Pauline McGibbon to jazz pianist Oscar Peterson, from Maureen Forrester to Wayne and Shuster, from Gordon Pinsent to Peter Newman, from Liona Boyd to Al Waxman. They all turned up in a ballooned and beribboned Studio Seven, bedecked with potted palms, a raised dance floor, flashing lights, and buffet tables piled high with Alaska king crab, lobster, shrimps, artichokes, hearts of palm, and an ocean of wine. Barbara Frum and I were hosts of the affair, tying together the serious news review of the 1970s, the interviews, and the partying.

Although we had known one another for more than a decade, this was to be the first of many times Barbara and I would work together as TV co-hosts. When I came up from Washington to be director of TV News and Current Affairs, Barbara had been hosting the local Toronto dinner-time current affairs program, *Week Day Journal*. At the time, my old colleague Don Cameron was executive producer of the program and he didn't like Barbara's on-air style. "Too argumentative," he said, and besides, with his news background, he wanted as host someone who "smelled of news." So he chose veteran reporter Ken Cavanagh to replace Barbara.

Actually, Cameron didn't fire Barbara but switched her from anchor to senior reporter, knowing, I suspect, that she might well feel the move was unfair and would quit. She did quit, saying, "There was a desire to limit my on camera performance," and blaming "higher-ups." I was one of the "higher-ups" Barbara may have had in mind, but in fact it was Cameron's call, with advice from news head Peter Trueman. I could have stopped it, though, and didn't because it was a central decision in Cameron's effort to make the dinner-time program more "newsy" and less current affairs. I felt badly, though, because in the process we lost the best interviewer on the CBC.

"It was a beautiful job," Barbara said. "And I loved it." Puzzled and hurt by her departure, she flirted with the idea of going into politics and both the Liberals and the NDP made overtures. "It's a tough decision," she said at the time. Wisely, she stayed in journalism, helped transform *As It Happens* into must listening for the nation, and in the process became an even more penetrating perfectionist in her interviewing techniques, paving the way for her future TV network hosting.

Now, she and I were on-air partners in a program that was unlike anything the CBC had ever done before, an exultant melange of news and show biz. Barbara and I were suddenly, even if only momentarily, treated as "stars" as we were chauffeured to the studio and found champagne and flowers in our dressing rooms. *The National* was never like this! As the three-and-a-half-hour program rollicked on toward the midnight birth of the 1980s, the news segments got less and less serious and the partying got zippier. Singer Nancy White forgot the lyrics of one song, a cameraman succumbed to the allure of the wine and took a spectacular tumble from the dance floor while shooting Veronica Tennant, and everybody sipped, munched, gossiped, and laughed at increasing volume.

Donald Macdonald, who had announced he would seek to replace Pierre Trudeau just before Trudeau changed his mind and decided to stay on as Liberal leader, told Barbara, "I wound up the decade with the shortest leadership campaign in history." Barbara and I introduced the taped items, chatted with each other, and interviewed people like Ontario Attorney General Roy McMurtry, Veronica Tennant, Fred Davis, Mavor Moore, Joe Schlesinger, Peter Kent, Bryce Mackasey, Barbara Amiel, Garth Drabinsky, and Max Ferguson. Bang at midnight, Barbara and I kissed the 1970s good-bye in front of the viewing nation and kissed hello to the 1980s. "Barbara and Knowlton's lips touched for a very long time," *The Toronto Star* tut-tutted the next day.

As our program began winding down and the party got noisier, I ripped off my tie and shrugged to the couple of million TV viewers, "What the hell!" For Trina McQueen that was the only lapse in the entire evening, and she later chided me for swearing on air.

The program ended at 1:00 a.m. but the party rolled on. During one turbulent dance after we were off the air, I found myself pulled away from Lorraine and, of all things, into the flailing arms of *Toronto Star* TV critic Ron Base, who, spurred on by the stimulation of the excessively flowing wine, twirled me about the dance floor in some macabre version of disco rock-and-roll until I whirled back to Lorraine. "What is there to be said, after all, about a decade that you end by dancing with Knowlton Nash," he wrote the next day in a somewhat chastened column, trying to remember what he'd done the night before.

Some durable celebrants stayed on until 6:00 a.m., but most of us were tucked away in our beds long before then, pleased with an unexpectedly and extraordinarily successful New Year's Eve show which, given the mix of serious news, entertainment, and partying, by all odds shouldn't have worked. But through some special combination it did (although I could have done without the dance with Ron Base).

Altogether, it was not an inappropriate ending to what had been an incredible first year for me as anchor of *The National*. Looking back on my anchoring at the end of that first year, I was certainly no Walter Cronkite, but at least I was better than when I started. Then I read too quickly and sometimes jerkily. I suppose I'd give myself a B rating, partly because I was not yet entirely comfortable in my own on-air work. Two things had surprised me about anchoring *The National*: one was the intensity of concentration needed on air; the other was the intensity of the media focus. If I was evaluating my work, so was everybody else. It was fascinating, if occasionally distressing, to read an incredibly wide range of evaluations.

"Canada's version of the Pillsbury Doughboy," said Tom McMahon of the *Windsor Star*. "Knowlton Nash, for my taste, would make an excellent funeral parlour director," said Sylvia Wigt in a St. John's, Nfld., paper. "But," said Bob Pennington of the *Toronto Sun*, "he radiates a relaxed expertise.... Critics routed, stature enhanced, Knowlton Nash approaches the '80's with renewed confidence and optimism." How I could be "cheerful" and "boyish" while at the same time being "a funeral parlour director" and "the Pillsbury Doughboy," I'll never know.

TV Guide portrayed me as some kind of journalistic Superman on its cover in a year-end story that noted "supporters shouting Cronkite" and detractors saying "underneath that bland exterior there's rice pudding." But, *TV Guide* concluded, "He may not be Superman, but he's a little less like Clark Kent now, too."

That was not as embarrassing as an article a couple of years later by *Toronto Star* columnist Joan Sutton in which she made me one of a dozen "sex symbols," saying "his gentle smile and air of reserve suggests a still water that runs very deep." Later, in another article, explaining to Sutton my passionate commitment to Canada and public broadcasting, things got a little out of hand and what emerged was a full-page story devoted to my "raging passions." Actually, her article was far more self-revealing than I ever dreamed it would be. With her innocent smile and sympathetic manner, I found myself lulled into saying things and being quoted about personal feelings that I would normally keep private. "I was brought up to restrain any show of emotion," I said to her. "There's a drawback to that, of course, in that as a result some people have concluded I don't have any emotions. But in fact, I have raging passions. But it's important to keep control and channel those passions so they are not damaging to yourself or other people." What I meant about "raging passions" was the depth of my commitment to Canada and public broadcasting, but it didn't come across that way.

As uneasy as I felt about seeing my remarks to Joan Sutton published, they at least were accurate, including the quotation at the end of the article. "But I'm an incurable optimist," I had said. "As a newscaster I see the awful reflection of the bad side of our society – the murders, the disasters, and the violence. But you have to keep a balance. Yes, there is tragedy and unhappiness in this life, but there is also happiness and triumph and joy, and on balance, I think life is a joyful thing."

At least most of the time. During much of my first year, the personal change and professional challenge of *The National* were accompanied by the continuing shrill agitation of CUPE complaining about me in the job. Trying to offset it, Trina McQueen had told *Maclean's* magazine, to my horror and embarrassment, "Just you wait. Five years from now in this country, Knowlton will be a saint." As if I didn't have enough problems, I now had to live down my anointed "sainthood" through ribbing by colleagues, radio talk-show razzing, and even "sainthood contests" begun by columnists. It was all good-natured fun, however, unlike the union attacks.

DAYS BEFORE I ACTUALLY went on air with *The National* in November, 1978, the union grievances had been taken to an independent arbitrator. He had before him three grievances against me, much rhetoric, and the CBC's strong defence. The arbitrator, George Adams, patiently waded through scores of documents, legal precedents, and endless hours of testimony lasting on and off from late November to mid-December of 1978. We sat in smoky, paper-littered hotel meeting rooms, the accusers on one side of the table, the defenders on the other, in surprisingly good humour most of the time in contrast to the bile of the accusations. I spent the mornings and early afternoons at the hearing and late afternoons and nights in the newsroom and studio.

The union case fell apart day by day, and in the end the arbitrator totally rejected all the grievances and accusations. In early winter of 1979 he handed down a ninety-six-page judgement saying the hiring process had been entirely fair and in conformity with the collective agreement; there was no "parachuting"; I clearly did not "appoint myself"; and the desirability of journalistic experience for *The National* anchor was "amply justified." "It's absolutely clear that a journalistic background can be most helpful ... and I find a requirement of previous journalistic experience is a reasonable requirement," the arbitrator said.

That was a gratifying ending to an idiotic argument. Equally satisfying was the finding that "when one reviews the procedures adopted by the CBC in relation to Mr. Nash's candidacy, there is no evidence of improper bias, discrimination, or the improper participation of Mr. Nash in the selection procedures directly affecting him."

I got the news in Ottawa in January, where I'd been covering a story. Before boarding the plane to come back to Toronto I called Trina McQueen from a phone booth. "You've won!" she exulted. "Congratulations." To reporters, Trina said, "We're delighted." To the same reporters, union official Barrie Davis said, "We're disappointed."

To nobody but myself, I breathed a great sigh of relief and Trina's words over the phone gave me a quiet moment of triumph. I felt that at least this unpleasantness was now over. But it wasn't quite. In spite of the official refutation of all the allegations, they still turned up in the occasional news story and column. Corrections and apologies were given when I or the CBC protested, but it was a lesson in the painful longevity of an accusation and the too easily forgotten clearance. Seven months later, as my first year on *The National* was drawing to a close, the union tried to overturn the arbitration award by appealing to the Ontario Divisional Court, a branch of the Ontario Supreme Court. It refused to hear the case. Another five months later, in April of 1980, CUPE took its arguments to the Ontario Court of Appeal, which after ten minutes of deliberation unanimously dismissed the case.

Finally, in October of 1980, the union went to the Supreme Court of Canada. It was impressive to see the black-robed justices, led by Chief Justice Bora Laskin, file into the court chamber and start talking about my case. In brusque language, the Chief Justice rejected the union request for a hearing and would not allow an appeal to be made, thereby, at long last, ending the case two years after it had begun.

After the hearing I walked out into the October Ottawa sunshine, relieved that the whole painful experience was at last over. There I ran into prominent criminal lawyer Eddie Greenspan, resplendent in his legal robes for a case of his own before the Supreme Court. "Congratulations," he said, "but you're lucky they don't have the right to appeal to the Privy Council in London any more, or else they'd probably have taken the case to England, too."

I smiled weakly and wondered then, as I have since, why the union tried so hard and with such a thin case. "I really thought we had a case," said the union's Barrie Davis, despite the judgements of the arbitrator and the courts. But I came to believe the union persistence was due to a combination of things. First there was George McLean's personal disappointment at not getting the job he'd wanted badly for fifteen years. He'd come to Toronto from CBC Vancouver in 1963 as a back-up *National* anchor to Earl Cameron and anticipated taking over if Earl left. When Earl did go, George was passed over, as he was four more times over the next decade and a half. He was always an announcer in the old tradition, never a journalist, and his interests were primarily in perfecting the high professionalism of his smooth, deep-voiced, friendly delivery. When George took early retirement from CBC in 1986 at age sixty-two, he was understandably still bitter about never taking centre stage with the news, and he never accepted the value of having a journalist anchor *The National*. Given George's strong feelings, the union wanted to demonstrate to its long-standing members that it would stand up for them. It was a very expensive exercise. Ironically, I paid for part of the legal assault against myself since I was, as a member of the announcing staff at CBC, a high dues-paying contributor to the union treasury. Altogether it had been a painful, blistering fire to have to walk through.

As I learned during that first year in the anchor chair, the pressure on and off the screen can be killing. On air, the split-second timing, the occasional technological snafus, and the last-second changes while the newscast is in progress can be intimidating as well as exhilarating. But for all the terrors, mistakes, and complexities of the anchor job and the off-camera demands for speeches, appearances, and interviews, I discovered the job was one of the most exciting, fulfilling, and enjoyable I'd ever had, what with the satisfying sense of reaching out in an instantaneous sharing of the day's news with millions of Canadians. To top it off I got paid for doing something I loved. Most of all, however, it was a fascinating time to be covering Canadian and world events, what with young and inexperienced Joe Clark pummelling the wily old Pierre Trudeau on the ropes as we headed for the 1979 federal election.

5 POLITICS AND POLITICIANS

My first passion as a journalist has always been politics – and the men and women who practise this extraordinary art. But for most of my professional journalistic life I covered the American scene, making only occasional forays back home to anchor elections or follow Mike Pearson and John Diefenbaker on the campaign trail. My first year in *The National*'s anchor chair, however, turned out to be a mesmerizing one for a political junkie.

The political news of 1979 was dominated by the David and Goliath confrontation of Pierre Trudeau, the most intimidatingly intelligent Prime Minister Canada has ever had – with the possible exception of Arthur Meighen – and the inoffensive, diligent, average-guy newcomer, Joe Clark, culminating in the May 22 election. It was the first time in years that I'd been on the campaign trail and I soon discovered that the life of a reporter/anchorman is far different from that of a more anonymous correspondent.

It was far different, too, from covering American presidential elections, which I'd done for a decade and a half out of Washington. American presidents are viewed with awe, while our prime ministers are viewed, at best, with scepticism. In U.S. campaigns, personality and perception are everything, but in Canadian electioneering, issues get at least a little more attention, even if we are lurching increasingly toward the American campaign style. Of all the Canadian politicians I've followed over the years, John Diefenbaker was clearly the most exciting with his fiery-eyed, arm-flailing politics of histrionics, no matter the fragility of his speech-making content. I'd covered Diefenbaker one way or another since he lost a Conservative Party leadership fight to George Drew in 1948, although not on a regular basis. With his quivering jowls and flashing eyes he always provided a good story, whether he was in government or out. He had called me the day before he died in mid-August, 1979, to complain about having an interview with him, which we had carried, shortened too much by editing. "I've been Gnashed!" the old exhausted Tory lion exclaimed to Mike Duffy, and later to me jokingly, but still somewhat upset. I intended to call him back again in a few days, but instead, Parliament Hill reporter John Drewery and I co-hosted his funeral service in Ottawa and his burial at the University of Saskatchewan in Saskatoon on a slope running down to the South Saskatchewan River.

But while in his heyday Diefenbaker electrified, he did not inspire as did his political contemporary in Washington, John F. Kennedy. Mike Pearson generated affection in the electorate while Lyndon Johnson ruled by fear and raw power.

Trudeau and Clark, however, seemed a clash between a cranky and exhausted king and a likeable nonentity. The campaign itself was a damp squib compared to the high emotions of the American ones I'd been following with their hero-worshipping, flag-waving fervour. Trudeau, with his bull-headed intellectualism, "always wanted to talk about the damn constitutional issues and federal-provincial relations," as Senator Keith Davey later told me, while Clark sailed along on the winds of a national "ABT" mood – Anybody But Trudeau.

During the 1979 campaign, my routine was to spend Monday to Thursday in the CBC Toronto newsroom and studios and Friday morning through Sunday night on the campaign trail, soaking up background for election night and doing weekly reports. I didn't spend much time with Trudeau, Clark, and Broadbent but rather went door-to-door and mainstreeted with various candidates. I attended candidates' meetings everywhere from a high school auditorium in Vancouver to a gymnasium in St. Joseph de Beauce on the south side of the St. Lawrence River in Quebec.

The single most impressive race I viewed close-up was in Halifax where three articulate, aggressive, and attractive up-and-comers, all friends, ran against each other: Alexa McDonough for the NDP, Brian Flemming for the Liberals, and George Cooper for the Conservatives.

Cooper, an energetic lawyer who had been the Maritime leader for Clark in his 1976 leadership race, and his wife Tia were the best on-the-stump campaigners I ran across in that eight-week campaign. Their enthusiasm and smooth-working togetherness reminded me a little of Robert Kennedy and his wife Ethel. The Coopers ran harder, faster, and longer than anyone else, jogging along streets to knock on doors and scampering up and down apartment hallways and stairs. They could do a six-storey apartment building in one hour. (While Cooper was number-one in the campaign running department, second place clearly went to John Roberts, who was the Secretary of State in Trudeau's cabinet. He literally jogged up and down the hilly streets of his north Toronto riding, losing twenty pounds in the process.)

The Coopers were impressive examples of the fact that campaigning takes not only energy but patience and discretion. One rainy Saturday morning in Halifax, an unshaved, underwear-clad young actor answered Cooper's knock on his paint-peeling front door by demanding, "What are you going to do about actors, marijuana, and Jerusalem?" Cooper replied that he'd work for more jobs for actors, thought marijuana was a sensitive issue, and would study the question of Jerusalem.

In this and other elections in Canada and the U.S., I've noted that significantly higher numbers of scantily clad women come to their doors in apartment buildings than in individual houses. I don't know whether or not it has some profound sociological implication, but every urban candidate has to deal with it. "The trick is to pretend you don't notice and go into your pitch," Cooper told me. "It's handy, too, to have your wife with you to hurry things along."

Cooper wasn't the only candidate that year to confront scantily clad constituents. Pat Carney, an old newspaper colleague of mine who later became a cabinet minister in the Mulroney government, told me when I visited her Vancouver campaign office that outside a hospital she had a 250-pound naked man leap onto her campaign car. He was dragged away by hospital guards. She also had a problem at her downtown headquarters, where several enterprising and politically active ladies of the evening sought to serve her campaign in their own way by, among other things, pinning Carney buttons on their clients.

The Halifax race was close, but Cooper won. He lost in the next election, however, and thereafter concentrated on his successful law career. Flemming had been an original 1968 backer of Trudeau and had worked in the Prime Minister's Office; after the election he, too, threw all his energies into a successful law career. McDonough stayed in active politics, becoming the NDP leader in Nova Scotia.

While I enjoyed following the politicians as they ran around their ridings and knocked on doors, I quickly found a real problem that plagues any journalist who's on television. I remember once watching in fascination during a San Francisco campaign stop with Lyndon Johnson as CBS commentator Eric Sevareid got mobbed by fans and as a result missed the press bus going on to the next stop. I didn't miss any buses, but I began to understand his problem as I was easily recognized as the anchor of *The National* and, indeed, often was introduced by the candidates at the doorways. Cooper, Roberts, and the others all took special pains to say I was just covering the campaign and not a supporter of theirs. Nevertheless, just being with them caused difficulties. Some Halifax Liberals protested that my presence with Cooper was unfair, and in the case of John Roberts, Toronto Conservatives made public statements charging I was helping the Liberal candidate.

In years past when I'd come up from my correspondent base in Washington to cover Canadian elections, it had been fun tagging along with Mike Pearson or John Diefenbaker. There would be some public recognition and they'd introduce me to people as they main-streeted through cities and towns. But these new protests weren't fun because they involved serious allegations that I was helping to win votes for the candidate I was with. After this election, I had to give up that kind of coverage of political campaigns. It's simply impossible now for anyone who has a relatively high visibility on television to go out door-to-door with the candidates and anonymously take notes on what happens.

I regretted that because I really had enjoyed that close-up view of political campaigning. And I'd done enough of it to know most of the rules in the campaigners' book of etiquette. For instance: always walk on the path or sidewalk in going up to a voter's home, never on the grass; uncut grass usually means that renters, not owners, live there; don't appear frightened by barking dogs; always shake hands bare-handed no matter how cold it is because gloves make it too impersonal; never, ever, let the cat run out the door; greet workers at the factory gate when they're going into work, not when they're coming out and in a hurry to go home; don't greet people coming out of a supermarket if you're a government party candidate because they'll blame you for the high prices they've just paid for their groceries; do more listening than talking; be quick, be confident, be deferential and smiling and never get into an argument – it wastes time and you can't win anyway; and give them a pamphlet so they'll remember your name.

And be patient, as I remember Cooper's Liberal opponent Brian Flemming was when he listened to the endless detail of a grizzled old World War I veteran in a Halifax veterans' hospital. The vet was telling him how a German bullet went through his wrist and into his stomach at Vimy Ridge. "One of the joys of campaigning," Flemming told me, "is meeting people like that who have lived through history. It's not a chore. It's a privilege."

For a political addict like myself, a campaign is the ultimate experience. And it bothers me when people dismiss all politicians as a bunch of bums. I remember seeing bumper stickers in Vancouver during that campaign that said, "Don't vote. It only encourages them." Unpopular as it might be to say so, I like to encourage them because, to my mind, politicians are as likeable, fascinating, hardworking, and dedicated a group of people as you'll ever find, and generally a lot more fun. Sure, there are rascals and charlatans among them, but for myself, I admire the vast majority of them – after nearly forty years of observation in Canada and the United States.

I'm not always a fan of their rhetoric, however, and if you're following the same candidate for days on end, you hear the same speech and the same jokes over and over again until you know them by heart. It was always the same whether I was following John Kennedy or Joe Clark. Actually, the most intriguing politician whose words I tried to report, usually unsuccessfully, was a one-time Toronto alderman and mayor, Allan Lamport, when I was in my early years as a reporter. He was the king of malapropism. "I deny the allegations and I deny the alligators," he once said. "If somebody's gonna stab me in the back I wanna be there," he said on another occasion. "You can lead a dead horse to water, but you can't make him drink," the irrepressible Lamport told another meeting. Nobody reached those heights of misspeak in the 1979 campaign.

There is a tempestuous, never-ending love-hate relationship between reporters and politicians as the candidates seek to shape our reporting to their objectives, sometimes economizing on truth in the process. Jody Powell, U.S. President Jimmy Carter's press secretary, once described political reporters as people "who watch the battle from afar and when it's over come down from the hills to shoot the wounded." While his comment reflected a universal feeling among politicians, most reporters are simply trying to report what they see, which does not necessarily agree with the self-image of a candidate.

On election night in Canada there are really two choices being made. In one, we vote for our choice of government; in the other, we vote for our choice of network. Much is at stake in both choices. For the networks election night is the ultimate test of their technological and journalistic qualities and of their ability to draw viewers. It sets a standard and strengthens the viewership of the winning network's news programs. And after the election is over we loudly boast about our triumphs. Reputations are made and broken, and it's no wonder the networks go for broke on this one night.

With its greater resources and more reporters across the country, CBC almost always provides more substantial, detailed coverage and better production values than CTV. "Competing with the CBC," CTV producer (and now Washington correspondent) Craig Oliver said just before the 1979 election night, "is like coming up against the entire Chinese Army." CTV, nevertheless, has beaten us on occasion with projection of the election result, sometimes being more daring than we in declaring a winner.

Serious preparation begins as soon as one election is over. Election night programs represent a monstrously complicated technological challenge. Reports are needed from every riding in the nation and a couple of dozen key centres on election night, such as party headquarters, the leaders' ridings, and critical points across the country. Over the years the CBC has developed an extraordinarily effective election team that not only plans federal elections but handles much of the planning for provincial elections as well.

The 1979 election was the ninth federal election covered by television and we'd come a very long way since Charlie Lynch sat puffing a cigar and chatted with Blair Fraser as they anchored the first network TV election night coverage in 1957. The results then were registered on blackboards, and Lynch and Fraser seemed buried under piles of paper as they expressed astonishment at John Diefenbaker's triumph. Now, the whiz-bangery of computers, satellites, and electronic gadgetry spew out the results so quickly it's all over before you know it.

There have now been a total of eleven TV federal elections and I've been involved as anchor, sub-anchor, reporter, and commentator in six of them and for most of the others was responsible for CBC coverage as director of News and Current Affairs.

In every campaign and increasingly so as TV began to dominate the process, all parties complain of unfair or inadequate coverage, insisting in effect that CBC should reflect their own image of themselves. The parties examine our coverage with a microscope and then loudly complain if they think we've been unfair. They keep meticulous track not only of the seconds and minutes given to their candidate, but of the kinds of cutaway shots (was it a cutaway to a cheering crowd or to a sullen crowd?), the calibre of reporters assigned to cover their candidate (was it the number-one Ottawa bureau correspondent or a lesser light?), facial expressions (did we use their candidate smiling or scowling?), and 100 other questions, all designed to intimidate us into giving them more air time and more positive pictures. Undoubtedly, one week one candidate will get more exposure than another or be seen smiling more. But overall, an intense effort is made to make sure the coverage is fair.

Occasionally things do go awry, however, such as a news release we put out near the end of the 1974 campaign on a public opinion survey we had done. The survey had projected a Liberal victory. In a masterpiece of stupidity and misinterpretation of the poll results, our news release on the survey said it projected a Conservative victory. Our erroneous release was front-page news across the country and it was a lamentable thirty hours before we corrected it. In an effort at explanation, we said "it was neither a simple nor a stupid mistake." In fact, it was both, as well as being mortifyingly embarrassing. From then on, all releases dealing with opinion surveys had to be triple-checked by the research department before going out.

Actually, the biggest problem of that 1974 election was not the parties but our chief parliamentary reporter, Ron Collister, who became a Conservative candidate in York-Scarborough, a suburban Toronto riding. "I've been watching politics for so long and my frustration has been growing," he announced. "Now I'd like to help shape things. . . . I want to be where the action is."

The forty-five-year-old veteran *Toronto Telegram* and CBC reporter, an old friend of mine, thus gave me a big problem as director of News and Current Affairs. Ron had been designated as our principal election reporter and election night co-host with Lloyd Robertson. The bylaws of the Corporation at the time specified that anyone running in a federal election had to resign. That, I thought, was unfair. I felt Collister should take a leave of absence, and if he won, then he should quit. If he lost, however, I didn't think he could go back to his parliamentary reporting job in Ottawa. No matter how professional he was in keeping his personal political thinking out of his reporting, he'd be perceived by both the public and the politicians as being biased. So my plan was to try to forestall his having to resign, but if he lost the election to move him to another beat.

The case became a cause célèbre both before and after his nomination. Many of my colleagues felt Collister had betrayed his journalistic professionalism and could never report anywhere again without a perceived bias. Several newspaper editorials also demanded he be fired. There was, however, much support for Collister, too, and other newspapers ridiculed the CBC bylaw that required him to quit. It was a front-page story from the start and controversy followed Ron throughout the campaign. His nomination meeting attracted a horde of reporters and party leading lights, including Conservative leader Bob Stanfield, and during the campaign even John Diefenbaker came to help him.

The publicity over his job problems with the CBC was handy fuel for Ron's campaign, especially as he portrayed the CBC resignation bylaw as victimization by an unfeeling, unthinking, uncaring bureaucracy. Privately, I sought to soften the Corporation bylaw, but publicly I had to go through the ritual of saying that when Ron formally advised the CBC of his candidacy he would have to resign. I also said, however, that we'd have him back if he lost, although probably posting him somewhere else other than Ottawa. Meanwhile, Ron kept stalling on formally advising us that he was running, even after his nomination.

Ron ran and lost and after a short stint as our Washington correspondent and a less than tranquil relationship with his chief news editor, Mike Daigneault, he quit, charging the CBC with political harassment. Ron took his Liverpudlian accent back to Ottawa where he became a political reporter for the *Toronto Sun* and later went west to help start the *Edmonton Sun*. Today he is a *Sun* columnist and a radio phone-in talk-show host.

Planning for what turned out to be the 1979 election had begun almost immediately after the 1974 race, and in a monumental piece of financial misguidance I firmly asserted in a memo to my bosses that a federal election was quite likely in 1978 and thus we did not need to worry about financing an election in the fiscal year of 1979-80. To our consternation there was no election in 1978, but we had to fund two in the 1979-80 fiscal year. Such are the perils of news budgeting in a parliamentary democracy.

Before I'd quit to become anchor of *The National*, we had whittled the election costs down from $1.3 million to just about a million dollars. But there was no way we could get it lower and still provide the kind of election coverage we needed for both the network and our local stations. A million dollars for our TV coverage was more than we'd ever spent on an election and it took an extensive campaign to persuade my bosses finally to agree to the figure. The costs broke down like this: $350,000 for election night itself; $160,000 as our English TV share of the cost of gathering the results, the total of which was split among English TV and Radio, and French TV and Radio; $40,000 for news specials; a rather small $30,000 for contingencies; and an allocation for regional stations ranging from an extra $600 for Sydney, N.S., to $30,000 each for Toronto and Montreal. The costs are puny by today's standards, but for those days they were fairly handsome. The network budget pays for reporters, producers, cameramen, and soundmen to accompany each of the party leaders, puts an "issues" team into the field, must account for their overtime and other extra costs, and must cover the costs of flying on the leaders' chartered planes, excess baggage, videotape cassettes, the election night set, special satellite feeds, computers, telephones, teletypes, and a thousand and one other items.

The 1979 election was going to be a particularly critical test for us because we knew CTV would be going all out in an effort to make up for their bad competitive showing in the previous two elections. (In 1974 the CTV computers broke down and we beat them by a mile.) Things I wanted especially to change this time were to put more emphasis on issues and less on the leaders and to provide more texture and insight on election night with less computer razzle-dazzle.

"The great thing in politics is to avoid mistakes," Mackenzie King once said, and that's true of TV election night broadcasting as well. A mistake can kill your credibility in the minds of the audience. As a result, fail-safe techniques such as double-checking of all results before they're announced and particular care in forecasting wins are vital necessities. Even so, mistakes happen, some "elected" turn out not to be elected and head-hanging corrections have to be made, chipping away at your image of authority. There are, in fact, very few of these goofs, however, and the wonder is there aren't more in all the confusing turmoil of election night.

For the 1979 election, which I'd helped plan and now would anchor, one thing we worried about was how much information we could put on the screen at one time and still have it absorbed by the audience. We didn't want to overload viewers, but our research showed a lot more could be absorbed than we used to think. So we had three different pieces of information going out simultaneously: one was what I and our commentators were saying; the second was the individual riding results displayed across the bottom of the screen as they came in; the third was a running total of seats won by each party shown up in the top corner of the screen.

As the May 22 election night approached we planned, dry ran, and rehearsed the program seemingly forever. In our election studio we game-played the whole vote, using our computers to monitor simulated results pouring in and having our reporters comment on the significance. In one rehearsal we pretended a Liberal victory, then an NDP win, and then a Conservative win. We also played out majority and minority governnment scenarios. It was all designed to test both our technology and our own knowledge of the political possibilities. All of us had read the polls that reported Clark and the Conservatives ahead, but still, Trudeau had been such a bastion of power for so long it was hard to imagine him being beaten. I still thought he might slip in with a small majority.

On election night something close to 1,000 men and women across the country were involved in collecting results for the CBC, projecting trends, providing editorial back-up, and handling the massively complex technological system from satellite feeds to the camera work in the election central studio. At thirty broadcast locations across the country, eighty-three cameras were in action, and there were computers galore. In France on election night, the TV network used to have a symphony orchestra standing by in an adjoining studio so that when there was a lull in the returns they could cut to the orchestra for a musical interlude. We didn't think we'd need any interludes.

A few hours before we went on air there was one final afternoon run-through in the CBC's big Studio 7. The place was a high-tech madhouse with its banks of TV monitors, clacking typewriters, whirling computers connected to other bigger computers, ringing phones, and young people clad in jeans rushing about with worried faces. About 5:00 p.m., with the run-through over, I strolled outside for a half-hour walk to clear my mind and psych myself up for the critical hours ahead. I had lived in terror for weeks that I'd catch cold, grow hoarse, or have incurable hiccups. But nothing like that happened and I was surprised that I was neither nervous nor tense, having done all the homework I could and having filled my head with statistics, history, and thumbnail sketches backed up by a fistful of reference cards. At 6:20 p.m. I walked around the studio shaking hands and wishing luck to my on-air colleagues and our cameramen. At 6:30 the butterflies were back momentarily as the camera's red light flickered on to indicate we were on the air in Newfoundland, where it was 8:00 p.m.

Throughout that hectic election night, veteran CBC correspondent David Halton was on one side of me and Don McNeill on the other, providing insight and background on the results flooding in. We were on a raised platform, and in a semicircle around us were five reporters covering each region: Mike Duffy, Atlantic Canada; Don Murray, Quebec; Larry Stout, Ontario; Peter Mansbridge, the Prairies; and Mark Phillips, British Columbia. Each had his own editor and computer and below all of us on the studio floor was a panel of experts moderated by Barbara Frum and CBC reporter John Blackstone. Behind David, Don, and me was a huge, lighted map of Canada. The heart of the program, unseen by the public, was the control room, jammed with people, electrified with tension, and alive with shouting instructions and the calm voice of director Bill Matthews talking quietly over our earphones to me, Halton, McNeill, or any of a score of other on-air people, giving us information on what we were going to do next, and sometimes we'd hear the less calm voice of producer Arnold Amber demanding "More energy!" and ordering new editorial direction for the program.

You have to subdivide your mind in anchoring an election because sometimes you find two or even three people giving you information and instructions at the same time on your earplug and an editor handing you some facts and figures on a sheet of paper while you yourself are talking on air. It's a challenge to absorb all these inputs and still make sense in what you're telling the audience.

My own adrenalin continued to surge as the hours flew by and the excitement built toward the era-ending Trudeau defeat. None of us left our seats, continuing to pour out results, provide analysis, do interviews, and chat with each other. This marathon performance makes the anchor chair tension on election night unlike any other TV experience. Everything revolves around that job of being host, policeman, guide, interviewer, reporter, and commentator. In fact, it's an impossible task, what with the million things that can go wrong. Yet all the time you're supposed to appear relaxed and in command. With never a moment of letdown, I understood why Walter Cronkite used to be called "Old Iron Pants" on election night coverage. But the endurance and the juggling of inputs are what make the job so much of a challenge and such fun. I've never known anyone who's done it, including Charlie Lynch, Norman DePoe, Lloyd Robertson, or Peter Mansbridge, who has not been exhausted but exhilarated at the end of the night.

One problem with Canadian elections is that they're often all over by the time the program hits the Manitoba border. The coverage begins in each time zone when the polls close at 8:00 p.m. local time. So half an hour after Newfoundland we pick up the Maritimes; then, an hour after that, Ontario and Quebec; then the Prairies, Alberta, and finally British Columbia. This time, it was 9:00 p.m. Eastern Time as we went on air in Manitoba and I said, "The CBC election desk projects a Conservative government." Normally, that would have made the rest of the night anti-climactic, but it was still unclear whether Clark would have a majority or minority government. Also, his defeat of Pierre Trudeau was such a political watershed that the tension and excitement sustained into the early morning hours.

After his defeat was clear, a wanly smiling Pierre Trudeau came into view as the cameras focused on him at a Liberal gathering in

Ottawa, and he told his stunned followers and an incredulous nation, conceding his defeat, "With all its sham, drudgery, and broken dreams, it's still a beautiful world." A short time later, to the cries of "Joe! ... Joe! ... Joe!" at an Alberta rally, we watched Joe Clark throw off his "Joe Who?" label to take on the mantle of our just-elected Prime Minister – at least for a little while.

As I watched Clark addressing both his victory rally in Alberta and the nation on TV, looking for all the world like an exultant chipmunk who'd just found a gigantic chestnut, my mind flashed back to a jammed and steamy Ottawa hockey arena three years earlier when I watched him become a surprise winner of the Progressive Conservative Party leadership with Brian Mulroney an embittered loser. At Clark's first PC convention after that, in Quebec City, I'd watched as his leadership had been enthusiastically upheld by a 97 per cent vote. In late December, 1978, I'd flown up to Ottawa to interview him along with correspondent Mike Duffy at the Opposition leader's residence, Stornoway. He and his wife Maureen were remodelling and we set up our cameras in front of a roaring living-room fireplace and moved some tables and chairs around to get a better picture. When Clark came into the living room for the interview and saw what we'd moved, his face fell and he gasped, "God, Maureen will kill me!" Fingering his blue polka-dot tie and, as usual, gesticulating with his hands and fingers, he talked of a "stimulative deficit" to get the economy moving again, a comment that later got him into political trouble during the campaign. But his comment was not serious enough to stop his election and now he was going to be Prime Minister of Canada.

In the early morning of May 23, when our election broadcast was all over, my legs nearly gave way as I stood up. I had sat there for seven and a half hours without once getting up. Now I realized how desperately I needed to go to the bathroom. No sooner was the program off the air and we had left the studio for a post-election party at a hotel across the street than producer Arnold Amber called us out to a meeting to plan the next night's election-aftermath program. It was 3:00 a.m. Reporters were dispatched across the country and details laid out for a news special the next night on the implications of Clark's victory. It was five in the morning before I finally got home for a few hours of sleep.

But I went to work later that morning with added zest because the newspapers not only recorded Clark's victory but clearly gave the nod to the CBC for the best election coverage. We felt we'd been much better than CTV, but it was comforting to see confirmation in the columns and later in the audience figures, which showed we had won a phenomenally big audience of nearly six million for our program, two million more than our competition. CTV had predicted a minority government a couple of minutes before we did, but the overall program strength of the CBC clearly outdistanced our rivals. And I was buoyed by the columnists: "Unflappable, non-partisan and splendidly informed while revealing flashes of dry humour," said Bob Pennington in the *Toronto Sun*. "Nash, ingratiating good spirits ... was more interesting," said the *Winnipeg Free Press*; " ... in complete command ... yet seeming to enjoy every moment," said the *Montreal Star*. There were, of course, those who disagreed. "Rather shrill," said the *Ottawa Citizen*. There was criticism, too, that my enthusiasm betrayed a Conservative bias.

The truth is that I became increasingly enthusiastic as the hours rolled on simply because I knew it was rapidly becoming one hell of a story: the end of an era; the astonishing change from Trudeau to Clark; and the arrival of a minority government, always a reporter's paradise for news stories. But that professional delight was mistaken by some for enthusiasm at a Conservative triumph.

A flood of mail poured in after the election expressing either joy or distaste at the results, with many letters picking up the criticism of me being "pro-Tory" in my on-air attitude. But what struck me most about the mail was the large and intense criticism of all politicians. A man from Chatham, Ont., wrote, "I think the nicest gift Canadians could give their country would be to vote out of office every incumbent Member of Parliament regardless of party or rank." A man from Killaloe, Ont., wrote me a six-page letter vividly expressing his distaste for politics: "Politics is anti-life. Politics is not news. Politics is a repressive coagulation that mucks up our gears and shortens out our creative circuits."

In early June I was in Ottawa for live coverage of the swearing in of Joe Clark on the eve of his fortieth birthday, followed by an hour-long news special that night and, finally, *The National*. Two particular memories of that sunny June day linger with me: one of Pierre Trudeau, now freed of his prime ministerial responsibilities, jauntily waving and smiling at reporters in his silver-grey Mercedes convertible, then, with his tires squealing, zipping up the driveway of the Governor General's residence after formally tendering his resignaton. The other is of Lily Schreyer, the wife of Governor General Ed Schreyer. She saw David Halton and me sitting at a desk in the ballroom of Government House chatting but didn't realize we were on the air live. She wanted to say hello and with a determined mien, ignoring the whispered warnings from her aides that we were on the air, she bore down on us and was about to break into our conversation when at the last moment she was blocked by a security guard who steered her off to the side. God knows what we would have said and done had she suddenly and noisily joined us on the TV screens of the nation.

A couple of weeks later I got to see Joe Clark in his new role at the Economic Summit being held in Tokyo. It would be his first appearance on the world stage as Prime Minister, attending a meeting of the leaders of the Big Seven industrial nations: U.S., U.K., France, Italy, Japan, West Germany, and Canada. The conference was preoccupied with the "oil shock," the dramatic increase in the price of oil and the feared world-wide economic tailspin of leaping inflation, unemployment, and slowdown.

As usual at these summit sessions, security was ferocious – 33,000 soldiers and policemen guarded the seven leaders. I'd been to Tokyo several times before and once again it was living up to its reputation as "The City of 9 c's": confusion, congestion, construction, contradiction, contamination, cars, computers, Coca-Cola, and cash. Especially cash. Four dollars for a cup of coffee and five dollars for a glass of orange juice were the going rates, and dinner could easily hit $100 per person. Lorraine had come with me and we met some old friends while at a Canadian embassy party who steered us to a more reasonable establishment near the Imperial Hotel, where we were staying, called "Curry In A Hurry" – the food was good and half the price of most Tokyo restaurants.

The night before the conference began I went along with half a dozen other reporters to Clark's hotel suite for an off-the-record interview. With his long thin fingers stabbing the air for emphasis, Clark reviewed his concerns about the world economy, alternating in appearance between Cheshire cat smiles and funereal solemnity. Clearly, he was a man thoroughly enjoying his new-found prime ministerial power. Since Clark was the new boy on the block among the Summit leaders and the youngest as well, in the moments I glimpsed him in public functions once the meeting was under way he seemed like a university freshman mixing with the upperclassmen.

The next day we opened *The National* from the grounds of the Akasaka Palace, where the conference was taking place. It seemed a bit odd, saying "Good evening" when it was a bright sunny morning in Tokyo, but time zones being what they are, it was necessary.

The most poignant moment of that conference was watching Prime Minister Clark eat with chopsticks. However successful he was at the conference table, he failed the chopstick test at a Japanese government luncheon. He waited until the others had started eating, watched

President Jimmy Carter particularly closely and sought to do what he did, but grabbed the sticks the wrong way, could hardly pick up anything, and, when he did, dropped it again. Finally he resorted to a kind of shovelling system for a few morsels before giving up entirely. All the while he chatted amiably, if distractedly, to his colleagues and smiled. Only the occasional grimace betrayed the fact that his mind was utterly preoccupied not with world affairs but with how to get the damn chopsticks to work. Unfortunately for Clark, Japanese television was broadcasting the luncheon on a closed circuit for the media and spent an inordinate amount of time focusing on our Prime Minister and his chopsticks. As a result of his vicissitudes he became a focal point to those watching on the closed-circuit TV. Every time he finally got hold of a morsel in his chopsticks, a roar of cheers would erupt among the TV-watching media, only to sink into groans as the morsel usually plopped back on his plate.

In wrapping up the conference we did a news special from Tokyo, editing the program through the night and into the dawn, ducking out of the TV station a couple of times to sample the wares at a Japanese Kentucky Fried Chicken restaurant across the street.

In the fall, Joe Clark finally called Parliament back to work and he faced his fellow MPs as Prime Minister for the first time. I flew up to Ottawa to do an interview with him, along with David Halton and Peter Mansbridge. He seemed fidgety and nervously jovial on camera but was relaxed and articulate off camera, much as he had been when I saw him at Stornoway less than a year before. It's a style problem that continually haunts Clark, who in public can appear jerky and ill at ease, like a young man trying to be a sombre funeral parlour director, muttering inconsequential comments to keep conversation going. But in private he becomes himself again – articulate, well-informed, friendly, and witty. In some ways he was much like the man he succeeded as Conservative leader, Robert Stanfield, whose sombre, boring public persona belied his private witty jocularity.

ALTHOUGH HE HAD only a minority government, Clark acted as if he had a majority in articulating his big plans for change. He was caught complacent and unprepared when he miscalcuated on a vote for Finance Minister John Crosbie's "small pain for long-term gain" budget. With his sudden defeat in the House of Commons on the budget we suddenly were plunged into another election campaign. Trudeau had announced his intention to resign as Liberal leader but hastily changed his mind as the polls showed the Liberals well ahead this time. So we prepared for Clark versus Trudeau, Round Two.

One of our pre-election news specials was a particularly memorable example of the vivid style of our news special producer, Arnold Amber. He's always shouting "More energy!" at his anchor, but this time he had a legitimate grievance, if not against me then against the program guests. They were Finance Minister John Crosbie, NDP Finance critic Bob Rae, and Liberal Finance critic Herb Gray, who were all surprisingly listless as we recorded a discussion. "Get more energy into them! This is godawful! Oh Christ!" were among Amber's comments tumbling into my earpiece as we talked. Finally, he ordered the taping stopped and I told our guests we would have to start over again. But before we could start, Amber came clattering down the steps from the control room above the studio, a thunderclap of seething distress. He shouted at the three guests in general but at the Finance Minister in particular. "It's just shit!" he proclaimed. "You've got to do better than that, for God's sake! What the fuck is the matter with you guys!"

Crosbie was uncharacteristically startled into silence, Gray looked dumbfounded, and Rae muttered to me, "Who in hell is that?"

"Our producer," I whispered back. "He wants more energy."

After a three-minute lecture, Amber went back up to the control room, the taping resumed, and Crosbie, Rae, and Gray dutifully fulfilled our producer's request.

On election night Barbara Frum co-anchored with me, taking time out from *As It Happens*. Essentially, I was the election night "policeman" moving the show along, doing the bridging between reports, and providing the latest results while Barbara concentrated on interviews and her own comments. We'd worked closely in the New Year's Eve extravaganza half a dozen weeks earlier, so we were comfortable with each other's style. But I had a fleeting problem with Patrick Watson of *This Hour Has Seven Days* fame, who was moderating a panel of experts. In one of our rehearsals, as we reacted to simulated election results, I learned of Watson's sensitivity to being called "Pat" on air. He didn't like it one bit. Several times in the rehearsal, after giving some results, I would throw it to him, saying, "For more comment on that, over to the panel and Pat Watson . . . Pat?" I noticed he seemed to grit his teeth every time I said his name and I couldn't understand why, until finally, in a tightly exasperated voice, he responded to me by saying, "Thank you, Knowltie." I grimaced and understood immediately. After that, it was always Knowlton and Patrick on air, even though it was "Pat" in private conversation, as it had been for a couple of decades.

In 1980, as I had the last time, I followed the politicians around the country Friday through Sunday (but not door-to-door this time) and occasionally during the week, while continuing to anchor *The National* Monday through Thursday. It made for lively ninety-hour weeks but, as usual, it was fun as well as necessary to build a reservoir of information for election night.

The big difference this time was that it was no horse race. The voters endorsed the old motto of students of power: "An army of stags led by a lion would be better than an army of lions led by a stag," and clearly they felt Trudeau was the lion leader and Clark the stag. In his prime ministership, Clark had been accident-prone but conscientious in everything he did while doing nothing notable. On the night of February 18, 1980, as soon as the results started trickling in from Atlantic Canada, it was clear that Trudeau would win in a walk. In fact, we'd been ready to project Trudeau as the winner about half an hour before we did but we wanted the comforting reassurance of the early Ontario and Quebec results before making the projection.

By the time we were on the air in Manitoba, we had projected a Trudeau majority government, which, in itself, was enough to encourage many westerners to turn off their sets. As usual, producer Arnold Amber kept shouting "Energy! ... Energy! ... Energy!" in our earpieces as the night wore on. Barbara and I and our reportorial colleagues tried to respond, although never to Arnold's satisfaction. The election, with the result apparent so soon, simply did not have the suspense of the previous spring.

There was "leakage," too, as some westerners in the know grabbed the results off the satellite beaming our program to eastern Canada, and journalists simply watched the CP teletypes in their newsrooms. Others caught the results on radio from the nearest easterly neighbouring time zone or tuned into U.S. border stations, which didn't worry about Canadian law prohibiting broadcasting returns while the polls were still open.

Vancouver Sun columnist Peter Wilson went to an election party at CBC Vancouver and watched our feeds from the time we went on air in Newfoundland, then wrote about his "law-breaking" experience. "I know it was wrong of me," he wrote. "I should have obeyed the Elections Act and the CRTC and all those other people who have my best interests at heart. Yet I couldn't help myself." He went on to ridicule the law, saying, "It's time for a change in the regulations. It's time to stop treating us like potentially wicked little children who will run out and change our votes if we know what's going on two or three time zones ahead of us."

But by the time the next election rolled around, still nothing had been done to change the law, with the same result that western Canada felt cheated as the TV networks came on the air in western time zones saying, in effect, "The election has already been decided and your votes can't change a thing." The present law treats westerners like children and should be changed, either by having a nation-wide common poll-closing time, or, more likely, simply by letting everyone else see the results as they actually come in. With satellite dishes and other technology, it soon won't make any difference anyway since anyone with the appropriate technology will be able to get the results when they're broadcast.

TRUDEAU'S RETURN TO POWER came just in time for him to take part in the Quebec referendum on sovereignty-association in the spring of 1980. This vote was far more critical than the federal election we'd just gone through because if René Lévesque won the referendum, it could well have been the beginning of the end of Canada, with Quebec trumpeting its nationhood and English-speaking Canadians drifting inexorably into the arms of the United States. In the weeks before the May 20 vote it appeared to be a close call, and our pre-referendum specials, which I anchored with David Halton, reflected a tense Quebec and a nervous nation. I was in and out of Quebec several times during the campaign and spent the final week in Montreal taking in what was, I believe, the turning point in the campaign: Trudeau's speech in the Paul Sauvé Arena five days before the vote. It was surely the greatest speech of his life, filled with scorn and ridicule for the separatists, soaring rhetoric, personal emotion, and hard argument. Never had I seen him filled with such passionate fire, for no topic more deeply aroused his soul than this one. The crowd in the arena went wild and even hard-nosed reporters were wide-eyed at their own unaccustomed, spine-tingling reaction to the Trudeau speech. Although the trend had been moving against Lévesque, I've always felt this one Trudeau speech did more than any other single event, or most of them put together for that matter, to defeat Lévesque's move toward separatism.

On the night of the vote, besides the flow of results from Quebec and interviews from across the country, we had a high-powered discussion panel in Toronto and one in Montreal led by Barbara Frum. She had demonstrated her intense concern about the future of the nation a couple of years earlier as host of a ninety-minute series called *Quarterly Report*. In the opening program of the 1978 season she examined the strains in the national fabric. "If we are to have a better and richer union," she said, " there are some things we'll have to accept. We are not a tightly knit, homogeneous society. We did not choose to build a unitary state like France or Britain. The French fact in Canada has survived and flourished despite the hope of some that it would go away.

"That's what we are not. What we are is a hardy and industrious people of 22 million inhabiting a vast and splendid land. We are a diverse people. Despite powerful central governments for more than 110 years, regional loyalties remain strong. And we are Canadians, maybe ready at last to make some sacrifices, to pay the price to make our union work. There are still great things to be done together. French and English, East and West, centralizers and regionalizers, if we want to. This country isn't finished yet. And the miracle is that after all these years of fumbling, stalling, patching or prejudice, blindness and neglect, we still do have another chance."

Amen! I shared that same sense of hope and belief in Canada, and few could have said it more effectively than Barbara. But now, on this nervous night in Quebec, the nation watched and was seized with the possibility of Quebec splitting Canada apart. Quebec writer-broadcaster Solange Chaput-Rolland said simply, "This country is sick," and Ronald Watts of Queen's University said, "Canada is like a roomful of gas."

David Halton and I were co-hosting the program from Montreal. As we went on the air, I said, "It's a historic night ... that will shape the future of Canada." Just under an hour later, the verdict was in and the separatists were defeated. As the evening wore on, I felt a rising joy that as a professional journalist I tried hard to suppress on air. But my personal sense of relief and pleasure inevitably broke through from time to time. In truth, I felt exultant, and ended the program by saying it was "a vote for Canada," and instead of saying good night I smilingly said, "Bon soir."

While the CBC and CTV were carrying the results (much to the loud protest of several of the CTV affiliates who preferred their network to show some Hollywood shoot-'em-ups), not all our competitors were interested in keeping the country informed of the vote. Global was broadcasting a game show called *Family Feud* and later a program called *What Will They Think Of Next?*

IN JULY OF 1980 I took a break from Canadian politics to return to my first love of American politics, going to Detroit for the 1980 Republican convention that chose Ronald Reagan as the party leader. It was the latest in a long string of American political conventions I'd covered since the Eisenhower and Adlai Stevenson conventions of 1956.

These events are democracy in the raw and I've been lucky enough to have been at almost all of them since then. Each one also is an enormous party for journalists, as we meet old reportorial friends and political contacts, gossip and drink long into the night, and enjoy the exciting spectacle of the choosing of a man who may be, and in this case was, the next President of the United States and the most powerful leader in the world.

This convention was unique not so much because of watching the choice of a one-time movie actor as the presidential candidate as in the choice of our living quarters during the convention. When we drove up to the American Plaza Hotel, I thought I was back in the aftermath shambles of the race riots that I'd covered in Detroit thirteen years before. To say the building was run down would be a severe understatement. It seemed to be almost falling down, with a wobbly card table as a reception desk, broken glass scattered about the floor, and broken windows here and there. Outside, there were loitering individuals you'd be leery of meeting in bright sunlight, let alone a dark alley.

A gentleman by the name of Mr. Eddy with a very large stomach and a very large German shepherd dog both snarled their greeting.

"Whataya want?" Mr. Eddy inquired.

As my colleagues and I explained we were from the CBC and were covering the Republican convention and had reservations, Mr. Eddy, who appeared to be the manager and sole employee, opened a drawer, pushed aside a revolver, and pulled out a long, dirty crumpled sheet of paper.

"Oh yeah," he said, swishing his unlit but well-chewed cigar to the other side of his mouth. "It's room 408 for Nash."

I picked up my bags and walked uneasily into a decrepit elevator. To my surprise it moved, albeit creakily and jerkily. The room was straight out of a lost weekend in the Bowery: a narrow, hard bed, a sheet, a horse blanket, a paint-peeling dresser, a string dangling down from an overhead light bulb, and a toilet that, when it occasionally flushed, let out a banshee howl of protest. There was a TV set that probably once worked and a window, which of course didn't open, overlooking the garbage-strewn, pot-holed street on which the hotel fronted.

Mr. Eddy, when questioned about the quality of the accommodation and the safety of the hotel, commented archly, "We ain't had nobody raped or any cars stolen for a week."

Our host was a little premature in his assurance, though. During the next few days there were a couple of rapes, one murder, and God

186

knows how many assaults and stolen cars within a one-block radius of the American Plaza. Even so, it probably would have been worse if there hadn't been a police station around the corner.

Coming home from the convention hall every night, it was hard to persuade cab drivers to go into the area. "Are you crazy?" the first one I picked shouted at me as he drove off. "I wouldn't go up there for anything. I value my life." But with a $10 bribe we would find, after a while, a cabbie with enough courage to make the ten-minute trip into what one Yellow Cab driver told me was "no man's land." I got a lot of work done at our convention hall news bureau because I didn't particularly want to go home at night, and when I did return to the hotel, I drifted into uneasy sleep amid the sounds of tinkling glass, screeching brakes, frequent shouts, and occasional shrieks. The hotel did open its bar for those in need, and this became a relatively safe refuge into which we would occasionally scoot after making it back to the hotel safely. It reminded me of a hotel bar in Santo Domingo in the midst of the Dominican Republic civil war of 1965, where we correspondents escaped each night after covering the fighting during the day.

Our CBC Radio colleagues had the wit to stay across the Detroit River in the Canadian safety of Windsor, Ont., but I and my television co-workers braved it out in Detroit. After it was all over I bought my colleagues T-shirts emblazoned with "I Survived The American Plaza."

While we were ensconced in our unusual digs, our American network friends cluck-clucked in supportive sympathy and then went home to rather fancier hotel rooms, accompanied by bodyguards in chauffeur-driven limousines. Dan Rather of CBS retired for the night to a $4,000-a-week suite while I paid $40 a night – too much, at that.

About a month after the Republican convention experience I flew to New York for the Democratic presidential nominating convention at Madison Square Garden to see the renomination of Jimmy Carter as the party candidate. It was a much tamer affair than the Reagan convention; perhaps the most interesting moment was when it ended – the delegates spontaneously rose and sang a final salute of "Good-bye Walter" to Walter Cronkite, who was anchoring his last political convention before his retirement. There was more enthusiasm in paying homage to Cronkite than in almost anything else at that convention, once again demonstrating the impact that someone like Cronkite had.

In the autumn of 1980 I was back to Canadian politics as the CBC provided what we called "wall-to-wall" coverage of the First Ministers Conference on the constitution. To my mind this was television at its finest, using the medium as an educational tool to show democracy in action. But by pre-empting our regular programming to show the political leaders, we caught hell in letters of protest from those who would rather see the Friendly Giant, Big Bird, and Mr. Dress-Up than Trudeau, Lougheed, Davis, and their colleagues.

I sought to enliven things as we began one morning by opening the program with, "Good morning Constitution fans from coast to coast . . ." I was later admonished for this light-hearted paraphrase of Foster Hewitt.

This meeting was a real battle, pitting Trudeau's implacable will and icy-eyed rhetoric about the national interest against the stubborn provincial rights advocates among the premiers. We heard little dialogue and a lot of monologues aimed at the opposition jugular.

Still, the constitutional conferences did have their lighter moments. At one afternoon session that was late in starting I was on the air filling time when Mike Duffy spotted New Brunswick Premier Richard Hatfield sauntering into the meeting room after a lengthy and liquid lunch. They conducted a decidedly loose, giggle-filled interview that undoubtedly confused more than it illuminated the audience. Later in the afternoon, Hatfield and Trudeau got into a discussion about sitting down together that night to work out some language in a proposal, and Hatfield quipped leeringly, "Your place or mine?" That night we invited Hatfield to join us at an Ottawa disco named Arnold's, but when he got there it was jammed and they wouldn't let him in, a slight he pointedly and poutingly noted to us the next morning.

For all his unique personal style, however, Hatfield made a significant contribution to the constitutional debate, displaying both a wide knowledge and a sensitivity. He rose above narrow provincial interests, often acting as a bridge between Trudeau and the premiers in trying to settle federal-provincial arguments. He deserves much more credit than he has been given for the eventual patriation of the constitution and the Charter of Rights.

A few weeks after this First Ministers Conference ended I again had a taste of American politics, spending some time following President Jimmy Carter and his challenger, Ronald Reagan. It was like old times again, in jammed meeting halls with noisy bands, emotional crowds, and singing and shouting just as I'd gone through a hundred times before when I was a Washington correspondent. It was a joy to get away from the Toronto studio from time to time on assignments like these, but I recognized, too, my absence interrupted the continuity

188

at the anchor desk. Hence, I tried to concentrate my out-of-town travel on weekends, sometimes including Fridays or Mondays.

Unlike my past experiences as a correspondent, this time it was more fun following the Republican challenger than the Democratic incumbent. There was a passionless, antiseptic atmosphere around Carter and his entourage. Reagan, on the other hand, with his emotional oversimplifications, his aw-shucks good-guy Hollywood image, and his flag-waving John Wayneish approach to world affairs, generated a mass magic that swept through the crowds and was going to sweep him right into the White House. Grinning through his anecdotal right-wing certainties and with his small-town mid-America virtues, Reagan was a confident, happy warrior in contrast to the responsibility-laden, seemingly uncertain distress of Carter. When CBC Washington correspondent Joe Schlesinger and I did an election night special, we were hardly on the air before the computer projections showed a Reagan landslide.

JOE CLARK WAS in about as much trouble as Carter. He'd been beaten by Trudeau the previous winter and now was under attack within his own party. In the winter of 1981, a year after his defeat, Clark faced a Progressive Conservative Party leadership review in Ottawa. While the delegates were voting, Ike Kelnick and his People's Choice band belted out "Happy Days Are Here Again." But they weren't for Joe.

Joe had become an obsession among the delegates, who ate, drank, talked, and dreamed of almost nothing else but Clark on and off the convention floor. Most of them – lawyers, motel owners, salesmen, executives, druggists, chartered accountants, MPs, and senators – voiced little criticism of Clark's policies and practically nobody admitted to voting against him. The undermining of Clark was rarely seen on television because it was done in private whispers and late-night conversations in which delegates sat around eviscerating their leader. While hardly anybody would say anything against Clark on the air, privately they clucked at his style and repeatedly I heard delegates quoting Liberal power broker Jim Coutts: "In this game you have to be a bit of a son of a bitch and Joe doesn't quite have it." Some more devastatingly quoted former Conservative Party president Dalton Camp, who had said, "When Joe Clark comes into a room, Conservatives can't make up their minds whether to stand up or send him out for coffee."

He left that convention with the endorsement of two-thirds of the delegates, a number that would come back to haunt him.

Two years later, in January of 1983 in Winnipeg, in another review Joe was fighting to save his political leadership by getting more support than he'd had in Ottawa. On the night of the vote, reporters of both networks were advised by "usually reliable sources" – meaning party officials who hadn't steered us wrong before – that it was Clark by a landslide. CTV trumpeted the expected Clark leadership triumph and CBC did, too, although our trumpeting was of short duration. As minutes ticked away delaying the vote announcement, CBC commentators led by Peter Mansbridge began to speculate the delay might be bad news for Joe. Finally, Pat Carney announced the stunning result that Clark had about the same level of support he'd had in the Ottawa convention, two-thirds of the delegates, and then, even more stunning, Clark called for a new leadership convention.

The Progressive Conservative leadership race was on. Until then Brian Mulroney had been hiding in the bushes while his supporters were quietly buttonholing support. Now all was in the open. The battle for delegates had never before been so visible to Canadians, who at times were shaken by the questionable tactics of both Clark and Mulroney campaigners. They packed meetings with "instant Conservatives," including derelicts and drunks, confused old men and unaware youngsters. Stories on *The National* revealing these new and controversial techniques of party membership recruitment were, at best, unappreciated by Clark and Mulroney, were pointed to with scorn by other leadership candidates, and were uncomfortably defended by Clark and Mulroney themselves.

All candidates of all parties are especially sensitive to what the media reports of their activities, and none more so than Brian Mulroney. Never have we had a political leader who so assiduously reads, hears, and watches what the media say about him. While other PC leadership candidates would have their aides call editors to complain from time to time about coverage, Mulroney himself seemed to be forever on the phone complaining and cajoling.

Most of the time he was smart enough to call to the newsroom and talk to the reporters and editors directly involved in putting out the news instead of talking to the more remote news executives. One Sunday night during the leadership campaign I was sitting in for Peter Mansbridge on *Sunday Report*. We'd done a piece on the leadership race, and Mulroney telephoned me in the control room just as we came off the air to complain about the way we described the size of a meeting he'd just held. "It was much bigger than your man said ... and God, you mentioned hardly any of the big names there ... people who are really influential and count. And it's not the first time I've been short-changed by you guys. I'm bloody mad about it!"

A few weeks later, he called again, complaining to me about being unfairly treated in a campaign story we'd carried. "I'm mad as hell!" he shouted. He calmed down, but ended the conversation saying, "It's just not fair. You're not giving me a fair shake." I thought that was the end of the matter, but around midnight after I got home from *The National*, he called me at home. "I'm still mad," he said. "The more I think about it, the madder I get." He began to sputter in indignation and then said, "Here, let me put Mila on and she'll tell you how angry I am." On came a soft-voiced, earnest Mila who told me, "Yes, Knowlton, he really is angry." Back came her husband, "You see, I told you I was mad!"

I could tell that he was, but we ended the conversation with her calming words and my assurance that I'd look over our coverage to see if it was indeed fair, as I felt it was. On the particular item about which he was complaining, it seemed to me to be a fair report, and on balance I thought our coverage overall had been reasonable.

By the time the voting started at the June, 1983, convention in Ottawa, it was a Clark and Mulroney race, with John Crosbie still a strong contender after a superb opening-night speech. But Crosbie's lack of French was deeply and, in the end, mortally wounding to him. As I roamed about the convention floor, chatting with delegates, old friends, and journalistic colleagues, it became clear this was unlike any other Conservative leadership convention. The Conservatives had now accepted the bilingual, multicultural reality of Canada, and most of them accepted the desirability of having a leader who spoke French as well as English and who was determined to make the Progressive Conservative Party a bilingual and multicultural party as it never had been before. That was a historic breakthrough for the Conservatives and it came thanks to Mulroney's persuasive tactic of saying the Conservatives can never again cede Quebec to the Liberals. His fluent, natural French was also a big factor. Joe Clark had also had a major role in changing the party attitude with his dogged and success-ful battle to learn passable French and to provide a Quebec presence in the PC Party.

Canadian political leadership conventions have become junior-size replicas of American presidential nominating conventions with much the same hoopla, polling, bands, parading girls, and buttonholing politicians. Even the campaign leading up to the convention has taken on some of the American hustling style of politics. Canadian politics is now out of the backrooms, where it had been for generations, and into the open in the living rooms of the nation, which is a bonanza for journalists and especially televison news: little, after all, escapes the penetrating eye of the TV camera. This strengthens the democratic process of choosing our leaders since everything – or almost everything – is happening where you can see it. It may be a lot tougher on politicians, who have to face the merciless glare of the TV camera, but it gives the public a chance to see just what's going on.

About ten minutes before the fourth vote tally was about to be announced I moved over on the jammed and steamy Ottawa Civic Centre convention floor to stand just below Clark's seat. I'd long felt that Mulroney would win the leadership, but I believed there was a deeper, more emotional story in watching how Clark handled seeing the destruction of his life-long dream before the eyes of millions of Canadians. Seven years earlier I had been in this same convention hall (actually, a hockey arena) and had watched Joe Clark win the leadership against, among others, Brian Mulroney. Clark was exultant then and Mulroney embittered. Now Mulroney was having his revenge.

Clark stood up in his box, holding hands with his wife Maureen, determinedly smiling, singing and swaying in rhythm to the music. But it was all over for him. He knew it, his supporters knew it, and the reporters knew it, but on he smiled and sang and swayed. Even though the fourth ballot result wasn't known, down on the floor young men and women with Clark buttons were already sobbing, and older Clark veterans were swearing and vowing some kind of future vengeance against Mulroney. The emotions were stronger than I'd ever seen at any Canadian political convention. "We'll get the bastard, somehow!" screamed Clark veteran and one-time CBC and CTV reporter Tim Ralfe, the same man who had done the emotional October Crisis interview with Pierre Trudeau. Ralfe was shaking his fist with red-faced hysteria at no one in particular, while sobbing youngsters in their first leadership campaign put their arms around each other, unsuccessfully trying to bite back the tears in their misery of bitterness and smashed dreams. You had to be made of stone not to be moved by all the raw, exposed emotions made all the more poignant by the raucous, delirious shouts of joy by the Mulroney supporters fifty yards away. Clark had led on all three previous ballots, but his strength had slipped just a little on each one while Mulroney's gained. With Crosbie out of the race after the third ballot, it was clear most of his votes were going to Mulroney.

Suddenly a wave of silence swept over the convention hall. The final vote was about to be announced: Clark, 1,325; Mulroney, 1,584. Even before Mulroney's figure could be heard a deafening roar of triumph erupted from the Mulroney delegates, drowning out the pain-laden boos and groans from the Clark side. His dream now shattered, Clark gulped at the announcement, his Adam's apple bobbing up and down as he smiled bravely but unconvincingly, and then he spent the next few moments shushing the booers and comforting the sobbers.

WITH THE INTERNAL THUNDERCLAPS of the Conservative Party now settling with Mulroney in and Clark out, it was the turn of the Liberals for leadership anxieties. There had been much speculation on whether Trudeau would quit before the next election and would-be replacements were quietly preparing their leadership races. On the last day of February, 1984, I was flying out to Calgary to speak to a conference of oil executives and journalists when, stepping off the plane, I met a sad-faced CBC public relations officer who had helped to arrange the trip and who now told me I had to turn around and go back to Toronto. Pierre Trudeau had just announced his resignation. I boarded the same plane on which I'd come out (meeting some surprised stares from the stewardesses who'd just said "Good-bye" and were now saying "Hello") so I could anchor that night's *National* with the Trudeau resignation story.

Trudeau had taken a "walk in the snow" the night before and decided to retire, ending one of Canada's most controversial eras, dominated by an intellectually arrogant and audacious Prime Minister who, I think, will be judged better by history than contemporary commentators have treated him. He had outraged so many with his fiery temper, cold insolence, and flamboyant disregard for tradition. And yet, his historic triumph over separatism in Quebec, his patriation of the constitution, and his Charter of Rights will reverberate through future generations of Canadians.

My personal encounters with Trudeau were relatively few but always memorable. To cover him professionally was journalistically profitable, for there always was a story. He was an extremely tough interview, however, interrupting questions, challenging assumptions, and most of the time seeking to make the reporter as uncomfortable as possible. His attitude seemed to be a product of his scorn for the intellectual prowess of almost all journalists.

At times the disdain was intensified by the action of reporters themselves. He never seemed to enjoy the annual Parliamentary Press Gallery dinners and what he considered the juvenile hilarity of such an evening of excessive eating, drinking, singing, and speech-making. It's meant to be an evening of poking fun at the politicians, but Trudeau never became addicted to it. I recall once I was one of the on-stage performers in a skit spoofing the media and politicians, and it was unnerving to stand on stage singing and making fun of Trudeau while he sat there in the front row, fifteen feet away, with his face frozen in boredom and a forced smile rarely and reluctantly creasing his face.

On another occasion of meeting the media at the urging of his aides, who wanted him to develop better relations, Trudeau reluctantly attended a luncheon in a Japanese restaurant with a couple dozen Toronto reporters, but it backfired. Trudeau's arrogance drove one columnist – Dennis Braithwaite of *The Toronto Star* – into a towering, red-faced rage. Braithwaite felt Trudeau was being "snobby and snotty" and shouted across the table that Trudeau could take his sushi and "shove it up your ass."

I remember a private two-hour breakfast with Trudeau in the mid-1970s with about half a dozen other senior journalist executives from radio, TV, and the newspapers where the Prime Minister showed his usual chippy belligerence in responding to questions. I wanted to discuss the problems of the "Americanization" of Canadian television, which was increasingly limiting the viewing opportunities for Canadian-made programs, and I pointed to pay TV as an example of the government acting in a way to increase the presence of made-in-Hollywood productions.

"What!" he scowled. "The CRTC has done wonders! There is much more viewing now of Canadian programs than ever."

"No," I ventured. "The growing availability of American TV programs has meant proportionately more viewing of American programs and less of Canadian, and besides . . ."

"Well," he interrupted, "do you want me to intrude in the free choice of Canadians? This is a democracy, you know."

"Then," I said, "you're prepared to take the heat on economic matters, but not prepared to take the heat to protect Canadian identity and culture."

"Well, look," he answered dismissively, "I know about economics, but I don't know about communications. I can't even go on the air sometimes when I want to. . . . The Opposition gets more air time than I do."

It was clear he simply didn't want to talk about the subject of Canadian TV programming and I wondered, in fact, if he actually knew or cared much about it. Like sports, it seemed that broadcasting simply didn't interest him.

Throughout the rest of our breakfast he was in the same argumentative mood, dismissing some thoughts offered by Don Hartford, who was then president of radio station CFRB in Toronto, and giving little credence to some economic suggestions from Martin Goodman, editor-in-chief of *The Toronto Star*. In the course of the conversation he expressed his anger at the premiers' demands for some tradeoffs in negotiations over patriation of the constitution. "All Canadians want patriation," he said. "Why should there be any tradeoffs?"

As we strolled out of the hotel suite after two hours of quintessential Trudeau at his disputatious best, one of my colleagues said, "You know, I almost feel like punching him in the nose." We all agreed, but we wondered, too, whether the style reflected an angry disposition or simply his love of an argument and his adamant insistence on winning it no matter what. My own sense was the latter.

In contrast to that intense Trudeau at breakfast, I recall a relaxed Trudeau at dinner in February, 1979. It was a relatively small group at a dinner party held in Ottawa's Rideau Club and it was strictly a quiet social evening to say farewell to Dick O'Hagan, an old friend of mine who was leaving his media relations post in the Prime Minister's Office. A smiling, relaxed Trudeau laughed about his media image and chatted amiably about his children. "My biggest problem is having enough time with the children," he told Lorraine and me with a gentle grin. "I enjoy them so much and this is a critical age for them." In his few comments at dinner, he poked fun at some of his colleagues and at himself, thanked them for their help, and exited early "to get back to the kids."

Trudeau could be an absolute charmer when he felt in the mood, but it was a side of him reporters seldom saw, especially in the years after the "Trudeaumania" of his early period had waned. He seemed to enjoy baiting reporters in interviews, sometimes being offhand with disdainful responses and shoulder shrugs, and generally reflecting something bordering on contempt.

Certainly no politician generated as much mail from the public as Trudeau, and I received some of it, mostly critical. Many accused Trudeau of being a Communist. "The CBC has played a leading part in imposing on this whole nation Trudeau's Masonic Marxist revolution," wrote a Toronto man. "There's a Trudeau plot to communize Canada," said an Edmonton letter writer. I was intrigued with the theme running through many letters that Trudeau was foisting communism on Canadians through adoption of the metric system. "Marx and his Russian communist inheritors are planning our destruction with metric," a Vancouver man wrote me. A man from Ottawa explained to me why he was so concerned about Trudeau's endorsement of metric: "Metric makes it easier for the Russians to use our bullets," he said. Another letter writer told me Trudeau's metric system was "converting us to hedonism."

While he undoubtedly stirred up emotions, no one could question Trudeau's nimble, forceful sagacity. Even though Canada is only a middle power, he gained world-wide respect with his sensitivity and intellectual creativity at the councils of world leaders, especially the annual economic summits of the world's seven major industrialized nations. At the Venice Summit in June of 1980, David Halton and I interviewed him on a hotel terrace overlooking the windswept Grand Canal. As gondolas and motorboats chugged past, Trudeau put away his normally chippy, combative style, occasionally fingered the red rose in his lapel, and responded smilingly to our questions about the world economy, Third World aid, and dealing with hostage-takers and terrorist hijackings. The only time he retreated to testiness was when David asked what he could do to protest the Soviet invasion of Afghanistan. "You mean like go to war?" he said crankily.

The high regard in which Trudeau was held in most nations was not, however, reflected in the White House of Ronald Reagan. They regarded him suspiciously as "a leftie" whose international attitudes didn't always mesh with U.S. policies. Nevertheless, after Reagan entered the White House in January, 1981, he honoured Trudeau by making his first foreign trip as President to Canada. He and Trudeau were about as dramatically opposite in style and substance as Kennedy and Diefenbaker had been, and they didn't get along any better. On this occasion, however, it was a simple get-acquainted visit, part of a "good neighbour" approach Reagan was seeking on this first visit to Canada of a U.S. President since Richard Nixon came nearly a decade earlier. Reagan smiled and reminisced through his visit, planting the usual silver maple tree at Government House, patiently suffering through the usual anti-American demonstrations on Parliament Hill, and including a few fractured French words in his speeches. When he spoke to Parliament he noted illustrious Canadians with whom he was familiar, such as Mary Pickford, Art Linkletter, Glenn Ford, Raymond Burr, Raymond Massey, and Walter Pidgeon.

One thing Trudeau particularly wanted to talk about during the Reagan visit was the complex process of trying to achieve peace in the Middle East, and this topic was scheduled to be discussed over lunch. Journalists weren't present but I was told by one of the participants that Reagan talked on through the meal with reminiscences, jokes, and anecdotes, including one about an unemployed lady in Chicago driving in her Cadillac to a welfare office to collect her unemployment cheque. He felt the story illustrated the dangers of unemployment insurance. Finally, Trudeau broke in with the comment, "Could we talk about the Middle East?" Immediately, Reagan said, "Yes, and I've got an idea on that."

At this point his Secretary of State, Alexander Haig, leapt in to say they could "deal later" with this. Undeterred, Reagan ploughed on, "No, I'd like to tell Pierre about it now."

As I was told by my source at the lunch, the conversation went like this: "You see," said Reagan, "if we could get all the God-fearing people together ... there are the Christians, the Jews, and the Arabs ... get them together to work against the Godless peoples ... the Communists. Then we'd have something." He continued like this for a few minutes as Trudeau's eyes rolled to the ceiling. Finally Trudeau, with his finger stroking his chin, said, "I see," and he summarized what Reagan had just said. "Yes. Yes," Reagan said excitedly. "You've got it exactly!"

"But," Trudeau went on in patient understatement, "I was there a couple of months ago and there are deep divisions even among the Arabs alone."

"Yes, but if we could just get all the God-fearing people together to oppose the Godless ..." Reagan went on.

As the conversation dwindled down, White House aide Michael Deaver leaned over to a Trudeau aide and whispered, "Well, we have our good days and we have our bad days."

Trudeau never really did break through Reagan's anecdotage, and while the Reagan White House admitted Trudeau's intellectual prowess he was never fully trusted.

NOW, THIS RIDDLE wrapped in a mystery inside an enigma, to quote Churchill on a different subject, was finally leaving the prime ministership. That winter day of 1984 as I flew back from Calgary musing about Trudeau, I was surprised at his resignation. I'd thought he'd stay on as Prime Minister for another year or so. In fact, I had confidently made that forecast in a couple of speeches to Canadian military personnel at NATO bases in Lahr and Baden Baden, West Germany, just a few weeks before he resigned.

Probably on a personal level and as a single parent, he did indeed want to spend "more time with the kids," and on a professional basis he possibly felt he had achieved much of what he had sought when he first came to Ottawa and now found the fire in his belly was banked. This time he meant it, unlike his petulant and temporary resignation back in late 1979.

Trudeau's impending departure set tingling the ambitions of many another Liberal politician, but soon the race boiled down to two men: John Turner and Jean Chrétien. In the end, the party establishment won out, supporting long-time heir presumptive and anticipated vote-getter Turner against Chrétien, whom the party regulars considered refreshing but déclassé.

During the campaign, the first thing that dumbfounded reporters was that Turner's God-like quality outside the political ring turned into a bundle of human frailties once he put on the gloves again. He was simply not used to the media of the 1980s. He was painfully rusty and nervous in the art of glad-handing voters, making speeches, and dealing with reporters. At local rallies it was occasionally embarrassing, but when shown on national television it became dangerously damaging.

At the Liberal convention in June, 1984, in the same arena where Conservatives had chosen Brian Mulroney a year earlier, there was a little less hoopla and a little less tension. It was not a foregone conclusion that Turner would win, but it was hard to find many bets against him despite his lacklustre performance. As I wandered about the convention floor talking to delegates, I kept hearing the same theme: private fear, especially among western delegates, of another French Canadian replacing Trudeau, despite Chrétien's totally different style. Nobody wanted to say so publicly, but delegate after delegate - except those from Quebec, New Brunswick, and a few from Ontario - repeated to me, "We can't win the West with Chrétien." As it turned out, they couldn't win the West with Turner either, but at the convention they thought they might. Chrétien suffered from what had become known as "the Flora Syndrome." Delegates smilingly and publicly slapped his back and wore his buttons, but in the privacy of the voting booth their prejudices ruled and they marked their ballots for Turner, just as eight years earlier Flora MacDonald saw many delegates wearing her buttons in the Conservative leadership race but also found that they voted against her in the booth, a fact that helped Joe Clark win in 1976.

Once the election campaign itself was under way, and with Turner succeeding Trudeau as Prime Minister, his rustiness became a significant liability. His every nervous laugh, twitch, and bottom pat were under the relentless glare of the media.

At the start, I believed the Liberals had a good chance of winning, at least with a minority government. But Turner's campaign began falling apart with his bum-patting penchant - "I'm a tactile kind of guy," he explained. But it was his acquiescence to Trudeau's final patronage appointments that fundamentally undermined his campaign. "I had no option," Turner said.

Within a couple of weeks of the start of the campaign his staff members were fighting each other and his gaffes bit deeply into his self-confidence. His campaign was blowing apart and finally he called in the old pro, "Rainmaker" Senator Keith Davey, who had masterminded the political success of Mike Pearson and Pierre Trudeau. His is the politics of sunshine; but he is a pragmatic somewhat left-of-centre Liberal with a ferocious determination to win. Keith and I have been personal friends since I was editor of a Toronto publication called *Canadian High News* and he was my sports columnist, displaying the same exuberance then as he brought to politics. In Keith's columns, a hockey player never simply scored a goal: he "dented the cords," "slammed home the rubber," or "dipsy-doodled the sphere into the netting."

Keith's irrepressible optimism was tried to the limit, however, as he sought to resurrect John Turner's sagging campaign. But it was much too late. In the final weeks Mulroney was so far ahead he never looked back. Even his off-the-cuff comment on the Liberal patronage appointments - "There's no whore like an old whore" (he was jokingly referring to himself at the time) - couldn't stem the momentum.

Both Mulroney's "old whore" comment and one made early in the campaign by Turner, about his economic disagreements with Trudeau and his reasons for resigning from the Trudeau cabinet some years earlier, were thought to be "off the record" by both Mulroney and Turner. In this journalistic day and age, however, it seems nothing is off the record. Mulroney became acclimatized much more quickly to the journalism of the 1980s than Turner did, although by the end of the campaign, when it was much too late, Turner was catching on. They both learned there really was no such thing as a private conversation with a reporter on the campaign trail, that everything they said would sooner or later be on television, radio, or the front pages. In turn, that made them much more cautious in talking to reporters and much more sensitive to the image they wanted to project. They recognized the unhappy truth of a comment made by Keith Davey that "in politics, perception has become reality." So the 1984 campaign became "perception politics," and in a very real way I think the public was the loser. We never really got to know the candidates, only their images. In a way it's our own fault as reporters because we pry so hard, watching every wink and nudge and reporting everything, that we force the candidate into a twenty-four-hour-a-day shell.

Canadian reporters for the most part are not nearly as aggressive in their prying as some American journalists. Gary Hart, for example, was forced out of the Democratic presidential race in 1987 by his self-invited media bedroom spying. To my mind, if the private life of a politician – or any prominent person, for that matter – seriously affects his or her public responsibilities, then personal misdeeds should be reported. If not, then to report them is mere sensationalism that doesn't belong in a newscast or newspaper.

I sometimes long for the days when there were many more truly off-the-record conversations with political leaders, who climbed off their pedestals in private. A reporter could get a sense of what the candidate was really like; at least, that certainly was the way it was in my experience as a Washington correspondent covering the Kennedys, Lyndon Johnson, Richard Nixon, and all their high-powered supporting casts. And it was that way in Ottawa, too, in the days of St. Laurent, Pearson, and Diefenbaker. The contemporary argument against off-the-record private conversations with the high and mighty is that they will corrupt the journalists, making them less objective. That may have been at least part of the objective of such off-the-record meetings, but if reporters could be corrupted so easily, then they weren't very good journalists in the first place. I think I was a better-informed reporter by having off-the-record conversations and private get-togethers with political leaders because, although I didn't quote what they said at the time, the information I learned in the process enabled me to provide better reportage than I otherwise would have.

A good example of that is a private Ottawa dinner Lorraine and I attended along with a dozen or so other couples. Our hosts were Prime Minister Brian Mulroney and his wife Mila. Since the dinner was a private social affair no announcement was made of it taking place, but several days later I was startled to see a couple of columnists fulminating that I (and *Globe and Mail* columnist Jeffrey Simpson, who also was there) had betrayed journalistic ethics by having a meal with the Prime Minister. One asked if I would have reported it if the Prime Minister had fallen into his soup. In all the off-the-record dinner parties and lunches I've attended in Washington, Ottawa, Toronto, London, Paris, Tokyo, and elsewhere, only one person has ever fallen into his soup. He was a fellow Canadian journalist in Washington working for *Maclean's* magazine, and I did not report the incident. Another columnist asked whether I would have reported it if the Prime Minister had made a major announcement. It's hardly likely he would choose a private social dinner to do that, but if he had, of course I would have reported it, social amenities suffering in the consequence. The other question that was raised involved the kind of relationship established by reporters with a prime minister and other political leaders. Obviously, to become one of the leader's cronies would dissolve the journalistic distance reporters must have from the subject of their reporting. But to be on a first-name basis, to have a meal or a drink with a political leader, is perfectly legitimate, indeed desirable, as long as both sides recognize their fundamentally different first loyalties. For the life of me, I've never been able to understand the bubbleheaded theory that a journalist should never get into such social situations with politicians, let alone presidents or prime ministers, because it would taint their journalistic purity. If someone can be won over so easily, he or she has no business being a journalist in the first place.

Unlike Mulroney, Trudeau was not one to pay much attention to journalists. By the time he left office, most Ottawa reporters were bitterly anti-Trudeau, a feeling that was certainly mutual. But when Turner came on the political scene again the high expectations of columnists and editorial writers, which had built up over the years because he "looked" prime ministerial, quickly dissipated. That gave Mulroney a media edge, in part because most journalists sensed a more exciting story for them if Mulroney took over with all the changes he would bring. When he became Prime Minister, there was something close to a honeymoon in his relations with the media, although it didn't last long. Only days after his election, Mulroney was asked by a CBC Ottawa reporter, "Is the honeymoon over yet?," to which he replied with a steely smile, "With you, it never began."

In Mulroney we had a Prime Minister who was totally different in his attitude toward journalists. Trudeau ignored the headlines, but Mulroney was obsessed by reading, watching, and listening to everything said about him. As I had learned during the leadership campaign, he knew our names and our work as Trudeau never did, and he is acutely sensitive to how the media portrays him. It was a new experience for journalists to have so attentive a Prime Minister, and this set the foundation for a long-running confrontation that soon would rival the Trudeau/media relationship for animosity.

NOT ALL OF MY journalistic peripatetions during my years on *The National* have involved the high seriousness and low comedy of politics. In fact, one of the highlights of my first four years on the job was when I anchored with Barbara Frum CBC's special coverage of the wedding of Prince Charles and Lady Diana, the "Wedding of the Century" as it was called. The wedding was set for 11:00 a.m. on July 29, 1981, and along with my colleagues I flew over to London a week before to prepare.

Lady Diana had captured the hearts of the world in what was billed as the most exciting and romantic courtship since Prince Charles's uncle, the former King Edward VIII, gave up his throne for "the woman I love." The easily blushing, beautiful blonde "young giraffe," as she was nicknamed by friends, or "Shy Di" as she was called by the media, became an instant star. No comment about her went unreported. Her father rather ungallantly described her to reporters as "a splendid physical specimen" and an uncle said, "She has an unblemished past." CBC reporter Larry Stout found out when visiting her home town that she was mad about chewing Hubba Bubba bubble gum and dutifully relayed this information to the presumably eager television audience.

The focus of this happy event was clearly not on the heir to the throne but on Lady Diana and what she said, what she felt, and what she did and on her 18-carat diamond, sapphire, and gold engagement ring. "I wouldn't take it off for anything," she told reporters, adding, "I want to be a good wife."

In the days before the wedding, as I walked about the history-laden streets of London, the city seemed in the grip of a fairytale. I have to admit to being a supporter of the monarchy as a non-political symbol of tradition and continuity, but even I was taken aback at the mass exuberance that seized the British capital that royal week. Smiles were everywhere and complete strangers uncharacteristically chatted with each other as Londoners shared the ubiquitous sense of joy and pride. It was somewhat similar to the spirit I remember on July 1st of our Centennial year. Souvenir salesmen all over London happily offered dish towels, plates, mugs, buttons, and even bumper stickers, some of them mischievously saying, "Di, Don't Do It!"

The wedding in St. Paul's Cathedral would be the greatest television spectacle in history, watched by 800 million people around the world on ninety-two television networks in sixty-one countries. Catering to the needs of thousands of reporters, editors, producers, and camera technicians was a monumental task, but with typical British efficiency the journalists were handled smoothly, given half a dozen different credentials and badges, supplied with hundreds of pages of information, and backgrounded in minute detail by the BBC, which was providing the basic coverage to all the foreign networks. The Americans were the royalty of the media; the U.S. anchors stayed at fancy Mayfair hotels and were chauffeured around town in Bentleys and

Rolls-Royces while the rest of us scrambled for cabs or took the tube.

The government genealogists had delved exhaustively back through time to find historic links for Diana and Charles. They had proven her related in one way or another to King Charles II, King James II, Mary Queen of Scots, Humphrey Bogart, and Rudolf Valentino. They said George Washington was her eighth cousin seven times removed. Prince Charles, we were breathlessly advised, is also a very distant relative of George Washington, as well as Dracula, King Canute, Old King Cole, William the Conqueror, William Shakespeare, "and probably," our briefing genealogy officer said, "Genghis Khan, too."

Barbara Frum and I were working together again, our most recent on-air association having been the 1980 Quebec referendum. This time we were co-hosts of the extensive CBC coverage of the event. We had to do a pre-wedding prime-time special the night before, along with our colleagues Peter Mansbridge, Larry Stout, and Eve Savory. In this show we would go over the wedding route, show the mood of London, air a BBC interview with Charles and Diana, and provide some background on their romance. Along with producer Arnold Amber, Barbara and I drove over the route from Buckingham Palace to St. Paul's and we videotaped our opening to the program on the steps of St. Paul's amid the crowds of curious bystanders.

Amber insisted we had to have one of the gold-and-black invitations to the wedding that had gone out to members of the royal family, the bride's family, presidents, prime ministers, kings, queens, princes, and a few royal friends. But we couldn't get one from the BBC or the Palace public relations people. I remembered that an acquaintance, Brigadier-General Dick Malone, a prominent Canadian newspaper publisher, was one of the twenty or so Canadians invited. Enlisting the help of Toronto *Globe and Mail* society columnist Zena Cherry, I tracked Dick down at the home of a friend of his and we took a camera crew over by taxi to shoot the prized piece of paper.

In the soft, warm night air of the wedding eve, Barbara and I did some of our "bridges" linking items within the program and the closing for the pre-wedding special to be sent by satellite back to Canada. Behind us was a Hyde Park backdrop and the most spectacular fireworks display Britain had seen in 200 years. All over town that night there were balls, parties, and receptions, but we went to bed early because of a pre-dawn start for the long day ahead.

The next morning at dawn, clutching hundreds of pages of notes and background material, we made our way through the gathering crowds to the BBC-TV broadcast centre where we were to host the four-and-a-half-hour CBC special. As Barbara and I entered the BBC studio our hearts sank. In contrast to the pomp and pageantry all over London, our studio, spartan to say the least, was a barren room in the BBC basement with makeshift tables, wobbly and creaky chairs, questionable technical equipment, and a technical crew not entirely dedicated to our needs.

We were working with BBC commentator Tom Fleming, who was doing the basic coverage along with BBC fashion commentator Barbara Griggs. Along the route and inside the church there were more than sixty BBC cameras, plus forty from Independent British TV. At 9:30 a.m. London time, we began broadcasting back to a pre-dawn Canada, but within seconds we had our first of numerous technological hitches. Barbara and I were supposed to open the program by voicing over a picture of exultant Londoners already jamming the parade route and then we were to go on camera in the studio for a minute or two of conversation before going back to "voice-over" the shots of the scenes of London.

But somewhere signals were crossed and while Barbara and I were peering intently at our respective TV monitors, shuffling through our notes and occasionally stretching, scratching, and yawning, we did what we thought was our "voice over." Later we discovered that for the first fifteen minutes, when we thought we had been off camera, we were in fact on camera, being seen live by millions of Canadians. We must have presented a most unusual sight, particularly since our TV monitors were at our sides and we therefore were looking at them, not at each other. We talked animatedly to each other about the pictures we were seeing, but which the audience wasn't.

A short time later, Barbara and I looked up to see the entire technical crew walking out of the studio. I couldn't understand what was happening until somebody explained they were simply changing shifts in the middle of the program, something we'd never experienced in Canada. That and a few other technological tribulations soon were overcome, however, although not before producer Arnold Amber was himself nearly overcome by his fury at the continuing mix-ups. Still, for once, he didn't have to keep barking into our earpieces "More energy!" because Barbara and I were fully energized by the excitement of the occasion itself.

Throughout the morning, we switched back and forth from our own commentary to the BBC or to Peter Mansbridge, standing just outside Buckingham Palace, Larry Stout, stationed at Canada House in Trafalgar Square, and Eve Savory, on the procession route at Temple Bar, the dividing line between Westminster and the city of London. As Barbara and I watched and commented, the glittering procession of gilded coaches and liveried escorts began the two-mile route from the Palace to St. Paul's with two million lusty-lunged, flag-waving royal enthusiasts cheering them on. The horses and coaches clattered down the narrow, straight, leafy Mall (which we were warned repeatedly to be sure to pronounce as "The Mell"), across Trafalgar Square where Margaret Trudeau and her three children watched from a window of Canada House, along the Strand and into Fleet Street, the so-called "Street of Ink" where New Brunswick Premier Richard Hatfield peered out of one of the upstairs windows of the *Daily Express*, and finally up Ludgate Hill to St. Paul's. Guests, of course, had arrived at the church well ahead of time, including the group, as we were told to describe them, of "minor royals," various earls, countesses, dukes, duchesses, marquises, and marchionesses who were, I suppose, in contrast to the "major royals," the Queen, the Queen's children, the Queen Mother, and the Duke of Edinburgh. Among the "foreign royals" were the Queen of Tonga, the Queen of Lesotho, the Prince of Nepal, three other queens, four kings, and scores of princes and princesses, dukes and duchesses. It was certainly the biggest display of royalty in a generation, if not two or three.

Barbara and I chatted about the spectacle, and with the help of our CBC colleagues we tried to put a Canadian perspective on the wedding. We talked of the Canadians on hand, including Prime Minister Trudeau, Governor General Schreyer, Dick Malone, Galen Weston, who played polo with Prince Charles when not selling his biscuits, and a handful of others, including a ninety-three-year-old World War I veteran.

We also talked about all the gifts Charles and Diana had received – some 3,000 of them – including such Canadian gifts as a four-poster antique bed from the Canadian government, a maple desk, fifty books by Canadian authors, "the world's largest wedding card" measuring 1.5 metres by 17 metres and signed by almost all the 45,000 residents of Welland, Ont., two Cowichan Indian sweaters from the government of B.C., a couple of deerskin jackets from Alberta, moosehide moccasins from Saskatchewan, and a painting of loons by wildlife artist Robert Bateman.

The biggest secret of the day was Lady Di's wedding dress, and we, along with just about every other reporter in London, had tried to pry loose the big secret of what the dress looked like. Nobody had succeeded, however, but we were promised a description before the ceremony. At 10:15 a.m. a breathless messenger ran into the studio with a news release marked in two-inch block letters: "EMBARGO. NOT TO BE PUBLISHED OR BROADCAST . . . BEFORE 10:35 A.M."

Being far from expert on wedding-dress styles, I quickly and gladly tossed it over to Barbara, who got word that the release time had been advanced to 10:15. So she went on immediately, talking about the ivory, pure silk taffeta and old lace, hand-embroidered gown with tiny mother-of-pearl sequins and pearls. It was made by a trendy young husband-and-wife designer team and, in a miracle of manufacturing accomplishment, $150 copies of the dress were in store windows on Regent and Oxford streets within hours. They had been copied from a "freeze frame" of the television pictures of the dress as Lady Di walked down the aisle.

When Lady Diana arrived at the church at 11:00 a.m., Barbara and I sat back and for more than an hour let the BBC commentary take over. We became just two of the millions of fascinated viewers as, among other things, we watched Lady Di mix up the full name of her husband, reversing the first two of his given names of Charles Philip Arthur George.

Then it was all over. The St. Paul's Cathedral bells rang out and the Prince of Wales and his bride got into their royal carriage for the trip back to Buckingham Palace to the joyously unrestrained cheers of the Londoners lining the way. We went off the air for a couple of hours while the royal wedding party sipped $50-a-bottle Bollinger champagne and sliced into their 220-pound, four-and-a-half-foot high, five-tier wedding cake, laced with rum and encrusted with fifty pounds of marzipan icing.

Then we were back on air, for without doubt what was the most boisterous moment of the entire day when the royal couple came out onto the balcony of Buckingham Palace to greet tens of thousands of cheering Londoners standing below them and hundreds of millions watching their television sets around the world. The noise was so great that Barbara and I could hardly hear Peter Mansbridge describe the moment from his post just across the street near the white marble statue of Queen Victoria.

Finally, Charles and Diana were off on their honeymoon in another royal carriage to which somebody had attached on the rear a hand-painted "Just Married" sign. They took a train to their Hampshire honeymoon retreat and Barbara and I signed off – to prepare a prime-time news special to be aired in a few hours in Canada, and I also had to lead off *The National*, being anchored that night by George Mc-Lean, with a report on the wedding. Fourteen tense and exciting hours after we'd first arrived at the BBC studios it was over, but I was still flying on adrenalin. Later, when I looked back over my notes and scripts, I felt I had been overly enthusiastic, with such phrases as "A truly thrilling moment in history"; "What a majestic ceremony it was"; "A day simply never to be forgotten ... a day of majesty, of romance, of history." Finally, as I signed off *The National* on the wedding night, I said, "Watching the culmination of this royal love story here in London, you just could not resist the overwhelming sense of pride and joy sweeping the country."

Perhaps fed up with all the usual news menu of strikes, recessions, terrorists, scandals, crimes, and disasters, I had overly luxuriated in a rare, truly happy story.

The next time I saw Prince Charles and Lady Di was not on a TV monitor in a BBC studio but in person two years later when they came to Ottawa. On a warm, June evening, Prime Minister Trudeau invited about 200 people to share grilled beefsteak, French fries, mushrooms, and champagne with "Chuck and Di" out at Mackenzie King's old retreat of Kingsmere. Lorraine and I flew up from Toronto with Gordon Pinsent and his wife Charmion King. We ate and drank handsomely and gossiped with the other guests on the sunlit grass, and Lorraine talked to Lady Di about their children. The royal couple smiled their way through the crowd and gnawed delicately on the barbecued beef, with Diana ever smiling shyly and glancing down, seeming to stoop to avoid looking so tall.

But as wedding week in London drew to its glittering close that event was off in the future. More immediate concerns awaited me and Barbara Frum on our return to Toronto. Soon she and I would be partners in one of the most daring experiments in Canadian television history, the fulfilment of a long-time dream of mine: the launch of a nightly prime-time hour of television journalism.

6 *A NEW HOUR*

I had been sitting behind the anchor desk of *The National* for a year and a half when Mike Daigneault, my one-time deputy and former chief news editor, made the announcement that *The National* would move to 10:00 p.m. to be followed by a hard-hitting current affairs magazine program of interviews, documentaries, and commentary. (Daigneault had recently moved back to Toronto after a stint as regional director of Quebec English broadcasting.) It was a dream come true for me, one of the most important long-term goals I'd set myself back in 1969 when I took on the job Mike now had as director of News and Current Affairs. In one way or another I'd been trying to sell the idea for more than a decade. In 1975, Patrick Watson and award-winning Ottawa producer Cam Graham developed a program idea for a Monday-through-Friday prime-time newsmagazine using satellites and mobile ground stations to do instant reports on news developments and interviews with newsmakers in Canada and around the world. It was exciting, expensive, and experimental, using the space-age technology for both breaking and backgrounding the news.

"But it's just too damn expensive," vice-president Don MacPherson had finally told me. "We simply can't do it."

Now it was five years later and this time the "can't do" had become "will do." In a way I envied Mike and his success in finally achieving what so many of us had tried to bring about for so long. But at least I could take satisfaction in my own efforts over the past decade to help make it happen, and now I would be part of the group actually putting it together and also fronting the new *National* at 10:00 p.m.

The move to prime time was an enormous risk, unquestionably the

208

biggest program gamble in CBC history. But after years of arguing, the CBC brass finally had been persuaded to bet the whole future of the CBC on one program throw of the dice. It would put an hour of CBC journalism smack against the biggest and best made-in-Hollywood mass-appeal TV shows on the other channels in prime time. But the hope and the hype was that we would substantially increase the number of people now watching *The National* at 11:00 p.m. – about 1.3 million Canadians out of a total 4.2 million watching TV at that time, or more than a quarter of the audience. Our research showed that 7.5 million people were watching at 10:00 p.m. – nearly double – so even if we lost audience share our total numbers should still go up. At least that was the sales pitch.

I wasn't so sure. In fact, I thought we would actually lose audience initially in face of the cut-throat competition from popular American shows on CTV and the other channels at ten, but that in a year or two our ratings would climb to 1.5 million and maybe more as the 10:00 p.m. *National* became a TV fixture. The CBC audience research department was similarly doubtful. "The historical precedents . . . are not good," it had advised in an extensive report outlining optimum and minimum models, audience flow, hypotheses, lead-ins, and lead-outs. "[T]he apparently limited appetite for news among young people, 2-34 years, negates at least part of the advantages of the higher overall viewing levels since a disproportionately high component of the increase comes from this age group."

But even before Daigneault made his announcement the cynics and sceptics outside the CBC were betting on failure. The possibility of moving the news to 10:00 p.m. had been discussed publicly by CBC executives for a year and a half and it had become an issue in the broadcasting industry. "In prime time, people want to escape the troubles of the day," an advertising executive told me. "The last thing they want is to hear it all again." His was the conventional wisdom of the day: one hour of prime-time journalism every weeknight was a noble cause that simply wouldn't work. We were betting the other way. We hoped Canadians, who are "infomaniacs" at heart, were prepared to engage the day in prime time and not just escape it. That was our gamble, our leap of faith. If we failed, not only would a lot of reputations and jobs be lost, but audiences and commercial revenue would plunge, criticism would grow louder, and the government might well start thinking the CBC wasn't worth the cost to the public.

No major U.S. network had dared such a move of news to prime time for fear of audience and commercial revenue loss. The American networks had flirted with prime-time news but never made the move.

There had been regularly scheduled newscasts in near prime time: at 7:30 p.m. on CBS in 1948, and at 7:45 p.m. on NBC the next year. But in 1957-58 the network news moved to 6:30, and in 1963, NBC and CBS moved to a half hour of news, including six minutes of commercials. The move away from near prime time was dictated by the commercial reality that an entertainment show could make much more money than news at the later time. In 1976, ABC talked of making the news an hour in length and the news departments of CBS and NBC were thinking along similar lines. But the commercial facts of life combined with the objections of forceful affiliates killed the idea. At the time, Donald McGannon, president of the Westinghouse group of network-affiliated stations, was an exception. He suggested the networks try a weeknight hour of journalism starting at 9:00 p.m. But the networks bowed to the pressure of the large majority of their affiliates and ignored the idea. A couple of decades later, Grant Tinker, chairman of NBC, picked up the thought again, saying it's "an idea whose time has come." But it never did, although some network officials still talk about it.

In Britain, however, the TV newscasts had always been in prime time, at first with both the BBC and the private network at about 9:00 p.m., but in 1967 the private network, ITV, expanded its thirteen-minute newscast produced by its news arm, ITN, to half an hour and placed it at ten o'clock. BBC then lengthened its news to about half an hour at nine. Over the years there had been discussion at both British networks about a daily prime-time journalistic program in addition to the news, but nothing ever came of the idea. Canadian private networks, given their commercial preoccupations, certainly didn't like the idea, although in its early years Global tried out news at ten and did well in audience terms but quickly moved to eleven because more money could be made with an American show at the earlier hour. A few independent local stations also put their news at 10:00. But the Global network's audience response was the most encouraging for us.

I had never felt the real reason for going to 10:00 p.m. was to add audience tonnage for the news, although that would be a wonderful bonus. The most important rationale was that the new time would offer an alternative to all the escapist couch-potato entertainment programming on the other channels. And I thought Mike Daigneault struck exactly the right note as he talked with reporters after releasing the announcement. "We're the public broadcasting network," he said, "and if we're going to properly service our viewers, then we should provide our most important program at a time when most of them are awake."

In his public comments Mike focused on *The National* – the most watched news program in Canada – and at least momentarily downplayed what would follow. He was using the established credibility of *The National* as the lever to open up the 10:00 to 11:00 p.m. time period, a commercial gold mine we could never have broken open for a nightly Current Affairs program alone. The lustre of *The National* and its recognition as "the CBC's most important service," as the CBC now boasted, publicly provided the weight that could sell the idea to the public, the media, and any doubting Thomases within the CBC itself.

After a decade of trench warfare the CBC brass had finally recognized that our journalism was good, popular, and the number-one priority for the Corporation. Mike Daigneault had fought many of the early battles with me when I had been director of News and Current Affairs, and Denny Harvey and Peter Herrndorf had been key figures as well. But it was now Herrndorf who became the central player. And once again, all his bureaucratic skills and forcefulness were needed. His taste for current affairs programming had been whetted when he ran that area for me before going to Ottawa as the CBC vice-president for Planning, and he had been lusting to get back to the program action at the network. Shortly after I took over as anchor of *The National* in late 1978, Peter returned from head office to work as deputy to Don MacPherson, vice-president of English-language radio and TV, and, in effect, the tsar of CBC programming. As Don's deputy, Herrndorf became the driving force behind the idea of an early *National* and a current affairs program to follow. He basically wanted to shake up the CBC schedule, and he knew starting *The National* in prime time would force a re-evaluation of everything else we did.

Methodically plotting his TV schedule revolution as he had earlier planned the birth of *Ninety Minutes Live*, Herrndorf appointed a "News Scheduling Study," which was nicknamed "the Three Wise Men" for the three senior program executives who conducted it. They were: Bill Morgan, the TV network program director; Vince Carlin, executive producer of the CBC Montreal local news program; and Mark Starowicz, executive producer of the highly successful CBC radio program *Sunday Morning* and, previously, executive producer of *As It Happens*. Their staff assistance was provided by Bruce McKay, assistant TV network program director. Their job was to examine the possibility of an earlier *National* followed by a current affairs program. So they holed up in a downtown Toronto hotel – The Four Seasons – sitting in a small conference room for thirty-five twelve- to fourteen-hour days through the summer of 1979. They sat around a green felt cloth-covered table and argued and wrote with the hotel room phone ringing constantly and advisers and researchers shuttling in and out all day and night with their reports.

Even before one word of the report was written, it was clear that the dice were loaded in favour of a news and current affairs prime-time program. The Three Wise Men all had journalistic backgrounds, and when their report was complete it spelled out a detailed recommendation for an earlier *National*. But they recognized the dangers of moving the nightly newscast, which for nearly three decades – through all the years of Larry Henderson, Earl Cameron, Stanley Burke, Lloyd Robertson, Peter Kent, and myself – had been at 11:00 p.m. "Moving *The National* is a major risk and still a leap of faith," they said in their 300-page report, which was submitted to Herrndorf on August 3, 1979. They also recommended that *The National* be followed by a current affairs program to expand on and explore the principal news events of the day.

By the fall of 1979, Don MacPherson had left to become president of a TV production company working through Global TV and Herrndorf took his place running English radio and TV. With Peter in charge and publicly giving newspaper interviews hardening his support for a 10:00 p.m. *National*, over in the newsroom our hopes soared. There was still opposition, however, as reflected by columnist Ron Base in *The Toronto Star*. Referring to Herrndorf's public comments on an earlier *National*, he wrote, ". . . those viewers [at 10 p.m.] are eagerly tuned into B.J. and The Bear. Suddenly to provide them with news in the same prime-time period and I'm willing to bet large sums of money that they stay eagerly tuned to B.J. and The Bear."

The Toronto *Globe and Mail* editorially took the same approach in its warning: "The implications of moving *The National* are profound and the safest bet to make is that it simply won't happen. It would take years to change such a deep-seated viewer habit as watching the news at 11:00 p.m. and if the CBC does change *The National*'s time slot, it will face a loss of audience and a loss of revenue. The network can't afford either." A lot of people still thought that, and as the move toward a 10:00 p.m. *National* gained momentum the opponents, both internal and external, belatedly realized that long-sought News Service dream was becoming an ominously real possibility.

The CBC commercial sales people were apprehensive about an earlier *National* because they feared it would mean as much as $6 million less revenue for the CBC with the unsponsored *National* soaking up a prime-time slot. The private affiliated stations were dead set against it because they were convinced their commercial revenue would sink with the smaller audience they foresaw with prime-time news. The CBC plant people, who organize and provide the technical studios and facilities, were uneasy at best because they feared the change would cause extraordinary havoc and complications in scheduling technical crews and would bring new demands for facilities they didn't have. And there were others in the internal power plays of the CBC who were against the idea because they felt a prime-time *National* would give the News Service too much clout. If *The National* and a current affairs program were scheduled every weeknight from 10:00 to 11:00 p.m., it meant some other programs would have to go and still others would face the stark reality that *The National* and the new current affairs program would soak up budgets, studio time, facilities, and, most of all, the attention of the senior executives and the public. With apprehensive producers, a reluctant plant, unhappy affiliates, a sceptical media, and worried financial officers, it meant Herrndorf still faced a tough job to make it all happen.

But he was unpersuaded and undismayed at the opposition of the apocalypticians, and through the early winter of 1980 he concentrated with bull-headed determination on getting approval for the project from president Al Johnson and the Board of Directors. The president and the Board were hesitant, however, because they realized the risks involved. Johnson also worried about there being too much journalism in prime-time already, with successful programs like *the fifth estate*, *Marketplace*, *Man Alive*, and *Newsmagazine*.

Another critical reason for the delay was Al Johnson's commitment to the idea of a second CBC-TV service – CBC-2. Herrndorf kept telling the Three Wise Men that there were "some problems" with their prime-time recommendation, but he provided no details. The "problems" were centred on the CBC president's desire to give priority to planning for CBC-2. Herrndorf could not ignore this presidential preference and kept stalling on any detailed planning for the 10 p.m. proposal. In fact, in December, 1979, four months after receiving the proposal, Herrndorf assigned Bill Morgan and Bruce McKay to work on CBC-2. The CBC was preparing an application to the broadcast regulatory agency, the CRTC, to seek authority to launch the second TV service. In January, 1980, Morgan and McKay began working on CBC-2, feeling the chances for the 10 p.m. proposal were slipping away.

They and their colleagues Mark Starowicz and Vince Carlin grew frustrated at the lack of substantial response to the 10 p.m. proposal and the delay was dubbed "the long silence." Originally they had been supposed to reconvene in September to further refine their proposal, but the reconvening never took place. Starowicz later said, "I thought it was all over.... I was ready to walk away."

None of the key decision-makers wanted to kill the idea of a daily prime-time *National* and current affairs program, however, even though the feeling at the Ottawa CBC headquarters was that CBC could not afford to do both CBC-2 and the prime-time hour. At this time, Herrndorf was telling his close associates that chances for the 10 p.m. proposal going ahead were "less than 50 per cent." Nevertheless, in quiet lunches and dinners with CBC Board members and other corporate decision-makers, Herrndorf kept the idea alive. At his compelling best, pulling every nationalistic heart string he could, Herrndorf began gaining support. Through the winter the CBC Board heard three different presentations from him and gradually became excited by the prospects he sketched. His argument was that CBC needed the prime-time hour to secure the immediate future of the corporation in providing a unique service – "an engine of reform," he called it – while CBC-2 was needed to ensure the CBC's long-term future. Besides, he argued, the cost of the prime-time hour could be handled without incremental funding. The financial projections offered were not overburdened with extensive detail or minute precision but they seemed to support that conclusion, and the debate over CBC-2 versus 10 p.m. was resolved with the feeling that both could indeed be done. (The CBC proceeded with its CBC-2 application, but a year later, in May, 1981, the CRTC turned down the application and the competition for resources between CBC-2 and 10 p.m. never arose.)

On March 13, 1980, after hearing the last presentation by Herrndorf (at which Starowicz made a brief appearance), Board member Dan Hays, a Calgary lawyer, said, "This is a terrific idea," and in an informal vote the Board said "Go!" It had been nine months since Herrndorf had launched his innocent-sounding "News Scheduling Study." The decision was made public by News and Current Affairs director Mike Daigneault two weeks later when he issued a press release and met the newsroom staff. "We've got to try some bold moves," Johnson said, as part of the announcement that *The National* would move to 10:00 p.m. as of January, 1981, nine months away. "Other changes in the evening program schedule are being developed in light of the decision to move the newscast earlier," the announcement said.

"Other changes" recommended in the report were accepted in principle and being evaluated in detail. They essentially sought to remake the face of CBC prime time. As well as *The National* at ten followed by a current affairs program, there would be one-minute news breaks at eight and nine, a four- or five-minute news recap at eleven, and from 11:05 to 11:30 a mix of local and network journalism. The 10:00- 11:30 period would thus become ninety minutes of journalism. All together, the changes would make the CBC "*the* information network as well as *an* entertainment network."

In developing their radical proposal for a prime-time journalistic "strip," Morgan, Carlin, and Starowicz had said, "This program should become, in a short time, the major marketplace of ideas and analysis in the country." As temporary names that simply described their concept, they variously called the new prime-time current affairs program "The Daily Journal," "The Nation's Journal," and simply "The Journal." For months Herrndorf kept asking Starowicz to confirm that "The Journal" was only a working title and that a proper name would soon be found. Starowicz and his colleagues always said "Yes," but they kept coming back to their working title. Eventually, the name *The Journal* stuck.

As expected, the local CBC stations objected to the proposal for the 11:00 to 11:30 p.m. local and network mix, arguing that it intruded into their local time. Al Johnson also was reluctant about the post-eleven proposal. Ultimately, its only vestige was a five-minute national news update at eleven. The update was important to us because it not only back-ended *The National* and *The Journal*, but more significantly, it gave us a competitive position opposite *CTV News* at 11:00 p.m. We didn't want to leave the national news field clear to CTV at that time. The "news break" idea also was eventually watered down to one thirty-second news break at eight, sometimes lengthened to one minute.

The "News Scheduling Study" had also suggested that when there was a heavy news night, *The National* could be extended beyond its normal time, thereby cutting into *The Journal*. It was a good idea, providing flexibility in the event a major story was breaking in Ottawa, Washington, or elsewhere, and letting the importance of the day's news dictate the length of *The National* instead of rigid scheduling. But in the end it never happened. The primary reason was a reluctance by *Journal* producers to give up any air time. So *The National* was locked into its allocated time no matter how big a news night it was. It was a case of territorial prerogative overwhelming editorial logic.

To be sure, there had been a long history of conflict between the News and Current Affairs areas, dating back to *Weekend*, the *Seven Days* affair, and beyond. Although much progress had been made in minimizing if not eliminating it, there was now a renewal of hostilities. The reasons were several. First, with the advent of *The Journal*, the

News Service specials unit would be severely reduced in the number of news specials it would produce. Second, the report had proposed that some existing elements of *The National*, such as the three- to four-minute special reports, be moved to *The Journal*. These special reports, however, were to be done at least in part by *The National's* reporters. Much more disquieting, this proposal assumed a *National* shorter than the current twenty-five minutes, but "If no efficient or practical way can be found to integrate elements of *The National* into *The Journal* we suggest that *The National* maintain its current length."

Apart from these two concerns, the News Service would lose *Newsmagazine*, the pioneering veteran of electronic journalism of three decades. To offset some of the News Service apprehension, the plan was to involve News reporters and correspondents in preparing items for *The Journal*. This, in fact, did come to pass.

The single issue that exploded newsroom emotions, and most particularly mine, was the proposed reduction in length of *The National*. Within minutes of the release of his March 27 announcement of the 10:00 p.m. start for *The National*, Daigneault came over to the newsroom to explain his plans. As the reporters, editors, producers, copy clerks, and office staff stood around the newsroom desks, Mike repeated his announcement and in the process clearly indicated *The National* would be chopped back from twenty-five minutes to twenty. Angry questions immediately erupted – one producer said it was "a kick in the ass for news" – and for seventy minutes the mood of the News staff went from apprehension to full-scale rage as Mike sought to explain his rationale. But the News people would have none of it, feeling they had been betrayed. Mike's own anger at this dyspeptic response rose as he stood at the side of the newsroom, tall and seeming even more gaunt and brusque than normal. Almost before our eyes he seemed to age beyond his forty years and his voice grew tighter and higher and his answers more clipped. When it was over, there was a red glow of anger in his cheeks as he left in a fury. "I'd never seen Mike so steamed up as when he came back from that meeting," Herrndorf later said.

The entire news staff was equally enraged, perhaps more united on this issue than they'd ever been on anything. To me, it was a simply intolerable cutback and a reversal of everything I'd fought for, and I left the meeting boiling. I hadn't taken on the anchor job in order to endure a shorter newscast. Within hours, in a reprise of my bureaucratic incarnation, I banged out a five-page memo to Mike and to Peter Herrndorf, saying such a cutback of *The National* was a flagrant violation of public commitments. I recited the public statements of Al Johnson pledging to the CRTC and to Parliament a longer *National* as well as an earlier one, and I noted an earlier report, co-authored by Herrndorf himself, urging more, not less, time for *The National*. The idea of reducing its length, I wrote, was simply incomprehensible and an insult to CBC journalists. *The National* was the basic information foundation for all our other journalistic programs. To weaken that foundation put at peril everything we did. A shorter program, I concluded in my note to Peter and Mike, "is a contemptuous rejection of our journalistic responsibility quite simply painful beyond articulation . . . and for me personally, it is not only insulting but deeply wounding."

A few days later, 120 members of the News Service, including myself, David Halton, Mike Duffy, and the entire senior team responsible for *The National*, sent a note to Peter and Mike. Less personal and less emotional than my memo, it laid out facts and figures that demonstrated the damage a shorter *National* would cause, including a warning of resignation by those "who have no intention of remaining in their positions while *The National* is undermined by CBC management."

Mike Daigneault was hurt and angry at the intensity of the newsroom response, and particularly mine. I couldn't really blame him because I knew the kinds of pressures he was under, having been there myself. He was in an impossible situation. He, in fact, never answered my memo except to tell me later with a rueful smile, "You sure were mad as hell!"

In face of the withering News Service rage, Mike began saying the shorter *National* was "only an option" and that he was "flexible" on the timing. He also faced rage from the Current Affairs side, where there were also threats of resignation if their program was cut back to satisfy *The National*. The decision was put on hold while "Bay Street," as the network headquarters was called, waited to see if the anger would die down. It didn't, and a couple of months later the newsroom sent another memo to Herrndorf and Daigneault urging no cutback in *The National*, harking back to the battles of the News Service and the program *This Hour Has Seven Days*.

Through the summer of 1980, into the fall, and on into the winter, as we raced against time to organize the new hour, I kept checking with Mike and Peter about the length of *The National*. "We'll let you know," they kept saying.

The excitement and agitation over the new program plans during the previous months had taken place amid a frenetic news period during which I anchored the 1980 federal election that returned Pierre Trudeau to power and the Quebec referendum vote to reject separatism. I also flew to Venice to cover the Economic Summit and spent time at the American presidential nominating conventions in Detroit and New York. The heavy run of news underlined my concern about any cutback in time for *The National*.

Finally, a year after the newsroom confrontation, the question of length was decided in a Solomon-like judgement. Mike announced he would split the difference with a slight edge to *The Journal*. *The National* would become twenty-two minutes in length, three minutes shorter but still two minutes longer than it would have been without the protest. This may sound like small potatoes, but an extra couple of minutes makes a significant difference not only in the amount of additional news possible, but in the rhythm and pacing of the program. Inevitably, a five-minute cutback would have meant that some of the longer, more thoughtful reports would disappear and reports from Canada's smaller centres would have been crowded out.

I was still angry at the adjusted cutback, but at least we'd salvaged something. So I and my newsroom colleagues grumpily acquiesced. *The Journal* forces, of course, felt they had been betrayed. Everybody hated the compromise, but everybody was prepared to tolerate it. However, it was a situation that seemed likely to lead to more problems as the preparations for the new hour progressed.

There was other unhappiness in the Current Affairs area. Some producers seethed at the loss of air time, money, and attention that was being soaked up by *The Journal*. "They're pumping money into it and bleeding everything else," one producer said. *The Journal* cost would run about $8.5 million a year, relatively modest for a nightly prime-time program, but tempers flared nonetheless. Programs such as *Ombudsman* and *The Watson Report* were axed to make room in the TV schedule, and *the fifth estate* worried the new show might shanghai its program rationale. At the same time every other show blamed the priority being given to *The Journal* for everything they didn't get, from more money to more resources. This resentment was reinforced by a feeling among Current Affairs traditionalists that *The Journal* would be "too newsy" and be more concerned with immediacy than with analysis.

In the early summer of 1980 while the battle was still raging over the length of *The National*, Daigneault made two key appointments that would ultimately determine the fate of the hour. Earlier, he had named Vince Carlin as chief news editor to replace Cliff Lonsdale, who had gone to CBC London to help run our European operations.

Now he and Herrndorf wanted to appoint Bill Morgan to head all Current Affairs programming, including *The Journal*, a job I'd tried to get him to take several years earlier. Bill was still reluctant, but Herrndorf intensified his persuasion, including an ardent plea as they strolled in the springtime sun on the roof of an exhibition hall in Cannes where both were attending a TV festival. Bill finally agreed; in his new role he would be the senior operational figure in shaping *The Journal* and fighting the boardroom battles for resources, money, and people. The forty-year-old Morgan had been the network program director and before that the director of TV at CBC Winnipeg. A thin, quietly hard-driving Australian with a dry wit who began professional life as a teacher, he had been the editorial page editor of the *Brandon Sun* before running local CBC radio and TV current affairs programming in Winnipeg.

The other appointment Daigneault announced was Mark Starowicz, the third of the Three Wise Men. Mark was a handsome thirty-five-year-old radio producer whom everyone called a "whiz kid." He had been running *As It Happens* and *Sunday Morning*. He was named as head of *The Journal*, an appointment many a veteran TV producer regarded dubiously since Starowicz didn't know a damn thing about television at the time. He'll put on, said one critic, "the greatest radio show ever seen on television." His appointment also evoked memories of the *Ninety Minutes Live* failure, where Alex Frame and Peter Gzowski had not translated their radio success to television.

Mark was born in England, raised in Argentina, and came to Montreal with his Polish parents at age seven not knowing a word of English. His family had a Polish military tradition and his mother had fought in the Warsaw underground in World War II. At McGill University in the 1960s he was an articulate, rabble-rousing student rebel. When not studying European and Chinese history, he was news director of Radio McGill and later ran the campus newspaper. He also worked nights and summers for the *Montreal Gazette* and after graduation for *The Toronto Star* before joining CBC Radio in 1970 at age twenty-four. By now he had given up his blue jeans in favour of conservative three-piece suits, but he remained an aggressive leader among his radio colleagues. A "wunderkind" to some, but an "enfant terrible" to others, Starowicz was both admired and feared. He was known to be audacious, occasionally outrageous in his comments and demands, and always determined. He thus had all the right qualifications to run what would become the most talked-about program on Canadian television.

Significantly, with the appointments of Morgan, Starowicz, and

Carlin, all of the Three Wise Men were now in a position to implement what they had recommended. Herrndorf's controlling hand could clearly be seen. He was taking no chances.

While revealing the new appointments Daigneault had one more announcement to make, and that was that the start of *The National* at ten would be delayed from January to September of 1981. The reason for the eight-month delay was that the project was proving a lot more technologically complicated than management had assumed. A major upgrading of outdated studio facilities was necessary, including major reconstruction of the studio *The Journal* would use and installation of new equipment, such as videotape recording facilities and microwave links to enable live satellite programming from some centres of the country. It also would take months to train production personnel to use the new state-of-the-art equipment. In fact, the earlier announcement of a January start had been wildly and impossibly optimistic. The network didn't really look at the facilities demand until after the Board go-ahead. As Morgan and Starowicz began planning for *The Journal*, Herrndorf was suddenly plunged into crisis when he found the capital expenditures for the prime-time hour had been underestimated by $3 million. The last thing in the world he wanted to do was to go back to the Board of Directors now to ask for more money. But he did, and after what he later described as "an extraordinarily unpleasant night" meeting with the Board, Herrndorf got his extra $3 million. In mid-June, Bruce McKay signed on the *Journal* staff and began developing detailed planning for *The Journal*.

There was only one more key appointment to be made before the new *National* and *Journal* leadership would be complete. Just about the time Morgan and Starowicz took over their new posts, Trina McQueen, who had brought me into *The National*'s anchor chair, left her executive producer job in News to become program director of the TV network. Into her place stepped Tony Burman, an aggressive, hyperactive, and ferociously determined thirty-three-year-old who had formerly worked for the *Montreal Star* and CBC in Montreal and who had been *The National*'s assignment editor and lineup editor. For the previous fifteen months, he had been the program producer of *The National*. Starowicz and Burman would benefit enormously in their new responsibilities in the prime-time hour by the fact that they had worked together before. They had known each other in Montreal as students when Starowicz was editor of the McGill paper and Burman was editor of the *Loyola News*. Burman had worked at the *Montreal Star* while Starowicz worked at the *Gazette*, and when Mark was producing his CBC radio shows, Tony occasionally provided items for them from Montreal.

As the man who ran *The National*, Burman inherited a large news staff, but by mid-summer of 1980 Starowicz had only about a dozen people working with him – "A bunch of pups . . . a sad and sorry little group," he later recalled. They were apprehensive about the enormous job before them and at their first full staff meeting in August in a boardroom borrowed from the Drama area, new Current Affairs head Bill Morgan looked around the table, softly smiled, and said, "Welcome to the first meeting of *The Journal*. In ten years, 500 people will claim to have been in this room." Bill won their hearts and boosted their morale, then went out of the boardroom to launch his battles with "Bay Street" as the master strategist of *The Journal*.

Starowicz flew out to Vancouver at about this time to talk with Alex Frame about his *Ninety Minutes Live* experience. Alex was now director of television in Vancouver and he and Mark had a long, late-night meeting at a Vancouver airport bar. Puffing a cigarette, Alex said something about the earlier experience that Mark never forgot: "Nothing got on the air the way it left my head. . . . Find out exactly what you want to do and then stick to it." Taking that warning to heart, Starowicz flew back to Toronto.

With Bill Morgan and Vince Carlin in the executive jobs and Starowicz and Burman on the front line, the stage was set to begin the most daring change in Canadian television history. Whether it would work depended on the creative leadership of Starowicz and Burman, the former a TV neophyte. At first sight the two were decidedly different: Burman, ever in jeans and sports shirt, Starowicz wearing his three-piece suits; Burman loud-voiced and excited, Starowicz always talking in a growl that betrayed little emotion. But both had driving energy, were experienced journalists skilled at bureaucratic infighting, shared a single-minded determination to succeed, and knew how to inspire their co-workers. Most important of all, they realized the value of working as a team. Each warned his staff against thinking of the other program as "the enemy," an attitude that still lingered among some junior and senior colleagues. And no wonder, given the fight already over the length of *The National*, the killing of *Newsmagazine* to make room for *The Journal*, and the near-disappearance of prime-time news specials.

There had been efforts in the past to blend programs of the News Service and Current Affairs. None had ever been a real success. Now sharing the same hour, both sides feared we would have two news programs within the same time period scrambling for the same stories, interviews, facilities, money, reporters, editors, and producers, but that style and policies would be fundamentally different. The degree of concern was heightened by the incredibly high stakes of this calculated program gamble. As much as the president, vice-presidents, and area heads might exhort the News and Current Affairs troops to work smoothly together, it really all depended on the leadership of Starowicz and Burman.

"No marriage was made in Heaven and this is no exception," Burman announced as he began detailed planning. "National TV News and Current Affairs are two separate and traditionally competitive departments and the potential for problems is limitless." To minimize the problems, in the late fall of 1980 the two executive producers started meeting together regularly. Mark wanted to use *The National*'s reporters for documentaries from time to time and Tony agreed, provided *The Journal* picked up the cost of any coverage off of the reporters' normal beats. They also agreed *The Journal* would not do news reports and *The National* would not do mini-documentaries. *The National* would be reportorial, *The Journal* analytical. Their objective was to make the two partners in the 10:00-to-11:00 time period complementary and reinforcing. It's an approach that lasted.

"I think we'll find that both units see themselves as natural allies," Burman told his staff after one five-hour session with Starowicz. "The futures of both our shows are linked together. We on *The National* have a direct stake in the success of *The Journal*. They have a direct stake in our success. The challenge that faces us both is to ensure that our operations, our attitudes, and our procedures work with this fact in mind."

That was exactly the kind of attitude Herrndorf wanted to hear since he saw the hour as a single program with two discrete but co-ordinated sections rather than as two totally separate programs overlapping each other. Nonetheless, Herrndorf's heart was with *The Journal*. *The National* already existed and had its own staff and approach. *The Journal* would be something totally new that could be moulded in the way he sought and staffed with people he favoured. But the program did not become Herrndorf's "executive sandbox," as Starowicz had initially feared. "He didn't really involve himself that much," Mark later said, although given Herrndorf's Current Affairs background Herrndorf felt more comfortable with producers from that area than with the more hard-nosed News staff. As a result, it was a usual occurrence to see him talking with *Journal* people and rare to see him talking with News people. "They were social visits," said

Morgan who, like Starowicz, did not want Herrndorf interfering professionally. But Herrndorf recognized the critical importance of *The National* at ten to the success of the program that followed. Nobody was going to tune in halfway through the hour.

In terms of the focus of corporate and media attention, *The Journal* was teacher's pet while *The National* was the low-profile stepsister. *The National* got precious little money for any new technology – "Use your imagination," network boss Norn Garriock had told us at one meeting where we pleaded for additional funding. But we almost didn't mind. The main thing was that we in the News Service were fulfilling our long-time dream of a prime-time *National*. Along the way we could at least pick up some better technical equipment by riding along on the crest of *The Journal*'s wave. Besides, we were sufficiently, even arrogantly, confident we could quietly pull off a major surprise with a new style and dash for the old Mother Hubbard *National*, a change that would have made Earl Cameron squirm.

Pulling it off, however, seemed a daunting challenge as 1981 began. It was "Get Ready Year" as we planned for a September 14 start. Now the CBC's bureaucracy and its technical bosses began to groan under the aggressive, exasperated pushing and shoving of Starowicz and Burman. Everything was running late as we nearly drowned in memos and meetings. Literally thousands of decisions were necessary, from colours for *National* and *Journal* sets to the design of the sets, whether there should be phones, typewriters, and teletypes on the studio floor, and the kinds of space-age technological equipment to buy. There were people to hire and the production and editorial style for the new hour to develop. As winter progressed, *The Journal* was rapidly falling far behind schedule in the installation of telephones and video lines, the purchase of desks, chairs, typewriters, and TV monitors. In February, *The Journal* didn't even have office space while arguments raged over where it should be located. The location was supposed to have been settled the previous November. "Frankly," Starowicz groaned, "it raises the horrible spectre of running this program out of twenty hotel rooms." But as winter turned to spring, space finally was found a half block from the TV building where the studios were located and where the *National* offices were. Starowicz and his colleagues moved in in May, still angry at the five-month delay. Those responsible "should be shot," he said.

Through intense eighteen-hour work days, drinking endless coffees and chain-smoking cigarettes, Starowicz juggled the administrative, technical, and creative emergencies while trying to shape *The Journal* with his key colleagues: Richard Bronstein, brought over from CBC

Radio, who concentrated on the editorial approach; and Bruce McKay, the only one of the three who knew television and its technology, who worked on ways to use the latest technological "toys" to bring drama, immediacy, and a "You Are There" feeling to the program. Mark called the whole process "editorial civil engineering."

There would be three basic elements in *The Journal*, they decided: first, the interview, which would be 60 per cent of the program; second, the pocket documentaries and field reports, which would carry on the tradition of *Newsmagazine* and take up 30 per cent of the program; and third, "The Journal Diary," comprising "back of the book" features in business, sports, arts, entertainment, science, and medicine in five- to six-minute reports.

Their concept married the styles of such programs as the old Edward R. Murrow *See It Now* on CBS, the ABC *Nightline* interview show with Ted Koppel, and the PBS *MacNeil-Lehrer Report* with the documentary style of the CBC's *Newsmagazine*. To this mix it added its own columns, features, and commentary ideas and wound up with something entirely new. In combination with *The National* this provided an hour of prime-time journalism unique in the world of television.

As spring arrived more staff began joining *The Journal*. If the program was going on the air in September, reporters and producers needed to be in the field gathering material within a couple of months to build up a bank of documentaries. Starowicz favoured young overachievers who would happily work sixty- and seventy-hour weeks at modest pay and who were attracted by the excitement of this high-profile TV adventure. "Okay, folks," Mark would tell potential staffers, "we're in the middle of a war here. Don't come to *The Journal* unless you're willing to fight." One of the first people he hired was my *National* anchor predecessor, Peter Kent, who'd gone off to South Africa for CBC News after his departure from *The National* in the fall of 1978. Shortly after, he had left CBC to join NBC in Johannesburg and now was coming back again to CBC as a producer/journalist for *The Journal*. Peter Jennings was also approached. In 1981 he was the roving chief correspondent for ABC, based in London. But Herrndorf, who made the approach, found him ambivalent and the overture wasn't pursued. Another Canadian considered as a possibility was Robert MacNeil of the *MacNeil-Lehrer Report*. Although he liked the program idea, he wouldn't leave PBS.

As the clock kept ticking for the September launch, attention was concentrated on who would host *The Journal*. Mark had decided the program would have two hosts: one to be the principal interviewer, the other to handle the continuity, introductions, and setups and act as a secondary interviewer. "We want a man/woman team," he said. Patrick Watson and Barbara Frum were two potential hosts who leapt to many minds, but I never thought the chemistry between them would work under the hosting plans. One would never have played second fiddle to the other.

Two study groups were set up, one the Host Committee and the other the Co-Host Committee, and Barbara was the unanimous choice for the principal host while the other committee decided on Mary Lou Finlay, then the co-host and co-producer of CTV's popular prime-time consumer show, *Live It Up*. "What are we going to do now?" Starowicz asked when faced with the recommendations for two women as hosts for *The Journal*. Then, slightly defiantly, he said, "Why the hell not!" In the choices, he certainly couldn't be accused of going for Barbie doll "twinkies."

Both women had impeccable journalistic credentials. Barbara, who had worked with Mark for years when he was executive producer of *As It Happens*, was the first one approached. At forty-four, she was both eager and uneasy: eager about the new challenge and responsibility the job held, but uneasy about the twelve-hour days, the pressures, and the intensity it would demand. She was also reluctant to leave her "perfect niche," as she described *As It Happens*. Overall, though, Barbara was worried about TV technology overwhelming editorial substance in the new program. She wavered back and forth for weeks, and in what Mark thought would be a clinching argument he took her into the half-finished *Journal* studio. But all the lights, cameras, monitors, and space-age technology she saw only reinforced her uneasiness. "That set us back a month," he later said.

Starowicz told her she would only have to work for a couple of hours in the afternoon doing interviews and then do the packaging of the program for a few hours at night. "What are you talking about!" Barbara exclaimed in one conversation. "Things never come through on time. There's the research, the lighting adjustments, the make-up time, the camera setups." Barbara guessed that, contrary to Mark's optimistic estimate on how many hours were involved each day in the job, it would be "a twelve-hour day any way you slice it." (She later said, "I was out by one hour. It's thirteen hours.") Barbara, in fact, knew much more about television than Mark. Having done many programs in the past, she knew it sometimes took a couple of hours to tape a couple of minutes for air because of all the technological complications. She was, however, worried about more than just the long hours. She worried that the rigid structure of the program, with its many elements and seriousness of purpose, would mean "I'd lose the ability to laugh . . . to be myself." She fussed to herself, too, about those who might criticize her by saying she couldn't translate her excellence on radio to television. Friends warned her health might suffer, and she thought of her husband Murray, who would have to adjust to her working at nights, with the inevitable elimination of most of their social life.

But with all the negatives, she still was attracted to the idea. In the end, she says today she agreed to do it because "I felt I'd be a coward if I didn't do it. I didn't want to be a coward."

In late spring Barbara said "Yes." "Leaving *As It Happens* was like getting divorced from myself," she said later. Although in radio as well as in her new job as anchor of *The Journal* she would be a slave to the clock, Barbara continued her refusal to wear a watch. "My little gesture of personal liberty," she said.

Shortly before Barbara said "yes," the blonde, blue-eyed, thirty-five-year-old Mary Lou was persuaded to come aboard starship *Journal*, although she, too, had been reluctant. When first approached, she demurred, saying she wanted to take things easier for a while and besides, she said, "I just bought this piano and I'm going to take up piano lessons." The Ottawa-born Finlay was one of the few *Journal* pioneers who had experience with daily television journalism, having been co-host of the CBC's afternoon information program, *Take Thirty*, as well as anchoring the early evening news at CBC Ottawa, and she had even been a guest host on *Ninety Minutes Live*. She, along with other reporters, producers, and editors, was irresistibly attracted to *The Journal*. "They didn't want to be left out of the Normandy invasion," Starowicz remembered.

As co-anchor, Mary Lou might be sitting at the same anchor desk with Barbara, but in media attention she played second fiddle. The focus was on Frum and whether she could translate her *As It Happens* success to TV. She herself wasn't certain, as she told me that spring, but she was damn well going to try. "I had to try it," she said. "If this program doesn't work, then the CBC doesn't work."

While Barbara had done TV before, never had she experienced the white heat of attention she did now. She spent the next few months in a crash course about the job, as did Starowicz himself, who knew nothing about TV when he began but was learning quickly. Mark also had to face the internal CBC critics of *The Journal* who viewed his adventure with malignant scepticism. Some scathingly called it "The Children's Brigade," a reference to the fact that most of his staff were young and unfamiliar with prime-time television. Fortunately, his immediate boss, Bill Morgan, knew a great deal about television and together they avoided most of the pitfalls.

With evangelical zeal, Bill and Mark charmed, pleaded, and cajoled the critics in Toronto and across the country, overcoming or at least neutralizing the opposition. Morgan was especially concerned about establishing good relations with the staff at CBC stations across the country who would help produce items for *The Journal*. Having run CBC-TV Winnipeg, he knew how damaging it could be to *The Journal* if it were seen as an "arrogant, know-it-all Toronto production."

The private stations affiliated with the CBC remained sceptical if not cynical about the whole project. At endless meetings with the network brass, including Herrndorf, Norn Garriock, Jack Craine, and Daigneault, they vividly expressed their doubts of success and their fears of commercial revenue loss. "No issue made them as wild as this one," Herrndorf later recalled. "They thought I was a Communist!" Three different presentations had to be made to the affiliates before they finally acquiesced. The five-minute update at eleven was also a sore spot with them. Eventually, most of the bigger private stations opted out while the smaller ones, along with our CBC local stations, carried it. It became a continuing battle waged by the local stations, and after a couple of years local news was upgraded to eleven with our news update following; later, it was killed altogether.

The affiliates were also pressuring for more commercials in the 10:00-to-11:00 hour. Normally there would be twelve minutes of commercials during this period, but now there would be only four or five. The affiliates claimed this cutback would cost them at least $3 million a year. The argument was a crucial one because the affiliates delivered about 35 per cent of the CBC's total audience, reaching areas where we didn't own stations. One proposal was for a commercial break between *The National* and *The Journal*, an idea that pleased not only the private affiliates but Norn Garriock and CBC's own commercial sales people as well. It would certainly have been a big money maker, but it would have been suicidal, as I and others strenuously argued. It would put up a barrier between *The National* and *The Journal* and would kill off much of the *National* audience that *The Journal* needed to inherit. At the first sign of a commercial between the two programs a large percentage of viewers would punch their channel changers and hop over to another station, never to return. "This would be the most expensive bit of hara-kiri ever inflicted on itself by a network! We've got to fight that tooth and nail for everyone's sake," said Starowicz. And Burman fully agreed, as did their bosses Morgan and Carlin.

It was Herrndorf who finally had to decide and, true to form, he went with his heart. "It really wasn't a hard decision," he later recalled. The commercial was put later, into the body of *The Journal*, which meant three minutes inside the program and two after it ended. To assuage the affiliates' fury, the CBC gave them some financial guarantees and other sweeteners that meant more money for them. Only in a public broadcasting system such as the CBC could that have happened. CTV is owned – lock, stock, and barrel – by its affiliates, and in the U.S. prime-time commercial revenue is so critical that there would have been no argument at all about putting a commercial between the two segments in the hour.

As spring of 1981 rolled toward summer, Starowicz, Burman, and their colleagues grew increasingly worried they might not be ready for a September start. At *The National* we began some dry runs to test out our new equipment and style, doing a dummy run of the 10:00 p.m. *National* at nine, and then doing the regular program after that. At *The Journal* Starowicz's thoughtful, pragmatic associate, Bruce McKay, who was the architect of that program's technical and production system, kept showing him schedule charts that discouragingly demonstrated how far they had fallen behind waiting for a decision on where they could set up shop.

In May, just as *The Journal* was moving into its offices, CBC technicians, locked in negotiating combat with CBC for months, went on strike. This put everything in jeopardy because without the technicians we couldn't do any rehearsals, test any equipment, or even seek their advice. Installation of the new equipment for *The Journal*, far from complete, came to a virtual standstill. Now there was no way we could make a September 14 start for the prime-time hour so the scheduled launch was postponed again. We figured we needed at least three or four months of testing and rehearsals once the technicians were back and, assuming the strike was over by fall, we now looked to a January, 1982, launch date.

There was another victim of the strike: *Newsmagazine*. The News Service's grand old lady of television journalism was ending anyway because its time period and money would be taken over by *The Journal*. But we'd planned a final salute to the oldest regular program still on Canadian television. It had begun on the opening day of CBC-TV in Toronto in the fall of 1952 and was to be taken off the air for good in June, 1981. *Newsmag* was special to me and to the News Service, having spawned and nurtured the careers of so many of us.

I had done reports for *Newsmag* from almost all over the world and had anchored the program from time to time over a period of twenty years. Its list of graduates included such illustrious electronic journalistic names as Morley Safer, Charles Wasserman, Norman DePoe, Bill Stephenson, Michael Maclear, Peter Kent, Peter Reilly, Joe Schlesinger, Ann Medina, James M. Minifie, Stanley Burke, and David Halton, as well as producers such as Don Cameron, Bill Cunningham, Bill Harcourt, and Harry Rasky. It had covered every major story in the world since September, 1952, when it began with Harry Rasky producing and Lorne Greene anchoring. That first program featured the Boyd Gang, a group of rampaging Ontario desperadoes who'd broken out of prison, and a story on the fighting in Vietnam, Laos, and Cambodia. *Newsmagazine* cameras were there for every Canadian election, every U.S. and British election, the Hungarian revolution, the Suez crisis, the Cuban missile crisis, the Soviet occupation of Czechoslovakia, the Middle East wars, the American civil rights battles, Watergate, the Iran hostages, our Centennial celebrations, separatism, and the constitutional arguments. Whenever and wherever something big was happening, *Newsmag* was there.

Ann Medina, the show's executive producer, and I wanted to do honour to this most revered of all Canadian news programs. Librarian Lillian Snider and film editor Ron Garrant culled the film library for weeks going through 1,200 tapes, picking out many of the highlights and some of the lowlights over thirty years. I was to host the final show planned for June 1, which we called "The Final Edition" - it was the 1,099th edition, in fact. But the realities of the technicians' walkout made it impossible to put the program on the air and the final edition of *Newsmag* became a casualty, ignominiously dying unseen and unheard.

But, as always, our focus was on what was coming, not on what had been, and we concentrated on the new hour. In some ways, the technicians' strike was a blessing in disguise because we now had time to think, plan, polish, and train. This training period was particularly important for *Journal* staffers, many of whom had to learn not only about television but about the complexities of the deadlines, feeds, and constraints of daily TV journalism - although with no facilities and no technicians, the training was all theory.

While *Journal* training sessions were under way that summer of 1981, *The National* brought its editors together for intensive training courses in writing. What was absolutely crucial, aside from the substance of the news reports themselves, was the way the words were put together. Over the years our writing for *The National* had grown stodgy and lumpy. It needed to be much more conversational, warm, friendlier, with short, simple sentences. There had to be pauses for breathing space, words that acted as signals of what was coming up and that indicated something important, interesting, and colourful was coming. George Orwell had some valuable rules on writing: never use a long word where a short one will do; if it's possible to cut a word out, always cut it out; never use a passive verb if you can use an active verb; never use jargon. We tried to adapt that advice for television.

When CBC began broadcasting newscasts prepared by our own News Service in the 1940s, the CBC's supervisor of broadcast language, W.H. "Steve" Brodie, advised news writers: "What we must have is good conversational English ... lively without being slangy, and above all, it must not sound stilted or pedantic ... that golden middle ground between glacial correctitude and shirtsleeve informality." Brodie's advice was still valid four decades later.

Not only did I want our writing to be more easily conversational, I wanted my own delivery to be more at ease. If I seemed to be comfortable in my style of delivery of the news, then the audience would be more comfortable, too. So in the summer of 1981 and again in the fall, I spent a couple of weeks with Tim Knight in the CBC Training Department, listening to *National* tapes as well as to tapes of CBS, NBC, ABC, and BBC newscasts. Tim, who is an old colleague, a former anchor himself, an ex-foreign correspondent and former local CBC executive producer in Ottawa, proved to be a sensitive but determined teacher. The most important thing he taught me was to relax, to "make friends with the camera" and to "share" the news with the audience instead of delivering the news like a formal speech. He had me slow down slightly in my reading pace and provide more "thinking pauses" in my delivery. The trick for an anchorman, of course, is to achieve a relaxing warmth without losing authority, energy, or the intense concentration that is so essential. "Don't push too much," Tim would say. "Be engaged, be concerned with the story."

We went over my old scripts, changing emphasis, trying to find ways of relaxing my delivery. In some cases I was choppy and tight or my speech rhythm more conducive to delivering an address from a podium than conversing with friends and sharing information on a little screen. With his help, I began to think of the camera lens as an old friend sitting in his living room where I was sharing with him the news of the day.

I had long been an admirer of dancer Fred Astaire for his seemingly effortless and utterly relaxed style, which had been a product of the most intense concentration and rehearsal. Now I began to scribble at the top of my script before going on each night, "Think Fred Astaire!"

It helped as a reminder to be relaxed in what is an inherently unrelaxed, tension-soaked environment.

As I honed my on-camera skills I recalled once in Washington when I ran into CBS commentator Eric Sevareid coming out of the CBS studio just as I was going in. Sevareid saw me and grimaced. "They tell you to be relaxed and easy," he muttered, shaking his big grey head at all the paraphernalia of television. "Amid all those damn lights and cameras focusing in on you, somebody counting and waving fingers at you and people all around concentrating on your every twist, twinge, and twitch. You're in Macy's front window, for God's sake, so how can you be relaxed?" It wasn't easy thinking of Fred Astaire.

DURING THE FINAL NINE MONTHS of 1981, while all the hectic planning and training for the new *National/Journal* was going on, I found myself galloping from story to story. In early summer I anchored coverage of the Economic Summit in Ottawa, watching Trudeau hosting world leaders. Then it was over to London for that memorable week of the royal wedding. What with breaking news, regular anchoring, and planning for prime time, there was not much holiday time that year.

There was time, though, for one happy event, which united my personal and professional life. Lorraine's daughter Francesca married the director of *The National*, Fred Parker. They took off for a one-week Florida honeymoon, which was all the time Fred could afford to be away from his key role in helping develop the new look of *The National*.

Fred concentrated on how the program would look and on its studio changes while Burman worried about everything from production values and editorial style to the nitty-gritty details of personnel, new technology, telephones, lines, and smooth relations with *The Journal*. Tony and Fred had gone to New York the previous fall and again in the spring to see what ideas they might borrow from the American networks. They were particularly interested in the quick, well-done graphics at ABC and the U.S. use of new technological "toys," including such things as "Addas," "Squeeze Zooms," "Vista 80s," and "Quantels," all visual means of translating complex stories into more easily understood information. When we went on air with *The National* at ten we didn't have one of the half-million-dollar Squeeze Zooms for ourselves but borrowed *The Journal's* for one hour a day. The Squeeze Zoom control panel is a three-foot-tall box about the size of a portable dishwasher with the top covered with buttons that light up in red, blue, green, yellow, and white, making it look like a midget version of a Tijuana taxicab. It connects to another floor where there is a package of Squeeze Zoom circuit cards about the size of two refrigerators. It animates charts, provides multiple images, and enables us to zoom pictures in and out or flip them like pages in a book. It's a key element in providing the high production values that make our reports more readily understood and visually exciting. In the control room, it sits beside the director and is operated by a technician known as a switcher, who is in charge of getting the right pictures on the screen.

Nowadays, *The National* has its own Quantel, which does much the same thing but looks a little less like R-2 D-2. These technological toys also electronically displayed preselected slides, and the computerized electronic character-generators enabled us to put texts, names, and titles onto the screen instantly, saving the hours once spent in putting up letters one at a time by hand. As I watched a demonstration of one of these expensive gadgets, I realized that for the first time the technology would let us make visually interesting reports out of what had hitherto been complicated and sometimes almost incomprehensible economic stories that television, with its demand for pictures and limited time, had never handled effectively.

When Burman and Parker saw the American networks close up, they almost literally salivated in envy. "God," said Parker, "they've got so much more of everything ... more money, more machines, more people, more time, more services." Where Parker had one script assistant and one production assistant, the director of *CBS Evening News* had nine; each network had three times the number of videotape editing machines as *The National*; twice as many graphic artists; four times more producers and writers; and a budget fifteen times the size of ours. "There are thousands of things the Americans have and use daily to present their newscast that we here at the CBC will never have ... at least not in our lifetime," Parker commented. Burman was especially impressed with the large number of reporters the U.S. networks had and noted that their assignment desks were larger than our entire newsroom.

We would have to do as well with much less. For one thing we wanted not only to enliven the nightly news visually with all the new technology we could get, but we also wanted to make it sound more contemporary. So we commissioned a new musical introduction. Burman and Parker spent hours talking to composers and listening to everything from symphony orchestras to a pick-up brass group. Occasionally I would join them in their listening. "Needs more high energy," one of us would say, or "That one's too complicated," or "Nice underlying tension in the horns." It may have been a poor imitation of Hollywood, but we felt the music was an important signal and had to reflect the urgency and immediacy of the news. Without being overwhelming or theatrical, it nevertheless had to get the viewer's attention. It also would tell every viewer that this was definitely a new *National*.

For years, *The National* had been introduced by music that accompanied electronic blippety-bloopety noises long ago nicknamed "The Bloops." I wanted to add new music but keep "The Bloops" because I felt they had become a tradition and a recognized signal that the news was about to begin. Most of my colleagues, however, wanted something entirely new, so we compromised by having a "bloopish" sound in the music itself. A final competition was held among four composers and we chose well-known Toronto composer Rick Wilkins to write the musical introduction. Once we'd approved his composition we hired the Canadian Brass to play it.

One thing Tony and Fred realized early was the need for a daytime production unit to start working on graphics and cells ten hours ahead of the broadcast. This would give *The National* more time to prepare a consistent, high-quality "uptown look," as Parker described it. We wanted the graphics and cells that appear just over the anchor's shoulder to illustrate a story to be simple, but to have a flair. The objective was to complement and reinforce my words and not overwhelm them. When a graphic or cell gets too complicated, it distracts the viewer from what's being said and thus, no matter how beautiful as a piece of art, it fails in its job of quietly and quickly reinforcing the news.

Burman and Parker's visits to the American networks reaffirmed the need for more videotape machines to handle incoming satellite and telephone-line feeds of news reports from our reporters. That would also mean more tape-editing capacity, which in turn would lead to higher overall production values. We got more of these machines, but they never seemed enough.

Another battle was over the studio from which *The National* was broadcast. When the prime-time *National* was announced we had hoped to have it come out of our fifth-floor newsroom in the TV building, where a new wing had just been erected. The building was one of the last acts of Don MacPherson before he left the CBC for Global and had been dubbed "MacPherson's Last Erection." But there was no money to put our full studio there, so we compromised on a new set for our old Studio Two with an upgraded control room. We could afford, however, to put a small "pocket studio" in the newsroom, which we planned to use for news bulletins, some news specials, and the new five-minute news update at 11:00 p.m.

Ideally, we wanted to have the studio used only for news, but we recognized we couldn't win that fight since several other programs used the studio, too. Our biggest problem was with, of all people, *The Friendly Giant*, the popular children's program that had been entertaining youngsters for nearly a quarter of a century and which had at one time been part of my program responsibilities. Since we shared the studio with Friendly, our *National* set had to be moved in and out every day. This meant inconsistent lighting, camera-angle difficulties, extra wear and tear on the set, and other problems. It was a long-standing annoyance for us. We needed more space but Friendly didn't want to give up any of the space he, Rusty the Rooster, and Jerome the Giraffe used.

Finally, shortly after Burman and Parker had come back from New York in the spring of 1981, a summit confrontation was held between the two sides after network management told us we could only have extra space if Friendly agreed. *The National* was represented by Parker, who had grown up watching the show and was somewhat awed and nonplussed to find himself as Friendly's adversary. At 5'11", Friendly was not really a giant but an amiable, white-haired, soft-voiced, and gentle sixty-three-year-old by the name of Bob Homme (rhymes with tummy). Nonetheless, he was very protective of his space.

As Parker entered a big boardroom for the summit confrontation, Friendly was standing at the far end of a long table surrounded by hard-looking aides ready to help defend his studio space. As it turned out, though, Friendly was indeed friendly, and after a half-hour discussion, Fred won agreement for the extra space and permanent *National* set. The deal struck was that *The National* could have permanent use of about one-third of the studio. This meant we could now achieve lighting and camera consistency and avoid damaging the anchor desk and chair each time we carted it in and out of the studio. So, finally, after nearly thirty years, *The National* had a genuine studio home, and even if it was only a third of a studio, it was our third. Ironically, *The Friendly Giant* was cancelled three years later and it went into repeats.

In addition to his concerns about the practical problems of the studio and the plant, Burman was especially worried about the reporters whose coverage would be affected by starting *The National* at ten instead of eleven. This meant new hours for both our foreign and domestic news bureaus since the feeds were needed an hour earlier each day. The worst problems were in Alberta and British Columbia. A ten o'clock *National* meant the Atlantic region program was at nine Eastern Time, six in Vancouver. That meant Vancouver reporters had to finish their filming by about three in the afternoon to have time for editing and feeding to the network centre in Toronto. One thing we pushed for, eventually successfully, was to have more electronic news-gathering (ENG) equipment installed in our bureaus. These not only improved the quality but meant that time-consuming stage of processing the film was no longer necessary. With ENG equipment we could, for example, keep shooting tape of a story up to 5:00 or even 5:30 p.m. in Vancouver instead of 3:00 p.m.

We also sought to bring a freshness and visual energy to the set where I sat anchoring the news. The old set was cold and sterile in appearance. What we needed was one that would look both comfortable and contemporary. The trick was to make these twin moods compatible. To help achieve that, I wanted a rich, mahogany desktop with a softening curve to it. I also wanted a large, comfortable soft-brown chair that conveyed a sense of ease but also had a look of authority. Parker and I spent weeks sitting in hundreds of chairs in stores all over Toronto. We made a decidedly odd sight to curious and gathering sales clerks and customers, with me sitting in the latest prospect pretending I was looking into a camera while Fred stood ten feet away squinting and visualizing what it would look like on air. "Just looking," we'd explain until we finally found the right one.

As we rolled through the summer, now looking toward our January, 1982, start, both *The National* and *The Journal* began focusing more on the editorial needs of the new hour. Starowicz had finally hired most of his staff. But his producers, correspondents, and technical crews were out around the world getting stories, building up items for the program. Among them was Ann Medina, who had gone over to *The Journal* when her job as executive producer of *Newsmagazine* disappeared with that program's cancellation. She was off in the Middle East. Another correspondent, Linden MacIntyre, was in the Arctic. Peter Kent was in Kampuchea, and others were chasing down stories all over North America. "The headquarters of *The Journal* is in an airplane," Starowicz commented wryly at the time.

Through the late summer days and nights Burman concentrated on the News Service editorial staff and style. He changed about 80 per cent of the *National* reporters across the country, wanting more aggressive and visually minded reporters. We'd also had audience surveys taken and had held special viewings with small test groups in which viewers rated what was important to them in a newscast – Canadian news was highest, followed by "knowledgeable reporters," and weather stories were rated high in importance, a surprise to us since we had felt the weather was much less important than politics or economic stories. International news got a relatively high rating, but Ottawa political news was rated surprisingly low. Viewers also wanted more coverage on medical and scientific stories.

Through these surveys and special viewings we got a good sense of how *The National* was viewed by the public. With that knowledge, we could tailor the new program to be a combination of what the viewers wanted to know and what they needed to know. While the surveys had recorded many complaints about our degree of coverage of national politics, such coverage was obviously essential. Our challenge was not whether to provide heavy Ottawa coverage, but rather how to do it in a way that would make it more interesting to viewers. We simply needed to echo that old Chinese proverb: "Tell me and I may forget. Show me and I may remember. Involve me and I will understand."

We learned, too, of the danger of underestimating the intelligence of the audience and of overestimating its knowledge of specific details of a particular event. And we learned of the importance of the last item in the newscast, often the best-remembered report in the program. As a result, we began to upgrade the quality of that last report.

As he examined the audience attitudes, Burman remembered the importance viewers had attached to a small segment of *The National* called "Across Canada Today." This was a device we had used a few years earlier to note a number of interesting but less than significant news events across the nation. We always started with an item from Atlantic Canada and then went east to west across the country with brief items. But some viewers felt this was unfair to the West. Finally, the venerable New Democratic MP from Winnipeg, Stanley Knowles, rose in all his dignity in the House of Commons to propose a motion that asked *The National* to "not always go from the East to the West, but once in a while to go from the West to the East or even to start from the North or from the Prairies as a gesture to the proposition that all parts of this country are equally important."

The MPs passed the motion unanimously. At *The National* we were stunned that anyone took our geographic approach so seriously. By way of explanation, Trina McQueen, executive producer at the time, responded, "If the sun goes east to west, there's no reason why the CBC shouldn't do the same." But after reflection, we decided to take Mr. Knowles and the House of Commons to heart and that night started "Across Canada Today" with an item from Calgary and ended with an item from Carbonear, Newfoundland. Ever after, we alternated the flow east to west, west to east, north to south, and south to north until, in time, we decided the segment was trivializing the news and killed it. It was, however, a good lesson in the close attention the audience pays to what we're doing on *The National*.

BY THE FALL OF 1981, the technicians' strike had ended and the pace of preparation accelerated as the countdown began in earnest for the January launch. Months before, Burman had begun issuing weekly progress reports headed with the warning, "26 Weeks To Go," then "25 Weeks To Go," and so on. Now, the weeks were galloping away and exhaustion loomed. Our eighteen-hour days were powered by coffee and adrenalin; nerve ends jangled, dry runs became more intense, and frustrations grew as we broke in the new equipment. At *The National* we not only were dry-running the new program but had to produce the regular newscast every night. Over in *The Journal's* offices, now nicknamed "The Bunker," Starowicz sought to meld his high-powered group of individuals into a smooth-working TV program team.

By mid-fall everyone was increasingly anxious to get on the air. "We're all sick of being pregnant with this thing," said Current Affairs boss Bill Morgan. If possible, Mark was smoking even more, and nervously stroking his black moustache.

The continuing problems with technical facilities infuriated him. The complex systems were having all the predictable teething problems, but even simple things were acting up. A little box designed to let *Journal* crews use normal telephones to feed in audio reports while in the field didn't work. A few weeks before the launch some *Journal* staffers found a make-do solution in an off-the-shelf item from a small electronics company in Texas. Half a dozen years later, it was still in use.

Starowicz was also getting annoyed at the amount of media attention. It zeroed in on *The Journal*, which became the target of an avalanche of accusations by anonymous critics both in and out of the CBC. They complained about wasting money, resources being taken away from other programs, hogging publicity, and stealing talent. Then CBC publicity added to the pressures with a public relations campaign proclaiming the move to ten o'clock as "one of the most significant programming changes in the history of CBC Television." It was that, but we didn't need to be reminded, and we began to fear excessive audience expectations. Mark was particularly sensitive to this danger. "The earth is not going to move, for God's sake!" he grumbled at one point. "Anyone expecting the Second Coming of Christ is going to be disappointed.... *The Journal* won't cure cancer [a comment made earlier by Barbara] or make your sex life better. My only concern is that people won't give the show time to develop."

Tony Burman was equally cautious about audience expectations. "We're not going to be a box-office hit that can blow away *Shogun* or the highest-rated American stuff at that hour," he said. We all remembered the intense build-up for *Ninety Minutes Live* and how the show never did recover. It had been the last great CBC television experiment. And, like *The Journal*, it had been powered by Herrndorf's determination. Playing it safe, Peter told reporters, "All of us are sure it's a great idea. But none of us are sure it will work. It's scary." What he and we were trying to do was concentrate our attention on getting the program ready for launch without being distracted by all the intrusive publicity, and at the same time trying to downsize audience expectations.

My own expectations had not changed since *The National* at ten had been announced a year and a half earlier. I still thought the new hour would be a long-distance runner, especially given the Hollywood competition on CTV, the American channels, and others. We were walking a tightrope, balancing on the one hand the desire to make Canadians aware of the new program at ten, and on the other, not wanting them to expect miracles. We didn't want to be immediately judged a failure if we dropped a couple hundred thousand viewers from the old *National* audience rating.

In November, Burman put out his "Bible," a forty-nine-page memorandum to the News staff that elaborated on his hopes and dreams for the program, laid down reportorial guidelines, and offered some locker room "Rah Rah" enthusiasm for the challenge ahead. No matter how dramatic and absorbing our production and presentation values would be with the new *National*, we knew the heart and soul of the program must be the quality of our journalism. Burman demanded that our news coverage be "sharper, faster, tougher ... first and best." Reporters, Burman urged, must be more creative in their news stories, using analogies that people can relate to. He didn't want any "Here they come, there they go" stories empty of editorial substance and content. He urged a better reflection of women in the news, greater use of our specialist reporters in law, labour, business, social affairs, and science and medicine and less use of American network reports. One key point he insisted on was a much better feedback system to provide reporters every night with an evaluation of their stories.

Tony got some sharp feedback himself from our Ottawa bureau

over a section in his "Bible" headed "Politics, Politics, Politics." He praised our many Ottawa scoops over the years but added, "we sometimes provide coverage that is totally empty of substance, meaning and interest...." That comment pitted Burman against Ottawa assignment editor Elly Alboim, who probably did and does know more about what goes on inside political Ottawa than almost any journalist in town and who naturally lusted after more "ice time" on air for his political reporters.

But we had to be as brutal and cold-blooded about the choice of political stories as we were about other stories, subjecting them to the criteria: Is the story new? Does the story matter? Why does it matter? It's the approach we adopted then and have held to ever since.

Over at *The Journal* the first full week of studio work began in mid-November, but problems with the new technical equipment continued. On December 7, full-scale dress rehearsal dry runs began. Full-length shows were done at 9:22 p.m., the start time for the first edition to Atlantic Canada. The rehearsals continued into the final weekend before the launch.

Suddenly, the "Get Ready Year" was over and we were in the last week of preparation before the January 11, 1982, launch. The media attention was overwhelming with the focus on the enormous risk the CBC was running with a nightly hour of prime-time journalism. News and Current Affairs director Mike Daigneault put it bluntly: "If this fails, the future of the CBC is bleak.... It will be much worse than a body blow to the CBC. It will be more like a TKO." That theme was picked up by *Maclean's* in a cover story on *The National* and *The Journal*, which stated, "At stake are not just the reputations of a handful of top CBC mandarins, but the very existence and essence of the CBC ... the Network is risking all...." Herrndorf was getting so nervous he even gave up his insatiable coffee-drinking in favour of tea because he couldn't take any more of the "high" from the caffeine.

The weekend before our launch, pictures of Barbara, Mary Lou, and me sprung up in magazines, newspapers, TV promos, and billboards across the country, as a half-million-dollar publicity and advertising blitz exploded with, among other things, full-page newspaper advertisements announcing, "10 p.m. The National. The Journal. A New Hour For Changing Times."

At *The Journal*, Mark, Barbara, Mary Lou, and the whole staff were dry-running through the last weekend, polishing and modifying. *The Journal*'s animation to be used at the top of the hour had arrived only two days before. Small pieces of the studio set were still missing, and engineers were still working around the clock on technical equipment.

Meanwhile over at *The National*, as Friday arrived we finished our dry-running and planned to rest through the weekend in readiness for the Monday launch. But our rest was abruptly halted by a brush fire that turned quickly into a major conflagration. The subject was *The National*'s new music and animated opening. Friday afternoon, Burman heard from chief news editor Vince Carlin that Daigneault was having second thoughts and now didn't like it. He wanted to get rid of it or drastically cut it down. "This is absolute bullshit!" said Burman. "Why are we into this kind of craziness on the eve of our launch?" But we were, and a first-class row broke out. Burman threatened to resign and heated meetings and phone calls erupted as the tensions got to everybody. Mike, who faced more strain than anyone, held firm, feeling the animation for *The National* as well as for *The Journal* went on too long. Burman argued that to remove the *National* animation and the musical theme from the opening would destroy the whole concept. The idea was to repeat the theme in "stings," on-air promotions, and other newscasts in order to provide an identifiable visual and aural linkage in all our news programs. Finally the battle was dropped into Herrndorf's lap. Sunday afternoon Burman had a phone call from Carlin to say Herrndorf had ruled *The National*'s music and animation, as proposed by Tony, would stay – the fight was over.

Now all the battles were over, all the planning was done, and we just had to put the thing on the air.

"THREE MINUTES TO AIR!" floor director Robert MacAskill shouted as I strolled into the cluttered, brightly lit Studio Two, inexplicably humming "Chattanooga Choo Choo." Maybe I was trying to hide my nervousness on this wintry night that I knew would see our gamble win or lose.

"You haven't got a chance in Hell!" CTV News vice-president Don Cameron had told me a few days earlier. "But I wish you luck." Perhaps my old friend and former CBC colleague was right.

"Two minutes to air," Robert said in a rising voice.

I recalled earlier that evening in the make-up room Barbara Frum had said, "Oh God, I wish there wasn't such a thing as a first night! I'd like to cancel it and get rid of all the tensions."

"Well, we're as ready as we'll ever be," added Mary Lou in her throaty, contralto chuckle.

We exchanged good luck and they gave me a hand-scribbled "Best Wishes Knowlton" note with a hastily scrawled Valentine heart and arrow and marked with the date.

Now we would find out whether all the blood, sweat, and tears of Herrndorf, Daigneault, Morgan, Carlin, Starowicz, Burman, and hundreds of others had produced a hit or a turkey. Would everything come together to produce compelling viewing?

To minimize first-night jitters and goofs, Starowicz had decided to begin taping *The Journal* well ahead of time, starting in the early afternoon. Late in the day I had popped into the control room, where *The Journal's* starship electronic technology was the most elaborate I'd ever seen. But now there were problems. Two pieces of equipment required to assemble the *Journal* "double-ender" interviews – the Squeeze Zoom and the edit-controller – were both down. Mark's troops were assembling the opening show more or less manually, and with painful slowness. With a cigarette dangling from his lips – he smoked four packs of Rothmans that launch day – a frown crinkling his forehead, and his hazel eyes narrowing, his nerves and frustration were crackling as he paced, puffed, and muttered. "He was a ball of nerves," Barbara said later. "For him, it was his whole life."

"Christ, the bloody technology is taking over the editorial," Starowicz grimaced. "It's dominating us. We can't do what we want. Christ!"

"Welcome to the world of television," I smiled at him.

While he muttered, director Bill Matthews gave crisply quiet direction to the cameramen and to Barbara and Mary Lou on the studio floor. It was a tense, apprehensive scene. "We'll never get through this!" Mark growled. "Sure we will, Mark . . . we're all in this together now," I whispered back.

Then I had tiptoed out and gone across the hall to *The National's* much more modest control room. Director Fred Parker and his crew were relatively relaxed. In a way, we could afford to be less tense than our *Journal* colleagues because people weren't expecting too much change in *The National*. Our problem was that it wasn't much of a news day. "What we really need is a big crisis to start things off," Tony had said. But little was happening except for a lot of bad weather across the country.

Now, as I sat in my anchor chair glancing at the clattering Canadian Press news wires behind me, my new seat felt comfortable and the set had a strong contemporary feel about it. We had, I thought, achieved the kind of look we had been seeking. I riffled through my script pages and my mind flicked back to two decades earlier when my colleagues and I first began the battle for a 10 p.m. *National* that was, at long last, climaxing on this night.

"One minute to air," floor director MacAskill smiled tensely.

I took a sip of water, pushed up my glasses, and remembered the production battles we'd had in the past two years over equipment, sets, people, story style, graphics, and animation.

"Thirty seconds!" Robert shouted as he and the three cameramen stiffened in anticipation.

I leaned over and picked up my direct telephone line to the control room to wish Fred Parker good luck. "Hey, and good luck to you, too, guy!" he said. "Don't worry, it'll be great!"

"Fifteen seconds!"

I checked the first page of my script one final time, straightened my tie, took another sip of water, cleared my throat, and focused my concentration.

The opening animation with its throbbing synthesizer sound and Canadian Brass horns, which had caused such controversy only hours before, now rolled by. Then the outstretched arm of my floor director was waving in front of me just out of camera range as he shouted "Stand by!" and his voice and fingers counted out "FIVE, FOUR, THREE, TWO, ONE!"

"Good evening," I smiled into the camera lens, "and welcome to a new hour."

Given the paucity of hard news, what followed was one of the most exhaustive weather reports ever seen on TV, with on-the-scene coverage of everything from raging blizzards and sub-zero temperatures in Ontario ("Frozen solid from Kapuskasing to Kingston," reported David Burt from a helicopter sweeping over the storm area) to snow in Quebec, snow in Regina, and snow in British Columbia, and bad weather in the United States, Wales, Belgium, and Poland. Other news highlights included a report on the marriage of female impersonator Craig Russell, who wore red slippers, and the first of a five-part series on the $8 billion drug racket in Canada by reporter Terry Milewski.

"... now, stand by for *The Journal*," I said after our inaugural twenty-two-minute Atlantic feed, heaved a gigantic sigh of relief, and thanked Robert and my main cameraman, Peter Peters, as well as the others. As Mary Lou did a *Journal* documentary on Jean Chrétien and Barbara stickhandled through a debate between Canadian Labour Congress chief Dennis McDermott and Manpower Minister Lloyd Axworthy, I scampered up a flight of steps to the control room.

"Well! Well! Well, we did it!" exclaimed a broad-grinning Parker, whirling around in his director's chair. We chattered and bubbled as we took the elevator up five floors to the newsroom. When we came into the room, the dozen editors and copy clerks burst into applause. It was the sweetest sound I'd ever heard, and we almost floated through our editorial meeting as we reviewed the program and made a few changes for the next edition of *The National* that would go out to Ontario and Quebec.

While we were reviewing the early edition of *The National*, the *Journal* staff had gathered in their office to watch their first edition going out to Atlantic Canada. Herrndorf had stopped by *The National* before the program began to wish us good luck and then walked down the street to the *Journal* office. As he entered the building, a stretcher on wheels came flying past him and a limp hand went up from the *Journal* staffer under the covers who had fainted from exhaustion. The collapsed staffer managed to smile wanly, lift himself up slightly, and say, "I'm sorry, Peter . . ." before falling back on the stretcher. "Holy shit! What a way to start," said an aghast Herrndorf. He went up to the third-floor office to join Starowicz, who was already pacing, puffing, and cracking jokes to relieve the tension. Groans greeted a couple of rough edits, but cheers erupted when the show ended.

At 9:45, up the street half a block away in the *National* newsroom once again I went down to the studio, took a sip of water, had a quiet, last-minute phone call of good luck to Fred Parker in the control room, and then at 10:00 off we were again. After that edition, we recorded the five-minute update for airing at 11:00 p.m. and then, still flying on adrenalin, we took the elevator up to a now almost empty newsroom. Just about everybody had gone over to the nearby Westbury Hotel for the "launch party" for *The National* and *The Journal* staff, and we quickly followed.

As Tony Burman, Parker, and I walked into the ballroom, the whole place broke into whistles and applause, catching all three of us off guard, for we certainly hadn't expected that kind of a reception nor had we thought there would be so many people from *The National*, *The Journal*, and from network headquarters. Once again, those chill thrills of pride went tingling up and down my spine. We really had pulled it off! The rest of the night was a blissful blur of smiling, handshaking, back-slapping, and repeated guffaws of "We really did it!"

What we really did was surprise everybody. When *The National* burst onto Canadian TV screens at ten o'clock with exciting new opening music and animation, dramatically new graphics, a conversational, fast-paced script, simple, sharper, more focused reportage, and better lighting and camera work, almost everyone was surprised. They had been so busy wondering what *The Journal* would be like they had figured *The National* would be its same old, slightly stodgy self. All of us on the news staff luxuriated in the surprise hit we were.

The next morning we grabbed every newspaper in sight to see the reaction. "CBC's Prime Time News A Hit," said the *Ottawa Citizen*; "a crackerjack performance . . . imaginative . . . stirring," said the *Montreal Gazette*; "There's a new, more urgent rhythm to The National . . . and The Journal was even brisker," said *The Toronto Star*, going on to say that "for a new baby, it sure had a lusty cry"; "An air of excitement," said the *Calgary Herald*; "the snazzier, snappier National is far easier to watch," said the *Edmonton Journal*, adding, "It's a tough job to draw Canadians from an hour of song and dance, but the CBC has created an imaginative chunk of nightly information. It's by far the best Mother Corporation has come up with in years." There was, however, some criticism about being "overproduced" and "mostly As It Happens with faces," as the *Winnipeg Free Press* said of *The Journal*, or "Like a trusty scholar uncomfortable in a flashy suit," as the Toronto *Globe and Mail* said of *The National*.

The criticism helped keep our rampaging egos in check, although we were all on a high from what we felt was an unqualified success. The day after the launch, Mike Daigneault poked his head into the boardroom where we were having our afternoon editorial meeting at *The National*, smiled, and said, "Congratulations. Everybody's absolutely knocked out about *The National*. It may be the sleeper of the year," meaning we'd surprised everyone. With that he quickly left, knowing that Burman in particular was still smarting from the weekend encounter over the opening animation. But now we wanted to know what the audience reaction was. How many had watched? At the time, Canada did not have any fast rating services, so we had to wait for close to three agonizing weeks for the first audience figures. We had guessed that the first night, with all the publicity attached to it, would be good; maybe, I thought, as high as 1.8 million for *The National*. But then we rationalized, partly out of fear and partly from realistic research advice, that the figure would drop back to around a million after the first night. Starowicz agreed, but added, "after a year, we'll be the cat's ass."

We were "the cat's ass" a lot sooner than that. The figures showed a first-night audience for *The National* of 2.3 million viewers. This jumped to 2.5 million on Friday, and for the week averaged an incredible 2.28 million. Our share of the total viewing audience was about 30 per cent and on one night hit 34 per cent. *The Journal* was not far behind, averaging 1.9 million for the week and hitting 2.1 million on

Friday. During that first week nearly 6.5 million different Canadians tuned into *The National* at least once, and 5.5 million for *The Journal*.

Peter Herrndorf had been in his office on a Sunday when an ominous sounding audience research official called him with the first figures. "Oh my God, it's going to be awful," Herrndorf later remembered thinking. "You will not believe it," said the official. "Uh huh," Peter muttered, nervously drumming his fingers on his desk, and then he whooped with disbelief when he heard the truth.

The whoops of exultation could be heard for blocks around. Burman didn't stop smiling for days, although in public, like all of us, he presented an image of cautious optimism. "We're certainly pleased," he told reporters. "But you can't on the basis of one week, particularly the first week, draw too many hard and fast conclusions. We have to be careful not to build up excessive expectations of how we're going to do."

The second-week figures were almost as good, as were those for the third and fourth weeks. In fact, *The National* and *The Journal* have averaged close to these same high audience levels ever since. On big story nights we sometimes get more than three million. What was intriguing and satisfying to me as a professional journalist was that most of our increase in audience came from new news viewers. *CTV News* did not really lose many viewers from its 11:00 p.m. newscast, and so the net result was that almost a million more Canadians were watching the news than before.

This meant that many people who hitherto had never devoted the time needed to read books and articles on major social, political, and economic issues were now regularly spending an hour a night viewing those issues. There is criticism that TV has taken people away from print, but I'd be willing to bet that insofar as *The National* and *The Journal* are concerned, it's had the reverse effect, sending viewers to print sources after they have seen something that pricked their curiosity.

The fact that two women were anchoring *The Journal* generated a lot of comment, especially in the letters that flooded in after that opening night. The comments in letters I received ranged from a complaint about "those two bimbo news hens" to "those wonderful, intelligent young ladies." There was intense attention paid to their clothes, hairstyles, and make-up, something women anchors have to face that men do not. But a man from Regina gave new meaning to criticism as he wrote me, "Barbara has marsupialized the cilia of the human spirit."

Two themes dominated the letters that flooded into *The National* after our launch. One was delight in the earlier time, which seemed to have changed the sleeping habits of the nation. "I'm going to bed the same time as the wife.... Now that may just be a bonus," said an Alberta man. "Moving *The National* to 10:00 p.m. is saving my marriage," wrote a Vancouver man, who also rejoiced in going to bed at the same time as his wife. A Stratford, Ont., woman saw other benefits for the earlier time as she wrote to me, "It will truly keep down the cost of food for the farmers can go to sleep earlier, get up earlier, feed the cattle, hogs, etc., and they, in turn, will grow faster and be more content."

The second major theme in the letters I got was one of discontent at the three "stings" we inserted into *The National* between news items to provide advance notice about upcoming reports, sort of like a newspaper boy seeking attention by shouting out the headlines. "Please let us find out for ourselves what is coming up," a woman from Paris, Ont., wrote me. "The present format gives the impression that you are afraid we will go away. We promise we won't." From Bruce Mines, Ont., a woman asked, "Must you have that horrible, noisy, so-called music rattling, banging, echoing around before and in between the news?" "The auditory and visual ballyhoo and pulsating noise and bugle blasts are enough to make me sick," said a Sudbury, Ont., man. Another viewer from Winnipeg protested "the ungodly thumping and pounding and tootling and banging and blaring," while a Montreal woman groaned, "Has the CBC lost its marbles? The banging, clashing, beating of drums, computer music, the mystery voice whispering 'Coming up next,' gives us a headache."

In spite of these and other complaints that the stings "made the news sound like 'a pinball arcade or disco hall,'" we kept them because they helped with pacing and we felt they heightened interest for the two million Canadians now watching. Indeed, as the Paris, Ont., woman said, we didn't want anyone to go away. The stings may have made some of the traditionalist viewers cringe at first, but they, as well as everybody else, quickly got accustomed to them and I haven't heard a complaint in years. We did, however, reduce their number from three to two and we toned them down slightly. Perhaps we were a bit too flashy at the start, but *The National* had become plodding. It was a wet sponge that needed squeezing. The high-impact production values gave it a shot of adrenalin just as they did for *The Journal*. And the technology never overwhelmed the editorial substance, tending rather to reinforce and heighten awareness and understanding of the news. That was something to which I was particularly sensitive as I assessed what we had done.

I recalled a conversation with CBC president Al Johnson one night in 1976. We were in Don MacPherson's office having drinks and arguing about *The National*. Johnson had said it "should be more like *The Economist*," the brilliantly written British publication, arguably the most erudite news magazine in the world. "No, it can't be and must never be," I had said. "We have a mass audience, not an elite audience. We would be failing our responsibilities if we became too nuanced, subtle, and detailed, pleasing the few but confusing and boring the many." The trick is to strike the balance so that we reach as big an audience as possible without oversimplifying. That was what we were trying to do with the new *National*.

The one major criticism I had of *The Journal* was that Mark didn't do the program live instead of taping large portions of it beforehand. It was obviously more convenient to tape Barbara's interviews ahead of time and gave the producers more control. But I felt the result was too slick, losing immediacy and squeezing out many of the humanizing facets of a live encounter that showed gaffes and all. So what if mistakes were made? It was live television and the viewers would understand. But Mark was and remains a conservative producer, wanting to minimize mistakes by maximum control. I was sorry, too, that a *Journal* deal with Patrick Watson hadn't worked out. The plan had been to have Patrick as a world-roving essayist to add "an Alistair Cooke presence" to the program, and a desk had been set aside for him in *The Journal*'s third-floor open-style office. One trip to Africa was cancelled at the last minute and Patrick never did do any items for *The Journal*. At the time, he had just signed on as host for the ill-fated CBS cultural channel, which in time succumbed to a lack of financial support.

But overall, I was exultant about the partnership of *The National* and *The Journal*. We were a success with the audience and with the critics.

Somewhat arrogantly for a neophyte television producer, Mark Starowicz had said, "Errors in television are the result of lack of preparation and road-building." Arrogant or not, he was right, and he and Burman built the roads that Barbara and I now use every night. But there had been much the same detailed planning for the ill-fated *Ninety Minutes Live* as for *The Journal*, and I wondered why one was a success and the other a failure. The answer, I think, was focus. Starowicz and his colleagues followed Alex Frame's hard-earned advice, decided what they wanted, and stuck to it. *Ninety Minutes Live* was often unsure of its focus, although given time, I'd always felt it would work. *Ninety Minutes Live* was a much more radical program in terms of content and sometimes sought to shock. *The Journal* protected itself with its comparatively conservative content and was buttressed by the tradition of *The National* airing as part of the hour. *The National* and *The Journal* were radical in the time they were aired, their nightly frequency, and their presentation, but not in their content.

With *The National* and *The Journal* we had achieved what we set out to do so many years before: to prove that news in prime time would be both popular and provide a significant contribution to a more aware, enlightened society. At the beginning, it seemed everybody had been against us: presidents, senior managers, middle managers, and bookkeepers. Nobody wanted to take the risks. In a kind of Chinese water torture process, our campaign continued drip by drip, year by year, persistently and patiently persuading one manager here, another there, slipping the idea into policy documents and presidential speeches, and finally winning the support of Peter Herrndorf, whose drive powerplayed the dream into a reality. As shown by the audience response and the critical comments, we had achieved the same level of impact with news and current affairs as we had a decade earlier with historical programs such as Pierre Berton's *The National Dream*, Vincent Tovell's social history, and Cam Graham's political series from Laurier to the Diefenbaker-Pearson years. And *The Journal* had finally laid to rest the ghost of *This Hour Has Seven Days*. *The National* at ten and *The Journal* had become a spinal cord of information for the nation and the most talked-about hour on the air.

7 THE TV NEWS MACHINE

The prime-time *National* and *Journal* may have journalistically united the country in a way never tried before, but there were still rumblings of discontent and remnants of old wars evident in the relations between them.

The *Journal* producers, more nervous than the *National* staff in the first few days after the launch, put up a sign outside their control room saying, "The Journal. Keep Out!" Our director, Fred Parker, immediately put up a sign outside our control room just across the hallway, saying, "The National. Everybody Welcome!" The *Journal* sign came down the next day. The *National* sign is still there. There is a difference, too, in the way each program describes the correction of a production or editorial mistake in the program, a change made for showing the program in the next time zone. The *Journal* producers tend to call this "an enhancement." *The National* calls it "a fix up."

A more serious difference between the News Service and *The Journal* arose within a couple of weeks of the launch over the coverage by the news specials unit of a First Ministers Conference. There was no argument about the news specials unit providing live coverage of the event itself during the day, but there were sharp differences over the coverage in prime time. Before the advent of *The Journal*, CBC would have carried a prime-time news special repeating the highlights of the day's debate plus analysis and interviews. Thus we would reach the vast majority of the audience, who would not have been watching during the day. In their report, "the Three Wise Men" had recommended "that most news specials be aired in this 10-11 time, so that *The Journal* or part of it would be pre-empted by such programming. . . ." But now, our bosses decided *The Journal* should handle any prime-time recap and provide the analysis and interviews. *The Journal* was of course reluctant to give up air time to news specials.

"No bloody way!" was the response of both news specials executive producer Arnold Amber and chief news editor Vince Carlin, who were proud of the in-depth coverage their specials unit had provided in the past and didn't want to be confined to the low-audience daytime schedule. The bureaucratic war began. Carlin fired off a bristling two-page memo to "Bay Street" and followed that the next day with another two-pager. Carlin and Amber felt the CBC was throwing away the superior experience of the news specials unit. But "Bay Street" felt the whole purpose of *The Journal* was to provide reviews, analysis, and interviews on the day's events and that we didn't need a special when we had *The Journal*.

Actually, I thought the battle to save prime-time news specials had been lost a couple of years before when the decision was made to go ahead with *The Journal*. But nonetheless, I felt *The Journal* didn't have the expertise or the time to provide the wrap-up of complex events such as a First Ministers Conference. What we needed on such occasions, I argued, was a prime-time edited version of the live coverage. "We simply cannot have a bias against unadorned fact," I wrote in a memo to Herrndorf. "We must show the Canadian public and in prime time when most of the public is watching TV, what has happened. Only after people see what has happened, can we then explain the background, the why, the implications and the nuances. To eliminate the reality and have only, or almost only the explanation, is to have all cart and no horse." Herrndorf sent back a note agreeing in principle, but nothing happened, and a now much-diminished news specials unit provides a prime-time special only occasionally, along with its major work of live coverage of daytime news specials and its unparalleled election coverage. Sometimes, though, News Service reporters and producers will produce a package of material on elections or other major events to be incorporated within *The Journal*.

What is still missing, however, is that full recapitulation of the live event itself, which prime-time audiences now too often see only in snatches on *The National* and *The Journal*. To a degree we are showing a "bias against unadorned fact," as I had said to Herrndorf, and the Canadian public is being short-changed on some of these significant conferences and events. CTV and Global, of course, do little or nothing in terms of prime-time recapitulations. In the United States, the big American networks seldom break into prime time for special news coverage and usually put their news specials at 11:30 p.m.

AFTER THE FIRST few exhausting months following the January 11 launch, it was decided *The Journal* would take the summer off to catch its breath and save some money. That was a mistake that became a disaster. At first there was newspaper speculation that *The Journal* had simply gone broke and needed the time off to save money. "No," said a CBC spokesman. But the *Ottawa Citizen* quoted Peter Herrndorf as saying money was, in fact, the reason. Then Starowicz said it wasn't. "We have no financial problems.... We aren't broke," he said. The CBC spokesman said again that it was: "We didn't want to go with a thin *Journal* in the summertime. We simply found it too expensive." In fact, a corporate budget cut had hit the network and the summer off was judged to be a good way to save money. No one, however, wanted to say that.

Mark grew increasingly angry at the nation-wide publicity about a nine-week summer holiday for *The Journal* and told reporters, "The irony of this is that we've got a unit which works fourteen hours a day and gets tagged as lazy." Privately, Mark simply called the critics "the bastards!"

But it was wrong to take the summer off and *The Journal* suffered for it, ridiculed in editorials, columns, and cartoons, and attacked in the House of Commons. It was, however, a lesson learned and never repeated.

Starowicz and his colleagues used the summer to refine the style and shape of *The Journal*, giving more room to documentaries and trying to make the set less "Star Wars" in appearance. Burman and his colleagues did the same thing as we rolled toward the fall, and he told me, "You know, dammit, we beat the hell out of *CTV News* through the summer." In fact, *The National* that summer was the CBC's highest-rated Canadian program, and in five of seven nights it was the highest-rated of all programs on the CBC, including American shows. "We're hot!" Burman smiled.

The success of the new *National/Journal* attracted a lot of attention, some of it from unexpected quarters. One night during our first year we got a phone call from the duty officer at the CIA in Washington, who asked, "What's wrong? We're not getting the program and I need it!" Apparently the CIA brought the program into its headquarters every night using its own satellite dish. That particular night, nothing came in. "There must be something wrong with your Anik satellite," the CIA man said. But after a check, we explained it must be a problem with their equipment, not ours. *The National* and *The Journal* had gone out as usual.

There was considerable interest from the American networks, which watched us carefully and borrowed graphic ideas and production techniques. Both Fred Parker and Tony Burman were offered other tempting jobs. They were riding the crest of their success with *The National* and Tony jokingly told Fred, "Maybe we've peaked too soon!" In the end Fred, still in his mid-twenties, turned down a CBS offer from Dan Rather to be a producer. But Tony couldn't resist the allure of becoming the senior CBC News producer in Europe.

Into Tony's shoes stepped tall, thin senior producer John Owen, who had been with Burman every step of the way in developing the new *National* and had been the principal daily liaison with the *Journal* staff. But even though our reborn nightly news was purring along beautifully, John was soon rubbing his bald head in bemusement at the kinds of problems he had to deal with in the new job. Fortunately, behind his gregarious manner there's a steely resolve. But sometimes what he needed most of all was a sense of humour.

Shortly after he took over John discovered the dangers of memo-writing at the CBC. He had issued a memorandum ordering reporters not to wear fur coats on air after one of our reporters had worn one while reporting on a seal-hunting story with a pile of dead seals behind her. Besides that, the economy was in recession, which added to Owen's distress at seeing his reporters on air in fur coats. In fact, we'd had a couple of nights when two or three stories in a row had seen reporters wearing expensive-looking fur coats, and he didn't like the image it projected. In his memo, circulated to all newsrooms across the country, John noted that it gave the impression that "We're rich and you're not!" He added, "No appeals please. The ban is permanent."

Any memo that goes out to CBC newsrooms across Canada is almost certain to wind up in a columnist's hands if some of the recipients aren't happy about it. Some weren't and this did. I thought John's memo made sense because fur-clad reporters can look overdressed and the audience attention is focused on the fur, not on the substance of what the reporter is saying. Canadian Press picked up the story, saying, "Mink is out and wool is in at CBC TV. . . . Reporters for *The National* have been ordered not to cosy up to the camera in fur coats because of the elitist image such garments project."

Columnists had fun with John's memo, some saying it demonstrated a socialist trend at CBC, others saying it showed CBC reporters were paid too much if they could afford mink and other fur coats. The *Washington Post* awarded CBC its prize for "the silliest story of the season" and NBC news even reported it. The *Edmonton Sun* splashed a cartoon across its editorial page showing Barbara, Mary Lou, and me all naked as a result of the new CBC dress code. Women's groups protested the memo was a male chauvinist plot against women and letters came cascading in, including one published in the Toronto *Globe and Mail* that suggested the "no-fur-coat" dress code could be expanded to achieve the objective of playing down on-air opulence by having "each reporter wearing a clearly visible tag on a sleeve ... discreetly worded to give the desired impression of poverty. For example, a woman reporter's garment might carry a tag, 'Coat borrowed from sister-in-law.' An expensive-looking man's suit could say, 'Still owe last four payments.'" Another letter protested, "Ever notice Knowlton Nash's suits. He's not wearing rags."

The Fur Council of Canada claimed Owen was discriminating against both women and the fur industry. It fired off a three-page letter of protest to Prime Minister Trudeau, his entire cabinet, CBC president Pierre Juneau, and a total of 100 others in the media, the fur industry, fishing and hunting organizations, and Inuit and Métis associations, demanding Owen's fur-coat ban be rescinded. The Fur Council said CBC was insulting four centuries of Canadian history since the English and French fur traders "truly opened up the land." Indeed, the Council said, "the ancient ancestors of our Indian and Inuit peoples were trappers and fur traders," adding, "to the spirits of the long departed pioneers of the fur trade, Mr. Owen's edict must seem strange and curious indeed." Furthermore, the letter went on to say we were endangering the livelihood of more than 15,000 people in the half-billion-dollar fur industry and also endangering $300 million in Canadian fur exports. "What next for Mr. Owen?" it asked. "Will female reporters wearing diamond rings be asked to remove them not to create the impression 'We're rich and you're not'? Where does this end?"

God knows what Prime Minister Trudeau thought of all this, if he ever saw the letter, or CBC president Juneau, for that matter. Owen, by now more than fed up with the story, simply told reporters, "I am not going to devote another second to this fur story." The story eventually petered out, although John was more careful about writing memos after that.

After that banner launch day of January 11, 1982, some of the key players changed, including Owen's move into *The National*'s executive producer job. Within a couple of months of going on the air with our prime-time hour, Mike Daigneault was wooed away from his job as director of News and Current Affairs to become editor-in-chief of Visnews, the international television news agency based in London. Bill Morgan was promoted from his job as head of Current Affairs to take over Mike's old role. There were changes, too, in getting out *The National*. For one thing, we began working more closely and harmoniously with *The Journal* in sharing assignment information. This avoided overlaps and sometimes saved money. While we remained two separate programs within the hour, we were co-ordinated more closely than any two News and Current Affairs programs had ever been before. The old wounds finally were healing.

But one thing hadn't changed: television news is an extraordinarily collaborative process involving literally hundreds of people around the world. In this respect, it is unlike the process of delivering the news in any other medium. Newspapers, for instance, can allow much more freedom to individual reporters and columnists in the preparation of a story (although the collaborative trend is noticeable there, too, with stories increasingly being researched by several journalists and written by others).

The sharp increase in production values in television news has meant a remarkably close interrelationship of many job functions. In no business I know is everyone so interdependent, from reporters to assignment editors to cameramen to graphic artists. And in no other news business do the desk editors, who evaluate, edit, and prepare reporters' stories for air, have as much control over how the stories are presented as in TV, especially at *The National*. There are both advantages and disadvantages to this. The advantages are seen on the screen with the reporters' words, pictures, and graphics all reinforcing each other to provide more readily understood newscasts. One danger is homogenization of the end product, making it characterless and bland, and it is the editors' job to make sure this doesn't happen. For the most part, I think, *The National* has succeeded in avoiding that and in providing a compelling newscast.

Every day on *The National* has its uniqueness, born of the blend of the actual news events themselves and the behind-the-scenes problems, human errors, and technological snafus that affect what is seen on the air. But the basic pattern remains the same, as is evident from one day I've picked at random to describe in detail. As it turned out, this particular day became not only especially newsworthy, but a good example of the many technological perils inherent in the complex process of getting out the nightly television news.

Thursday, April 30, 1987

7:00 a.m.
Joan Andersen, a tall, cheery, brown-haired veteran reporter and editor arrives at the nearly empty fifth-floor TV newsroom in downtown Toronto to begin her day as acting foreign assignment editor (standing in for George Hoff, who is in Japan on a scholarship). Her responsibility is to assign and handle all foreign coverage by CBC correspondents in Beijing, Washington, Paris, London, Jerusalem, and Moscow, plus any roving reporters who may be out of the country on foreign assignments. She also deals with foreign free-lance reporters and handles liaison with other networks around the world, making deals for joint coverage or exchanges of stories. It's quite a beat for a girl from Govan, Saskatchewan (pop. 397).

Desks are scattered higgeldy-piggeldy about the newsroom, on almost every one of them a typewriter and a computer. But most of the desks are empty this early in the morning and the newsroom, about the size of a small hotel ballroom, is almost eerily quiet as Joan flicks on her computer, glances up at the four TV sets on the wall beside her, and then takes a quick read of the Associated Press, Canadian Press, Reuters, and Agence France Presse news agency wires. Next she peruses the script of the 6:00 a.m. CBC Radio newscast and looks at the overnight messages sent to reporters evaluating their reports on last night's *National* and telling her who's where. While doing all this, with one eye she's watching the 7:00 a.m. newscasts on CBS, NBC, and the CNN all-news channel.

Joan is not the first person into the newsroom this morning, however. A couple of writers and the lineup editor for the newscasts of *Midday*, the noon-hour version of the prime-time *National/Journal*, have been here for an hour preparing for the first *Midday* broadcast that is sent to Atlantic Canada at 11:00 a.m. While Joan is making the first preparations for tonight's *National*, they and their half-dozen *Midday* news colleagues, who are now trickling in, prepare the first of four newscasts. As Joan picks up the phone to make her first call of the day, it may be 7:00 a.m. in Toronto but it's 3:00 p.m. in Moscow, 1:00 p.m. in London and Paris, and 7:00 p.m. in Beijing. It's time to check what's happening in those and other cities in her global beat.

7:15 a.m.
Joan's first call is to the foreign assignment desk at CBC Radio News, located in a CBC building next door, to see what coverage plans Radio News has for tomorrow's May Day celebrations in various countries.

7:20 a.m.

She calls the foreign assignment desks at CBS and NBC in New York and CNN in Atlanta to check their May Day coverage plans. CBS and NBC will be just picking up coverage provided by Soviet TV, but CNN is considering doing a report by its correspondent in Moscow. Polish TV will also have coverage of its May Day parade in Warsaw.

7:30 a.m.

With her glasses perched atop her head, Joan taps out a telex to CBC Moscow correspondent Michael McIvor asking him to prepare a voice report to go with the visual material she's collecting on May Day from Moscow and Warsaw.

7:40 a.m.

Joan phones the CBC Jerusalem bureau and talks of story possibilities with Middle East producer Don Dixon. Correspondent Don Murray has just arrived from Paris to take on a new assignment in the Middle East and is planning coverage of Israel's Independence Day celebrations on Sunday. Joan also discusses with Dixon a feature report by Murray for a June 5 air date pegged to the twentieth anniversary of Israel's Six Day War with Egypt, Syria, and Jordan. She and Dixon also talk of correspondent Terry Milewski's plans for departing Israel and going to a Washington assignment before going back to his normal base in Ottawa.

8:00 a.m.

Joan calls the CBC London bureau and London producer Kelly Crichton and researcher Valma Glenn tell her, "No spot story today," which means there is no big news breaking on this day in the U.K. It's just as well because London correspondent Sheila MacVicar is busily editing a piece on Ethiopia, where she and Crichton have just spent two weeks covering a new famine in that strife-torn country. MacVicar will also do a report this Sunday about an unemployment demonstration across Britain organized by several groups protesting Prime Minister Thatcher's labour policies. During this call Joan also learns what the BBC is doing, what news reports are being carried on the European TV networks, and what, if anything, her London team thinks we should pick up for tonight's *National*.

8:15 a.m.

Joan calls Johannesburg correspondent Michael Buerk, who works for the BBC but does special reporting for CBC-TV News and who today has a political story on a right-wing challenge to the South African government that is cutting into President Botha's political support. (A week and a half later, Buerk will be expelled from South Africa because the government felt his reporting was too critical.)

8:20 a.m.
Domestic assignment editor Suzanne Howden arrives to start her day. She's a seasoned reporter, writer, and editor and looks like a tomboy version of a young Doris Day. Suzanne is responsible for CBC coverage on *The National* throughout the country except for Ontario and the Ottawa bureau. As she takes her seat a couple of desks away from foreign assignment editor Andersen, her first move is to reach for the phone to check with reporters and CBC regional newsrooms across the country on what stories are breaking in their areas. She starts with Newfoundland reporter Kathryn Wright and then moves west to Halifax, Montreal, Winnipeg, Regina, Edmonton, and Vancouver. There are about twenty domestic CBC-TV news bureaus to be checked at one time or another during the day, plus occasionally the newsrooms of the private affiliated stations. But not much is happening on her beat today.

8:30 a.m.
While Andersen and Howden are pounding the phone, Bob Waller, the meticulous, brown-bearded assignment editor in charge of Ottawa coverage, Ontario, and all of *The National*'s specialist reporters, arrives to begin his day of orchestrating reporters and camera crews – "shooters," he calls the cameramen. Having heard the CBC 6:00 and 7:00 a.m. radio newscasts and gone through the *Globe and Mail* en route to work on a commuter train, Bob's first call is to the Toronto CBC local assignment editor, with whom he works closely to co-ordinate assignments, exchange information, and make sure *National* reporters don't cover the same story as local reporters, unless it's a particularly big event. But Bob already knows that the big story today is a conference at Meech Lake outside Ottawa, where Prime Minister Mulroney and the ten premiers are trying to work out a deal to get Quebec to sign the constitution, something it has refused to do since patriation in 1982. The conference begins at noon, but Ottawa reporters David Halton, our reliable, well-connected chief political correspondent, and his rotund, mischievous, and knowledgeable colleague, Mike Duffy, and their telegenic, hard-working teammate, Wendy Mesley, are heading out of town to Meech Lake shortly. Bob makes logistical arrangements with Ottawa assignment editor Elly Alboim and producer Don Dickson. As he discusses the story with Alboim, they decide that Wendy will do a sidebar story on Quebec while Halton will do "the header" - the main story - and Duffy a "talk-

back" or interview with me on *The National* that night. We've already set up two editing suites in a building a mile from the meeting site and a microwave truck to send – or "feed" – the signal to a satellite truck a mile away. The satellite truck will then beam the signal up to the Anik D1 satellite and it'll be brought down in Toronto for insertion into *The National*. At the end of this technological chain of events the newscast will be beamed up to a satellite for distribution across the nation.

The technology required to cover any story for TV is considerable, which makes planned news events like this one much more certain of air time than, say, a sudden development far from the nearest news crew.

With Alboim concentrating on Meech Lake, the coverage of the day's events in the nation's capital is co-ordinated by Maureen Boyd, normally a reporter, who assigns reporter Bill Casey to cover the emergency farm debate in the House of Commons. Altogether there are nine reporters and three producers assigned to *The National*'s Ottawa Bureau.

8:45 a.m.

Foreign assignment editor Joan Andersen is writing notes. One is to colleagues in the Resources area, who arrange feeds with the satellite and phone companies, and she requests a couple of overseas feeds. Another is to executive producer David Bazay, suggesting our own camera person be sent to Moscow so that we don't have to borrow a U.S. network cameraman all the time. Yet another urges *The National*'s program producer David Nayman to call correspondent Don Murray in Jerusalem to discuss future stories. Then she talks to TV News financial officer Graham MacFarlane about the costs of covering the June Economic Summit meeting in Venice, an event that will be covered by correspondent Joe Schlesinger and producer John Grier from Washington and David Halton from Ottawa, along with both their camera crews. Given the logistics and high cost of TV news, advance planning is essential.

9:00 a.m.

Andersen now calls the NBC station in Providence, Rhode Island, to set up editing and feeding facilities for a future story that Halifax *National* reporter Kevin Evans plans to do on a Canadian sailor who's been in the BOC round-the-world yacht race but who, after a mishap, has had to sail 4,000 miles around the bottom of South America without a mast. He's due to arrive in Providence in three or four weeks.

9:45 a.m.

Andersen now calls Washington producer John Grier to talk about the Washington visit today of Japanese Prime Minister Yasuhiro Nakasone and U.S. trade policies. She wants a story on this for tonight's *National*. But it's not a subject that appeals to Joe Schlesinger; besides, he's done a trade story the night before that mentioned Nakasone's visit. Joan still thinks we should have a fuller story for tonight. For now, the decision is left hanging.

10:00 a.m.

Joan Andersen, Suzanne Howden, and Bob Waller, *The National's* story assignment team, meet with producer David Burt and the two researchers to have a "dayside" story meeting. They discuss whether last night's Mozambique famine story by Michael Buerk should be followed up in Canada for reaction from Canadian aid groups and politicians, but they decide against it for now. Joan phones the *Journal* news desk and is told they plan to run a long Buerk piece on Mozambique tonight that went on BBC earlier and follow it with an interview about Canada's aid role.

11:00 a.m.

Joan talks to Joe Schlesinger about the Washington trade story and he's unenthusiastic. "How much of the same story do I have to do?" he says. "I had Nakasone on last night. Maybe I should have saved him."

"No," says Joan. "You had to use him last night." Joan, who admires Joe's sardonic style and knows how to handle his sometimes prickly temperament, says how much she liked his piece of last night and eventually they agree Joe will do a story for tonight on the Japanese Prime Minister and a trade vote in the U.S. House of Representatives. She suggests he do about a two-minute report.

11:30 a.m.

Domestic assignment editor Bob Waller has assigned business specialist Der Hoi-Yin to do a story on a House of Commons Finance Committee report coming down at 3:15 p.m. on the question of giving Montreal and Vancouver special status for foreign banking. Reporters and producers in Ottawa, Vancouver, and Montreal are also gathering material to fold into her story. Ottawa reporter Jason Moscovitz, who's in Toronto from Ottawa, calls in with a progress report on his efforts to track down a potential scandal in land development at the Toronto waterfront, but he can't get any confirmation as yet. (He will give up the story later in the day.)

12:00 noon

Waller makes more phone calls to Elly Alboim in Ottawa about Meech Lake, to Maureen Boyd in the Ottawa bureau, and to Quebec City, where legal specialist reporter Vicky Russell is doing a story on the newest appointee to the Supreme Court of Canada, Claire L'Heureux-Dubé, who will be sworn in Monday morning. Russell is one of five specialist reporters we have; they cover science and medicine, business, labour, social affairs, and law. Medical specialist Eve Savory is shooting material for a report on vaccine-damaged children, labour specialist Allen Garr is covering a fishermen's union story in St. John's that we plan to use tomorrow night, national reporter Dan Bjarnason is arranging a swing west for three feature pieces, and social affairs specialist Karen Webb is flying from Vancouver to Kamloops today for an abortion debate story for use tomorrow night. Waller decides to hire a charter to fly her to and from Kamloops because, while the charter costs $300 more than regular air fare for Karen and her crew, it will get them back to Vancouver that same night and will thus save on hotel and meal expenses. The saving will more than offset the additional charter charges.

The high cost of news coverage is always preoccupying, whether it's $300 extra for a charter from Vancouver to Kamloops, $20,000 to charter a jet to get into an earthquake-stricken San Salvador, or $100,000 to get a crew into Ethiopia. The TV news business is costly not just in getting the reporters, producers, and camera crews to remote areas, but also in the everyday costs of hotels, food, local transportation, production facilities, and satellite feeds at $2,500 for five minutes from Tel Aviv or Paris. To save money, *The National* and *The Journal* sometimes go on joint assignments, and deals are made frequently with BBC, NBC, CBS, CNN, and others to share costs and exchange material.

12:10 p.m.

The graphics meeting. Director Fred Parker arrives for the daily meeting on the graphics to be used for the day's major stories on tonight's *National*. With producer David Burt, he sits down in the newsroom boardroom with the three graphic artists, Pierre Clouâtre, David Kimpton, and Ray Rix. Burt describes the main news items of the day and after fifteen minutes he leaves, while Parker and the artists discuss how best to illustrate them for the graphics that will be seen over my shoulder as I introduce our coverage. For Schlesinger's report, they decide on portraits of Reagan and Nakasone amid a couple of packing cases to illustrate trade, with the American flag draped over one case, the Japanese over another. For the Meech Lake story, they decide on a partially unrolled scroll tied with a red ribbon, with the words "Constitution" printed on it in formal capital letters. Standing at the side will be a blue fleur de lis with legs, to make it look like a person. In all, eighteen graphics will be agreed on. After three quarters of an hour, the artists leave to start their work.

12:45 p.m.
Business specialist Der Hoi-Yin gets a tip from a banking source that Canadian banks are raising questions about a deal to sell Dome Petroleum to an American oil giant, Amoco, for $5.1 billion. Waller decides to take her off the other banking story about Vancouver and Montreal and switches her to the Dome story. He sends out reporter Claude Adams to do the Vancouver and Montreal story and starts getting reaction material for the Dome piece from Edmonton, Calgary, and Ottawa. Already tonight's news is taking on a different shape, as it usually does as the day progresses.

1:00 p.m.
Lunch. Waller eats a roast beef sandwich at his desk, Joan a chocolate bar, and Suzanne has nothing at all. Throughout the day, whenever a spare moment arises, they go through the newspapers, such as the *Manchester Guardian*, *Financial Times* of London, *New York Times*, *Wall Street Journal*, *Ottawa Citizen*, *Toronto Star*, *Globe and Mail*, *Montreal Gazette* (and other papers from across the country), as well as watching the newscasts of NBC, CBS, and CNN and checking with CBC Radio news and the CBC French network news. All three assignment editors are getting ready for the daily 2:15 p.m. meeting with the "nightside" editors and producers who are responsible for putting out *The National*. This is when the nightly *National* will finally begin to come together.

1:05 p.m.
I come off the elevator and walk into the newsroom, greeted by a low hum of voices at one of the quieter moments of the day for *The National*. Throughout the morning while my colleagues have been chasing after stories and arranging coverage, I've been at home checking news contacts, researching, and doing some writing. Now, I head to my cubbyhole office to pick up messages and mail, read through the news agency wires and the newspapers, and gossip with fellow workers. I tell Andersen how much I liked Michael Buerk's report last night on starvation in Mozambique. "Yeah ... very gutsy," she says.

2:25 p.m.

Bob Waller walks to the middle of the newsroom with his slightly military bearing and shouts out to one and all, "Meet! Meet! We're ready!" and about a dozen and a half of us troop into the small newsroom boardroom for a report from the three assignment editors on the day's news menu – editors, producers, and researchers sit around a T-shaped table and occasionally look up at the graphic pictures from old *Nationals* that hang on the light brown, grass-cloth walls of the boardroom or at the photographs of our reporters on the back wall. This is the critical meeting of the day for *The National* as the dayside essentially hands the reins over to the nightside, explaining the story assignments that have been made and why, and what other stories are developing.

As we settle into our chairs, Joan Andersen starts off with a review of the international story offerings for tonight. "Joe will file on Nakasone's first full day in Washington and Joe warns it'll have a similar feel to last night," she says. She tells us Sheila MacVicar's report from Ethiopia is being satellited in from London for tonight, as is a report from Michael Buerk from Johannesburg on the growing role of the far right in South African politics. Joan also says there will be material available from both Visnews and the U.S. networks on the Pope's visit to West Germany today, and she notes there is a news report about Terry Waite being seen in Lebanon, one about an underground U.S. nuclear test in the Nevada desert, and a statement issued about the British ferry that sank off Belgium. A shorthand language is heard during these meetings. "McIvor has a uni after the Viz bird. . . . It's a thumb-sucker, but it'll give him some ice time," the foreign assignment editor may note. The translation is that Moscow correspondent Michael McIvor is filing a report that will be sent first to London and then satellited to Toronto and we're paying the full cost of the transmission – no sharing. It will arrive by satellite just after the regular satellite feed from Visnews in London. His report will be primarily a background evaluation and not a hard news story, but it will give him an appearance on air.

The National's curly black-haired, pencil-thin producer, David Nayman, who is operationally in charge of the whole program, wants to know about a train derailment in West Berlin. "One killed, a couple injured . . . nothing serious," says nightside editor-writer Peter McCluskey.

Domestic assignment editor Bob Waller takes a quick wipe of his gold, wire-rimmed glasses and reports on the Dome deal story and on Vancouver and Montreal as banking centres. He also notes, "Casey's doing the resumption of the farm debate, but if you're heavy you may decide to just boil it down to vo." That means Bill Casey's report may not be used and we'll only use some of his visual material for me to briefly "voice over."

"Elly called from Meech Lake to say his government sources tell him chances look good for a deal tonight," Waller says. "It could go on late into the evening," he warns, signalling that *The National* may have to be updated for the western time zones if the story doesn't break until after 10:00 p.m. Eastern Time. That will mean another late night. Waller also reports that our microwave dish at Meech Lake, which had been blown over by the wind, is now back up and the signal restored.

Waller's colleague Suzanne Howden now reports on what's happening in Atlantic Canada, Quebec, and the West. The regions have little to offer. Some Innu hunters in Labrador have been found guilty of illegal hunting. "It's pretty thin out there. Basically, that's it, folks," she smiles.

There is a quick review of the previous night's *National*, noting Michael Buerk's report on starvation in Mozambique. "Beautifully written," says producer David Burt, who oversees the dayside production work, including preparation of the graphics and cells for *The National*, and also works with reporters in producing their items. We all agree that Buerk's spare but emotion-packed script was terrific.

2:45 p.m.
Since this is Thursday it's the day for a review of the coming week – "The Dreaded Look-Ahead meeting" as it's called because it usually keeps us an extra half to three-quarters of an hour. We've also now begun an occasional "Year-Ahead" review. As *National* producer Nayman says, "We always should be looking at least a month or two ahead." While these "look-aheads" take time, they are essential in planning the deployment of reporters and camera crews and for getting a sense of what the news menu will be like in the days and months ahead. But we'll do the "Year-Ahead" tomorrow. Today, it's only the next week we'll be thinking about.

One problem immediately arises over an item now scheduled for Friday night on *The National*. It's a report by Vancouver reporter Jane Chalmers on the first anniversary of Expo '86. "It's a matter of principle," says weekend assignment editor Karen Gelbart. "It should run on the Saturday, the day of the anniversary. . . . Medina's unhappy about it going Friday," Karen adds, reporting the displeasure of Saturday *National* anchor Ann Medina, who thinks it's a good item and wants it for her program. Later it's decided to move the report from Friday to Saturday.

The assignment editors (Andersen, Waller, and Howden) go through the main stories coming up in the week ahead and who's covering what. Then come the questions. "How are we going to cover the coming political crisis in Israel?" "When does the death penalty debate start?" "When is Joe going to do his setup piece on the Iran arms scandal hearing?" "How about a story on Drapeau at UNESCO – let's shoot the pictures for future use even if we don't use the story." "How about a quick and dirty on the Glenn Gould awards?" (meaning a quickly done and short item without spending much time on a lot of production values for the item).

"Looks like the dog days of summer are already here," Nayman comments, as he looks over the relatively slow news outlook.

Discussion turns to the need for more stories about the problems facing big cities. Doodling tight circles and lines on a piece of paper in front of him, the quiet but tough-minded Nayman says, "What's missing here are urban stories. Most of this stuff has hills and lakes, yet most of us live in cities." There is a discussion about doing urban renewal stories as the assignment editors make notes to talk to their reporters about this.

3:30 p.m.

The Look-Ahead meeting ends and it's back into the newsroom as the next couple of hours see the assignment editors revising and refining instructions to reporters reflecting "the appetite" of the meeting for various stories, dropping some, adding others, in the continual changes of the selection process for the news that will appear on *The National* tonight. At this point the lineup editor, Mark Bulgutch, prepares a tentative lineup of the stories he plans to use in tonight's *National*. A thin, boyish, junk-food-loving Montrealer with an infectious laugh, Mark's job is to decide what news items go where in *The National*. He checks with program producer David Nayman and then has his list of tonight's probable *National* items photocopied.

At this point in the day the heartbeat of *The National* moves from the assignment desks at the front of newsroom, where it's been since 7:00 a.m. when Joan Anderson arrived, to the far end about twenty-five feet down the greyish-carpeted floor to the desks of the nightside writers, Bulgutch, Nayman, and myself, which are pushed together in a U-shaped form. Now the day's real countdown begins for the first edition of *The National* that goes out at 9:00 p.m. to Atlantic Canada.

4:30 p.m.
An Evening News Syndication (ENS) service goes out at 4:30 p.m. to all our stations in Atlantic Canada providing them with national and international news reports for inclusion in their local dinner-hour programs. It's prepared by a team of writers and editors working apart from *The National* in a newsroom across the hall from our newsroom.

4:35 p.m.
I leave the newsroom for a brief meeting with a former Canadian diplomat who is now a businessman in Los Angeles and visiting Toronto to talk with associates about implications for his business of the free-trade negotiations between Canada and the United States. Later I spend half an hour at a committee meeting in downtown Toronto discussing sending books to Third World countries in a literacy campaign run by Canadian Overseas Development Through Education (CODE), of which I'm honorary campaign chairman.

4:40 p.m.
The Visnews satellite feed comes in from London with ten minutes of general reports on the main world news of the day. Bulgutch and Nayman don't think we'll use much, if any, of it.

4:50 p.m.
A "uni" of Sheila MacVicar's Ethiopian report follows "the multi" – meaning the general feed is for all news subscribers to the Visnews feed while the "uni" is exclusively for the CBC. Bulgutch and Nayman think her piece looks good and we'll use it tonight.

5:30 p.m.
The second Evening News Syndication (ENS) service goes out to stations in the rest of Canada for their dinner-hour news programs.

5:40 p.m.
Bulgutch and Nayman discuss the lineup for tonight's *National,* which is beginning to take shape. They talk about the desired length for the reports from the meeting at Meech Lake and the length of my "talkback" with Mike Duffy.

5:45 p.m.
I grab a quick dinner at home with Lorraine and then head back to the CBC.

6:15 p.m.
The make-up room is my first stop in coming back from dinner. As I get powdered, Barbara Frum pops out of her *Journal* dressing room

next door and wonders how late we'll be staying tonight to cover the breaking news from the First Ministers Conference. "How many updates do you figure tonight with Meech Lake?" she asks. She's hoping to do an interview with one of the provincial premiers after the meeting breaks up.

"Not more than five!" I respond, knowing it's going to be a late night for both of us. Then I take the elevator up to the fifth floor to the newsroom. There writer Angus Dalrymple, a tall Englishman who is a successful fiction writer in his off hours, hands me the script of a thirty-second "mini" newscast to be aired shortly. I read through it, make a few changes, and then we time it – it has to be precisely thirty seconds.

6:30 p.m.
"Dan [Rather] is waving his hands around a lot tonight," says editor Peter McCluskey as we watch the U.S. network newscasts coming in on the bank of TV sets on the side wall of the room. Since we have direct satellite feeds from the U.S. networks, we sometimes watch Rather or Tom Brokaw in their last-second preparations before going on air. Often we'll see Brokaw repeatedly tugging and pulling at his tie, generally making it worse than when he started, and scowling into an off-camera mirror before coming on with his smiling "Good evening." Or Dan Rather quickly putting on his jacket with fifteen seconds to air.

Tonight, all the networks lead with Japanese Prime Minister Nakasone's visit to Washington. While we've had reports from the U.S. "nets" during the day on what they're airing tonight, they're monitored closely and a sober, squinting Nayman makes judgements about what, if anything, we might use from their programs tonight. Usually it's one or possibly two items, although we operate on the theory that the fewer the better. "None would be ideal," smiles lineup editor Mark Bulgutch, brushing some cookie crumbs off his short-sleeve polo shirt. The only U.S. network material we'll use tonight is about a dozen seconds from CBS on the Pope in West Germany, which we combine with about twenty seconds of Visnews material from Germany for a brief voice over by me on the Pontiff's trip. The first edition of *The National* is now two and a half hours away.

6:50 p.m.
I walk up to the front end of the newsroom just beyond the assignment area to a "pocket studio" to do the "mini" newscast. This is also where the *Midday* news is anchored by Sheldon Turcott. The "mini" is going on air at 7:00 p.m. tonight for the feed to the Maritimes, where

it's 8:00, and Newfoundland, where it's 8:30 p.m. It will be replayed in Ontario and Quebec at 8:00 p.m. and at 8:00 in each of the western time zones. Tonight, however, the CBC is carrying a hockey game in Quebec so I'll later do a one-minute newscast for viewers in that province. It will be aired after the second period in the game. This "mini" over, I leave the pocket studio and go back to the other end of the newsroom to edit and read through the Quebec "mini."

7:00 p.m.

For months we've been getting a call in the newsroom from a person we have come to call "The Laughing Hyena," a woman who calls at seven every night and says nothing but laughs hysterically for a couple of minutes and then hangs up. Tonight, however, she doesn't call and we wonder if she's sick. We kind of miss her.

7:10 p.m.

A satellite feed comes in from St. John's, Nfld., with a report on the guilty verdict against the Innu hunters, which we plan to use on tonight's *National.* "Nice pictures," says Bulgutch.

7:15 p.m.

Nayman talks to Elly Alboim at Meech Lake about the possible news scenarios tonight: agreement among the First Ministers; near agreement, but not final; complete breakdown. They discuss how we will adjust our coverage for each eventuality.

7:25 p.m.

There are four editor-writers around the night desk tonight: Angus Dalrymple, Peter McCluskey, who will be handling the reports from Meech Lake, Tom McFeat, who will be handling Joe Schlesinger's report among others, and Paul Moore. McCluskey and McFeat are on the phones with reporters polishing scripts, Moore is banging out a story introduction on his typewriter, while Dalrymple is heading downstairs to work with the videotape editors in cutting a report that has come in on Visnews.

Sitting across the desk from Nayman and Bulgutch, who are both in their mid-thirties, and alongside the tall, bespectacled McCluskey, I concentrate on editing the scripts already written, reading through the Reuters wire, Associated Press, and Canadian Press, and discussing story approaches with Bulgutch, Nayman, and the writers. McFeat is on the phone to Schlesinger, discussing his script. Joe can be touchy about what he's written and there's usually an argument about some of the wording. Once when Nayman complained about Joe using a cliché about President Reagan employing a "carrot-and-stick" approach to foreign policy, Joe insisted on using it. The next day he had a grocery store send Nayman a bunch of carrots, along with a note saying "from me never the stick, always the carrot." There were no problems tonight, however.

7:45 p.m.
"When's Halton's script coming in?" asks Mary Bidinost, one of the two editors who write the captions for the special CBC service for the deaf provided by *The National*. She wants as much time as possible to caption the words David will use.

"You're not going to get scripts in time," says Nayman. "You'll just have to wing it. They'll be writing to the last minute." That's the way it often is on breaking stories.

7:55 p.m.
On one of the TV sets on the wall, smiling quizmaster Alex Trebek, host of a program called *Jeopardy!*, peers out to announce "the final Jeopardy," the last question in his show. Bulgutch usually insists we all take out three minutes to listen to the question and try to guess the answer. It's a tension-releasing break as we sprint toward 9:00 p.m. Trebek is a former CBC announcer who went to Hollywood nearly two decades ago. Tonight, though, we're too busy, even for the infectiously enthusiastic Bulgutch.

8:00 p.m.
"Any danger of getting any scripts in?" Nayman sings out drily as he worries about the editor-writers being slow in finishing writing their story introductions.

8:15 p.m.
Forty-five minutes to air.

"What'll Duffy and I concentrate on?" I ask Nayman in connection with the conversation we're going to have on air about the Meech Lake meeting.

"Depends on what Halton says," he responds.

"When will we know that?"

"When we hear what he says as he says it at nine."

"Oh," I say, knowing how many things can go wrong with live reports.

I've tried to get in touch with Mike to talk about our on-air interview but he's been too busy chasing his contacts for last-minute information, so I scribble some notes for myself. If we're lucky we'll have a few seconds to get organized just before we do the "talk-back." Fortunately, we've done this sort of thing many times before.

8:20 p.m.
We decide not to do a one-minute "mini" newscast in the Quebec hockey game, turning the time over to the Montreal newsroom to do a special report on the Quebec provincial budget that is unexpectedly coming down tonight because of a news leak in a Montreal TV station newscast. It's a big local story in Quebec.

8:25 p.m.
Writer-editor Peter McCluskey gets a call from Halton, who gives him a sense of what he's going to say in his Meech Lake report. Running his hand through his thinning red-blond hair, McCluskey reads Halton the introduction he's written to the story. Halton says it's fine.

8:28 p.m.
Thirty-two minutes to air.
   Copy clerks start "splitting" the script. This means dividing up the original and six carbon copies of each page of *The National's* script into seven different copies – one for Nayman, the commanding officer, one for Bulgutch, his second in command, one for the script assistant who keeps track of our timing, one for studio floor director David Ritchie, one for the director, Fred Parker, one for the autocue operator, and one for me to use as a back-up in case the autocue fails. It's happened before.

8:34 p.m.
At a desk behind me, the script assistant checks through her copy, reading it aloud to check her timing.

8:35 p.m.
"Washington coming in on channel seven!" shouts John Benn, who advises when the feeds are expected. Eyes around the news desk flick up to see Joe Schlesinger's report on Nakasone come in from Washington via satellite.

8:36 p.m.
Ottawa assignment editor Elly Alboim calls from Meech Lake with an update on what's happening there. He "thinks" Halton will be ready on time to lead *The National*.

8:37 p.m.
Twenty-three minutes to air.

8:38 p.m.
"I don't know the physical contact with Duffy," Nayman says. "Is he calling us or do we call him?"

Nobody knows.

8:38 p.m.
Schlesinger calls to see if we're happy with his report. "We're happy, Joe," he's told, although in truth Nayman, Bulgutch, and I were so busy we hadn't given it more than a passing glance as it came in. His script had been well vetted beforehand, though. It runs 2:05. "Nice and tight," says Bulgutch.

8:39 p.m.
I get my copy of the script and start a final edit of it, advising Bulgutch, the script assistant, and director Fred Parker of my changes. There have been a lot of changes since assignment editors Joan Andersen, Bob Waller, and Suzanne Howden left. The Dome story that Waller and reporter Der Hoi-Yin had been working on much of the day had been killed because we had too much material from Meech Lake and elsewhere. It has been reduced to a twenty-second copy story that I'll read. Also killed was the banking story reporter Claude Adams had worked on all day. It was reduced to a twenty-eight-second copy story. Bill Casey's report on the parliamentary farm debate also bit the dust, winding up as forty-four seconds of copy to be read. But Joe Schlesinger's Nakasone trade story has made it, and at 2:05 in length it is just five seconds longer than the figure Joan Anderson had given to Joe nearly nine hours earlier, and Sheila MacVicar's Ethiopia report would also make it tonight.

8:40 p.m.
"How long is Halton going to be?" asks Nayman.

"About 2:30," says Peter McCluskey.

"Hey, God, that's light!" says Bulgutch, knowing that's not a usual problem with David's reports. "You and Duffy may have to talk a lot longer," he laughs at me. "But I've got a plan. I've got three versions of Buerk, long, short, and in-between, and so we can juggle that way, and Bob's your uncle; it'll be perfect."

8:41 p.m.
Alboim calls again from Meech Lake with a report on how Halton's lead piece is coming. He'll be ready.

8:42 p.m.
Eighteen minutes to air. I hand to a copy clerk the finally edited script of *The National*. He runs downstairs to the control room with it to the autocue operator, a compact, black moustached Portuguese, Paul Franco.

8:44 p.m.
New script pages are written: Nayman wants a couple of changes.

8:46 p.m.
More new script pages are written.

8:47 p.m.
"Actually, it looks like a good little show here," says Mark, who in his genial way is ferociously competitive, always pushing to be better. Nayman's major concern now is whether Halton's Meech Lake report will make it on time and whether there'll be any technical foul-ups with the Duffy talk-back. He takes a minute to move from that immediate worry to skim through the whole newscast to make sure that it flows together and to spot any errors in the copy.

8:49 p.m.
I leave the newsroom to go down five floors to the make-up room for a quick powdering.

8:51 p.m.
A copy clerk catches me in the hallway en route from make-up to the control room and hands me a couple of new script pages.

8:54 p.m.
Six minutes to air. I realize I've forgotten to get my earphone plug for the interview with Mike Duffy and rush back up to my office.

8:56 p.m.
Slightly out of breath, I'm in the control room again for a quick check with director Fred Parker on any changes and to give him the new script pages and to give a couple of editorial changes to Paul at the autocue. Ever calm, Paul is laying out the pages on the autocue desktop platform and says, "I've got this new waterbed and it's terrific." Waterbeds are not my preoccupation right now and I mutter "uh huh" and leave.

8:57 p.m.
I clatter down the flight of stairs to the studio, walk past the coffee-maker and a punching bag hanging by the studio side wall on which the studio crew occasionally vent their frustrations, wave and smile at my three cameramen - Peter Peters, Sid Gertler, and Rick White - who've been with *The National* for years, turn on my Canadian Press teletypes, and, as I sit in my chair, clip a microphone to my tie and plug in my earpiece so I can hear Duffy for our talk-back.

8:58 p.m.
Two minutes to air. There's trouble on my earplug and I can't hear Duffy, although he can hear me and his voice is coming into the control room all right. We try to fix the problem but can't.

8:59 p.m.
One minute to air. Since Mike can hear me, I tell him I'll ask a general question about what was going on behind the scenes at Meech Lake and I'll know when he's finished by watching to see when his lips stop moving. So much for modern technology. This is going to be more fun than usual.

8:59:30 p.m.
Thirty seconds to air. Crisis. We now have lost phone contact with Meech Lake and can't get Halton's report in to lead *The National*. Meech Lake was supposed to feed it in a few minutes before nine to be recorded and then played back. When we called the Meech Lake feed point to find out where the report was, we got a busy signal. Up in the newsroom, David Nayman gets a call from Meech Lake and hears the producer there say he's only getting a busy signal in phoning "The Pit," the videotape centre in Toronto where their feed would be recorded and almost instantly played back to lead *The National*.

8:59:45 p.m.
Nayman calls the control room and "The Pit" to tell them the problem. "I have Meech Lake on the line," he says. "They can't get you."

9:00 p.m.
We're on the air with the animation and music and the previously recorded voice of the announcer saying what's on *The National* and *The Journal* tonight.

9:00:30 p.m.
The feed from Ottawa now will have to roll live into *The National* from Meech Lake, but how will Meech Lake know when to roll? Nayman, who's up in the newsroom, and Bulgutch, now in the control room, decide Bulgutch will hold up the phone receiver so Nayman can hear Fred Parker's "Roll tape!" shout right after my introduction. That way Nayman will hear it on one of the two phones and then be able to relay the cue on the other, directly to Meech Lake. The "electronic highway" is not usually like this.

9:00:50 p.m.
"Good evening," I say as I come on camera for the Atlantic edition of *The National*. "The discussions are continuing tonight at Meech Lake

where the Prime Minister and the ten premiers are trying to bring Quebec into the Constitution. . . ."

9:01:12 p.m.

The instant I introduce Halton with his report, Parker in the control room yells "Roll tape!" Nayman hears his words on one phone and yells to Meech Lake on the other, "Roll!" Meech Lake rolls the tape and the signal carrying the Halton report travels 22,000 miles in 250 milliseconds up to the Anik D1 satellite and then comes back down again in another quarter of a second to the CBC in Toronto. Then, since it's going live into *The National*, it is sent back up again to the satellite and finally bounces down onto the viewers' television sets in Atlantic Canada. From the time Parker shouted "Roll!" it's taken a second and a half. In the seemingly interminable delay, we all agonize before finally seeing Meech Lake. But, as Parker says, "At home, they'll never know."

9:03:15

Meanwhile, I still can't hear Duffy, so after the Halton report ends I introduce him and ask my question. Mike responds and keeps on talking for a couple of minutes. I thank him and then it's into a report on the Quebec budget and the rest of the news.

9:12 p.m.

While the "sting" previewing what's coming up on *The Journal* is running for half a minute, lineup editor Mark Bulgutch calls me from the control room: "Kill the South African voice over and use the Buerk intro," he says. We're light because Duffy was shorter than we'd planned so now we'll run the longer, full report from Michael Buerk in Johannesburg.

9:15 p.m.

While the Buerk item is running, Mark is on the phone again to me: "Kill pages 15-A and 16 . . . Now we're heavy." The Buerk report was longer than the time we needed to make up from Duffy being short, so in order to get off on time, we had to cut a bit. Autocue operator Paul Franco quickly switches the pages around so everything will be in order when I come on air again.

9:21 p.m.

Mark again: "We forgot a page was out. Now we're light. Do a recap of the top story before saying good night."

9:21:59 p.m.

". . . and now, *The Journal*," I say as the Atlantic edition of *The*

National ends just one second light. That's not a problem, though, because we can be up to ten seconds light or ten seconds heavy and *The Journal* will adjust accordingly because it has about thirty seconds of extra "pad" at the end of its program.

9:22:15 p.m.
"Stay here," floor director David Ritchie tells me. "We'll try to tape Duffy."

9:24 p.m.
After fiddling with the sound in my earplug I can now hear Mike so we are ready to tape the talk-back.

9:35 p.m.
After a couple of false starts, Mike and I have our one-minute-and-forty-two-second chat about what happens behind the scenes at Meech Lake and then I scamper upstairs for our between-newscasts editorial meeting. This is where we make changes for the next edition of *The National*.

9:42 p.m.
Not many changes are needed, although we'll rewrite the Quebec budget story to give more details of the provincial tax changes and prune a couple of the copy stories. A quick check of the May 1 *Globe and Mail*, which has just been delivered, shows the *Globe* has nothing we don't.

9:51 p.m.
I head down to the make-up room again, have a quick word with Barbara Frum about whether an agreement will be reached by the Prime Minister and the premiers on bringing Quebec into the constitution, and then go up one flight to the control room to chat briefly with Fred Parker and with Paul Franco at the autocue. As I leave, Fred says, "Okay now, remember, guys. This is the one Trina watches!" Even though she's not been executive producer of *The National* for six years, Trina McQueen's intense scrutiny of *The National* remains a vivid memory, verging on newsroom folklore.

10:00 p.m.
The opening animation for *The National* rolls and fifty seconds later it's "Good evening," and we go through the newscast once again – this time without the feed problems we'd had on the Atlantic edition with the Meech Lake report from Halton.

10:19 p.m.
Suddenly, with the program nearly over, we get a phone call from Prime Minister Mulroney's press secretary, who tells us there is a deal on getting Quebec to sign the constitution. A quick story is typed in the newsroom and rushed down to the studio, where I just have time to add the eighteen-second report on the agreement as *The National* ends.

10:23 p.m.
It's back upstairs for another editorial meeting for the 11:00 p.m. edition going to Manitoba, which will now lead with the Meech Lake agreement.

10:30 p.m.
David Nayman is on the phone to Meech Lake arranging new feeds on the breaking story of an agreement reached between the Prime Minister and the premiers. Halton will do a new piece saying what the agreement means, Duffy will do a new talk-back with me, and Wendy Mesley will do a report on the Quebec implications of the agreement. This is turning into a marathon night for our Ottawa team as well as for us.

"But now we're in a box with Quebec," Nayman says. The trouble is that the CBC in Quebec is carrying the Montreal Canadiens-Quebec Nordiques hockey playoff game. Montreal is ahead by one goal and it looks like the game will end shortly after 11:00 p.m. If so, *The National* must follow immediately. The "box" we are in is that we can't go live at 11:00 to Manitoba and live shortly after 11:00 to Quebec. One province will have to watch a tape of the 10:00 p.m. *National*, which means one region will get only a brief end-of-program reference to the agreement reached at Meech Lake instead of the full new story. Since the story is more important to Quebec, Nayman decides Manitoba will get a tape and Quebec the live program.

10:45 p.m.
Quebec has scored to tie the game with six minutes and twenty-three seconds to go in the game, raising the possibility of overtime. We keep open the option of going live to Manitoba instead of Quebec if the game is still going at 11:00.

10:48 p.m.
As I head for the control room Quebec scores again to take the lead in the hockey game with less than five minutes to go.

10:55 p.m.
When I reach the control room, Fred Parker tells me the game is going to go past 11:00 so we'll go live to Manitoba and do a "split tape." That means we'll record the program on two tapes, and if the hockey game is over before we are off the air in Manitoba with *The National*, we can run the first tape with the opening ten minutes of the newscast to Quebec thus ensuring that Quebec will get the full new story on the constitutional agreement and then pull the second tape into synch with the first as it ends to show the last half of *The National*. It sounds complicated and it is, at least to me.

10:58 p.m.
As I put on my microphone and earplug, I now find I can't hear Mike at Meech Lake, but he can hear me. This simply is not our day.

10:59 p.m.
Now I still can't hear Mike, but I am getting a feed in my ear of Wendy Mesley's report.

10:59:45 p.m.
"Well, lets hope it works," says floor director David Ritchie as he then shouts, "Fifteen seconds!"

11:00 p.m.
We're on live to Manitoba.

11:01:30 p.m.
I get a sudden change in Wendy's introduction script: a new fact, which I add.

11:06 p.m.
I start talking to Duffy and we both hear each other perfectly as Mike delivers an impressive two-and-a-half-minute Meech Lake summary in answering my three questions.

11:09 p.m.
We're running heavy because of the Meech Lake stories so we change to a shorter version of the Michael Buerk piece on South Africa.

11:18 p.m.
We're still running heavy, so we kill a couple of paragraphs on Sheila MacVicar's introduction.

11:20 p.m.
The hockey game is over in Quebec (Quebec has won) and we're now running the first half of *The National* on the split tape to Quebec while

we're finishing the last half of the same program live to Manitoba.

11:22 p.m.
The National to Manitoba ends and I head up to the control room and then take the elevator to the fifth-floor newsroom.

11:27 p.m.
"Halton's putting in some new pictures and changing it just a bit. . . . It'll be slightly longer," says David Nayman. The new pictures will show more of the premiers after they'd reached the agreement and will be more up-to-date. So now we'll do *The National* again at midnight for the Alberta edition.

11:35 p.m.
Because Halton's piece is longer this time, we have to cut elsewhere to make room. We decide to take out Michael Buerk's report from South Africa and use a much shorter film report with my voice over it. We now will have used all three of the versions of Buerk that lineup editor Mark Bulgutch had set aside three hours earlier "just in case."

12:00 midnight
We're on the air with *The National* to Alberta.

12:22 a.m.
". . . and now, *The Journal*," I say, signing off for the last time.

12:23 a.m.
I loosen my tie, stand up, and stretch.

12:24 a.m.
"And that's a wrap," booms Fred's voice over the loudspeaker on the studio floor. He means there are no new developments so British Columbia will get a tape of *The National* we just did and we can go home. Often with breaking news like tonight we go live into British Columbia, too, so we can keep up to date. But for tonight, the story's now over.

12:26 a.m.
I head up to the newsroom, chat briefly with Mark Bulgutch and David Nayman. David is typing a note to assignment editor Bob Waller about follow-up coverage tomorrow on Meech Lake. I hand my now somewhat tattered script to a copy clerk for filing and go back downstairs to take off my make-up.

12:39 a.m.
"Good night," the front door security guard sings out as I go out the door, with *The National* of April 30, 1987, now finally over.

THE FAIRLY TYPICAL DAY just described dramatically underlines the much more intense, co-ordinated, production-oriented, desk-controlled approach to *The National* compared to the days when I was a correspondent in Washington in the 1960s. Then, we correspondents in the field did news reports for radio as well as TV and paid far less attention to production values than is now the case. We usually didn't work with a producer, often with just a cameraman, and generally did the stories we wanted to with little or no direction from the news desk at network headquarters. Today no story is done without a producer approving it and then vetting the script.

In the old days I would frequently do a couple of radio reports, another one for the early evening TV news, still another for *The National*, and also prepare material for *Newsmagazine*, all in a single day. Now there are field producers, two- or sometimes three-person camera crews, and a tight leash from the producers and editors from the assignment desk and the night desk, all putting an emphasis on production values that we never dreamed of. With the new *National*, all scripts from correspondents are checked, edited, and argued over by editors at network headquarters. The idea of checking our scripts with the desk when I was in Washington wouldn't even have occurred to me or my colleagues, such as James M. Minifie, Norman DePoe, Michael Maclear, or Stanley Burke. We were graduates from the print media and much more independent than the new breed of correspondent. The greater production values, tighter desk control, and visual sensitivity have led to far more polished and comprehensive news reports, but less reportorial flare and individuality.

I had talked about these changes shortly before the *National/Journal* went on the air in 1982 with my old correspondent colleague and former *National* anchorman Stanley Burke, who was then a visiting professor of journalism at the University of Saskatchewan at Regina. I was at the school to talk on journalism ethics in making the inaugural lecture in what would become the annual James M. Minifie Memorial Lecture series in honour of my late colleague. I was delighted Minifie's home province had decided to honour my old friend and mentor from Washington days, the man who taught me more about integrity and honesty in journalism than everybody else put together.

"Don," as he was called by his friends (his middle name was Macdonald), was a British-born but prairie-raised farm boy from Saskatchewan who went on to one of Canada's most illustrious journalistic careers. He had interviewed everybody who was anybody from Mussolini and Franklin Roosevelt to Churchill and Lyndon Johnson, and he had covered innumerable wars, revolutions, elections, riots, and assorted crises.

At age sixteen, Minifie had talked his way into World War I with the Canadian Army. Later he was a Rhodes Scholar and then spent a couple of decades with the *New York Herald Tribune* and covered the Spanish Civil War, where he was captured by the Moors of the Franco forces just outside Madrid. During World War II he covered the Battle of Britain and lost an eye in the Blitz. After the war he reported from Washington for both the *Herald Tribune* and CBC Radio. A cherub-faced enthusiast, Don was a man of great loves and great hates, a passionate person who despised those he called "the fat cats," whether political, social, or economic. He had a cultivated pugnacity, a true gentleman who was at the same time fiercely competitive in a cut-throat game. Don's old bald head was filled with more knowledge of the classics and contemporary life than any of us. He added lustre to our journalistic profession.

He never did, however, really come to terms with television. Although he would never admit it, he hated all the lights, cameras, and production techniques that he felt distracted him from his main job of delivering the news. He was, in fact, contemptuous of producers, not to say editors, too, whom he alternately called "the young buggers" or "the dishwashers of television." Don got his revenge once on a Lyndon Johnson campaign train swing through the U.S. Midwest when he ignored his cameraman and producer totally, leaving them to play cards and drink throughout the trip while he went about gathering the news. His reports for *The National* consisted of pictures of him standing at a train stop and talking for two minutes about what had happened with no accompanying pictures.

Minifie had taught me much about the necessity of never relenting in the passionate search for journalistic truth, of the need for dogged hard work, how to exploit lucky breaks, and the importance of style. He always provided just enough personal flavour and the right number of pungent phrases without editorializing. He was my professional anchor and, most important of all, a friend whom I missed and remembered.

Over dinner and wine before my lecture honouring Minifie, Stan Burke and I reminisced about Don and about Norman DePoe, another old colleague who had died earlier that year. Minifie and DePoe were the best of the veteran reporters of the CBC, charismatic, knowledge-able, totally devoted to their craft. Norman, first as the senior Ottawa reporter and later as a roving correspondent, was a special pain in the ass to CBC bureaucrats, who weren't prepared to accept his unique attitude and didn't appreciate his talents. He did not suffer fools gladly, to say the least, and woe betide any politician who tried to bafflegab his way out of a problem. Norman never was your average squeaky clean, blow-dried, mellow-voiced, sweet-faced, buttoned-down television anchorman. He smoked like a chimney and drank like a fish, cursed like a Trojan and caroused like a Roman. He had a face that looked like it had been up all night and often was, a raspy growl, the product of fifty cigarettes a day, a love of gin and late-night Press Club harmonizing.

With his furrowed brow, military moustache, and sergeant-major approach developed during his wartime years in the Canadian Army, DePoe was simply unbeatable when he came on television as a reporter or anchorman to give you the inside story of what was going on in Ottawa. Beyond the tough demeanour there was a brilliant mind that held an encyclopedic knowledge of Canadian politics. He could and did quote Plato to Pierre Trudeau and Gerda Munsinger to John Diefenbaker. He could put more information and insight into a two-minute report than his rivals could in thirty minutes or three columns. He could out-drink, out-sing, out-think, and out-write anybody in the business. In short, Norman was the best and the last of a breed.

The first memo he ever received as a reporter from a CBC boss was after he'd covered the 1952 Republican presidential convention in Chicago. It read, "What you said was excellent. The way you said it was unacceptable." There was a lot that was bureaucratically unacceptable about Norman, and he literally went out swinging. He had been shoved over to radio news from television because he and his TV boss, chief news editor Mike Daigneault, were utterly irreconcilable. Mike, a young, new-style editor, was outraged at what he felt were Norman's unreliability and lack of respect, while Norman was contemptuous of any "young kid" telling him what to do. It boiled into an office hallway confrontation with, some observers claim, wild swinging, but which DePoe later described as only "an acrimonious dispute."

After that, it was radio for Norman, but his heart really wasn't in it. He was cut adrift by the end of 1976. Always a loner, even with his boisterous late-night camaraderie, Norman told me, "I've had it." I was director of News and Current Affairs at the time and I regretted Norman's loss to broadcasting, but I understood the problems of managing Norman's increasing impetuosity. Even his last assignment saw a quintessential, liquid-fuelled confrontation with one of his bosses, whom he ordered out of the Montreal newsroom when he was reporting the 1976 Quebec election. "Never did like the pompous ass," DePoe said later.

DePoe's paycheque had been chicken feed (about $30,000 at the end of his career) compared to the TV anchor salaries, but he never complained. "Look," he said, "I never wanted a big salary. I never wanted to be a millionaire. Where the hell else could I have done exactly what I like doing and get paid for it?"

On his last day at CBC, Norman went on *The National* as we ran a brief retrospective report on his career, and then he shook hands a little nervously with the new breed of TV journalist, Peter Kent, who was anchoring *The National* then, so utterly different from Norman in his demeanour and his sense of using the picture as much as the word to tell a story. After three decades with the CBC as Canada's best-known journalist, Norman faded away into the night. He had planned to do his autobiography, but never did manage to finish it.

I would run into Norman from time to time after his retirement and was saddened to see how both he and the CBC had wasted such a rich talent. He could have done so much more. He was the most tempestuous, sensitive, demanding, brilliant TV journalist Canada ever produced. "All I ever tried to do," he said, "is report as honestly as I could . . . to tell as much of the truth as you can get into a minute or two or three."

Shortly before Norman died in 1980 of his self-inflicted lifestyle, we met as he was striding along Jarvis Street outside the CBC in downtown Toronto. He was older now, more subdued, greyer and slower, but still defiant, ignoring his doctors orders about drinking and showing flashes of the old DePoe, as he complained about the quality of writing on *The National*, denounced the bureaucrats, and mischievously smiled at remembered triumphs. Rakishly tilting his hat and waving his Irish cane at me, he said, "You know, I've had a dandy life, thank you. All I want on my tombstone now are the words: 'He was a good reporter.'"

That he was.

Stan Burke and I agreed that the only correspondent who came close to DePoe in tempestuousness was our old friend Peter Reilly, who also was an old-school broadcast journalist. To his Irish charm and sensitivity, his Irish anger and melancholy, Reilly added a talent for puncturing stuffed shirts with his honest, polished journalistic craftmanship. He, Stan, and I had all been correspondents together, along with Minifie and DePoe, as Reilly covered the United Nations beat and travelled the world. Like DePoe, Reilly was hard to take for some of his colleagues, but he inspired love, too, as demonstrated by

Warner Troyer, who worked with him as a co-host (along with Adrienne Clarkson) when *the fifth estate* began. When Reilly died in 1976 at age forty-four from his excessive lifestyle, Troyer said, "Partly we love him because he made us think more of ourselves, think and speak more honestly." In a bar late one night, I asked Peter why he drank so much. With his mischievous grin and dancing eyes, he said, "Because it tastes so damned good!" Reilly at times was one hell of a lot of trouble to his friends as well as his adversaries, but he was always worth it.

While DePoe, Minifie, and Reilly were quintessential examples of the best of the old school of broadcast journalist, for whom words remained more important than pictures, their colleague Michael Maclear was the first-generation TV correspondent who knew how to combine words and images to achieve greater impact on a mass audience than any of his CBC correspondent colleagues.

An often sickly beanpole Englishman, Maclear's losses at the gambling tables of Macao, Nassau, or the private clubs of London were as legendary as his journalistic coups. He scooped the world with the first interview of American prisoners of war in North Vietnam and the death of Ho Chih Minh (his reports to CBC-TV on Ho's death were picked up by the networks of eighty-four countries), and he conducted one of the first interviews in the Sierra Maestre Mountains with Fidel Castro in 1958 just before Castro launched his successful battle for power. Whether Maclear was interviewing Jawaharlal Nehru in the marble halls of an Indian government palace in New Delhi or dodging bullets in the Middle East, his gaunt face conveyed a compelling, involving realism. He was a consummate TV professional, shooting delicately nuanced film and marrying cinema vérité emotions with the words while the rest of us largely concentrated on the words alone. He knew the art of writing lean scripts that let the pictures carry the story. The result was high emotional impact. He went on to become an award-winning TV documentary producer.

Minifie, DePoe, Reilly, and Maclear were characteristic of that hard-drinking, swashbuckling generation now replaced by a generally better educated, certainly better paid, and probably more stable new breed of correspondent. If anything, Maclear was a kind of bridge between the old and the new. The new breed included women such as Ann Medina, whose personal friendliness and professional toughness endear her to colleagues and viewers alike. She, like all the new correspondents, has a much better feel for the visual values in TV reporting than did most of the old breed.

Medina's journalistic roots go back to her teenage years when she started a high school newspaper. While gaining degrees in philosophy at Wellesley College and the University of Chicago, she worked part-time and summers for ABC News and then became a full-fledged U.S. network reporter. She was sent to Canada for an assignment and stayed for romance and a husband. I met her more than a decade ago after she joined *Newsmagazine* as a correspondent. She went on to become executive producer of *Newsmagazine* and, later, a sterling field correspondent for *The Journal* and a weekend anchor of *The National*, bringing outstanding journalistic polish to both programs.

Medina never, or hardly ever, felt nervous as a woman correspondent and some leaders, such as the PLO's Yasser Arafat and Israeli Prime Minister Menachem Begin, admired her spunk and gave her interviews after turning down her male competitors. With her deep voice and no-nonsense approach to what is a rough and tumble, often dangerous business, Ann never lost her distinctiveness either in her high-quality reporting or her well-tailored look in the field. Ann never has been a journalistic crusader. "You report what you see, what you know, and what you touch, which is after all what reporters are all about," she says. While she loves reporting from Beirut, Tel Aviv, Nicaragua, Northern Ireland, Uganda, or China, she worries about getting "burned out," as so many correspondents of the bygone era did. "I wanted to pace myself so that didn't happen," she says of her decision to come in from the field and anchor *The National* on Saturdays and substitute for me during the week from time to time. She still covers stories for her Saturday program and occasionally does documentaries for *The Journal*, but life now is a little less hectic as she reaches out for a kind of "normalcy" and now feels she may even try to stop smoking. Ann never regarded herself as one of the old-fashioned newswomen who acted as hard-boiled "dames" trying to out-macho the men.

Nor did Adrienne Clarkson, who was the most successful of all women journalists in the growing middle years of television. As host of the CBC afternoon program *Take Thirty* for nearly a decade, she displayed a sparkling on-air presence and a desperate desire to get into prime-time TV. When I was director of News and Current Affairs we developed a prime-time program for her called *Adrienne At Large*, which took her around the world by jet, camel, boat, and car, interviewing everyone from the King of Sweden to refugees in Hong Kong. She was an earlier version of Ann Medina and later was an original and certainly the most well-known host of *the fifth estate*. She became an icon of television journalism, a cool, crisp, beautiful, elegant, but unstoppable presence. She resented columnists who criticized her for being so clothes conscious and once told me, "Just because I'm interested in Yves Saint Laurent doesn't mean I'm not interested in Nietzsche." Years later, columnist Allan Fotheringham would write that Adrienne "has a wardrobe that makes Imelda Marcos look like a bag lady."

On both *Adrienne At Large* and *the fifth estate* she hurtled from continent to continent, so much so she sometimes forgot where she'd been, telling more than one customs official who asked where she was coming from, "I have absolutely no idea.... Here's my passport, you figure it out."

Born in Hong Kong, she was a driving, ambitious, witty, and sometimes cutting reporter who could charm the pants off even the most belligerent or reluctant interviewee. She also had an ego of not insignificant proportions. Fotheringham once said Adrienne was the only woman he knew (and he is an old friend of hers) who "struts sitting down," adding, "And her alarm clock doesn't ring, it applauds." But even with her healthy ego, she never demanded "star treatment" and gave her producers no serious problems.

At one point the government considered her as a possible executive director of the Canadian Film Development Corp. (CFDC), and she didn't blink an eye as she told a reporter, "The presidency of the CBC or any arts agency isn't something I'd seek out. But for me, it's either the top job or nothing. I'm bilingual and ... I think I could do the CFDC job or I wouldn't give it a second thought." With her tongue only slightly tucked into her cheek, she added that she would "love to tap dance" on TV and also that "I'm not an actress, but if they were doing a series about a brilliant archeologist who raises hair from cattle in her spare time and is a champion handball player and was a fashion model for Balmain, I'd be perfect for the part."

Certainly Adrienne had no evident sense of insecurity about herself and she had a magical presence in front of the camera, not in the slightest worried about "performing" as some TV journalists are, and she could be professionally demanding in the studio about lighting and camera positions. During her *fifth estate* years she was sought out to be host of the CBS show *60 Minutes*. Executive producer Don Hewitt flew her down to New York twice for interviews and wanted her for the show. So, too, did Mike Wallace, who thought she would make a perfect co-host and colleague.

"We wanted her and thought she'd be terrific," Wallace told me years later. But *60 Minutes* co-host Morley Safer, a one-time CBC news correspondent, didn't share the enthusiasm of Hewitt and Wallace. "Morley was against it," Wallace told me. "He never really did say why, but he was so strongly against her we reluctantly gave her a pass. Too bad."

So Adrienne stayed with the CBC until she was willingly plucked from her $70,000 *fifth estate* hosting chores by the Ontario government, which made her the province's representative in Paris in 1982. She came back to Canada five years later as publisher of McClelland and Stewart. That isn't running the CBC, but it probably is almost as difficult given the precarious economics of Canadian book publishers.

While Adrienne was a clear extrovert, loving the glamour of dashing around the world and the lights of the studio, Peter Kent was a prime example of the new breed of globetrotting reporter, an introverted extrovert, if such a thing is possible. Shying away from the glitter, but nevertheless secretly enjoying it, too, Peter as a CBC correspondent and anchorman was a handsome, visually sensitive, quietly aggressive journalistic jewel for the CBC. He is also typical of the kind of reporter the American networks like and twice left CBC for foreign correspondent jobs with NBC, first in South Africa and later in Central America. He now works for NBC out of Miami.

Nothing could stop his peripatetic fireman's pace, whether he worked for CBC or NBC, although he admitted to being slowed down on one occasion as he scampered from Kampuchea to Uganda and along the way caught amoebic dysentery. That and malaria are the constant threats correspondents have to face in their travels. "When you're on a tight shooting schedule, it slows you down," he said dismissively.

AMERICAN NETWORK talent scouts always keep a close watch on potential Canadian prospects like Kent and have snapped up an extraordinarily large number of them over the years. Correspondents like Morley Safer from Toronto, Robert MacNeil from Montreal, Peter Jennings from Ottawa, Don McNeill from St. John's, Mark Phillips from Montreal, John Blackstone from Goderich, Ont., Doreen Kays from Charlottetown, Allen Pizzey from London, Ont., Mike McCourt from Saskatoon, Hilary Brown from Ottawa, and more than a dozen others found varying degrees of fame and fortune with the American networks. In truth, though, they left Canada for neither, but rather for the bigger resources, the Lear jets, more satellite feeds, and a sense of being in "the Big Leagues." At one point, in Johannesburg covering the South African story, the three American networks were represented by three Canadians, Pizzey for CBS, McCourt for ABC, and Kent for NBC. But the competition was tougher with the U.S. networks, the on-air "ice time" was less, and some got discouraged and came back home.

The U.S. networks wanted Canadians in part because a Canadian passport got a correspondent places Americans couldn't go – such as China, for a while – and in many parts of the world – Nicaragua, for example – it was safer to be a Canadian than an American. Our correspondents also are generally better trained in both journalism and TV production than many of their American counterparts and have more knowledge of the world at large, especially compared to the younger would-be correspondents in the U.S. whose training is gained mainly in the slapdash superficiality of most of the local U.S. stations. Our Canadian accents are fully acceptable in the U.S. – although Peter Jennings was warned when he started anchoring the news at ABC to stop saying "zed" and to avoid pronouncing "out" and "house" with what was perceived to be too much of a Canadian "oo" accent – and we're more knowledgeable about the United States than any other country of English-speaking non-Americans.

Another CBC correspondent who went to "the Big Leagues" was Brian Stewart, who had been an outstanding Ottawa reporter before being assigned to London and adding sheen to our foreign correspondent corps. A quiet, serious man, Stewart was more emotionally stirred by stories he covered than most of his colleagues. Speaking long after the first time he was under fire as a foreign correspondent, he said, "I can remember vividly as the shells crashed with this horrendous bang and my face buried in a dirty ditch, and I could see blades of grass quivering as the shells came in. I was struck by something I had read by the First World War poets ... the intensity of detail, how small details were sort of frozen in time, and I could see the little puffs of dust coming up between the blades of grass. ... What amazed me most was that here ... on a vast stage like Beirut, what was fascinating to me was the little puffs of dirt."

Freezing moments in time is what Stewart and all foreign correspondents do, whether in Beirut, El Salvador, Belfast, Vietnam, or Ethiopia. They risk their lives, fight lying officials, try to outsmart censors, and argue with editors back home in their determination to tell the story. "Some of the best reporting in war I've ever come across," Stewart has said, "was the First World War poets who wrote quite dramatically and eloquently of the sound of battle, the sound of shell fire ... the chaos and smell of battle, the weariness and fatigue ... the slowness of movement, the troglodyte existence of the people who are fighting ... the gut-wrenching fear that goes on from morning through the evening."

As a youngster Stewart had dreamed of becoming a sports reporter so he could "get a free ticket to the World Series." But watching the

Suez crisis and the Hungarian revolution unfold on television in the fall of 1956, he changed his mind. "I was flabbergasted," he later said, recalling his youthful innocence, "that people were actually paid to be in the first row of history."

But in covering the shooting in Northern Ireland, El Salvador, and Lebanon, he found no glamour. In a compelling CBC documentary, *The War Reporters*, he called El Salvador "the most evil place I've ever known in my life." He remembered awakening in a luxurious downtown San Salvador hotel every morning and having breakfast, which "was the last moment of decent civilized behaviour for the rest of the day.... In would charge our driver to say, 'Come quick. Finish up. We've got bodies ... more bodies during the night.' "

In Lebanon, Stewart was a friendly rival to CTV's Clark Todd, who was killed by shellfire in that war-torn excuse for a country. After Todd's death, Stewart visited his widow Ann, who, as the typical wife of a foreign correspondent, never knew when she and the children would see him. Like most correspondents, Todd was away from home three-quarters of the time. On his fatal, final assignment to Lebanon, he'd left his home outside London at dawn and Ann remembered, "We never said good-bye to him because he left before we were even awake." In this respect, the new breed of correspondent is no different from the old.

He'd been wounded in Northern Ireland but it wasn't serious. But in a village in the Shouf Mountains outside Beirut he and his crew came under fire and he got what his cameraman described as "a small neat round hole close to his heart." Todd's last words as he lay on a bed in an abandoned, bomb-shattered house were, "It's not death that scares, it's the embarrassment." Before dying, he penned a last message on his blood-stained pillowcase: "Please tell my family I love them." Commenting on this story, Brian Stewart said, "There's nothing glamorous whatever about lying bleeding to death in a remote Lebanese mountain village.... I'm damned if I can see the glamour in it."

Reflecting on what he called "all the oozing evil of the Middle East ... concentrated in Beirut," Stewart later confessed, "I keep having this image of Beirut in the nighttime rain and thinking of T.S. Eliot's poem 'The Wasteland': 'We are in rats' alley where the dead men lost their bones.' "

Brian Stewart refuted the stereotypical image of the hard-bitten, unemotional foreign correspondent, and his sensitivity had its ultimate test when he covered the starvation in Ethiopia as the first North American reporter to work on the story. He found there a nightmare of ragged children, swollen bellies, emaciated bodies, swirling dust, and death everywhere. He spent one chilly, sleepless night in a room on the edge of a refugee camp, hearing strange cries and howls through the night. "Sort of a barnyard scene out of a medieval world," he later said. When light came at 5:15 a.m., he went outside to see "all along the road a line of people moaning and groaning in their freezing starvation. . . . This was about as close to Hell as one can probably find anywhere on earth."

Stewart was in Ethiopia with producer Tony Burman, fresh from guiding the new *National* to its successful launch. Together, they viewed the Ethiopian starvation story as the greatest professional challenge of their lives. When Stewart got back to the comfort of his London home he used to have nightmares, "images of small starving black kids scurrying about the floor."

NBC had been so impressed with Stewart's Ethiopian reporting that they wooed and eventually won him. The day he walked into the NBC newsroom in New York in 1986 he was dispatched to Libya and he had kept running ever since. But Ethiopia had seared his soul and he never was the same again. After a year based in the NBC Frankfurt bureau, at the age of forty-four, he felt his luck, his legs, and his soul could take no more, and he left the job to come back to Canada to think, to write, and to nurse the psychological scar tissue that correspondents accumulate. "I just hope my sensitivities haven't been dulled," he said. It's a dilemma for all foreign correspondents, and some keep going forever until they drop, as most of the old breed did, while some, like Stewart, Medina, and, indeed, even myself, quit, perhaps while we still don't have too much scar tissue.

Stewart, Todd, Medina, Kent, DePoe, Minifie, Maclear, Burke, myself, and hundreds of other broadcast correspondents all have their roots in what's known as "Murrow's Boys." This was a happy band of journalistic warriors who were broadcasting's first foreign correspondents, put together in the late 1930s and early 1940s by the icon of broadcast journalism, Edward R. Murrow of CBS. Murrow's Boys, such as William Shirer, Eric Sevareid, Alexander Kendrick, Bill Downs, David Schoenbrun, and Howard K. Smith, set the standards that all broadcast correspondents are measured against today. They were reporting during an extraordinary news period, with Hitler on the march and then on the run. Their broadcasting brought to people an immediacy never before experienced. Having heard it crackling over the airwaves from a London air raid, who could ever forget Edward R. Murrow's terse, emotion-laden, "This . . . is London." All of Murrow's Boys injected their personalities and sometimes their opinions into their reports, so unlike the modern style of cleansing reports of opinion and personality in pursuit of objectivity. A few people, like Mike Duffy in his CBC reports from Ottawa or Joe Schlesinger from Washington, can effectively inject their personalities into their stories, but they are exceptions.

Murrow's Boys thought of themselves as teachers with a mission, but today's broadcast correspondents essentially think of themselves as fact reporters with good-paying jobs and lots of travel. What's been lost is a richness and a flavour. What's been gained is less bias and more objectivity. Emotionally, I yearn for the colourful, visceral reportage of those earlier days, but intellectually I know today's correspondents are presenting a better balanced and fairer reflection of reality.

The contrast between these two approaches was clearly evident in the difference between Edward R. Murrow, the thoughtful analyst, and Walter Cronkite, the front-page action man. Although both worked for CBS News and sometimes were together on major stories, they never were comfortable with each other. As Murrow's star descended at CBS, Cronkite's rose, and he became the best-known anchorman in the world. In Sweden, the name for a news anchor on TV is "Kronkiter." I'd known Walter when I was a correspondent in Washington. Later, when he retired in the spring of 1981, I flew down to New York to interview him for *Newsmagazine*. In private he was basically the same as on the TV screen – a comfortable, reliable, knowledgeable "Uncle Walter." But one thing not seen was his intense competitiveness. Nobody in the news business was more intent on beating the competition than Cronkite, a character trait probably from his days as a United Press news agency reporter, which was part of my background, too.

"I'll miss getting my hands into the product every day ... that's been my life," he told me. When I asked this "most respected man in America," as opinion surveys had declared him, his feelings about the enormously high audience impact of TV news, he replied, "It's far beyond reason ... far beyond acceptability.... What we can do is a bare microcosm of what the people need to know." He, of course, was right.

He worried, too, about "showmanship" in TV news – the "giggle factor," he called it. "Are they hiring people to be news people or are they hiring people to be comedians?.... 'Showmanship,' we don't need it." The "cult of personality" for newscast anchormen alarmed him, too. "I'm worried all the time about it. It's silly ... it's no damn good," he told me.

Walter Cronkite had worried about the "show-biz" cult of the TV anchor personalities, but that tends to be much more of an American local station problem than a British or a Canadian problem. Bubble-headed, chit-chatty news anchors are relatively rare in Canada because we view our newscasters more seriously than most of the local stations in the U.S. Driven by advertisers' desire for high ratings, the American stations often fall victim to the old Hearstian smash-and-grab journalism, playing up fires, rapes, and murders and largely ignoring city hall and significant social, economic, and political issues. The difference is also evident between Canadian and U.S. networks. In war stories, NBC, CBS, and ABC more often go after "bang-bang" coverage, as for example in Vietnam, the Middle East, and Nicaragua, than does the CBC. Admittedly, one reason is money. We often can't afford to be there when the "bang-banging" breaks out, so to make a virtue out of necessity we tend to do more explanatory backgrounders called "situationers," picking up battle footage from the American networks to buttress our reports.

A cost squeeze now has overtaken the American networks, however, as each of their news departments faces heavy pressure on its $300-million-a-year news budgets (ten times what CBC spends on news). They have all been taken over by the bean counters of conglomerate corporations with a mindset of profit, not service. Even so, the U.S. network budget-cutting may have the value of forcing them to have fewer news crews, gallivanting superficially around the world using Lear jets and satellites, and put more emphasis on textured explanation and less on immediacy at all costs.

Our problem at the CBC and for all the broadcast media in Canada is that we've never had enough money to cover the world properly. It's critically important for the Canadian networks to have their own correspondents abroad and not take the cheap and easy way of picking up U.S. network reports for much of their foreign coverage. Aside from their proclivity for immediacy over texture, the U.S. network correspondents are reporting to an American audience and naturally using American reference points and relating their stories to American history and policies. One of the Canadian networks' big failures – including, and perhaps especially, the CBC, given our public broadcasting mandate – is the relatively small number of full-time foreign correspondents we have in places like Beijing, Washington, Moscow, London, Paris, and Jerusalem. There are many other parts of the world where we are unrepresented. Even the TV networks in a country like Sweden have more foreign correspondents than we do.

DURING MY NEW YORK conversation with Cronkite, I'd mentioned James M. Minifie, whom he had known in both his CBC and his *New*

York Herald Tribune days, and we agreed that Don's three key professional qualities had made him an ideal journalist: an implacable demand for accuracy; an insatiable curiosity; and an irrespressible joy in being a journalist.

When I gave the James M. Minifie Memorial Lecture at the University of Saskatchewan in Regina, I echoed the theme of that conversation with Cronkite. I talked about the media and its responsibilities. I told the students that journalism is, in effect, the glue that holds together our democratic society: "We stake everything on a rational dialogue of an informed public, and only journalism can reach the mass of the people to provide information they must have for that rational dialogue. Journalism, in effect, is a message centre communicating back and forth between the governed and the governing, and without an independent journalism, you simply cannot have a democratic society."

The effectiveness of journalism, though, is challenged by two factors. First, what I like to call "the Cleopatra Syndrome." The idea is that the bearer of bad news is somehow to blame for the severity of the message. And yet, as I said in my lecture, a key part of journalism's job is to make people aware of uncomfortable problems and to provide a fair reflection of reality in our reportage. There must always be freedom for the thought you hate. Part of the journalist's job is to be the bearer of bad news.

The second challenge for effective journalism, I told the students, is credibility. It's the heart and soul of our business. We get that credibility, and the respect and power that go with it, only by being a socially and professionally responsible agent for the public. British Prime Minister Stanley Baldwin once attacked some of the more sensational Fleet Street journalists by saying they had "power without responsibility . . . the prerogative of the harlot throughout the ages." That stinging accusation underlined my own attitude that the media have enormous responsibility in their role of messenger in a democratic society and must, therefore, be fair, honest, accurate, comprehensive, and fearless. We must report social co-operation as well as social confrontation.

The media have improved enormously since the shameless superficialities of the flashy fedora and trenchcoat days of *The Front Page* and of American publishing buccaneer William Randolph Hearst's abdication of truth and taste. But the idea still lingers, especially among some of those in television, that the news business is show business, and consequently there still are journalists ignoring their professional responsibilities by pandering to the lowest common denominator and emphasizing theatricality over substance with flash-

and-trash reporting and lazy, shallow, sensationalized, and simplistic journalism. Our role is not that of the hootchie-kootchie girl at an old-time carnival show.

To be credible we must present factual, straightforward news. We cannot be little moral thermometers slashing out against every perceived wrongdoing. There is a role for journalistic crusaders and zealots, but they belong not on the newscasts or the front pages but in the columns of the editorial "op ed" and feature pages and in broadcast commentaries, where there is a clearly defined dividing line between straight news and opinion.

The factual, straightforward journalist, however, has a problem when governments and politicians lie. They all occasionally lie, distort, shield, and dissemble. Sometimes they claim to do this for the sake of the country, which can be quite legitimate, but too often it is done for political reasons masquerading as national security. This is unforgivable. Democratic governments simply cannot use the excuse cited by one of Arthur Koestler's characters in *The Yogi and the Commissar*, "In this war, we are fighting a total lie in the name of a half truth."

There are total lies, half-truth lies, cover-up lies, policy lies, and the occasional personal lie. There are black lies and white lies. There are the Joseph McCarthy lies, the Watergate and Iran arms lies, and the RCMP "dirty tricks" lies. Columnists and commentators can "har-rumph!" to their hearts' content about all this, but the straight reporter has a harder job. He or she can and must only reflect the claim, although providing whatever context is needed so readers, viewers, and listeners can make their own judgements based on the evidence. We don't resolve the conflicts of society, we report them, and in doing so we highlight those conflicts, inevitably distressing some of the participants, who may not like to see any public reflection of an adversary's argument.

It's no wonder, though, that journalists become sceptics in the course of their tempestuous, never-ending, love/hate relationship with those in authority. All too often journalists encounter high principles and low practices in the same individual. A recent survey in *U.S. News and World Report* showed a high degree of public scepticism of the veracity of political leaders in the U.S., noting that the public believed leading politicians always or almost always tell the truth only 30 per cent of the time and the President of the United States only 38 per cent of the time. The survey reported network anchors had a 54 per cent rating for truth-telling and, at the top of the list, doctors had 75 per cent.

As I hope the Regina students understood in my lecture, independent and responsible media are critical in a democracy as an invaluable monitor of governments in particular and society in general. But if the media are the watchdogs of governments, acting as agents for the public, the public equally must watch the watchdogs to be sure we print and broadcast journalists fulfil our social and professional responsibililties.

The comments I made in Regina encapsulated the underlying philosophy of responsible journalism as practised by a Minifie, a Murrow, a Cronkite, an Ann Medina, or a Brian Stewart. When I had been director of News and Current Affairs for the CBC, it was a theme I reiterated in many meetings and memos. I didn't want our journalists lusting after ego-satisfaction, glamour, and sensationalism in a show-biz crusade of one kind or another. I worried that the romantic appeal of Watergate's "Deep Throat" stories would lure younger reporters into the murky and jerky so-called "New Journalism" with its emphasis on style over substance, on impressionistic cynicism, rather than on the plodding, detailed work of quality investigative reportage. We need to remember that our primary job is explanatory rather than accusatory. Let the politicians do the accusing; we'll do the reporting.

I do not, however, believe reporters can be totally objective in their stories. They are, after all, thinking, concerned humans and more curious than most about what makes society tick. But I do believe we must continually strive for objectivity in our reporting and try to come as close to it as humanly possible, simply to be fair.

Over the past couple of decades in Canada there has been a veritable revolution in the concern and quality of broadcast journalism as well as in its quantity and prime-time availability. "More is better," Cronkite once said. Although TV will never match the print medium for detail, it can provide an informative and emotional involvement for millions as a form of adult education. In Canada, we have some of the best television journalism in the world, but there is still much more to be done.

8 21ST CENTURY TELEVISION

As the 10:00 p.m. partnership of *The National* and *The Journal* rolled through its second year it was beginning to become an electronic informational spinal column for the nation. Not every night was great, but the close to two million Canadians watching every weeknight were getting a better news service than they'd ever had before. There were more documentaries, more special reports, more interviews, more hard-hitting news reports. We were proving that a prime-time hour of Canadian-produced journalism could stand up against any competition even though we were offering something demanding, not just distracting.

Among the first major documentaries done by *The Journal* was Peter Kent's moving report from Kampuchea showing the murderous tragedy caused by that country's civil wars. It brought back the best of the old *Newsmagazine* "reporter-in-the-field" documentary tradition. So did the program's coverage of the Falklands War and the sinking of the *Ocean Ranger* off Newfoundland. *The Journal* broke new ground, too, for Canadian TV with its linking of such places as Moscow and Washington, with officials in those cities talking to Barbara Frum in the Toronto studio and talking to each other. Cementing relations with *The National* while making good use of talent, *The Journal* assigned documentaries to a number of News correspondents including, as time went on, a revealing two-part retrospective on Vichy France by Joe Schlesinger and another by Joe on the Spanish Civil War, and Paris correspondent Don Murray did an examination of Vietnam a decade after the war. The costs of correspondent Brian Stewart's reports on the Ethiopian famine were shared between *The*

National and *The Journal,* and his searing reports on the newscast were matched with a couple of major documentaries from Ethiopia shown on *The Journal.* The traffic went the other way, too, when *Journal* correspondent Ann Medina would do reports for *The National* while out on a documentary assignment.

Not everything always went perfectly, however. On the last *Journal* of the first season the entire audio system in the control room broke down. Nobody could hear what Barbara and Mary Lou were saying down on the floor as they did the program. In a panic, director Bill Matthews called a colleague in his office and had him turn up a TV set and put the phone beside it. That way Matthews, with his ear glued to the phone and his eyes on the screen watching Barbara and Mary Lou, could at least hear what was going out on the air and know when to roll tapes and animation. "It went flawlessly," Starowicz later said, and although everything was rolled about a second late the audience at home probably didn't notice a thing.

After the first couple of years, Mary Lou began to feel limited and studio-bound in her co-hosting role and wanted to get into the field more frequently to make documentaries. At the same time, Peter Kent had become a new father and was anxious to slow down his travelling for a while. So Mary Lou began spending more time in the field and Peter began sitting in as Barbara's co-host in Mary Lou's absence. When Barbara was away, Peter would sit in for her, too, although he was not altogether comfortable in the inquisitorial role. "I just don't like it much," he told me.

There never was any doubt that Barbara was the dominant on-air presence on *The Journal.* Studio director Steve Hyde had taken to calling her "Boss lady." At times Mary Lou had appeared uneasy and subdued in a second-fiddle role. In fact, they both appeared more smoothly at ease when Peter was co-anchor than with each other. By the end of 1984, as the third year of *The Journal* came to a close, Mary Lou won a scholarship for a year at Harvard. When she came back to *The Journal* she preferred to concentrate on her documentary work. Peter Kent also left, rejoining NBC as its Central American correspondent based in Miami. Barbara then had a series of male co-anchors who shuttled between documentary work and the studio, including Bill Cameron, who came over to *The Journal* from anchoring the late-night news on Toronto's CITY-TV, Keith Morrison, who had been the weekend anchor on CTV's national news at 11:00 p.m. and finally Paul Griffin, a smooth, silver-haired Vancouver CBC radio reporter who became Barbara's regular co-host. Peter Mansbridge, who anchors news specials and sits in for me on *The National* when

I'm away, also went over to *The Journal* from time to time to replace Barbara when she was on assignment or on holiday.

Another change in the first years was in the atmosphere of the relationship between the *National* and *Journal* producers and editors. The thunder had quieted with the diminished role of the news specials unit fading into history. Gradually relations became increasingly close between the two staffs as the co-operation and co-ordination grew. Much of the credit for that went to *The National's* executive producer, John Owen, with his finely honed diplomatic skills. All the exhortations of the past, including my own fifteen years earlier, to get News and Current Affairs working together had had only modest success, but actually working together within the same hour every weeknight had made full-fledged partners out of hitherto uneasy partners and sometimes bitter rivals. We were now a long way from the painful battles between News and *This Hour Has Seven Days*. The audience was the beneficiary of all this with more and better coverage, *The National* covering the breaking stories and *The Journal* providing complementary analysis and background.

There were other changes, too. In the fall of 1983 we all were jarred by the abrupt departure of Peter Herrndorf from the CBC. He had been vice-president in charge of English radio and TV programming and of all CBC English-language regional broadcasting, a job of enormous responsibility and opportunity that he loved. It made him the single most important cultural executive in Canada, aside from the CBC president himself. Peter had always wanted full control over his own "space," or as much as he could get, and had been frustrated sometimes when Al Johnson exercised his presidential prerogatives. The frustration had increased when Johnson's successor, Pierre Juneau, decided on a corporate reorganization that saw much of Herrndorf's empire pulled away from him and concentrated in Ottawa or split up into smaller units. As a result he lost both radio and the regions, along with his autonomy in other administrative areas. In the end, Peter was left with the English television network, a mammoth job in itself and one where he, in any event, had always concentrated his energies.

At the time, I had never heard either Herrndorf or Juneau publicly or privately attack the other, and even through Herrndorf's very public departure they both displayed a respectful awareness that any wound the other may have felt should not be spoken of. Nevertheless, it had been clear for some time that while their objectives were the same, their styles of management were profoundly different. Pierre wanted Ottawa to have much more decision-making involvement with the network and Peter wanted Ottawa to have less. Herrndorf's discomfort grew to the point where he began listening to outside offers, finally deciding to take the plunge after seventeen years with the CBC and move into the magazine world as publisher of *Toronto Life*. An enormous outpouring of affection and respect for Peter immediately flowed out of the creative community, with many suggesting that he would be an ideal candidate for president of the CBC at some future date. "The contribution of Peter Herrndorf . . . is appreciated by Canadians everywhere," Juneau said following Peter's resignation. Peter himself said simply, "I loved the job."

Without his leadership, the prime-time *National* and *Journal* never would have happened. And he was certainly going out in grand style because of the continued success of the new hour. When Peter left we were riding high in audience numbers.

Another measure of success was international recognition. Programs in the United States and Australia copied our format, and *Journal* documentaries were picked up by networks the world over – twenty-five by the BBC in an average year, thirteen by West German television, fourteen by PBS in the United States. Even the Chinese television network did a report praising *The National* for its presentation of the news, although it didn't indicate any desire to follow our approach.

WITH THE BATTLES FOR PRIME TIME won and the CBC French network following our example in 1983 with its own hour of prime-time journalism, we now focused on improvements in the quality of the two programs. Our lives settled into a routine pattern. There was, however, another battle suddenly swirling around us with the coming of the fall of 1984, a battle that occupied a good deal of my attention.

The election of the Conservative government of Brian Mulroney in September, 1984, brought slashing budget cuts for the CBC. Seventy-five-million dollars were chopped, which meant more than a thousand jobs killed and numerous programs diluted or cancelled. It was a devastating blow not only because of its size but, more worryingly, because of the accompanying government rhetoric. The Tories' action raised old fears about erosion of government support of the very principle of public broadcasting. Was the new Mulroney government convinced the CBC was nothing more than a bloated, bureaucrat-filled waste of taxpayer money? Was it so preoccupied with the budget deficit and so thirsty for revenge, believing it had received ill-treatment over the long years out of political power, that it would sacrifice public broadcasting? Was it uninterested in the cultural identity of

Canada and persuaded that CTV, Global, and the private TV stations with their central focus on American programming could do just as good a job at no cost to the taxpayer?

A lot of those concerned with the survival of public broadcasting, myself included, worried that the whole foundation of public broadcasting, established half a century earlier by a Conservative government, could simply go gurgling down the drain. What the new Minister of Communications, Marcel Masse, was saying about the need for an overhaul and "new look" at CBC did nothing to calm our fears. In this atmosphere, I recalled something Al Johnson had once told me: "Any government that wants to kill an institution like the CBC would never just close it down because that would be politically impossible. No, it would starve it to death slowly over a period of years." I wondered whether this was the beginning of the starvation. What made the whole situation more alarming was that the government's pronouncements were met by no immediate public outcry. It seemed that the many advocates of public broadcasting were momentarily stunned into inactivity. Within the CBC itself a mood of black despondency fell over the staff. Worry about jobs and survival of the organization itself encouraged bureaucratic conservatism and promoted creative stultification. It was the most morose period I ever recall at the CBC.

But as the implications of the budget cuts sank in, faint stirrings of counterattack were beginning to be felt. Newspaper editorials warned against damaging the CBC. "The CBC may change, but it must endure, nay flourish," said the *Globe and Mail*. Authors such as Pierre Berton and Margaret Atwood expressed public concern, and associations of producers, unions, and cultural groups began a rumble of protest. A few weeks after the CBC budget cuts were announced, I was master of ceremonies at a fund-raising dinner for Ethiopian famine relief where External Affairs Minister Joe Clark was the featured speaker. I sat beside him at dinner with my wife Lorraine on his other side, and throughout the meal we both peppered him with our worries about the future of public broadcasting. "No. No. You worry excessively," he said. "We strongly support it, and the budget cuts reflect a concern over the deficit, not over the principle of the CBC." His words were encouraging but I wasn't sure how representative of his colleagues they were. We could only hope he would transmit our worries to them in Ottawa. As it turned out, Lorraine and I were firing an opening shot in what would become a campaign involving many concerned people to persuade our new governors that the survival of Canada was in large measure dependent on a strong cultural heartbeat. This we firmly believed would be provided primarily through public broadcasting for the mass of Canadians.

Broadcasting has become the principal source of entertainment, information, and culture in general for most of us. It's amazing to reflect that this cultural preoccupation only really began in the 1920s with the arrival on the scene of a new-fangled thing called radio. Suddenly our undefended border seemed not a border at all as a deluge of American radio programs threatened to drown Canada in what would be, in effect, American cultural annexation. In the twenties and early thirties, Canadians were tuning in to such American programming as *Amos and Andy* and *Major Bowes' Amateur Hour*, for only 60 per cent of us were even able to receive Canadian stations. Half of those stations were in Toronto and Montreal and 80 per cent of all programs listened to by Canadians were American.

Ever since then it has been a story of attack and counterattack on the Canadian cultural front as public broadcasting was born and grew. In 1928, in the first clear enunciation of the principles that have guided cultural nationalists to this day, the Aird Commission concluded, "Canadian radio listeners want Canadian broadcasting," and it proposed establishment of a public broadcasting network. This would be paid for by a licence fee for each household radio, from government subsidy, and from what it called "indirect subsidy" in the form of programs sponsored by companies but during which there was to be no mention of any specific product. Provincial directors would be appointed to run the network. However, the stock market's 1929 "Black Thursday" crash and its tidal wave of economic repercussions came a month and a half after the Aird Report was published, and the public and the politicians put aside their cultural fears to focus on their economic terrors.

But one group of social activists, led by Graham Spry, the determined and irrepressible national secretary of the Association of Canadian Clubs, kept pressuring Prime Minister Bennett. Spry and fellow "do-gooders" such as the wealthy young social activist Alan Plaunt and Brooke Claxton, who later became a Liberal cabinet minister, set up the Canadian Radio League and campaigned tirelessly in speeches in church basements and school auditoriums, to service club meetings and conventions, in magazine and newspaper articles, in private meetings and buttonholing in the corridors of power. Finally, in 1931, they persuaded Bennett to follow up on the Aird Report. The result was Canada's first coast-to-coast radio network, which by the mid-1930s reached just under half the population, operating on nights and on Sunday afternoons with a mixture of French and English programs.

But a better broadcasting service was needed, and on November 2, 1936, the Mackenzie King government established the Canadian Broadcasting Corporation with a staff of 132, eight of its own stations, and fourteen private affiliates. The government had decided to save money by having some private stations carry the CBC programs instead of constructing more CBC stations, thereby building in a long-term problem as the affiliates over the years sought to push the CBC into a more commercial ethos.

Television arrived in September, 1952. (The Toronto opening was somewhat marred, however, by the CBC coming on the air with the station slide upside down. The co-ordinating producer responsible was a man called Murray Chercover, who later became president of CTV.) With the rapid spread of CBC-TV, thanks to the engineering wizardry of Alphonse Ouimet and his colleagues, most Canadians could now see (as well as hear) Canadian programs. But as broadcasting became a power in the land, the politicians became uneasy, especially if its journalism did not reflect what they thought was appropriate. John Diefenbaker accused the CBC of sheltering "a nest of Liberals" out to get him. After he was Prime Minister, investigative commissions were appointed, the CTV network born, and a new broadcast regulatory agency established. The Diefenbaker government put pressure on the CBC to raise more of its revenue through commercials, a development with long-lasting effect. Then in the late 1960s came the *Seven Days* affair, which again catapulted CBC into nation-wide controversy. For the next two decades there were almost endless royal commissions, special committees, reports, and investigations into the CBC as governments wrestled with the problem of how to finance and control the impact of broadcasting on the country.

Now, in 1984, another government was taking action that would deeply affect the programs Canadians see on TV. In effect, the $75 million budget cut would mean less Canadian TV programming for Canadians to watch. This would have been bad enough, but the government also planned a continuing budget haemorrhage, the inevitable result of the decision to deny the normal inflation-rate increase to CBC. In effect, that meant real cuts of $50-$60 million every year since salaries, rents, heating, air fares, and all other costs keep going up.

In CBC corporate terms, budget chops of $75 million or $60 million sound ominous but somewhat antiseptic. But down at the program level they've been devastating. The CBC was forced to let go talented radio and TV producers, kill programs, shorten series, and water down everything else, all to the detriment of the viewing public. The News and Current Affairs and Drama areas were given a priority, but even so they were affected as we cut back on foreign assignments, where we most needed to grow.

Perhaps the most worrisome impact of the budget cuts has been the assault on so much of what makes public broadcasting special. Significant reductions had to be made in arts programming, opera, ballet, classical drama, and plays and musicals from Canadian theatre. The CBC in the past offered the only national outlet for this type of programming. When the CBC doesn't do it, nobody does because these programs are expensive, only rarely generate audiences in the millions, and thus are not lusted after by advertisers.

In 1984, another factor was at play as well as money. The government was also pondering the power of public broadcasting, especially in the journalistic area. Beyond the daily pin pricks and embarrassing revelations from aggressive journalists, some in government worried that TV journalism, with all its resources and huge audience, was setting the agenda for society instead of the governing party. To a large degree that was true, since most Canadians got their news from television. And in some ways the bigger the success of *The National* and *The Journal*, the more the government worried.

The worrying was shared in other countries, too. In fact, broadcasting was and is in crisis everywhere in the world for the twin reasons of cost and fear. Politicians fear the power of TV and seek to control its messages to reflect their self-image. In London, Margaret Thatcher was determined to trim the sails of the BBC and was making headway; in France, the government was selling off most of its public broadcasting to private entrepreneurs; in Belgium, the government authorized its French-language public broadcaster to contract out its entertainment programming; in Washington, Ronald Reagan was dramatically chopping back the budget for public broadcasting; and fundamental changes were happening, too, in Spain, Japan, Australia, New Zealand, and elsewhere.

It was against this troubling background that the Mulroney government, preoccupied with the huge deficit it faced, zeroed in on the CBC. The efforts Lorraine and I were making to talk to people about the implications of the government's budget cuts were only a tiny part of a much larger campaign to make the decision-makers aware of the loss to Canadian viewers caused by those chops.

Within a few months of the cuts, as the ramifications sank in, the cultural counterattack was under way. Many people were moved by the implications for the very principle of public broadcasting. The CBC Producers Association in Toronto, led by its president, Ray Hazzan,

Mark Starowicz, drama producer Jeannine Locke, Louise Lore, executive producer of *Man Alive*, and others, had been among the first to recover, and Lorraine and I became involved almost immediately. We talked with members of the House of Commons Broadcasting Committee and chatted with influential Conservatives, such as former party leader Robert Stanfield, seeking to impress on them the importance of public broadcasting to Canadian viewers and listeners. Lorraine helped organize a trip to Ottawa by producers and others, such as Pierre Berton, to meet MPS, have lunch with Communications Minister Marcel Masse, and hold a news conference. Soon that early effort was accompanied by a much broader coalition known as the Friends of Public Broadcasting, which launched a large advertising campaign, and a group of 300 writers, performers, directors, and culturally concerned people also "marched" on Ottawa to protest the budget cuts for the CBC and other cultural groups.

DURING THAT 1985 winter of cultural discontent, the main focus of my concern was on any dilution of government support for the principle of public broadcasting, and I had the opportunity to talk privately with Marcel Masse a few times, as did a number of others when he consulted them in an attempt to find out what all the fuss was about. At one point I found myself at a late-night dinner in a downtown Toronto steak house owned in part by Michael Meighen, former Progressive Conservative Party president and a grandson of one-time Tory Prime Minister Arthur Meighen. Masse was in an expansive mood and we spent almost three hours talking about public broadcasting and the CBC and listening to a lot of inside gossip of Conservative politics and the new government from some of our half-dozen companions around the table, all of whom were backroom Conservative power brokers. I was surprised at the intimate knowledge Masse had of politics in English Canada, particularly Ontario politics, and at his insatiable curiosity.

"You know, you've got a bad reputation for wanting to kill the principle of public broadcasting," I began as we sliced into our steaks.

"No, no!" he smiled back tightly. "That's just not true. I support public broadcasting. I may want to change it to meet the changing environment, but fundamentally I strongly support public broadcasting."

"If that's the case," I said, "then the message is not clear. That's not what people think. You need to find the right kind of forum to make a speech saying precisely that and that you recognize the importance of the CBC."

As we finished our meal and said our goodnights, Masse said he was hearing from a lot of people with the same advice; it seemed to me the cultural counterattack was beginning to get through. A couple of months after that dinner Masse made a carefully crafted address to a cable industry audience in Toronto giving strong support to the principle of public broadcasting and announcing the appointment of a task force to develop recommendations for the Canadian broadcasting system and especially the CBC, recommendations that would take broadcasting into the next century. "This country deserves a broadcasting system which is equal to its greatness," he said. "It deserves the continued right to see itself through its own eyes."

It was a theme that I felt had to be reinforced by specific government actions. Along with our colleagues, Lorraine and I continued to talk to anybody of influence we thought could be helpful. One good opportunity for that came in December, 1985, when Lorraine and I were invited to a private black-tie dinner being given by Prime Minister Mulroney at 24 Sussex Drive in Ottawa. Joining the Prime Minister and Mila would be about a dozen other couples, including the Galen Westons of the business world, the Doug Bassetts from private broadcasting, and a number of other business and government leaders.

Over the years since his assumption of the Conservative leadership and his angry phone calls to me about our coverage of that event, I'd seen him in action and chatted with him several times, mostly during the recent election campaign. But I still remembered the thin skin he'd shown in that late-night call during his successful leadership campaign. Clearly, he was a man who could swing quickly from friendly gregariousness to black rage, and I wondered as we walked up the snow-cleared front steps of the prime ministerial residence what mood would dominate this night.

It was the first time in years I'd been at 24 Sussex Drive. No one was outside when we arrived, and I wasn't sure whether we simply knocked on the PM's front door as we would our neighbours, or what. Before my question could be answered, the door swung open and we could hear the sound of a tinkling piano and laughter wafting down from the living room. As we entered, coming down the stairs to greet us was Mulroney himself, his Irish face broadly grinning. He gave me a shoulder-grabbing bear hug and then said, "Knowlton, how are you? It's great to see you," and then he shook Lorraine's hand and kissed her cheek. He whisked us into the living room, asked what we wanted to drink, and introduced us to painter Alex Colville and Chief Justice Brian Dickson. Then he was off to greet someone else with equal exuberance. Mila came by in a black v-neck, long-sleeved dress looking like a model, a fact we commented on. "I only wish," she laughed as she cradled in her arms the latest member of the Mulroney family, an inquisitive, quietly gurgling three-month-old Nicholas. We chatted about children and holidays and then she took him off to bed.

But amid this happy social scene, the subject of broadcasting wasn't far from our minds, or the Prime Minister's. In fact, he had just arrived home from Chicago where he had given a major speech about Canadian culture, echoing what most of the public broadcast supporters had been saying: ". . . cultural sovereignty is as vital to our national life as political sovereignty." Now he displayed ebullience at the positive reaction his speech had met in the cultural community. "I feel I can talk to you after that speech," Lorraine said to him, smiling sweetly and only half-joking.

We all trickled across the front hall from the living room to the dining room. As we sat at the dinner table, the other three pyjama-clad Mulroney children watched us through the window of an adjoining study until their father nodded to let them come in and say goodnight to their parents and meet the guests.

During dinner, Lorraine sat next to the Prime Minister. As the meal drew to a close he made a few remarks to his dinner companions in which he referred to his conversation with Lorraine: "She lectured me through the fish, the veal, and the salad" on broadcasting and culture. "I'm almost cultured out. You win, Knowlton," he joked. "Whatever you want, it's yours." Perhaps the point might at last be getting across, we thought, even if he was treating it light-heartedly.

After dinner he took first the women and then the men on what he called "the fifty-cent tour" of the prime ministerial residence, telling some of his male guests mildly risqué stories about its previous occupants. Then liqueurs were poured. Throughout he was the solicitous, joking, charming host he had been all evening, making sure he chatted with everyone, mostly in a light, self-mocking vein. "When I first got to Ottawa, I didn't know a damn thing," he laughed. "Never had been on the House of Commons floor and didn't even know where the men's room was. I didn't know the process . . . didn't know a damn thing. I didn't even know the purpose of Question Period in the House of Commons was not to get an answer but to be seen asking a question. It's all theatre. Once I understood that, I was all set."

Through the evening we talked of Marcel Masse, about the possibility of a Canadian edition of *Time*, of culture in general and the CBC in particular, about the Queen ("a very nice person . . . I like her"), and about how demanding the job of Prime Minister is. "I never had any idea of the demands, of how many people you have to see," he said. "I come home about seven, spend an hour and a half with Mila and the kids, have dinner, relax, and then it's back to work again. You just got to have that break. I don't know how you could do it without it." But always in my mind was the subject of public broadcasting and how important I believed it to be to the survival of Canada.

Whatever else it was, the dinner provided a chance to have some quite direct conversations with Mulroney and some of his guests, including an old friend of mine from my Washington days, Peter Roberts, who had been a diplomat stationed at the Canadian embassy there and now was the new head of the Canada Council. Another guest was Paul Tellier, the Clerk of the Privy Council and the top public servant in the government.

Every year Lorraine and I have a series of Christmas parties at home for friends and colleagues, and this year Marcel Masse came along to one of them. We were able to combine a festive brunch with talk about public broadcasting and its future that involved Masse and everyone from CBC executives to TV personalities, producers, and diplomats. It all was in aid of gaining support for a stronger Canadian broadcast system. While we, along with many others, were trying to win friends and influence people on the importance of public broadcasting, the task force that Marcel Masse had set up was travelling across Canada in as intensive examination of broadcasting as Canada had ever seen. It was known as the Caplan-Sauvageau Committee, after the two co-chairmen, Gerald Caplan, former staff director of the NDP, and Professor Florian Sauvageau of Laval University in Quebec.

Ottawa shelves are piled high with a succession of reports of royal commissions, special committees, and task forces, all on the future of broadcasting and culture in Canada, from the Aird Commission in the 1920s to Massey to Fowler to Boyle to Clyne to Applebaum-Hébert and finally to this latest incarnation. The question of Canadian programming versus American, and of public broadcasting versus private, dominates the tens of thousands of pages of research, analysis, and recommendations of the commissions, committees, and task forces. This Himalaya of paper, testimony, and criticism made the CBC, as former president Alphonse Ouimet once said, "the most damned, slurred, supported, inquired into, ignored, blamed, upheld, detested, praised organization I know." While some attacked the CBC for failing to provide enough Canadian programming or particular kinds of programming, every one of them down through the decades powerfully endorsed the basic principle of a strong public broadcasting system.

Perhaps the most vivid articulation of that principle had come from Conservative Prime Minister R.B. Bennett, who told Parliament more than half a century ago, "First of all, this country must be assured of complete control of broadcasting from Canadian sources, free from foreign interference or influence. Without such control radio broadcasting can never become a great agency for communication of matters of national concern and for the diffusion of national thought and ideals, and without such control it can never be the agency by which national consciousness may be fostered and sustained and national unity still further strengthened. . . . Secondly, no other scheme than that of public ownership can ensure to the people of this country, without regard to class or place, equal enjoyment of the benefits and pleasures of radio broadcasting. . . . I cannot think that any government would be warranted in leaving the air to private exploitation and not reserving it for development for the use of the people."

Ever since then governments have echoed those sentiments but welshed on the financing of them. They have overmandated the CBC but underfunded it. The underfunding and government encouragement to get more commercial revenue (starting with John Diefenbaker's regime) had led CBC into a greater reliance on the popular American TV programming that advertisers wanted in prime time. The first major assault to reverse that trend came in 1977 when CBC president Al Johnson raised the battle cry of "Canadianization." He issued an emotional *cri de coeur* on the future of the CBC called "Touchstone," which was the first full-scale articulation of guiding principles and objectives for CBC, laying out the kind of programming he felt the public deserved to see. And I was lucky enough to have been intimately involved in developing it in the year before I left my job as director of TV News and Current Affairs. Al had asked me to write what he called "my credo" and he had asked me to come to Ottawa to talk about what I would compose on his behalf. As we chatted easily in his spacious but relatively utilitarian office, he cut off all phone calls and office "drop-ins," threw off his role as president and boss, and became a boyishly enthusiastic armchair philosopher. It was late afternoon, and after an hour or so he broke out one of his beloved but carefully rationed martinis and meditatively stirred it with the sterling silver swizzle stick he always carried with him.

He told me a favoured motto I was to hear from him many times: "Dream no little dreams. They have no magic with which to stir men's souls." It was his adaptation of the words of turn-of-the-century visionary American architect Daniel Burham, who was quoted as saying, "Make no little plans; they have no magic to stir men's blood." He wanted to apply that same thought to broadcasting.

For a couple of weeks, locked away in an Ottawa hotel room with a suitcase full of research documents and notes on consultations with colleagues and others, I scribbled away. Taking Johnson at his word, I began the first of the 100 pages I wrote for him as his ghost writer: "(This) is a confession in that I believe we in the CBC have failed to play our proper leadership role in the national battle for Canadianism ... for our national heritage.

"It is an accusation in that I believe successive governments and their agencies have failed to provide the policies and funding necessary to safeguard Canadians and our culture through broadcasting – especially in English Canada. And we in the CBC have failed to be sufficiently forceful in dramatizing the need for appropriate policies and funding. . . ."

Picking up his own emotionalism, "Touchstone" added, "You develop a culture with passion, not passivity. In this plan for Canadian culture and public broadcasting in Canada and its reinforcement of our nationhood, I am going to be as fighting, aggressive, bold, loud and honestly nationalistic as I am capable of being."

There were scores of recommendations, but the crucial ones revolved about "Canadianization" of English TV by adding more Canadian prime-time programming and proposing a second CBC television channel to give Canadians more choice in their TV viewing. In writing the statement for Johnson, I drew on a number of the old philosophical memoranda and proposals I had made over the years in my bureacratic career. One of them included a second TV channel, which had been a long-time dream of mine and others at CBC. Five years earlier, I had put together a thirty-two-page presentation to my senior colleagues for a CBC-2 as, essentially, an all-news channel. Nothing much happened at the time, but now, in 1977, we were able to push the idea again in Al Johnson's statement.

In preparing "Touchstone," I wanted to make certain it underlined what I felt was the reality – that journalism was the CBC's number-one priority. Thus the document included phrases such as: "the Broadcasting Act cites the first responsibility of informing Canadians about events and issues shaping our lives"; "Our journalistic programming carries the greatest responsibility for responding to the immediate issues in the current national crisis"; and "the single most important service the CBC provides is its journalistic service and especially *The National* and *Téléjournal* [the French network news program]." One pledge I wrote into "Touchstone" was to have *The National* in prime time. This commitment in principle, endorsed by Johnson and agreed to by the Board of Directors, led to Johnson's public endorsement of the idea at the CRTC hearings in 1978. In a way, Johnson, with his

"Touchstone" statement, thus set in motion the chain of events that led to *The National* at ten and *The Journal*.

In "Touchstone" I also wrote on Johnson's behalf of concern about the commercial environment, which sometimes infected CBC programming and scheduling judgements: "Too often public broadcasting needs are overridden by commercial considerations. The CBC will stay in the commercial business, but public service needs always must come first for the CBC." These and other statements drew fire from various internal vested interests, but in the end they remained in Johnson's "Touchstone."

In the final days and nights of rushing to meet a deadline, I was working through the night, dictating last-minute revisions to my secretary, Jean Bruce, in a borrowed office at CBC corporate headquarters in Ottawa. About 9:00 p.m. one night the phone rang and it was Al asking how we were doing and worrying if we'd had any dinner yet.

"No," I said, "but maybe we can find a hamburger place open later on when we finish."

"Oh dear, no . . . that'll never do," said the president. "I'll see you there shortly."

Three-quarters of an hour later, he and his wife Ruth showed up in the office, laden down with pots, pans, dishes, and cutlery. With sympathetic words about being hungry and working late, Ruth plugged in one hotplate and Al another and together, squatting on the floor, they stirred their pots and laid out napkins and plates. Then, to our astonishment, the president of the CBC and his wife knelt on the floor to ladle out a sumptuous stew. Looking up anxiously, Johnson asked, "Is it all right?"

It was a side of Al Johnson rarely seen in bureaucratic Ottawa.

"Touchstone" laid down a specific plan of action to increase the number of Canadian programs in prime time and reduce American shows on CBC. Using the plan as a rough guideline, U.S. prime-time hours on the CBC fell during the next decade from about ten a week to six.

I'd found it enormously satisfying to prepare "Touchstone" for Johnson and also later in doing some speech-writing for him because it gave me a chance to argue with him and incorporate in his statements a lot of the ideas that I and many of my colleagues had been championing for years in endless numbers of memos and meetings.

NOW, EIGHT YEARS AFTER "Touchstone" was presented to the CRTC and the government as a path for the future, we were at it again with the Caplan-Sauvageau Task Force going over much of the same ground.

308

The man who succeeded Johnson as CBC president, Pierre Juneau, wanted to lay out his view of the broadcasting future for the Task Force and government, and he asked me to help write it for him. Juneau had come to the CBC as Johnson's successor with a powerful reputation as an unflinchable supporter of public broadcasting and a man whose ideas on how the CBC should serve Canada were clearly on record through his term as chairman of the CRTC and as a deputy minister. Many of us felt that if anybody could wring support from the government, he could. I'd met him a number of times, but my most hopeful memory of him was a brief encounter when he was still chairman of the CRTC. As he came out of a Toronto TV studio where he'd just been interviewed about the future of broadcasting, he told me, "Like in *Hair*, you've got to 'Let the Sun Shine In.' You've got to try new things. Be adventuresome." As I reflected on that conversation, I thought, maybe Juneau as CBC president could bring off his "Let the Sun Shine In" approach.

Working on Juneau's statement (which we named "Let's Do It!") in the late fall of 1985 was like old times, as I left my anchor chair on *The National* for a couple of weeks to knock heads with old bureaucratic colleagues and some new ones, arguing, writing, and rewriting. I had never before worked closely with Pierre and was intrigued with his working style of intense concentration on issues and twelve- to fourteen-hour working days, often including weekends. His reputation as a cold, austere mandarin was not in evidence and I found him, if not anxious for argument, at least prepared to listen.

"Canadian broadcasting is crackling with change and opportunity," our final 188-page document began. We urged co-operation among all broadcasters, public and private, to bring about "Canadianization" of the TV tube. In writing the statement for Juneau I wanted to emphasize that the answer to our challenge was not to stop American shows coming into Canada, "but we have a right to see Canadian programs. . . . Our job, quite simply, is to amplify the culture of Canada – to maximize the value of all of Canada's cultural investments in theatre, dance, music, film and opera. The battle cry must be 'Equal Time For Canada' on our television screens. We must aim at a Canadian broadcasting system that carries, in total, more than 50% Canadian programming by 1990."

That was an ambitious objective and it remains to be seen how close we'll come to it. For the CBC, our proposals recommended ten hours of prime-time Canadian drama every week; establishment of a second CBC channel to showcase programs of the regions, provincial broadcasting organizations, and independent producers as well as "second-chance" viewing of some of the programs on the CBC main service; a Canadian television channel in the United States to provide Americans with a regular, daily sense of Canada, which we thought could be a profit-maker; and, most important insofar as I was concerned, the creation of a Canadian all-news TV channel.

In terms of Canadian programming, the CBC likely will be close to 90 per cent Canadian in prime time by the 1990 target set in "Let's Do It!" but the real question is how far the private TV stations will progress in offering viewers Canadian programming in addition to their American fare.

This ambitious program of change obviously would cost more than the current CBC budget, but even in the midst of the Ottawa budget slashing we felt it necessary to take the long view. Our sweeping proposals for the reform of Canadian television were meant to demonstrate how the objectives of the Broadcast Act and the policy directives of every government since the days of R.B. Bennett could finally be fulfilled. The additional costs, as we estimated them in 1985, were, in fact, relatively modest – an extra $75 million to bring about the changes to television, for example.

In working on "Let's Do It!" I emphasized, as I had so many times in the past, the critical importance of our news programming, noting that "The single most important service the CBC provides is its journalistic service." I singled out *The National* and *The Journal* and their CBC French network counterparts, adding, "Journalism is the hinge of our democratic society."

With my keen interest in news programming, I was delighted to see the Caplan-Sauvageau Report, when it came out almost a year later, endorse our proposal for a Canadian all-news channel. The Report also supported the broad theme of Juneau's "Let's Do It!" statement, strongly urging more Canadian programming and asking the government to provide the funding needed either through larger grants or additional small taxes on cable services. For the most part, it echoed what just about every such report has urged for the past sixty years, since the Aird Report of 1928.

MY YEARS ON BOTH SIDES of the TV camera have reinforced my passionate belief in the importance of public broadcasting to Canada's survival as a nation identifiably different from our southern neighbours. CBC journalism has done its part, giving Canadians something distinctively theirs, and our broadcast journalism is arguably the best in the world. But while we are a success story in reporting our facts, we still import most of our fantasies, and they are primarily American

310

ones. Ironically, entertainment programming was the crown princess of early Canadian television and the news the unwanted stepchild. That has dramatically changed in the past two decades. Now the central challenge for the CBC and for Canadian television in general as we move toward the twenty-first century is to bring about the same kind of revolution in Canadian entertainment programming that has occurred in journalism.

This idea is not new. In 1951 the Massey Report said, "Many Canadians in the 1920s ... began to fear that cultural annexation would follow our absorption into the American radio system just as surely as economic or even political annexation would have followed absorption into the American railway system 50 years earlier." And television in the late 1980s has far more impact on Canadians than radio in the 1920s.

Like it or not, television today is the single greatest cultural force the world has ever known. More than half of our leisure time is spent watching TV: an average of nearly twenty-four hours a week in front of that mesmerizing box of wires, tubes, and circuit boards. All the time we spend reading books, newspapers, and magazines, going to the movies, ballet, the symphony or to hockey, baseball, or football games, or just relaxing doing nothing, does not add up to the time spent watching TV.

In our current contemplation of television and its impact, a great many old myths are fighting new realities. One old myth is that nobody watches Canadian TV programs. The reality is that they do, in the millions. In fact, when given a fair choice, Canadians generally prefer watching Canadian programs, as the success of *The National* and *The Journal* in the heart of the fierce prime-time competition from American shows has proved.

A single performance by the Royal Winnipeg Ballet seen on CBC-TV will be watched by more people than would attend two years of nightly performances at Toronto's O'Keefe Centre. *Charlie Grant's War*, about an unsung Canadian war hero, had a bigger audience for the one night it was on than all of the top-ten grossing Canadian feature films combined in the whole year of 1985. Stratford's 1986 production of *Twelfth Night* got a larger audience on CBC television than attended all of Stratford's productions in the entire previous season. *Anne of Green Gables* brought five million viewers to the CBC.

The trouble is that our TV industry does not produce enough drama, so we are overwhelmed by the excessive availability of American programs, especially in prime time. Of a total of 52,000 hours of English-speaking television programming available to Canadians in a year, there are only about 370 hours of Canadian drama, most of it on the CBC. And drama is what we watch most, from *The Young and the Restless* to *Masterpiece Theatre*. The pervasiveness of U.S. drama is now unquestionably the greatest single challenge for Canadian broadcasting.

By the time children reach the age of twelve, they will have seen about 12,000 hours of television, nearly twice as much time as they will have spent in their classrooms. All this time spent watching the box makes TV a massive cultural conditioner. It gives young and old alike much of our sense of self, reinforces or weakens our values, provides many of our role models, helps define our expectations, and is our most important source of knowledge of what's happening at home and abroad.

Some argue the old myth that it really doesn't affect our sense of Canadian identity to watch so much American entertainment programming. But the new reality is that most Canadians today know more about the American system of justice than our own because of everything from *Perry Mason* to *Hill Street Blues* or *Miami Vice*. Our kids know more about the Alamo and Gettysburg than about the Plains of Abraham or Lundy's Lane.

Others argue that "After all, it's only television," and people really aren't affected by it. If that's the case, why are Canadian advertisers spending a billion dollars a year on television commercials in trying to affect the buying habits of the nation? Why do politicians and social activists of all kinds rate television as their primary way of getting messages across to the public? Indisputably, what we see on television can and does affect how we think about people, issues, and events both of the past and the present. The high impact of television today is an irrefutable reality, and for that very reason television must be the central focus of our cultural policy and must reflect Canada and Canadians. It must give us Canadian reference points and Canadian touchstones.

Another old myth is that there is not much difference between the CBC and CTV, Global, and the independent private stations in Canada. The reality, however, is that there is an enormous difference - one need only compare the TV schedules. Not only is there a huge quantitative difference, with the CBC currently showing around 80 per cent Canadian programming in prime time, but a huge qualitative difference, too. One must look long and hard to find much Canadian drama anywhere but on CBC - or ballet or serious music or comedy. And nobody carries as much documentary programming and so much current affairs and news as the CBC does. Pay TV movies, of course, are

312

overwhelmingly American and seemingly aimed at the numb and the dumb.

When the private stations and networks appear before the broadcast regulators and other public bodies, they make impressive promises cloaked in much righteous rhetoric about the Canadian programming they're going to do. But their pledges are almost all chiselled in water. Their seemingly conscientious public posture contrasts sharply with their actual program achievement. Their TV entertainment listings primarily consist of programs made in Hollywood and schedules made in New York. The private networks and stations do well in giving Canadians news and sports programming, but the paucity of their reflection of Canada in drama, variety, and other performance programming stems from simple appetite for profit. Dramas they do produce usually are cleansed of Canadian reference points so as to be more saleable to American TV stations.

Since its inception, private TV has returned handsome dividends to investors in the form of before-tax profits. In the past ten years these have ranged from 17 to 20 per cent on average; and some stations have done substantially better. It would be all but impossible to sustain that happy level of profitability if the private stations substantially increased their output of Canadian programming because Canadianization is expensive compared to buying video junk food off the Hollywood shelf. A U.S. program can be bought for $30,000-$40,000 an hour on average, but it would cost at least ten to twenty times that to produce an hour of Canadian drama or variety. A big prime-time show like *Dallas* can be bought for about $50,000, but it costs $1.5 million to make.

Besides these daunting financial figures, advertisers are wary of Canadian programs; so there might be some commercial loss, too. Understandably, given their basic profit motive, the private stations are queasy about Canadianization. Nonetheless, facing Canadianization demands from the CRTC, they have begun to improve in the past couple of years.

Since people invest in private broadcasting to earn money, the preoccupation with profit is appropriate and inevitable. But the profit motive also induces a mindset that encourages the use of lowest-common-denominator shows in order to sell products. Using television as an educational medium doesn't sell soap. As a British public broadcaster commented at a meeting of broadcasters held in Canada, "We make programs, they make money." Sometimes it seems there is not even enough mediocrity to go around, as shows add to their "jolts per minute," in broadcast critic Morris Wolfe's felicitous phrase, to stop viewers' fingers from flicking over their channel-changers – zapping, zipping, and muting the sound and pictures.

One favourite old myth about Canadian broadcasting is that the CBC is wasteful, inefficient, ineffective, and bloated with bureaucracy. The reality is that the CBC today is leaner and meaner than it's ever been, and in some ways leaner and meaner than it should be. But the myth of huge waste is so pervasive and persistent that it seems people prefer the comfortable familiarity of their anecdotal fantasies to reality. Yet the money provided to the CBC now falls significantly short of demands placed on it; consequently, the creative soup is being watered down, a fact re-emphasized in the Caplan-Sauvageau Report.

In any big organization, to be sure, whether General Motors, Imperial Oil, the Royal Bank, or the CBC, there inevitably is some waste and managers must go to war against it constantly and ferociously. As a creative organization, the CBC must be particularly concerned because every bureaucratic dollar wasted is a creative dollar betrayed. There is nothing more repulsive than bureaucratic dollars squeezing out creative dollars, a theme I constantly kept in mind during my years as a bureaucrat.

The CBC spends more than a billion dollars a year, mostly taxpayers' money. That works out to about nine cents a day per Canadian, around one-third of the cost of a daily newspaper and certainly much cheaper than a bus fare. Where does it go? For one thing, our geography is very expensive. The Massey Report noted in 1951 that the BBC reached 50 million people with 975 miles of landline while in Canada CBC Radio needed 15,000 miles of telegraph and telephone lines to reach 14 million people. Today it costs about $150 million a year just to send out the signal on satellites and transmitters to reach 24 million. Of all the money the CBC gets, $743 million goes to programming. English television spends almost $370 million of that; French television, just over $211 million; English radio, a little more than $101 million; and French radio programming, $61 million. The CBC is the single greatest supporter of the arts in Canada. About $150 million a year goes to Canadian composers, musicians, writers, actors, dancers, and others, most of whom, without the CBC, would be drawing unemployment cheques from the government or be down in Hollywood.

Another old myth says, why can't CBC be more like PBS in the United States? The reality is that for the CBC to become "PBS North" would downgrade, not upgrade, our programming. PBS produces much less programming than the CBC – less than half of the drama CBC produces, for example – and it costs much more to run than the

CBC English TV network, which is its counterpart. In fact, PBS costs about as much as the whole of the CBC: French and English, television and radio, the Northern Service, the overseas service, and the regions. There is no PBS news service, and although the MacNeil-Lehrer public affairs hour is good, it's not as good as *The National* and *The Journal* at 10:00 p.m. The CBC-TV English network delivers about three times the product of PBS for much less cost.

Still another misconception is that technology has made public broadcasting irrelevant in contemporary society because we now can pull in signals from all over the United States and elsewhere through cable and satellite dishes. In fact, the modern technology makes a public broadcasting system in Canada more needed today than ever before. Technology is rendering geography meaningless and endangering sovereignty. Satellites have become cultural border-busters. The sad truth is that the new technology has made Canada today a culturally occupied country. If it weren't for the programming of the CBC, we would have practically nothing Canadian on the air in prime time except for news and sports.

With satellites, with cable, and with Canadian private stations essentially regurgitating made-in-Hollywood shoot-'em-ups and situation comedies, 75 per cent of our total viewing time is spent watching American programs. In drama alone, 98 per cent of the program offerings are American.

We have a right, of course, to see those American programs. But we have a right, too, to see Canadian programs: to see Canadian role models, Canadian heroes, Canadian history, Canadian people and places. On the basis of past history, that's only going to come in any significant way from a public broadcasting system in Canada. The private system is simply not going to do it. All the promises made in the licence applications inevitably fade in face of the profit imperative.

There can be an argument, of course, that we don't need a public system, and some do make it. Who cares if all we see is *The Love Boat* and *The A-Team* and all the other made-in-Hollywood products? Who cares if we are a culturally occupied country? Who cares about "safeguarding, enriching and strengthening . . . the fabric of the country"? There are some who feel Canadian independence is a waste of money, that it is inevitable and maybe even desirable for Canadian traditions, institutions, economy, and culture to become homogeneous with those of the United states and, in time, to be fully absorbed by our seductive and successful American neighbours.

I think most of us, however, do care about remaining Canadian. When we think about it, we are concerned about safeguarding our sense of Canadianism, even if it does cost money to do so. Our independence has cost us throughout our entire history, from Sir John A. Macdonald's national dream of a transcontinental railway to the current day.

We probably could save money if we allowed the disintegration of those things that mark us as distinctively Canadian. But a majority of Canadians simply would not tolerate that. I think we have a deep, if quiet, pride in our country. We recognize that if the economy is the engine of our society, our culture is its heartbeat. The kind of television we have has become the best measure of our cultural pulse, the primary medium of culture for most Canadians.

But there are no free lunches in Canadian broadcasting. In the "Let's Do It!" statement, we estimated it would cost an extra $75 million to eliminate American commercial TV programming on the CBC; to air ten hours of Canadian prime-time drama every week; to provide more documentaries; to establish a CBC-2; and to make other changes to further Canadianize television. Looking only at prime-time TV, Caplan-Sauvageau estimated it would cost the CBC an extra $10-$12 million a year to achieve 85 per cent Canadian content; $20-$24 million for 90 per cent; and $30-36 million for 95 per cent Canadian programming between 7:00 and 11:00 p.m. But additional program funding by Telefilm, the government agency set up to stimulate independent TV production, and possible loss of commercial revenue could increase the total costs for Canadianization to as much as three times those figures. To pay this bill, the Report proposed a combination of tax adjustments and increased government grants to public broadcasting.

A few years ago *The Toronto Star* had a contest in which readers were asked to complete the following phrase: "As Canadian as ..." The winner was, "As Canadian as possible under the circumstances." For Canadian television, until now "the circumstances" have given us a mostly American culture on Canadian TV. With the foresight and political courage of a Sir John A. Macdonald, the government must introduce "circumstances" to give Canadians a better chance to see themselves on television – at least a fifty-fifty chance. Nothing less will give Canadian TV equality with American TV on our screens

While the focus of the broadcast debate is centred on the Canadianization of the TV schedules, there remains one more news battle. The success of *The National* and *The Journal* in prime-time has clearly demonstrated the Canadian public's keen appetite to be informed. But *The National* and *The Journal*, as well as the *CTV News*, are irritatingly delayed at times for sports events, especially during the hockey playoffs. Also, while both CBC and the private broadcasters provide excellent news programs that reach millions of Canadians, they do so at specific set times. Increasingly, Canadians want to check in on what's happening on their own timetable. Currently they can do that only with the CNN channel out of Atlanta, Georgia.

Beyond that, the viewers of today not only want their news on demand, but more and more they want to witness events as they unfold to increase their awareness of what's happening in their world. And that, too, they can do on CNN, watching coverage of a hurricane in Florida, a fire in Philadelphia, a plane crash in Houston, or a presidential news conference in Washington. They can't, however, watch similar events in Canada unless the networks interrupt regular programming, which causes other viewer aggravations and has commercial implications.

Journalism is one of the greatest strengths of Canadian television – "First and foremost," said a survey reported by the Friends of Public Broadcasting; "The great Canadian TV success story," said Caplan-Sauvageau. What we need to do is to capitalize on that success.

The CBC today is the biggest news organization in the country with two television networks, four radio networks, and the regional stations, producing 400 newscasts a day and 1,000 hours of other journalistic programming a week. This rich reservoir of news would be the ideal foundation for a Canadian news channel.

A CBC all-news channel would improve the regular CBC News Service, open up better coverage of the regions of Canada, put more foreign correspondents in places not now covered, provide extended live coverage of major events, and give a valuable "second window," a second chance to view many programs from the main CBC channel such as Man Alive, the fifth estate, Venture, Journal documentaries, Marketplace, and The National. By the time this book is published we'll likely know whether an all-news channel will be approved by the CRTC and whether it will be operated by the CBC.

Wayne Gretzky once said, "I skate to where the puck is going to be, not to where it's been." It's a good guide for broadcasting as well as hockey, and Canadianization of our television screen, including an all-news channel, is where the puck is going to be in the years ahead. It is as vital to the cultural and political health of Canada as the railways were for the economic and political health of Canada a century ago.

Television news will never and should never replace the printed word of newspapers, magazines, and books, and if it's doing its job in the years ahead it must stimulate people's interest so that they read more, not less. But there is no doubt that TV news increasingly will be the primary source of news for Canadians, whether we like it or not. The most vivid evidence of this I've ever run across was in a conversation with a man in Winnipeg at a CBC "open house." He told me he had a satellite dish in his backyard and every night he watched *The National* as it went out to every time zone. "Five times every night!" his wife exclaimed. "It drives me nuts."

GIVEN THE EXAMPLE of *The National* and *The Journal*, it's now clear that quantity of audience can go hand in hand with quality of product. That was the theme on Monday, January 12, 1987, when we celebrated the fifth anniversary of our twinned programs. It was a subdued celebration that emphasized how the hour of nightly prime-time journalism, so radical a risk when we started, had so quickly become an accepted fixture. What had been revolutionary was now almost ordinary. Late that afternoon a group of us gathered in the *Journal* boardroom, sipped wine from plastic cups, and talked of our feats of derring-do five years before, to the bemused, often sceptical stares of newer staff members. Al Johnson, now teaching at the University of Toronto and president of the Canadian Broadcasting League, was there for the reunion, relaxed in a sports jacket and slacks, slapping backs and beaming proudly. *The National* at ten and *The Journal* had been the single greatest program achievement of his CBC presidency, a shining example of his philosophy of Canadianization of the TV schedule.

Peter Herrndorf was also on hand for the fifth-anniversary celebrations, chatting with former colleagues about past battles and triumphs, almost like a wartime colonel meeting old soldiers at a veterans' reunion. All of the Three Wise Men who had developed the concept of the prime-time hour of journalism were there, too. Mark Starowicz, now puffing a pipe instead of his cigarettes, circulated, smiled softly, and talked earnestly. Vince Carlin chatted with old friends about his days as chief news editor and about his new job as chief correspondent for CBC Radio News. And the behind-the-scenes master strategist of the program, Bill Morgan, relived his days of hotel room arguments, Current Affairs responsibilities, and his succession to become overall head of CBC-TV News and Current Affairs. Tony Burman, who had been the executive producer of the new *National*, was there, too, having returned from London to become the senior documentary producer at *The Journal*. Barbara Frum chatted with colleagues, who noted she had just begun wearing a watch for the first time in many years. Somehow she felt more at ease with a watch now, and besides she got it from her husband Murray. "It's quite nice to know what time it is," she said later.

Later that evening, Tony joined a dozen of us who gathered in the TV newsroom shortly before *The National*. The group included other veterans of the launch of *The National* at ten in 1982: John Owen, who had been senior producer at the launch and then had taken over from Burman as executive producer and now had become the CBC's chief news editor; director Fred Parker; Vince Carlin. But our little gathering was somehow awkward. Most of our newsroom colleagues didn't share our common cause of the prime-time launch of *The National* and drifted away to continue their work on this night's *National*. As usual, the deadlines were immovable and the party quietly ended.

Anchoring *The National* that night, I had a sense of déjà vu. One of our major stories was about the weather, just as it had been on launch night five years earlier. "Nearly all of Europe is still shivering under the deepest freeze in decades," I reported, and went on to inform two million Canadians of extraordinary cold and snowy weather in Atlantic Canada and unusually mild weather in Alberta. *The Journal*, too, that night grappled with meteorology as Barbara reported on "What's wrong with the weather." As it had been five years before, it was a slow night for news.

We had come a long way, as has broadcast journalism in general, from that day in November, 1924, when an announcer uttered these opening words on the first-ever BBC radio newscast: "It is my intention tonight to read this bulletin twice, first of all rapidly and then slowly, repeating on the second occasion, when necessary, details upon which the listener may wish to take notes."

Although, as is our tradition and penchant, we Canadians seldom salute our achievements, we have produced a world-class broadcast journalism, and *The National* and *The Journal* are unquestionably at the top of the class. It has happened thanks to a clutch of bureaucratic battlers, from Dan McArthur and Gene Hallman to Peter Herrndorf, Denny Harvey, Don Macdonald, Mike Daigneault, and Bill Morgan, as well as the creative verve of Tony Burman, Mark Starowicz, John Owen, Fred Parker, and hundreds of producers, editors, reporters, and the supportive help from so many others. My own contribution, as a correspondent, director of News and Current Affairs, and anchor of *The National*, if I can try to be objective, was essentially to provide an unrepentant and irrepressible optimism in spite of times when it felt like I was on a treadmill to oblivion, combined with a healthy dose of common sense and an awful lot of patience and persistence. As a nation, I believe we stake everything on a rational dialogue of an informed public and my job has been to help provide the basic material for that dialogue. I'm at one with Graham Spry, the 1930s leader in the fight to establish public broadcasting in Canada, who said, "Information is the prime, integrating factor, creating, nourishing, adjusting and sustaining a society."

On the night of our fifth anniversary, as I contemplated the past couple of decades of TV news, my mind reeled back to that winter night twenty-one years before when my rambunctious colleagues Don Cameron and Bill Cunningham phoned me in Washington: "we're getting screwed," they had said. "Things have just got to change. . . . We need a revolution, for Chrissakes!"

Well, we had one, old friends. It took a lot longer than we ever dreamed, but it worked. And it isn't over yet.

INDEX

329

Date Due